SAFETY FROM FALSE CONVICTIONS

Safety from False Convictions

Boaz Sangero

To Professor Rinat Kitai-Sangero, the spirit of my writing.

Contents

Acknowledgments

I WOULD LIKE to thank Professor Rinat Kitai-Sangero, who helped me during all the years of the work on this book and who made this book possible. Her remarks and suggestions regarding each draft were a tremendous contribution.

I am also grateful to Professor Alex Stein and Dr. Daniel Hartmann for their support and advice, and Ms. Dana Rothman-Meshulam for her super professional editing work.

Boaz Sangero
Jerusalem, Israel
2016

Acknowledgments

Introduction

IMAGINE THE FOLLOWING airline advertisement:[1]

> Our airplanes are exceptionally comfortable and offer very spacious passenger
> seating. Gourmet in-flight meals are served, and our staff and crew members
> are exceptionally professional and courteous. Newly released movies are shown
> on flights, and massages are offered to passengers for their comfort. Our prices
> are the fairest on the market, and our planes are only rarely involved in crashes,
> with an only 1 percent accident rate.[2]

Even with the very attractive flight conditions and terms offered, no reasonable
person would fly with this airline given its 1-in-100 flights crash rate. Yet although
false convictions occur at a far more prevalent rate than this 1 percent accident rate,
criminal law, in contrast to other spheres that generate risks to human well-being
and life, lacks any form of a modern safety theory.

---

[1] This example is taken, with some modifications, from Boaz Sangero & Mordechai Halpert, *A Safety Doctrine for the Criminal Justice System*, MICH. ST. L. REV. 1293 (2011).

[2] Others have also compared wrongful convictions to plane crashes. *See, e.g.*, Barry Scheck & Peter Neufeld, *Toward the Formation of "Innocence Commissions" in America*, 86 JUDICATURE 98 (2002).

It is most convenient for us to hold our criminal law system in high regard, to the point of calling it the "criminal justice system." It is convenient for us to think that everything runs as it should in this system. And even if certain doubts creep in at times, we tend to repress them and stand firm in our ignorance.

The state can inflict no greater injustice on a citizen than to falsely convict him when he is innocent. In the past, it was possible to call into question the actual occurrence of false convictions and consider this, at most, a negligible phenomenon. However, today such skepticism has no place and likely derives mainly from ignorance. This is principally due to the "DNA revolution" and the first Innocence Project at the Cardozo School of Law at Yeshiva University in the United States. In the framework of this Innocence Project, genetic comparisons are conducted between samples taken from inmates and samples that have been preserved from crime scenes. On the basis of the testing initiated by the original Innocence Project (today there are similar additional projects, both in the United States and elsewhere), over three hundred false convictions have been exposed, the majority of which were for the serious offenses of rape and murder, which carry the harshest possible penalties: life imprisonment or capital punishment. Moreover, in many of the cases, genetic testing even led to the identification of the true perpetrators of the crimes, who had roamed free due to the false convictions and, in some cases, even continued to commit crimes. In addition, recent studies have shown that false convictions are not an uncommon phenomenon. These findings make a renewed, more realistic consideration of the issue imperative.

On this background, this book explores ways of reducing the false conviction rate. The view advanced here is that the criminal justice system can be categorized as what is termed in safety engineering a "safety-critical system."[3] As systems of this type entail matters of life and death, any system error is likely to cause severe harm to both individuals and society at large. A false conviction is no less a system error and accident than a plane crash, not only from a metaphorical perspective but also in the very realistic terms of economic cost.[4]

This book argues for the formulation and application of a safety theory in the criminal justice system.[5] But this would not be a simple matter of raising the beyond-reasonable-doubt bar, thereby increasing the number of acquittals and

---

[3] In a coauthored article with Dr. Mordechai Halpert, we have suggested applying this term to the criminal justice system, Mordechai Halpert & Boaz Sangero, *From a Plane Crash to the Conviction of an Innocent Person: Why Forensic Science Evidence Should Be Inadmissible unless It Has Been Developed as a Safety-Critical System*, 32 HAMLINE L. REV. 65, 70 (2009). *See also* Sangero & Halpert, *supra* note 1, at 1300–01.

[4] Sangero & Halpert, *supra* note 1, at 1304–05.

[5] *See also id.* at 1325.

decreasing the number of convictions. Rather, implementing care and safety in the system will entail implementing reasonable safety measures whose costs are lower than their expected harm, due to the resulting reduction of both the number of false acquittals *and* the number of false convictions.[6]

Modern safety began to develop following World War II. Until then, the safety approach in the field of aeronautics had been "Fly-Fix-Fly": an airplane would be flown until an accident occurred, the causes of the accident would be investigated and the defects repaired, and then the airplane would resume flight. This method was based on a system of learning from past experience to repair product defects and flaws and prevent future mishaps. However, such a system does not safeguard against future mishaps that can be caused by other, as-yet undetected defects. This approach became clearly inadequate with the rapid advances in aviation technology and rising costs of airplanes. This made learning from experience too expensive, leading to a shift in approach over a half century ago, and the birth of modern safety.[7]

At this point, the primary objective in the safety field became preventing accidents before they occur, thereby avoiding the high costs of learning through experience. The "Fly-Fix-Fly" approach was thus replaced by the "Identify-Analyze-Control" method, with its aim of "First-Time-Safe." Under the latter approach, there is systematic identification of future hazards, analysis of the probability of their occurrence, and a complete neutralization of the risk or at least its reduction to an acceptable level.[8]

The central proposal put forth in this book is that the First-Time-Safe approach be adopted in the field of criminal justice. The history of modern system-safety will be described by tracing its development in fields such as military aviation, engineering, and medical diagnostic devices. The book suggests how the legal system should and can learn from the engineering field. For example, there is a duty in engineering safety to report not only accidents but also "incidents," defined as situations in which there was potential for harm to be caused and it was averted purely by coincidence. It is important to recognize the fact that near-miss conditions, if not rectified, most likely will develop into accidents at a later point. In contrast, "incidents" in criminal law are completely ignored. Even worse, accidents are not always investigated either.[9]

The obvious question that arises is why safety measures have yet to be implemented in criminal law. Moreover, why has the system never even adopted a Fly-Fix-Fly

---

[6] *Id.* at 1301.
[7] *Id.* at 1296–97.
[8] *Id.* at 1297.
[9] *Id.* at 1299.

approach? The answers to these questions are related to the general inability to detect the occurrence of false convictions, which are typically indiscernible. This can account for the optimistic false impression that false convictions are a very rare phenomenon. Despite all indications of a conceivably very high rate of false convictions, policymakers and the public alike are certain and confident that the system performs well and that there is no need to invest resources in safety measures.[10] This aspect of criminal law is so fundamental that it amounts to a principle: what I have termed elsewhere, with Dr. Mordechai Halpert, the "Hidden Accidents Principle" of the criminal justice system.[11]

The book explains why implementing safety in criminal law is necessary both morally and economically. A definition of safety is proposed, and the Hidden Accidents Principle is elaborated on. As risk assessment is an important component of any safety theory, the risk of a false conviction is analyzed. The book also proposes some key general principles for the incorporation of safety into the criminal justice system.

In addition to drawing on modern safety practices and methods from other fields, the book suggests ways to incorporate safety into specific evidence contexts: DNA testing, fingerprint comparisons, confessions, and eyewitness identifications. The current lack of safety in these particular contexts is analyzed and discussed, and possible safety measures are suggested. Finally, the book demonstrates the absence of safety mechanisms in criminal procedure, which is reflected and manifested in police and prosecutorial negligence and misconduct, plea bargains, and faulty post-conviction proceedings. Safety measures will be proposed to rectify this situation as well.

This book constitutes an attempt to set the groundwork for developing a modern theory of safety for the criminal justice system, by drawing on the modern safety methods in fields with more experience in "doing safety" than the criminal justice system. The suggested safety theory presented in this book is, moreover, universal, rather than being applicable only to certain criminal law systems. I believe that every criminal law system can benefit from adopting it. The first two chapters of the book present modern safety and show the need for the criminal justice system to derive insights from other fields. The four chapters that follow propose general safety principles for the criminal justice system and illustrate the application of the general theory in various criminal evidence and procedural contexts. Chapters 1 to 4 are, of course, universal in content and scope. Although Chapters 5 and 6 illustrate the

---

[10] Another possible explanation is the erroneous idea that whereas unsafe airplanes pose a risk to all of "us," an unsafe criminal justice system is a risk only to "them"—that is, potential criminals.

[11] Sangero & Halpert, *supra* note 1, at 1314–16.

suitability of the proposed theory for the American criminal justice system, suggesting avenues for improvements in criminal evidence and criminal procedure, this model is suited also to many other, non-American criminal law systems.

Incorporating into the criminal justice system a modern safety theory that is commonly accepted in other areas, such as space, aviation, engineering, and transportation, is an idea that was developed jointly by myself and Dr. Mordechai Halpert and presented in a number of coauthored articles, particularly *A Safety Doctrine for the Criminal Justice System*.[12] This book was intended to expand on the preliminary proposition and engage in the application of the modern safety theory in the criminal justice system. In addition to drawing on the accepted academic research on the subject, the book is built also on my own experience gained through two decades of teaching the seminar "Convicting the Innocent—Causes and Solutions" at the College of Law & Business in Ramat Gan, Israel. I delved into many of the notions and ideas presented in the book in innumerable discussions with my students, from whom I also learned a great deal. During the course of the research for this book, I attended a course on modern safety at Ben-Gurion University in Israel instructed by Dr. Daniel Hartmann, who also enlightened me on the vast body of rich professional literature in this field. Among other things, he directed me to the work of Professor Nancy Leveson, whose books have become canon in the field. Both Dr. Hartman and Professor Leveson read parts of the draft of this book and contributed important insights as experts on safety. Also of great assistance in writing the book was Professor Rinat Kitai-Sangero, who read the draft in its entirety and whose many insightful comments greatly improved it, and Dana Rothman-Meshulam, who did not suffice with language editing and provided helpful comments on the contents as well.

The following is a description in brief of the central topics that will be discussed in each of the six chapters of the book:

Chapter 1 considers the need for safety in the criminal justice system. It describes the enormous harm that is caused by false convictions—to the innocent defendants, their families, and friends, but also to society as a whole. In order to show that false convictions are not a rare or negligible phenomenon, several ways of assessing the false conviction rate are suggested.

I next progress to the moral duty to adopt safety measures, addressing social theories, such as the social contract theory, and legal doctrines, such as the state-created danger doctrine. The conviction of an innocent person is an enormous injustice. One of the central justifications for the state's failure to invest all available resources in safety in other contexts, such as improving road infrastructures, is the lack of

---

[12] Sangero & Halpert, *supra* note 1. *See also* Halpert & Sangero, *supra* note 3.

sufficient funds to optimally achieve all of the government's objectives, such as security, education, and health. The book takes a close critical look at this argument, showing why it does not hold in the context of the criminal justice system.

The first chapter continues with a proposed economic justification for adopting safety measures in the criminal justice system. This rationale draws on, among other things, proven cost-benefit analyses of safety in aviation and other fields. The chapter closes with addressing possible objections to my main argument.

Chapter 2 describes the fundamentals of modern system-safety. It begins with a history of system-safety and then sets out the basic definitions applied in this field and the three basic stages of the system-safety process: Identify, Analyze, and Control. This is followed by a description of the process, in which risk assessment is vital, for it produces meaningful data to guide in prioritizing hazards, allocating resources, and evaluating the acceptability of risks associated with these hazards. I then present fundamental safety concepts and common methods of system-safety. Special attention is given to the notion of redundancy, to the duty to report accidents and incidents (near misses), and to the preferability of system-safety engineering over "black-box" testing. I discuss also safety in medical diagnostic devices, as the safety requirements strongly resemble those needed for forensic science equipment. Finally, I consider the most progressive system-safety method currently applied, known as "System-Theoretic Accident Model and Processes" or "STAMP."

Chapter 3 suggests seven principles that could form the foundation for a core safety theory for the criminal justice system.

First, as the book initiates a new line of discussion, it is necessary to provide a definition of safety in the criminal justice system. The proposed definition is constructed on how safety is defined in other fields, such as aviation, adapted to the particular needs of criminal law.

Second, I discuss the Hidden Accidents Principle in criminal law, under which effective feedback for the criminal justice system is implausible, even in theory. The only way to introduce safety into this system, therefore, is through comparison with fields in which mishaps are seen and can be detected. The Hidden Accidents Principle is evidence of the inadequacy of the Fly-Fix-Fly safety method for criminal law, because of the extreme difficulty of learning from the experience of past accidents in the system when they are a hidden phenomenon.

The third general rule built on safety considerations is that a conviction must not be based on any single piece of evidence. In this context, I present medical diagnostic concepts, such as error rate, sensitivity, specificity, and positive predictive value, and a probability calculation. The latter is shown to lead to the conclusion that not only are the classic types of evidence such as confessions and lineup identifications insufficiently accurate to establish guilt beyond a reasonable doubt, but even the strongest scientific evidence, including fingerprint and DNA matches, may suffer from flaws.

The fourth general rule adapts the beyond-reasonable-doubt standard to a safety doctrine by adding the requirement that all reasonable measures be taken to ensure that a conviction is safe.

Fifth, I demonstrate how the conception of the certainty of a suspect's guilt (and, at later stages, the guilt of defendants, appellants, and convicted inmates) according to which all we (police/prosecutors/society) must do is find evidence confirming this conception, results, time and again, in failures in the criminal justice system. I therefore suggest adopting a general safety principle that frees the system from this conception of the suspect's guilt, applying insights from psychological research.

Sixth, I demonstrate, in brief, that if we look at the history of evidence law, there is a realization in every era that excessive weight was accorded to specific types of evidence in the preceding era. Today, we know that no type of evidence is completely error-free. Accordingly, I propose a general safety principle of the need to pursue an ultimate goal of gathering and submitting accurate evidence.

Finally, although the Fly-Fix-Fly method is not a modern safety method, and much better approaches have been developed, such as Identify-Analyze-Control, in a criminal law system in which not even accidents are always investigated, starting out with the Fly-Fix-Fly approach would be progress.

Chapter 4 focuses on learning modern safety from the field of engineering. It begins with suggesting the establishment of a Safety in the Criminal Justice System Institute: a centralized federal body for overseeing safety in the criminal justice system, similarly to how the National Highway Traffic Safety Administration and Food and Drug Administration function in their respective fields. The duties of the Institute would include investigating accidents (false convictions) and incidents (near misses) in the criminal justice system and formulating concrete recommendations to prevent such occurrences.

I then propose instituting an accident (false conviction) and incident reporting duty as well as compulsory safety-education and safety-training, and fostering the development of a culture of safety in the criminal justice system. I demonstrate how the fundamentally important Identify-Analyze-Control method can and should be implemented in the system, using Leveson's STAMP model. Other important principles suggested are the need for an ongoing process of improvement and redundancy in the system.

Chapter 5 describes the current state of unsafety in *criminal evidence* and suggests possible safety measures regarding the four main types of criminal evidence: DNA testing, fingerprint comparisons, confessions, and eyewitness identifications. It addresses also "junk science," which is yet another enemy of safety in the criminal justice system. The safety suggestions are based both on an analysis of each individual type of evidence in line with current research on the subject and on modern safety theory and its implementation in the criminal justice system in accordance with the principles outlined in Chapters 2, 3, and 4. I focus first on different types of scientific evidence, as the overall safety solutions for them are similar, and then look at the two central pieces of nonscientific evidence: confessions and eyewitness identifications.

Chapter 6 points the way to safety in *criminal procedure*, addressing specifically police and prosecutorial negligence and misconduct, plea bargains, and post-conviction proceedings. I examine first the current state of unsafety in each of the procedures chosen for discussion and then propose possible safety measures to contend with this. The latter are based on analyses of each procedure in line with current research and on modern safety theory as I propose applying it in criminal law.

It is important to note that I offer only some possible safety methods. Developing an all-encompassing, comprehensive safety theory for the criminal justice system will entail much additional interdisciplinary scholarly research, which I recommend be conducted and consolidated in the framework of the proposed Safety in the Criminal Justice System Institute.

Finally, the Conclusion wraps up with the assertion that given the Hidden Accidents Principle in criminal law, the legal system must apply modern system-safety methods that were developed in other fields. It must make greater use of scientific research and of other disciplines, such as psychology, and rely less on so-called common sense and "past experience." This will enable an assessment of the risks built into the system and generate possible ways, in both evidence law and criminal procedure, to eliminate those risks without undermining the objectives of criminal law. Only once this has been accomplished will society have a criminal legal system in which more actual criminals and fewer innocent people are convicted.

1   The Need for Safety in the Criminal Justice System

I. General

Safety-critical systems have been defined as "systems whose failure could result in loss of life, significant property damage, or damage to the environment."[1] A failure of such systems could result in catastrophic damage. Accordingly, engineering methods designed to reduce such risks are imperative in their development and manufacture. The legal system is one such safety-critical system.[2] As it deals with matters of life and death, any error in this system is likely to cause grave harm to both the individual and society in general. A false conviction is no less an accident than a fighter airplane crash. As will be shown, this analogy is not only metaphorical, in terms of the economic tolls both entail, but quite literal.[3]

---

[1] J.C. KNIGHT, SAFETY CRITICAL SYSTEMS: CHALLENGES AND DIRECTIONS (2002). *See also* Mordechai Halpert & Boaz Sangero, *From a Plane Crash to the Conviction of an Innocent Person: Why Forensic Science Evidence Should Be Inadmissible unless It Has Been Developed as a Safety-Critical System*, 32 HAMLINE L. REV. 65, 70 (2009).

[2] Halpert & Sangero, *supra* note 1.

[3] *See infra* Part 4.

An error such as a false conviction is likely to cause deprivation of liberty in the form of imprisonment or even loss of life through the death penalty. There have been cases in which inmates sentenced to death have emerged as innocent[4] or where innocent defendants have been executed.[5] But even when human life is not at risk, the deprivation of liberty through imprisonment constitutes a horrific injury to the individual. This possibility justifies classifying the criminal justice system as a safety-critical system just like any system that is likely to cause injury (and not death).

As a safety-critical system, the criminal justice system also requires safety measures. From the perspective of those engaged in safety in other spheres of life, it would seem indisputable that safety is required in criminal law. But modern system-safety has not been introduced into the criminal justice system, and there is no common discourse of safety terms. Thus, as this book addresses primarily those who are engaged in law and not safety, I will begin here by justifying the incorporation of safety into criminal law on three rationales: (1) the unrecognized high rate of false convictions, (2) the state's moral duty to implement safety measures in the criminal justice system, and (3) the economic rationale for safety in the criminal justice system. I will also address possible objections to this justification and offer some conclusions.[6]

II. False Convictions Do Occur, and at an Unrecognized High Rate

Risk assessment is an integral part of safety. For many years, however, there was complete denial of the phenomenon of a false convictions. Thus, the first prong of the justification for incorporating safety into the criminal law is the actual incidence of false convictions and the rate of their occurrence, which I will estimate below.

A. FALSE CONVICTIONS HAPPEN

There has been a tendency in the past to cast doubt on the possibility that a significant number of innocent persons are convicted of crimes they did not commit. In

---

[4] Michael Risinger, *Innocents Convicted: An Empirically Justified Factual Wrongful Conviction Rate*, 97 J. CRIM. L. & CRIMINOLOGY 761 (2007).

[5] *See, e.g.*, Hugo A. Bedau & Michael L. Radelet, *Miscarriages of Justice in Potentially Capital Cases*, 40 STAN. L. REV. 21, 72–75 (1987).

[6] Parts of this chapter are based in part on the two following articles: Boaz Sangero & Mordechai Halpert, *A Safety Doctrine for the Criminal Justice System*, 2011 MICH. STATE L. REV. 1293; Halpert & Sangero, *supra* note 1.

England,[7] the long-standing prevailing view was that no such phenomenon exists.[8] This conservative approach was soundly shaken with the renowned Birmingham Six[9] and Guildford Four[10] cases, in which the wrongful convictions of Irish individuals who had fallen victim to "predatory" British investigators were uncovered. In the wake of these cases, the Runciman Commission was appointed and, following its 1993 report,[11] the English approach to false convictions shifted considerably. This included the establishment of the Criminal Cases Review Commission (CCRC), an independent public body with the mandate to examine any claim of wrongful conviction.[12] The CCRC conducts its own inquiries and transfers cases it deems suitable to the courts for reconsideration.[13] In a considerable number of these cases (dozens a year), falsely convicted individuals have been acquitted and released from prison.[14]

In the United States,[15] too, courts have tended to be dismissive of the possibility of false convictions. In fact, for many years, a considerable number of jurists believed false conviction to be a virtual impossibility. Learned Hand's oft-quoted description of the phenomenon as an "unreal dream"[16] is reflective of this predominant approach. Despite clear research and empirical evidence of a significant number of wrongful convictions,[17] skeptics have remained doubtful.[18]

The great difficulty in detecting false convictions can be explained by what Dr. Mordechai Halpert and I term the "Hidden Accidents Principle" of criminal

---

[7] Boaz Sangero, *Miranda Is Not Enough: A New Justification for Demanding "Strong Corroboration" to a Confession*, 28 CARDOZO L. REV. 2791, 2792–93 (2007).

[8] *See, e.g.*, CLIVE WALKER & KEIR STAMER, JUSTICE IN ERROR 16 (1993) (acknowledging this approach and expressing reservations about it).

[9] R. v. McIlkenny, (1991) 93 Cr. App. R. 287.

[10] R. v. Richardson, 1989 WL 651412 (C.A. Crim. Div. 1989).

[11] ROYAL COMMISSION ON CRIMINAL JUSTICE REPORT: PRESENTED TO PARLIAMENT BY COMMAND OF HER MAJESTY, JULY 1993 (HMSO 1993) [hereinafter RUNCIMAN COMMISSION REPORT].

[12] *See* the CCRC website at http://www.ccrc.gov.uk.

[13] *Id.*

[14] *Id.*; Lissa Griffin, *The Correction of Wrongful Convictions: A Comparative Perspective*, 16 AM. U. INT'L L. REV. 1241, 1275–78 (2001); Lissa Griffin, *Correcting Injustice: Studying How the United Kingdom and the United States Review Claims of Innocence*, 41 UNIV. TOLEDO L. REV. 107 (2009).

[15] Sangero, *supra* note 7, at 2793–94.

[16] United States v. Garsson, 291 F. 646, 649 (1923).

[17] *See, e.g.*, Hugo Adam Bedau & Michael L. Radelet, *Miscarriages of Justice in Potentially Capital Cases*, 40 STAN. L. REV. 21 (1987); Arye Rattner, *Convicted but Innocent: Wrongful Conviction and the Criminal Justice System*, 12 LAW & HUM. BEHAV. 283 (1988); Richard A. Leo & Richard J. Ofshe, *The Consequences of False Confession: Deprivations of Liberty and Miscarriages of Justice in the Age of Psychological Interrogation*, 88 J. CRIM. L. & CRIMINOLOGY 429 (1998).

[18] *See, e.g.*, Gerald M. Caplan, *Questioning* Miranda, 48 VAND. L. REV. 1417, 1457 (1985); Laurie Magid, *Deceptive Police Interrogation Practices: How Far Is Too Far?*, 99 MICH. L. REV. 1168, 1190 (2001).

law.[19] This principle refers to reality in which accidents in criminal law—false convictions—tend to remain concealed. In contrast to aeronautics, for example, where an airplane crash is an open fact, no one—except the person accused, who is almost never believed—ever knows or can know that a defendant has been wrongly convicted. This enables legal decision-makers to optimistically assume the system is close to perfect, and makes it virtually impossible to prove otherwise.

But with the initiation of the groundbreaking Innocence Project at the Cardozo School of Law, it was no longer possible to deny the significance of false convictions as a phenomenon and brand it mere supposition. From this dramatic point onward, disputing the possibility of a false conviction became synonymous with ignorance. Through its work, the Innocence Project has with DNA testing exposed over three-hundred wrongful convictions.[20] Only in a small proportion of cases in which an inmate claims he or she was wrongly convicted is there sufficient physical evidence available to conduct post-conviction DNA testing. It can thus be safely assumed that those convictions that are actually exposed as wrongful through DNA testing are merely the tip of the iceberg.

One of the most impactful works on the exposure of wrongful convictions is Samuel R. Gross and Michael Shaffer's study, entitled *Exonerations in the United States, 1989-2012—Report by the National Registry of Exonerations*.[21] The researchers gathered data on the exoneration of wrongfully convicted defendants in the United States, including exonerations based on DNA comparative testing, but not only such exonerations. Gross and Schaffer were extremely cautious—I believe, too much so—regarding which cases were included in their database: they looked only at cases in which the authorities had officially recognized the wrongful conviction of an innocent defendant and exonerated him or her . This is despite the fact that the researchers had data on many additional cases in which the wrongfulness of the conviction was nearly certain. Gross and Schaffer stressed that by applying this very narrow condition of official exoneration by the law-enforcement system, they had managed to collect data on only some of the relevant cases; this is, in fact,

---

[19] Sangero & Halpert, *supra* note 6, at 1314–16. This will be discussed in greater detail in Chapter 3.

[20] *See* INNOCENCE PROJECT, KNOW THE CASES, http://www.innocenceproject.org/know/Browse-Profiles.php (last visited April 14, 2015 – 329 exonerations). Even though the results of DNA testing could lead to exoneration, they do not necessarily do so, however. Rather, what usually happens is that the police reopen their investigation of the case. A convictions is then overturned only when the police discover in the reopened investigation that the defendant is innocent, or the person who actually committed the crime is identified, or errors in the evidence-gathering that led to the conviction are discovered. For a case (George Allen) in which the defendant was not exonerated for years despite DNA test results pointing to his innocence, see Boaz Sangero & Mordechai Halpert, *Proposal to Reverse the View of a Confession: From Key Evidence Requiring Corroboration to Corroboration for Key Evidence*, 44 U. MICH. J. L. REFORM 511 (2011).

[21] SAMUEL R. GROSS & MICHAEL SHAFFER, EXONERATIONS IN THE UNITED STATES, 1989–2012, REPORT BY THE NATIONAL REGISTRY OF EXONERATIONS (2013).

they stated, only the preliminary stages of a database that is expected to expand greatly with the addition of many more cases of false convictions that have yet to be identified. Regardless, the database encompasses an impressive number of exonerations: 891 exonerations of individuals, of which approximately one-third were based on DNA comparisons, and an additional 1170 individuals cleared in "group exonerations";[22] altogether these amounted to a total of 2061 official exonerations of wrongly convicted, innocent defendants who were sentenced to prison or even death. These numbers remove any doubt as to the occurrence of false convictions. The question now, however, is with what frequency they occur, and what can be done to diminish their incidence.

As noted, the Hidden Accidents Principle is what facilitates many optimists about the criminal justice system to compellingly claim that false convictions never occur, or else understate their frequency. In *Kansas v. Marsh*, for example, Justice Antonin Scalia referred to an earlier Gross study,[23] which exposed 340 wrongful convictions.[24] He indicated that in his view, false convictions are a marginal phenomenon, citing a prosecutor who had claimed in a newspaper article that the rate of false convictions reaches, at most, a mere 0.027 percent.

> [L]et's give the professor the benefit of the doubt: let's assume that he understated the number of innocents by roughly a factor of 10, that instead of 340 there were 4,000 people in prison who weren't involved in the crime in any way. During that same 15 years, there were more than 15 million felony convictions across the country. That would make the error rate .027 percent—or, to put it another way, a success rate of 99.973 percent.[25]

Below, I set out a theoretical model—developed by Dr. Halpert and me for estimating the false-convictions rate, which is based on the fundamental risk inherent to the standard of proof required in criminal law. Using this model, I will demonstrate that from a theoretical perspective, Scalia's optimism about the system is unfounded. I will then apply findings from empirical studies to further challenge this view.

---

[22] These group exonerations were in the framework of twelve different instances of police corruption, where in each case, police officers had deliberately and systematically incriminated innocent citizens with false claims and fabricated evidence in order to gain promotions. *Id.*

[23] Samuel R. Gross et al., *Exonerations in the United States 1989 through 2003*, 95 J. CRIM. L. & C. 523 (2006).

[24] 548 U.S. 163, 196–98 (Scalia, J., concurring).

[25] *Id.* at 197–98 (quoting Joshua Marquis, *The Innocent and the Shammed*, N.Y. TIMES, Jan. 26, 2006, at A23).

B. THE FALSE-CONVICTION RATE BASED ON THE CRIMINAL
STANDARD OF PROOF

Under[26] Blackstone's 1:10 ratio, which is the prevailing rule in American law, there must be a 90 percent certainty of a defendant's guilt in order to convict.[27] Indeed, as he famously declared, "better that ten guilty persons escape, than that one innocent suffer."[28] A survey of judges on the required threshold of proof in criminal law found the most common response to be a 90 percent certainty of guilt,[29] which is in line with Blackstone's ratio. If we take this to be the actual average ratio,[30] this is a significant divergence from the optimistic estimate of over 99 percent reliability in conviction.

To illustrate, let us take the 2012 figures for convicted prisoners in the United States of 1,571,013,[31] and assume a uniform distribution of the probability of guilt, from a minimum threshold of 90 percent to a maximum of 100 percent. This would make the average true conviction rate 95 percent, that is, the median between the 90 percent threshold level and 100 percent ceiling, and mean that 5 percent of the 1,571,013 convicts—78,551—were wrongly convicted. This exposes the logical

---

[26] This section is based on Sangero & Halpert, *supra* note 6. I have modified the calculation, and responsibility for any error is solely mine.

[27] Alexander Volokh, *n Guilty Men*, 146 U. PA. L. REV. 173, 174 (1997); Sangero & Halpert, *supra* note 26, at 1316; Daniel Epps, *The Consequences of Error in Criminal Justice*, 128 HARV. L. REV. (forthcoming 2015); Edward K. Cheng, *Essay: Reconceptualizing the Burden of Proof*, 122 YALE L.J. 1254, 1275–76 ("the beyond-a-reasonable-doubt standard has often been (informally) quantified as 0.90 or 0.95"); Brown v. Bowen, 847 F.2d 342, 345-46 (7th Cir. 1988) (0.9 or higher); Andrea Roth, *Safety in Numbers? Deciding When DNA Alone Is Enough to Convict*, 85 N.Y.U.L. REV. 1130, 1176 (2010) ("most scholars, judges, and jurors would place the numerical equivalent of 'beyond a reasonable doubt' in a typical case involving qualitative evidence at closer to 95 percent certainty of guilt or lower").

[28] Volokh, *supra* note 27.

[29] The average response was 90.3 percent, and the median response 90 percent. C.M.A. McCauliff, *Burdens of Proof: Degrees of Belief, Quanta of Evidence, or Constitutional Guarantees?*, 35 VAND. L. REV. 1293, 1324–27 (1982). *See also* Sangero & Halpert, *supra* note 26, at 1316–17. For an overview of other surveys showing similar results, see Lawrence M. Solan, *Refocusing the Burden of Proof in Criminal Cases: Some Doubt about Reasonable Doubt*, 78 TEX. L. REV. 105, 125–29 (1999).

[30] This is a questionable proposition, for defendants are often convicted on a single piece of evidence, such as a lineup identification, their confession, or one item of scientific evidence. The "fallacy of the transposed conditional" (or "false positive fallacy") is likely to arise in such cases, and the probability of guilt is much lower than would appear. *See* Boaz Sangero & Mordechai Halpert, *Why a Conviction Should Not Be Based on a Single Piece of Evidence: A Proposal for Reform*, 48 JURIMETRICS J. 43 (2007). A judge's estimation of a 90 percent certainty of guilt is, moreover, subjective, and there is no reason not to assume that in reality, a much lower certainty of guilt was proven. In addition, in the context of juries, "When explicitly instructed to use a standard-of-proof threshold of 90 percent, simulated jurors reported using an average standard of 85 percent, which appears to have been a compromise between the instructed threshold and the one they reported absent an instruction (78 percent)." DAN SIMON, IN DOUBT—THE PSYCHOLOGY OF THE CRIMINAL JUSTICE PROCESS 185 (2012).

[31] U.S. DEP'T OF JUSTICE, OFFICE OF JUSTICE PROGRAMS, BUREAU OF JUSTICE STATISTICS, CORRECTIONAL POPULATIONS IN THE UNITED STATES, *available at* http://www.bjs.gov/index.cfm?ty=pbdetail&iid=4737 (last visited Oct. 13, 2014). *See also* Erica Goode, *U.S. Prison Populations Decline, Reflecting a New Approach to Crime*, N.Y. TIMES, July 25, 2013.

inconsistency of a 1:10 ratio for the beyond-reasonable-doubt-threshold, which pre-dicts a 5 percent rate of wrongful convictions and shows the fallacy of the optimistic contention, held by many, that the legal process and law-enforcement system are safe, with only a negligible rate of error: Alongside the rightful convictions of many guilty defendants, a not-insignificant amount of innocent defendants are convicted of crimes they did not commit. Consequently, it is vital that resources be devoted to turn the system into a safer one.

It could be argued that this calculation fails to take into account the fact that most convictions are the outcome of plea bargains,[32] which allegedly have a significantly lower error rate than court verdicts.[33] This claim, however, does not take into account safety considerations. For rather than improving overall safety in convictions, plea bargains in fact entail greater risks, as they do not require 90 percent proof of guilt. It is sufficient to close a plea bargain for a defendant to confess, without any further proof of his or her guilt. In fact, offering a defendant a plea deal is often justified on the fact that the prosecution does not have strong enough evidence to convict at a full trial.[34] In turn, innocent defendants are often tempted to accept the deal for fear of harsher con-sequences if they go to trial.[35] Thus, it is quite possible for a conviction to be false even if the defendant has confessed as part of a plea bargain.[36] A prominent example is cases of widespread police corruption, where many innocent suspects are brought to trial and the majority plead guilty, as in the LAPD Rampart scandal[37] and Tulia scandal.[38]

---

[32] *See* Sangero & Halpert, *supra* note 26, at 1317–18. Plea bargains are discussed extensively in Chapter 6.

[33] Morris B. Hoffman, *The Myth of Factual Innocence*, 82 CHI.-KENT L. REV. 663, 672 (2007). *See* Sangero & Halpert, *supra* note 26, at 1317. *See also* the interesting debate between Allen and Laudan and between Risinger in Ronald J. Allen & Larry Laudan, *Why Do We Convict as Many Innocent People as We Do?: Deadly Dilemmas*, 41 TEX. TECH L. REV. 65 (2008), and D. Michael Risinger, *Tragic Consequences of Deadly Dilemmas: A Response to Allen and Laudan*, 40 SETON HALL L. REV. 991 (2010).

[34] Joachim Herrmann, *Bargaining Justice: A Bargain for German Criminal Justice?*, 53 U. PITT. L. REV. 755, 756 (1992).

[35] GEORGE C. THOMAS III, THE SUPREME COURT ON TRIAL—HOW THE AMERICAN JUSTICE SYSTEM SACRIFICES INNOCENT DEFENDANTS 40 (2008); James Vorenberg, *Decent Restraint of Prosecutorial Power*, 94 HARV. L. REV. 1521, 1535 (1981); Phil Fennell et al., *The Convergence of the Continental and the Common Law Model of Criminal Procedure*, 7 CRIM. L. F. 471, 474 (1996) (book review).

[36] Brandon L. Garrett, *Judging Innocence*, 108 COLUM. L. REV. 55, 74 (2008). *See also* the study conducted in Virginia, *infra* note 54 and accompanying text, which examined all cases in which DNA samples were preserved, but without distinguishing between cases culminating in a plea bargain and those in which no plea bargain was made. The DNA testing revealed that even in plea bargains, wrongful convictions occur (fn 6 on page 4 of the study).

[37] Gross et al., *supra* note 23, at 534–36. In the LAPD Rampart scandal, a corrupt police officer who was await-ing trial for dealing in cocaine revealed how he and his colleagues in the unit had incriminated defendants by fabricating evidence, false testimony, and more. At least one-hundred defendants were incriminated and convicted in this way, with most pleading guilty to the charges against them. *See also* JUSTIN BROOKS, WRONGFUL CONVICTIONS CASES AND MATERIALS 190 (2014).

[38] Gross et al., *supra* note 23, at 534–36. In the Tulia scandal, thirty-nine defendants were tried for drug offenses as a result of a single piece of false testimony given by an undercover police detective. Most of the defendants pleaded guilty and were convicted.

C. ESTIMATING THE FALSE-CONVICTION RATE BASED
ON EMPIRICAL DATA

The preceding sections presented studies confirming the actual occurrence of false convictions, as well as a theoretical calculation of the rate of false convictions, based on the proof threshold in criminal law. This section will now show how the false-conviction rate can be estimated based on actual empiric data.

Michael Risinger conducted a groundbreaking study on false convictions[39] using data gathered from Innocence Project cases, which found a 3.3 percent minimum rate of factually wrongful convictions in the 1980s for capital rape-murder.[40] He calculated this minimum rate using the known number of false convictions within a reference group with similar characteristics as the numerator and total number of convictions within the same reference group as the denominator.[41] To form a reliably sized reference group, Risinger observed a group of eleven cases[42] of false conviction for capital rape-murder between 1982 and 1989 that had been uncovered by the Innocence Project and where DNA samples had been preserved.[43] He then excluded 5 percent of the cases based on the possibility that some of the defendants had been guilty despite indications to the contrary from DNA testing. This left 10.5 relevant cases for analysis.[44] During the period of time relevant to the study's cases, there had been 479 capital rape-murder convictions in the United States.[45] The Innocence Project data showed no DNA samples had been preserved in one-third of the cases.[46] Accordingly, it could be predicted that post-conviction DNA testing could be possible in only two-thirds (319 cases) of the 479 convictions,[47] yielding a 10.5/319 = 3.33 percent minimum false-conviction rate.[48] This was determined as the minimum, as it was unclear whether all 319 convicted defendants had requested post-conviction DNA testing.[49] Risinger assumed, however, that at least half of the 391 would have requested DNA testing, as this would be their last hope for

---

[39] Michael Risinger, *Innocents Convicted: An Empirically Justified Factual Wrongful Conviction Rate*, 97 J. CRIM. L. & CRIMINOLOGY 761 (2007). For a description of this study, see Sangero & Halpert, *supra* note 26, at 1318–19.

[40] Risinger, *supra* note 39, at 780.

[41] *Id.* at 768.

[42] *Id.* at 773–74.

[43] *Id.* at 774–78.

[44] *Id.* at 774. In my opinion, this conclusion is overcautious. *See supra* note 20.

[45] *Id.* at 778.

[46] *Id.*

[47] *Id.*

[48] *Id.*

[49] *Id.*

exoneration.[50] This assumption yielded a 6.4 percent upper boundary,[51] but because of the lack of accurate data, Risinger set a "fair threshold" of 5 percent.[52] As opposed to the lower boundary, which was well supported by the data, the upper boundary and fair threshold were solely estimates and could have been set even higher.[53]

In fact, a recently published, fascinating empirical study, initiated and funded by the State of Virginia,[54] supports an even higher estimate of the false conviction rate, in excess of 5 percent. Similar to Risinger's research, this timely study was based on recent DNA testing conducted in relation to convictions from the 1980s, in an attempt to identify false convictions. Unlike Risinger's study, however, the database was not comprised of exonerations in the framework of the Innocence Project. The Virginian study began with the Innocence Project's attempt to obtain a biological sample from the crime scene of a particular convicted defendant who claimed to be innocent. No sample could be found in the court files, but a thorough investigation discovered that a sample had been preserved in the laboratory where the defendant's blood type had been tested at the time of the investigation. The lab serologist, Mary Jane Burton, it emerged, kept samples in the lab from all the cases she worked on. Following the uncovering of this reserve of samples, the governor of Virginia ordered, in 2005, that genetic comparisons be conducted on all the pairs of samples that had been found (in every pair of samples, one sample is taken from the crime scene and the other from the defendant's body) that were from cases ending in conviction for rape, sexual assault, murder, or manslaughter. This critical decision set in motion the first wide-scale testing of samples remaining after conviction—and not limited to cases in which inmates have requested the testing but, rather, in a "test-them-all" approach. Data were gathered on 634 cases, of which 422 were convictions for rape or other sexual assault offenses between the years 1973 and 1987. In about half of the sexual assault cases, it was possible to ascertain whether there was a match between the DNA from the crime scene (from the victim's body, clothes, etc.) and the convicted defendant's DNA. In about half of the cases, no such determination was possible, for a variety of reasons, including insufficient genetic material.

---

[50] *Id.* at 779.

[51] *Id.*

[52] *Id.* at 779–80.

[53] *Id.*; Sangero & Halpert, *supra* note 26, at 1319.

[54] John Roman, Kelly Walsh, Pamela Lachman & Jennifer Yahner, Post-Conviction DNA Testing and Wrongful Conviction (2012) (research report submitted to the U.S. Department of Justice).

The investigators performed genetic comparisons and examined all the data in the files and, after meticulous study, reached the following four results:[55]

(1) In 40 out of 422 cases, the DNA comparison negated the possibility that the body of the person convicted of the crime was the source of the DNA taken from the crime scene—9 percent of the 422 cases.

(2) In 33 of those same 40 cases, not only did the DNA comparison negate the possibility of the crime-scene DNA sample belonging to the convicted defendant, but the examination of the relevant case data known to the researchers showed it to be exculpatory evidence—8 percent of the 422 cases.

To illustrate the difference between the first and second categories of cases, take the case of joint offenders who were both convicted of the crime in question, where it is possible that the DNA taken from the crime scene belongs to the one but not the other. In the first category of cases, it is still possible, based on other evidence, that both are guilty of the crime. In the second category of cases, however, the circumstances point to exculpatory evidence: for example, if it is known that there was only one assailant in the rape, and the sperm found at the crime scene has a genetic profile that does not match either the defendant or the victim.

(3) In 40 of the 227 cases in which the DNA comparison could determine whether the convicted defendant was the source of the DNA sample taken from the crime scene, the answer was in the negative—18 percent of the 227 cases.

(4) In 33 of those same 40 cases, where the DNA comparison determined whether the convicted defendant was the source of the DNA, not only was the answer in the negative, but the examination of the relevant case data known to the researchers in fact indicated exculpatory evidence—15 percent of the 227 cases.

---

[55] *Id.* at 5–6. It should be noted that the study examined also cases of conviction for manslaughter. Naturally, however, the number of cases in which genetic samples were found at the crime scene and then preserved is far lower for manslaughter than for rape offenses, where sperm samples are taken from the victim's body as a matter of routine. In addition, in cases of rape by a stranger, where the defendant cannot claim consensual relations, the genetic sample is an indicator of guilt or innocence far more often than in cases of manslaughter. In the course of the Virginia study, not enough data were collected on the manslaughter cases to allow for any productive statistical analysis. *Id.*

Which figure is relevant to assessing the false-conviction rate? Let us begin with a different question: Had we been able to perform genetic testing in the past (in those same years in which these defendants were convicted), how many innocent, wrongfully convicted defendants would have been saved from this horrific fate? This question can be easily answered: 9 percent if we are willing to suffice with the negation of a match to the convicted defendant by a genetic comparison, and 8 percent if we want to be more precise and examine whether, given the aggregate of evidence in the case, the convicted defendant still could be guilty.

In my view, however, this is not the interesting question. My aim is not to "promote" DNA testing. Thus, those cases in which the DNA does not enable a determination of the defendant's guilt are of no interest to us. In attempting to estimate the rate at which innocent defendants are wrongfully convicted, we must look only at the 227 cases in which the genetic testing allows a determination as to whether this is the right person. Accordingly, the pertinent finding is either 18 percent, if we are willing to suffice with the negation of a match with the convicted defendant by the genetic comparison, or 15 percent, if we want to be more precise and examine whether, given the aggregate of evidence in the case, it is possible that the convicted defendant is indeed guilty. These are alarming results. **Fifteen (or even possibly eighteen) out of every 100 people convicted of rape (or some other sexual assault) are in fact innocent!**

I will try to illustrate in an additional way why, in my opinion, from the various data presented in the Virginia study, only the data on the cases in which the DNA sample enabled a significant finding regarding guilt or innocence are relevant to our purposes. Assume that all 422 trials were conducted in hazy conditions, preventing us from knowing if the conviction was the correct outcome. Then assume that we somehow manage to secure a "magic" lamp that shines light on some of the trials, but only randomly so. We could take this lamp into all 422 courtrooms, but it would work in only 227 of them and clarify whether the defendant is rightfully being accused. Assume that we would find strong evidence of innocence in 15 percent (or even 18 percent) of these "illuminated" cases. What, then, would be the expected rate of conviction of innocent defendants at trials (at least for rape and other sexual assault offenses) that were conducted in Virginia during the period examined by the study? Taking account of various methodological doubts regarding this study,[56] the answer could possibly be 15 percent (or 18 percent).

---

[56] I should note that the researchers who conducted the study were wary of asserting that the more significant figure is 15 percent (or 18 percent), reasoning that it is impossible to know whether the 227 cases in which it was possible to determine if there was a match between the crime-scene DNA and the convicted defendant constitute a representative sample of the 422 convictions or of all convictions for rape and sexual assault in that same period in Virginia. *Id.* at 56. Yet as they do determine that the 422 convictions are a representative

In 2014, Gross et al. published their study on "Rates of False Conviction of Criminal Defendants who are Sentenced to Death."[57] They found that capital defendants who are removed from death row but not exonerated cease to benefit from the high level of attention given to death row inmates. Thus, innocent inmates who are released from the threat of death are far less likely to be exonerated than had they remained on death row. Given this, the proportion of death-row inmates who are exonerated must be far lower than the proportion of false convictions among other inmates, as "the intensive search for possible errors is largely abandoned once the threat of execution is removed. In other words, the engine that produces an exoneration rate that is a plausible proxy for the rate of false conviction among death-sentenced prisoners is the process of reinvestigation and reconsideration under threat of execution."[58] The researchers found that with time, the majority of the death-sentenced inmates are taken off death row and resentenced to life in prison. At that point, the chances of exoneration appear to return to (or close to) the background rate for all murders. A better estimate of the rate of false capital convictions can be calculated, therefore, based on the rate of capital exonerations if all death sentences are "subject for an indefinite period to the level of scrutiny that applies to those facing the prospect of execution."[59] Accordingly, the researchers gathered data on 7482 death-sentenced inmates in the United States between 1973 and 2004. Of these, 117 who were sentenced to death after January 1, 1973, were exonerated by legal proceedings that began before the end of 2004. The researchers used "survival analysis" to model the expected effect ("the intensive search for possible errors is largely abandoned once the threat of execution is removed"). They estimated that if all death-sentenced defendants were to remain under sentence of death indefinitely, at least 4.1 percent would be exonerated, but concluded this to be "a conservative estimate" of the proportion of false convictions among death sentences

---

sampling of all convictions for these offenses in Virginia in that particular period (completely coincidentally, the tests were conducted in Mary Jane Burton's laboratory and not in another laboratory), and as they found no factor accounting for a divergence between the false-conviction rate in those cases (approximately half) in which the DNA sample enabled a determination and the rate in those cases in which a determination could not be made, there is no good reason to assume that the 227 cases are not representative. Moreover, even if they are not representative, is it not possible that the false-conviction rate in those cases where no determination can be made is in fact higher? So long as we do not know the results of the testing, the very fact that in a given case, genetic comparison can (or cannot) determine whether the right person has been caught bears absolutely no relevance to the question of whether the defendant is guilty or innocent and rightfully or wrongfully convicted. Either way, I concur with the authors' assertion that even were the false-conviction rate for these offenses "only" 8 percent, such a finding, too, is extremely distressing and requires a meaningful action to improve the criminal justice system. *Id.* at 58.

[57] SAMUEL R. GROSS, BARBARA O'BRIEN, CHEN HU & EDWARD H. KENNEDY, RATE OF FALSE CONVICTION OF CRIMINAL DEFENDANTS WHO ARE SENTENCED TO DEATH 111 PNAS 7230 (2014).
[58] *Id* at 7231.
[59] *Id.*

in the United States, and that it is almost certain that the actual proportion is significantly higher (i.e., 4.1 percent is the greatest lower bound). The researchers detail in their article some of the many factors for this 4.1 percent rate of false convictions and conclude with the following interesting finding and assessment:

> Interviews with jurors who participated in capital sentencing proceedings indicate that lingering doubts about the defendant's guilt is the strongest available predictor of a sentence of life imprisonment rather than death. It follows that the rate of innocence must be higher for convicted capital defendants who are not sentenced to death than for those who are. The net result is that the great majority of innocent defendants who are convicted of capital murder in the United States are neither executed nor exonerated. They are sentenced, or resentenced to prison for life, and then forgotten.[60]

D. SUMMARY

There can be no doubt that false convictions occur. Due to the Hidden Accidents Principle in criminal law, many people continue to have great faith in the system and are confident that the rate of false convictions is low. Yet as the hypothetical calculation presented above shows, this is hardly the case. This illustration demonstrated that a 90 percent probability of guilt under the reasonable doubt standard, as judges estimate it to be, yields a 5 percent false-conviction rate. This has the catastrophic implication that at any moment in time, almost eighty thousand innocent convicted prisoners are locked up in U.S. prisons.

This hypothetical calculation is supported by estimates made based on empirical data. Risinger found, for example, a minimum 3.3 percent rate of false conviction in capital rape-murder cases. But we must add to these detected cases of false conviction those cases that go undetected due to the Hidden Accidents Principle. Gross et al.'s study, in turn, which was based on the exoneration of death-sentenced inmates, concluded that a 4.1 percent false-conviction rate is a conservative estimate of the actual proportion of false convictions among capital convicted defendants. Moreover and even more startling, are the findings of the Virginia study, that in 15 percent (or even 18 percent) of all sexual offense cases in which a DNA sample was preserved, the DNA evidence pointed to the convicted defendant's innocence.

Thus the false-conviction rate in all criminal cases—not only in murder and rape offenses—can be reasonably estimated as somewhere between 5 percent and 10 percent. And as it is reasonable to assume that courts are less cautious with regard to less

---

[60] *Id.* at 7235.

serious offenses than those examined in the studies reviewed above, it is likely that the false-conviction rate is significantly higher than 5 percent.

A primary objective of this book is to convey the urgency of understanding and internalizing the need for modern system-safety in criminal law, but I do not want this understanding to be contingent on any particular estimation of the false-conviction rate. Thus despite the findings and data noted above, the discussion throughout the book will suffice with what is emerging to be the conservative assumption of a false-conviction rate of 5–10 percent in general and 5 percent for the most serious offenses.

III. The Moral Duty to Adopt Safety Measures in the Criminal Justice System

A state can inflict no greater injustice on its citizens than a wrongful criminal conviction.[61] This holds especially if not enough was invested or done in preventing a false conviction.[62] The falsely convicted individual bears the primary injury in the very fact of being convicted, the accompanying stigma, and the actual punishment, which can range from a monetary fine to imprisonment, to loss of life in jurisdictions allowing the death penalty. Studies have been conducted on the harm caused by imprisonment for many years, but only in the last decade have the particular harms of *wrongful* imprisonment, some irreversible, been researched. In their article *"Framing Innocents: The Wrongly Convicted as Victims of State Harm,"* Saundra Westervelt and Kimberly J. Cook applied David Kauzlarich et al.'s general model of six characteristics common to victims of state crime to a group of wrongfully-imprisoned individuals they interviewed for the study.[63] Something that emerged from the study was the impact of the central role played by the state that created the injustice on how the wrongly convicted feel and the harm caused to them. The study points to both the harm caused by the false conviction and ensuing false imprisonment (and, at times, the time spent on death row) as well as the great hardships that former inmates experience after exoneration and release: difficulties in sustaining themselves, housing, health, employment due to the residual stigma despite their exoneration, adapting to freedom and their new reality, and in repairing old relationships and forming new ones.[64] These difficulties, along with

---

[61] Parts of this section are based on Sangero & Halpert, *supra* note 6, at 1301–04.
[62] I thank Prof. Alon Harel for this observation.
[63] S. Westervelt & Kimberly J. Cook, *Framing Innocents: The Wrongly Convicted as Victims of State Harm*, 53 CRIME L. & SOC. CHANGE 259 (2010). *See also* David Kauzlarich, Rick Matthews & William Miller, *Toward a Victimology of State Crime*, 10 CRITICAL CRIMINOLOGY 173 (2001).
[64] *Id.* at 260–63.

the lack of assistance and compensation from the state, whose agents do not tend to apologize to exonerees, lead to additional difficulties following their release, which reinforce their sense of grief and loss and lack of self-confidence, particularly in public places, and self-identity.[65]

Another study focused on the mental problems that result from false convictions, pointing to how these problems are further exacerbated by the difficulties exonerated convicts experience after their release: financial dependency, employment obstacles, and the struggle to re-establish family relationships after so many years and the changes people naturally undergo with time.[66] The study surveys other studies that found evidence of post-traumatic stress disorder suffered by wrongly convicted exonerees after release, which shows that the mental damage is more severe than what guilty inmates experience: immediately after imprisonment, exonerees are in a state of shock and disbelief, followed by feelings of helplessness and hopelessness, a sense of injustice and "soul death," and a loss of self-identity and dignity.[67] After release, these are joined by "Post Traumatic Stress Disorder, anxiety, depression, obsessive-compulsions, phobias, paranoia … fears of re-arrest, sleep-disturbances, trouble adapting to life on the outside, and problems trusting others."[68]

A brief description of some specific instances can give insight into the tremendous injustice that society causes to each individual who is wrongly convicted and wastes a significant part of his or her life between prison walls. Ronald Keith Williams is one such illustrative instance. Williams was falsely convicted and sentenced to death for a rape and murder he did not commit, acquitted only after nine years in prison. During his imprisonment, he became so depressed that he tried to hang himself. As was standard practice in Oklahoma at the time, upon release, he received only $50 from the state to begin his life over. After his release from prison, he suffered from nightmares, fear of loud noises, and sleeping in the dark.[69] A similar case is that of Michael Anthony, who was convicted at age sixteen for the rape of his tutor and imprisoned for over twenty-four years—more than half his life—until being exonerated and released. After his release from prison, he experienced alienation from his family and tremendous isolation, and struggled with a lack of basic skills, such as driving and

---

[65] *Id.* at 263–68. On the tremendous difficulties faced by exonerees after their release, see also Heather Weigand, *Rebuilding a Life: The Wrongfully Convicted and Exonerated*, 18 Pub. Interest L.J. 427 (2009); Mary C. Delaney, Keith A. Findley & Sheila Sullivan, *Exonerees' Hardships after Freedom*, 83 Wis. L. Rev. 18 (2010); James R. Acker & Allison D. Redlich, Wrongful Conviction—Law, Science, and Policy 590–606 (2011).

[66] Leslie Scott, *"It Never Ends": The Psychological Impacts of Wrongful Conviction*, 5 Am. Univ. Criminal L. Brief 10 (2010).

[67] *Id.* at 13.

[68] *Id.* at 14.

[69] *Id.* at 10, 12.

using computers and cellular phones, as he had been imprisoned as a mere youth.[70] Similarly, Neil Miller was convicted for a rape he did not commit and was imprisoned for ten years until his release. Before his conviction and imprisonment, Miller had had very strong relationships with his four sisters, daughter, and some of his aunts and cousins. As he held women in great esteem, being accused specifically of rape caused him tremendous mental anguish. His daughter was only a three-year-old when he was imprisoned, but thirteen when he was released ten years later. His wife never brought their daughter to visit Miller in prison, telling her that her father was guilty of the crime he had been convicted of. Thus, the false conviction destroyed Miller's relations with his wife and daughter. After his release, he told the researchers that he felt homeless and at times even wished he could return to his old prison routines.[71]

Finally, David Quindt's case illustrates the deep suffering that false conviction and imprisonment cause almost immediately as well as its long-term consequences even after exoneration. Although he spent only fourteen months in prison until his exoneration, Quindt tried to kill himself twice while imprisoned. Then, after being exonerated and released, he lost the job that he had finally managed to find because due to a court error his charges had never been expunged.[72] Thus, every false conviction that results in incarceration is tragically harmful to the individual, but also, directly and indirectly, to his or her family and friends. Wrongful convictions also cause significant harm to society as a whole, as the actual offender roams free to commit more crimes. According to the data collected by the Innocence Project, at least 40 actual offenders in the cases investigated committed serious crimes in the period that the people falsely convicted in their stead were locked up in prison, with 56 of those crimes rape and 9 murder.[73]

In 2014 the National Academy of Sciences published a very important report, titled The Growth of Incarceration in the United States—Exploring Causes and Consequences.[74] The report concludes that "[t]he increase in incarceration [from prison population of about 200,000 in 1973 to 1.5 million in 2009, let alone about 700,000 that are held daily in local jails[75]] may have caused a decrease in crime, but the magnitude of the reduction is highly uncertain and the results of most studies suggest it was unlikely to have been large."[76] The report shows that the effects of harsh penal policies

---

[70] Id. at 10–11.

[71] Id. at 11–13.

[72] Id. at 12.

[73] BRANDON L. GARRETT, CONVICTING THE INNOCENT—WHERE CRIMINAL PROSECUTIONS GO WRONG 232 (2011).

[74] THE NATIONAL ACADEMY OF SCIENCES, THE GROWTH OF INCARCERATION IN THE UNITED STATES—EXPLORING CAUSES AND CONSEQUENCES (2014), available at http://www.jjay.cuny.edu/_images/NAS_report_on_incarceration.pdf (last visited Dec. 7, 2014).

[75] Id. at 2.

[76] Id. at 4.

in the past forty years have fallen most heavily on blacks and Hispanics, especially the poorest;[77] and that it has a wide range of unwanted social costs, which are felt most acutely in minority communities in urban areas already experiencing significant social, economic, and public health disadvantages.[78] The report recommends: "Given the small crime prevention effects of long prison sentences and the possibly high financial, social, and human costs of incarceration, federal and state policy makers should revise current criminal justice policies to significantly reduce the rate of incarceration in the United States."[79] Indeed, the report does not deal with innocent prisoners, but with the subject of incarceration at large. Nevertheless, its findings regarding the huge costs of incarceration to the prisoners, to their families, to their communities, and to society at large are obviously most relevant also to innocent convicted prisoners.[80]

Although many are willing to accept rare occurrence of wrongful convictions as an unavoidable phenomenon, sooner or later it will become common public knowledge that not only are false convictions not a rarity, but the law enforcement authorities make no significant effort to diminish their incidence. This is likely to strongly shake existing public confidence and trust in the criminal law enforcement system, which is still referred to as the criminal justice system. In other words, even disregarding due process,[81] if we want to preserve public faith in the criminal justice system so that it can continue to perform its function of crime control, it is vital that safety standards be implemented to decrease the rate of false convictions. In this context, Kenneth Kipnis proposed an important distinction between "aberrational injustice" and "systematic injustice."[82] Aberrational injustice occurs as a result of human error: "judges, jurors, lawyers, and legislators with the best of intentions may make errors in judgment that result in mistakes in the administration of punishment."[83] Systematic injustice, in contrast, results "from structural flaws in the criminal justice system itself.... [T]he system itself is not well calculated to avoid injustice."[84] The systematic failure that Kipnis refers to is the plea-bargaining system, which will be addressed further on in the book, along with other systemic failures.

---

[77] *Id.* at 5.

[78] *Id.* at 7.

[79] *Id.* at 9.

[80] *See also* OLIVER ROEDER, LAUREN-BROOKE EISEN & JULIA BOWLING, WHAT CAUSED THE CRIME DECLINE? (A report of the Brennan Center for Justice at New York University School of Law, 2015, *available at* http://papers.ssrn.com/sol3/papers.cfm?abstract_id=2566965 (last visited Feb. 21, 2015) ("This report aims to spur discussion of what constitutes effective policies to deter crime. It aims to use science, law, and logic to break the myth that has fueled mass incarceration and resulted in harm to our communities, our economy, and our country. More incarceration does not lead to *less* crime. The United States can simultaneously reduce crime and reduce mass incarceration." *Id.* at 10.)

[81] HERBERT L. PACKER, THE LIMITS OF THE CRIMINAL SANCTION 149–73 (1968).

[82] Kenneth Kipnis, *Criminal Justice and the Negotiated Plea*, 86 ETHICS 93, 102 (1976).

[83] *Id.*

[84] *Id.* at 103.

The state's failure to invest all of its available resources in safety in any given area is often justified by the fact that it does not have the funds necessary to optimally attain all of its objectives (security, education, health, and so on).[85] In the context of the criminal justice system, however, this does not hold as it does in other contexts. With road traffic, for example, there was a preexisting risk of accidents when the state implemented mandatory safety standards to diminish that risk. The risk of false convictions, in contrast, is created by the state itself: when it prescribes what constitutes criminal behavior in its laws, when it directs focus onto a specific suspect and puts him or her on trial, when it relies on problematic evidence and inaccurate equipment to prove guilt, and when it convicts defendants and imposes harsh sentences on them. Under principles of both tort and criminal law, the agent that creates a dangerous situation bears a duty to eliminate or reduce as best he or she can the risk of harm from that situation. Applying the same logic, the "state-created danger doctrine" imposes a similar duty on the state when its action creates a risk.[86] Given this, not only does the state bear a moral duty to implement safety in its criminal justice system, regardless of the resources this entails, but also a legal duty.

Social contract theory also provides a rationale for imposing a moral duty on the state to institute safety in criminal justice. Under this theory, the state was created in order to safeguard the rights of society's members, not to cause them injury,[87] and as noted, false conviction is the greatest wrong that a state can inflict upon its citizens. Thus, from the social contract perspective, the state, as the creator of the risk of false convictions, bears a heightened moral duty in the context of criminal justice—as compared to other contexts—to take safety measures to alleviate this risk. Yet beyond its theoretical declaration that guilt must be proven beyond a reasonable doubt, the state makes no meaningful attempt to reduce the risk of an innocent person being falsely convicted.[88] Criminal law in fact lacks even the most basic concept of modern system-safety,[89] with not even the most rudimentary and simple safety measures implemented to reduce the risk of false convictions.[90]

This is despite the fact that there is a particularly straightforward solution to funding safety in the criminal justice system. Law enforcement measures are

---

[85] Sangero & Halpert, *supra* note 6, at 1302–303.

[86] *See, e.g.,* Erwin Chemerinsky, *The State-Created Danger Doctrine*, 23 TOURO L. REV. 1 (2007); Rinat Kitai, *What Remains Necessary following* Alabama v. Shelton *to Fulfill the Right of a Criminal Defendant to Counsel at the Expense of the State?*, 30 OHIO N. U. L. REV. (2004) 35, 57.

[87] Rinat Kitai, *Protecting the Guilty*, 6 BUFF. CRIM. L. REV. 1163, 1172–79, 1186–87 (2003); Sangero & Halpert, *supra* note 6, at 1303.

[88] Sangero & Halpert, *supra* note 6, at 1303.

[89] For some groundbreaking articles in this direction, however, see Halpert & Sangero, *supra* note 1; James M. Doyle, *Learning from Error in American Criminal Justice*, 100 J. CRIM. L. & CRIMINOLOGY 109 (2010); Sangero & Halpert, *supra* note 6.

[90] This will be expanded on in Chapters 5 and 6.

contingent on what budget is allocated for this purpose, and safety precautions should be included as an item in that budget.[91] Assuming a fixed budget, this means that safety measures in the system could be funded at the expense of fewer criminal proceedings, for society's objective is not maximum enforcement per se, which would severely hamper individual freedom and make life intolerable, especially in a system that many argue already tends towards over-criminalization.[92]

Finally, George Thomas has offered another rationale for imposing a moral duty on the state to safeguard against false convictions:

> [T]he prime directive of a criminal justice system is to protect the innocent, at a reasonable cost. The American criminal justice system has both a moral and a legal duty to take reasonable steps not to convict the innocent and to review convictions with an eye toward correcting wrongful convictions. The moral duty comes from the principle that the state can justify imposing sanctions only on proof that the defendant threatens the orderly functioning of society. A false accusation of crime does not provide that proof.[93]

In the next section, I will proceed to demonstrate the benefits that other fields have reaped from investing in safety, even under a narrow economic analysis that excludes any moral considerations. I will then explain why this economic justification hold no less for the criminal justice system.

IV. Economic Justification for Investing in Safety in the Criminal Justice System

There is no dispute that a cost-benefit analysis justifies investing in safety in the fighter plane context, for it would simply be too expensive not to do so.[94] As an illustration, a total of $5 million was invested over a ten-year period in the safety program in developing the F-14 fighter plane. At the time, it cost $15 million to

---

[91] Sangero & Halpert, *supra* note 6, at 1303–04.

[92] SANFORD H. KADISH, *The Crisis of Overcriminalization, in* BLAME AND PUNISHMENT: ESSAYS IN THE CRIMINAL LAW 21 (1987); JONATHAN SIMON, GOVERNING THROUGH CRIME: HOW THE WAR ON CRIME TRANSFORMED AMERICAN DEMOCRACY AND CREATED A CULTURE OF FEAR (2007); DOUGLAS HUSAK, OVERCRIMINALIZATION: THE LIMITS OF THE CRIMINAL LAW (2008); GO DIRECTLY TO JAIL: THE CRIMINALIZATION OF ALMOST EVERYTHING (Gene Healy ed., 2004); Lucian E. Dervan, *The Symbiotic Relationship between Plea Bargaining and Overcriminalization,* 7 J. L. ECON. & POL'Y 645 (2011).

[93] THOMAS, *supra* note 35, at 2. Thomas further notes: "[A] deeper value than truth is the protection of the innocent." *Id.* at 2–3. *See also* Susan A. Bandes, *Protecting the Innocent as the Primary Value of the Criminal Justice System,* 7 OHIO ST. J. CRIM. L. 413 (2009).

[94] Parts of this subsection are based on Sangero & Halpert, *supra* note 6, 1304–05. I have modified the calculation, and the responsibility for any error is mine alone.

build one F-14 plane. Thus, even if in practice it were to prevent only a single plane crash, the $5 million investment in safety was economically justified.[95]

No less significant or quantifiable is the economic cost of error in the criminal justice system. Numerous plaintiffs have been awarded vast sums of money in damages over the last two decades, as in *Limone*, where $101,750,000 in compensation was awarded to four falsely convicted men and their immediate families. This amounted to $1 million for each year each man spent in prison.[96] Based on the outcome in this decision, then, the erroneous "solving" of one crime that leads to the wrongful conviction of a given number of individuals can create economic harm in excess of $100 million, which is close to the cost of an expensive modern fighter plane. Moreover, courts have awarded even more damages per year in prison in other cases. For example, Juan Johnson was awarded $21 million for eleven years of false imprisonment,[97] which means nearly $2 million for each year of incarceration. Given this, it is economically justified to invest millions of dollars in safety measures even if they in practice prevent only one false conviction. This premise is even more plausible given the fact that false convictions are, as shown, no isolated or negligible occurrence.

The economic harm false convictions create for society might be claimed to be less than what I argue here as the majority are never uncovered, and society therefore does not need to compensate for this harm. However, economic harm is most definitely created by the state, and its costs are borne, unjustifiably, by the individuals who are falsely convicted, not by society. The state imposes grievous harm yet refrains from taking any precautionary action to prevent its occurrence. In fact, if we multiply the *Limone* outcome of $1 million per year of incarceration[98] by the 78,000 estimated falsely convicted inmates[99] in U.S. prisons at any given moment in time, the economic costs of false convictions could be a staggering $78 billion a year.[100]

Many states in the United States have passed legislation setting a cap on the amount of compensation that can be awarded to exonerees, while federal legislation has set a ceiling of $100,000 for each year of false imprisonment in the case of a death sentence and $50,000 for someone sentenced "only" to imprisonment.[101] In

---

[95] Halpert & Sangero, *supra* note 2, at 89.
[96] Limone v. United States, 579 F.3d 79, 102 (1st Cir. 2009); Sangero & Halpert, *supra* note 6, at 1304.
[97] Ben Meyerson, *Record Verdict: Former Gang Member Awarded $21 Million for Wrongful Conviction*, CHI. TRIB., June 23, 2009; Sangero & Halpert, *supra* note 6, at 1305.
[98] *Limone*, 579 F.3d at 104–05.
[99] Based on a false conviction rate of 5 percent; *see supra* Part II.
[100] Sangero & Halpert, *supra* note 6, at 1305.
[101] 28 U.S.C. § 2513 (e) (2004); ACKER & REDLICH, *supra* note 65, at 591.

my opinion, this "stingy" legislation does not reflect the full extent of the damage caused to the wrongly convicted, as I showed above, but rather is intended to protect the state coffers from a realistic awards judgment, and is contemptuous of human liberty in attributing to it a value of $4167 a month, $139 for twenty-four hours.[102] Putting this aside, however, if we accept the measure of only $50,000 per year of incarceration and multiply it by 78,000, we arrive at the not-negligible annual sum of $3.9 billion. Added to this is the average annual cost of $31,286 to incarcerate one inmate, which amounts to $2.44 billion annually to incarcerate 78,000 innocent inmates.[103]

Moreover, the costs of conducting legal proceedings that culminate in the wrongful conviction of 78,000 innocent defendants each year must also be taken into account. We can assume that the majority of these convictions are the product of a plea bargain, which can cost between thousands to tens of thousands of dollars. Some of these convictions are the outcome of a full trial, whose costs can range between the tens of thousands to hundreds of thousands of dollars. And, finally, some of those convicted at trial are handed down a death sentence, which entails millions of dollars in costs. If we suffice with a conservative estimate of $12,000 for every false conviction and multiply this by 78,000, we arrive at an annual cost of approximately $1 billion.[104]

There is no need to actually add up all of these amounts—the direct damage to the wrongfully convicted inmate, the costs of unnecessary incarceration, and the costs of redundant legal proceedings—for it to be clear that wrongful convictions cause direct economic harm in the billions of dollars annually. This astronomical harm not only justifies but even mandates, from an economic perspective, allocating significant economic resources to making the criminal justice system safer. The extremely conservative calculation presented above indicates damage of approximately $10 billion annually. The allocation of only 1 percent of this amount would

---

[102] Worse yet is the fact that some states have even passed legislation explicitly denying compensation to exonerees, on a variety of unclear grounds, such as the fact the exonerated inmate confessed to the crime and is therefore to be regarded as guilty as convicted. ACKER & REDLICH, *supra* note 65, at 591. This is, of course, outrageous, especially in light of the extensive evidence that innocent suspects are coerced into confessing under the pressure of the police interrogation, discussed in detail in Part IV of Chapter 5.

[103] CHRISTIAN HENRICHSON & RUTH DELANEY, THE PRICE OF PRISONS: WHAT INCARCERATION COSTS TAXPAYERS 9 (2012), *available at* http://www.vera.org/sites/default/files/resources/downloads/Price_of_Prisons_updated_version_072512.pdf (last visited July 11, 2014).

[104] A possible counterargument is, of course, that at least some of the proceedings conducted against innocent defendants are not redundant, but rather should have culminated in acquittal. This is the case, for example, when there is weighty evidence against an innocent defendant that mandates conducting a trial. I have factored this consideration into my conservative estimate of the costs of legal proceedings.

enable $100 million, with which it would certainly be possible to "purchase" significant safety.

These calculations do not, of course, include the harms and costs created by leaving the actual perpetrators of the crimes for which others were wrongly convicted free to commit new crimes. The immense proportions of these costs justify allocating considerable resources to reducing the harm.

Finally, another possible justification for investing significant resources in creating safety in criminal justice does not focus on the harm caused by wrongful convictions, but rather on the system's overall financial turnover. The criminal justice system—from the police investigation and forensic lab work, to the work of the prosecution, defense, and courts, and up to the punishment stage, which centers on imprisonment—is a huge and expensive system. It entails an enormous annual budget, which likely amounts to at least $100 billion annually. The two simultaneous goals of the system are to punish the guilty while refraining from punishing the innocent and causing them injustice. It is unfathomable that the entirety of this enormous budget be channeled only to punishing the guilty, and not even one-thousandth (pro mil) of this sum devoted to the no-less important objective of refraining from punishing the innocent. One-thousandth of an annual budget of $100 billion amounts to $100 million a year. Such funds would ensure the implementation of meaningful safety in the system.

V. Possible Objections

The need to adopt safety measures in the criminal justice system has been justified by the high rate of false convictions, harm that they cause, moral duty of the state to implement safety in the system, and economic considerations. Objections to all four of these rationales are certainly possible. But before addressing each aspect separately, I will offer an overall decisive response to any objections to my claim: namely, it is vital that modern system-safety approaches be incorporated into any safety-critical system—systems where critical accidents can be expected to occur—and the burden of proof is borne not by those who wish to implement safety to prevent false convictions but by those who object to doing so. It is the latter who must prove that despite the consensus regarding the necessity of safety methods in other spheres of life, no such need arises in the criminal justice system.

At this point, it is important to stress that although modern system-safety did first develop within the field of aeronautics in the mid-twentieth century, today, modern safety theory is generalized and applicable to all areas of life. Accordingly, Nancy Leveson, a leader in the field of safety, did not deal with only astronautics, aeronautics, and transportation in her recent book, appropriately entitled *Engineering a Safer World*.[105] As demonstrated in her book, safety does not relate only to technology and machinery but also, and perhaps even principally, to social systems (and, of course, socio-technical systems) in which people act and, as a course of nature, make mistakes. There is a need, therefore, to develop safety rules that will prevent the immediate conversion of human error into heavy damage to human beings, the environment, and property.[106]

A conceptual transformation similar to what I am suggesting in the criminal law arena occurred around 2000 in the medical field. In this field, too, there was insufficient awareness in the past regarding the importance of modern system-safety. It was mistakenly thought that system-safety relates only to machinery and not to human actions. One of the central fruits of the conceptual shift in medicine was a detailed 2000 report prepared by the National Academy of Sciences, *To Err Is Human: Building a Safer Health System*.[107] The report stated that errors in healthcare are a leading cause of death and injury[108] and explained why these errors occur.[109] It set forth a comprehensive approach to improving patient safety,[110] recommending the development of a culture of safety, which should include: building leadership and knowledge for patient safety, establishing and funding a center for patient safety,[111] instituting error-reporting systems (both mandatory and voluntary reporting),[112] setting performance standards and expectations for patient safety,[113] and creating safety systems in healthcare organizations.[114]

Famously exemplifying the crucial importance of safety practices is Ignaz Semmelweis's discovery in the nineteenth century that handwashing by medical staff reduces the incidence of puerperal fever, which caused the otherwise-avoidable deaths of thousands of women during childbirth.[115] This simple, cheap practice dramatically reduces the mortality rate of patients, making it a significant safety measure. Dismissed by his contemporaries as insane, Semmelweis's discovery went

---

[105] NANCY G. LEVESON, ENGINEERING A SAFER WORLD: SYSTEMS THINKING APPLIED TO SAFETY (2011).

[106] *Id.*; *see especially id.* at 198–209 ("Safety Control Structures in Social Systems").

[107] NATIONAL ACAD. OF SCIENCES, COMMITTEE ON QUALITY OF HEALTH CARE IN AMERICA, INSTITUTE OF MEDICINE, TO ERR IS HUMAN: BUILDING A SAFER HEALTH SYSTEM (Linda T. Kohn, Janet M. Corrigan & Molla S. Donaldson eds., 2000).

[108] *Id.* at 26–48.

[109] *Id.* at 49–68.

[110] *Id.* at 17–25.

[111] *Id.* at 69–85.

[112] *Id.* at 86–108.

[113] *Id.* at 132–54.

[114] *Id.* at 155–61.

[115] *See, e.g.*, Ignaz Semmelweis, Wikipedia, *available at* http://en.wikipedia.org/wiki/Ignaz_Semmelweis (last visited July 13, 2014).

on, years later, to influence many in the medical field and, apparently, prevent the unnecessary deaths of countless people. Florence Nightingale also contributed considerably in the nineteenth century to the awareness of the imperativeness of hand hygiene among medical staff.[116] However, tragically, in the twenty-first century, we are still forced to battle infections that result from improper hand hygiene in hospitals.[117] This is only one example of how safety practices in the medical field can save many lives.

The medical system and criminal justice system have a great deal in common. Both are systems that are based primarily not on machinery, technological devices, or computer programs but on human beings. Many errors that arise in these systems are human errors and not technological failures. There is a need to plan the system in advance so as to decrease the number of errors, and so that when an error does occur—and humans will always err—it will not cause the system to collapse. Just as the pioneers of safety in medicine knew that they must look to fields such as aeronautics, astronautics, and transportation to learn about modern system-safety, so must criminal law enforcement agencies do today, and quickly, for they are already a generation behind medicine and generations behind the engineering fields.[118]

I will now return to the four fundamental rationales on which I have justified a need for safety in criminal law: the high false-conviction rate, the harm caused by wrongfully convicting innocent defendants, the state's moral duty to adopt a safety approach, and economic justifications. I hope that my claims were convincing with regard to each of the individual factors rationales. But there is no need to accept all of my premises—certainly not in their entirety—in order to reach the inescapable conclusion that it is imperative that modern system-safety be introduced into the criminal justice system. This conclusion can be reached solely on the basis of the state's moral duty, or solely on the basis of the economic calculation. It seems an incontestable fact that a false conviction causes significant damage to the innocent defendant, his or her family, and society as a whole. There may be some dispute over the false-conviction rate. As discussed, despite my assessment that the rate exceeds 5 percent (likely closer to 10 percent), for the purpose of my calculation of the damage caused, I have sufficed with an assumed 5 percent rate, which, given the finding of recent studies, is a conservative estimate. But even the most conservative of conservatives, who, despite these studies and despite the data from the Innocence Project, will still estimate the false-conviction rate to be no more than 1 percent,

[116] See, e.g., Florence Nightingale, Wikipedia, available at http://en.wikipedia.org/wiki/Florence_Nightingale (last visited July 13, 2014).

[117] Didier Pittet, Improving Compliance with Hand Hygiene in Hospitals, 21 INFECTION CONTROL & HOSPITAL EPIDEMIOLOGY 381 (2000).

[118] Halpert & Sangero, supra note 89; Doyle, supra note 89; Sangero & Halpert, supra note 89.

would have to concede this to be a considerable amount. Of the approximately 1,600,000 convicted prisoners in the United States, at any given point in time at least 16,000 will be innocent. We would most certainly decline the offer of a free ticket to fly on a plane whose chances of crashing are 1 percent.

I will show, further on, that significant improvements can be made to the criminal justice system at negligible or zero cost—such as improving lineup identification protocols to prevent errors and wrongful convictions—leading to the inevitable conclusion that there is no justification for refraining from adopting modern safety theory in this system. Moreover, even if the situation were far better than my conservative estimate assumes, and only a fraction of a percentage of convictions were wrongful, were a certain error to consistently repeat itself that could be prevented through reasonable means, we would be obligated to take such measures from both a moral and economic perspective—under a cost-benefit analysis.

A final possible objection to my proposal that must be addressed is that practicing safety in the criminal justice system will impair its ability to fulfill its function. One response to this objection could be based on the fact that under American law's prevailing liberal-democratic approach, although the purpose of criminal law is not to punish but to guide behavior in advance so that people will not commit crimes, the criminal law enforcement system has the two following objectives: "A. Those (and only those) individuals who are clearly guilty of certain serious specified wrongdoings deserve an officially administered punishment which is proportional to their wrongdoing.... B. Certain basic liberties shall not be violated in bringing the guilty to justice."[119] In other words, the criminal justice system is aimed equally at enforcing the criminal law and upholding human rights. Neglecting safety in criminal law, which leads to the conviction of innocent people, amounts to at least significant negligence (if not actual awareness of wrongdoing) in protecting human rights, including the basic right to freedom.

As an intuitive matter, the notion of safety in the criminal justice system could be understood as the prevention of false convictions by raising the evidentiary threshold for conviction.[120] Under such a conception, some would likely object to implementing safety mechanisms in the system. An innate problem in criminal justice is, indeed, risk allocation and finding the optimal balance between wrongful acquittals and wrongful convictions.[121] As a social value, wrongful convictions are a greater concern than wrongful acquittals; thus, society would rather have many

---

[119] Kipnis, *supra* note 82, at 101–02.
[120] Sangero & Halpert, *supra* note 6, at 1300.
[121] *In re* Winship, 397 U.S. 358, 371 (1970) (Harlan, J., concurring); *see also* ALEX STEIN, FOUNDATIONS OF EVIDENCE LAW 14 (2005); Sangero & Halpert, *supra* note 6; Epps, *supra* note 27.

guilty defendants acquitted than one innocent person convicted.[122] Yet the extreme situation in which all defendants are acquitted so as to ensure a zero false-conviction rate is also undesirable, as it would mean a total abandonment of criminal justice.[123]

Increasing safety in the criminal justice system does not necessarily entail increasing the number of acquittals of guilty defendants. Under Packer's two-pronged model of the criminal process—crime control versus due process[124]—the process tends to be perceived as a zero-sum game: greater due process and fewer wrongful convictions come at the expense of less crime control and more wrongful acquittals. However, incorporating safety into the criminal justice system could be a win-win situation, as resources could be allocated to assessing and identifying hazards and risks, and instituting safety measures to reduce both wrongful convictions and wrongful acquittals. Thus, as safety would increase (with, for example, the improved reliability of certain types of evidence), and the hazard of convicting the innocent reduced, efficiency in convicting the truly guilty would increase.[125] In this way, the criminal law system would be equally striving for and achieving its two main objectives of punishing the guilty and protecting the innocent from injustice.

---

[122] Volokh, *supra* note 27, at 174; Sangero & Halpert, *supra* note 6. Posner maintains that the above question must be determined by the costs of the various errors. According to Posner, the cost of a wrongful conviction is greater than the cost of a wrongful acquittal, for every conviction, be it justified or wrongful, imposes great suffering on the defendant and significant costs on society—the costs of the proceedings and the punishment. Therefore, the utility from a justified conviction is relatively low: the utility from promoting deterrence and preventing further crime minus the cost of the conviction. In contrast, the cost of a wrongful conviction is relatively high: the injury to deterrence due to the undermining of public confidence in the criminal justice system added to the injury to prevention and the costs of the proceedings and punishment. Richard A. Posner, *An Economic Approach to Legal Procedure and Judicial Administration*, 2 J. LEGAL STUD. 399 (1973). Dworkin, for his part, maintains that the calculation of the above costs should include also the moral harm caused by convicting an innocent person, making the disparity between the harms caused by the two types of error even greater. RONALD M. DWORKIN, A MATTER OF PRINCIPLE 92 (1985).

[123] Sangero & Halpert, *supra* note 6.

[124] PACKER, *supra* note 81, at 149–73; Sangero & Halpert, *supra* note 6, at 1301.

[125] Sangero & Halpert, *supra* note 6.

2 Fundamentals of Modern System-Safety

I. The History of System-Safety

In 1937, a terrible catastrophe occurred, which had a tremendous impact on safety in the pharmaceuticals field. The S.E. Massengill Company, which manufactured and successfully sold the safe-for-use drug sulfanilamide in pill form, began to manufacture and sell the same drug in liquid form, calling it "Elixir Sulfanilamide." However, Massengill did not test the safety of the new drug, mistakenly assuming that no significant difference between the two forms of the drug could be expected. The terrible outcome was the deaths of 107 people after taking the drug in its liquid form.[1] In order to prevent similar occurrences, Congress passed in 1938 the Federal Food, Drug and Cosmetic Act,[2] which requires, inter alia, safety testing and government approval of all new drugs before they can be distributed and sold to the general public. About two decades later, in 1962, another scandal shook the pharmaceuticals field, when the drug thalidomide, which was sold as safe for pregnant

---

[1] Steven R. Salbu, *Regulation of Drug Treatments for HIV and AIDS: A Contractarian Model of Access*, 11 YALE J. REG. 401, 407 (1994).

[2] Pub. L. No. 52–717, 52 Stat. 1040 (1938).

women, caused serious birth defects in thousands of newborn babies whose mothers had taken the drug during their pregnancies.[3] This similarly led to amendments to the law,[4] which mandate more rigorous pre-approval testing of drugs than originally required under the 1938 Act, including a series of clinical tests.[5] Moreover, in recent years, the deaths and serious illnesses caused by food poisoning have triggered efforts to promote food safety.[6] A 2011 amendment to the law expanded significantly the Food and Drug Administration's authority to conduct testing on food and to recall products.[7] Likewise, in the 1980s, a series of industrial catastrophes, including the Chernobyl, Three Mile Island, and Bhopal disasters, raised serious awareness as to the need for developing safety in this field.[8] Finally, the space shuttle Columbia catastrophe further prompted the development of safety rules. In addition to the tragic loss of human life, when all seven members of the space shuttle's crew were killed, tremendous economic harm was caused by the crash. The physical reason for the shuttle's disintegration upon re-entry (alongside an analysis of the organizational reasons, among others) is described as follows in the National Aeronautics and Space Administration (NASA) investigation report following the accident:[9]

> The physical cause of the loss of Columbia and its crew was a breach in the Thermal Protection System on the leading edge of the left wing, caused by a piece of insulating foam which separated from the left bipod ramp section of the External Tank at 81.7 seconds after launch, and struck the wing in the vicinity of the lower half of Reinforced Carbon-Carbon panel number 8.

---

[3] Salbu, *supra* note 1, at 408.

[4] Pub. L. No. 87–781, 76 Stat. 780 (1962).

[5] *See* Salbu, *supra* note 1.

[6] Caroline Smith DeWaal, *Food Safety and Security: What Tragedy Teaches Us about Our 100-Year-Old Food Laws*, 40 Van. J. Transnat'l L. 921 (2007); Richard J. Durbin, *Food Safety Oversight for the 21st Century: The Creation of a Single, Independent Federal Food Safety Agency*, 59 Food & Drug L.J. 383, 384 (2004) ("The Centers for Disease Control and Prevention (CDC) estimate that as many as seventy-six million people suffer from food poisoning each year. Of those individuals, approximately 325,000 will be hospitalized, and more than 5,000 will die.").

[7] Debra M. Strauss, *An Analysis of the FDA Food Safety Modernization Act: Protection of Consumers and Boon for Business*, 66 Food & Drug L.J. 353 (2011); FDA Food Safety Modernization Act (FSMA), 21 U.S.C. § 2201, Pub. L. No. 111–353, 124 Stat. 3885 (2011).

[8] James A. Squires, *Regulating Safety Culture in the Railroad Industry: The Time Has Come for Broader Horizons*, 27 Transp. L.J. 93, 95 (2000).

[9] Harold Gehman, Columbia Accident Investigation Report, U.S. GAO, Aug. 2003, at 9. *See also* Nancy G. Leveson, *Technical and Managerial Factors in the NASA Challenger and Columbia Losses: Looking Forward to the Future, in* 2 Controversies in Science and Technology (Daniel Lee Kleinman, Karen A. Cloud-Hansen, Christina Matta & Jo Handelsman eds., 2008).

During re-entry this breach in the Thermal Protection System allowed super-heated air to penetrate through the leading edge insulation and progressively melt the aluminum structure of the left wing, resulting in a weakening of the structure until increasing aerodynamic forces caused loss of control, failure of the wing, and break-up of the Orbiter. This breakup occurred in a flight regime in which, given the current design of the Orbiter, there was no possibility for the crew to survive.

Catastrophes such as these[10] could have been prevented had proper safety-critical system practices been followed.

A safety-critical system is a system "in which a malfunction could result in death, injury or illness, major economic loss, mission failure, environmental damage, or property damage."[11] Airplanes, space shuttles, drugs and pharmaceuticals, medical devices, railway control systems, and automobiles are all such systems,[12] as are the aeronautics of airplanes and antilock braking systems in automobiles.[13] Failure in a safety-critical system could lead to damage of catastrophic proportions, and thus, engineering methods for reducing such hazards must be used in developing and manufacturing such systems.

Safety engineering developed as a separate discipline in engineering only after World War II, even though engineers had long been concerned with the safety of their products.[14] Until this point in time, the standard approach to safety had been

---

[10] For other examples, see Nancy Leveson & Clark S. Turner, *An Investigation of the Therac-25 Accidents*, 25 IEEE COMPUTER (1993) (discussing six software-related accidents that occurred between June 1985 and January 1987 involving the Therac-25 computerized radiation therapy machine, which caused massive overdoses of radiation resulting in deaths and serious injuries); Steven Goldberg, *The Space Shuttle Tragedy and the Ethics of Engineering*, 27 JURIMETRICS J. 155 (1986–1987).

[11] Mordechai Halpert & Boaz Sangero, *From a Plane Crash to the Conviction of an Innocent Person: Why Forensic Science Evidence Should Be Inadmissible unless It Has Been Developed as a Safety-Critical System*, 32 HAMLINE L. REV. 65, 70 (2009); Frances E. Zollers et al., *No More Soft Landings for Software: Liability for Defects in an Industry That Has Come of Age*, 21 SANTA CLARA COMPUTER & HIGH TECH. L.J. 745, 751 (2005).

[12] Halpert & Sangero, *supra* note 11, at 70; NEIL STOREY, SAFETY-CRITICAL COMPUTER SYSTEMS 1–2 (1996); U.S. DEP'T OF DEFENSE, MIL-STD-882E—STANDARD PRACTICE FOR SYSTEM SAFETY (2012), *available at* http://www.system-safety.org/Documents/MIL-STD-882E.pdf [hereinafter MIL-STD-882E]; U.S. AIR FORCE, SYSTEM SAFETY HANDBOOK (2000), *available at* http://www.system-safety.org/Documents/AF_System-Safety-HNDBK.pdf [hereinafter USAF HANDBOOK]; U.S. FEDERAL AVIATION ADMINISTRATION, SYSTEM SAFETY HANDBOOK (2005), *available at* http://www.faa.gov/library/manuals/aviation/risk_management/ss_handbook [hereinafter FAA HANDBOOK].

[13] Halpert & Sangero, *supra* note 11, at 70–71; STOREY, *supra* note 12, at 1.

[14] Halpert & Sangero, *supra* note 11, at 71; NANCY LEVESON ET AL., EFFECTIVELY ADDRESSING NASA'S ORGANIZATIONAL AND SAFETY CULTURE: INSIGHTS FROM SYSTEMS SAFETY AND ENGINEERING SYSTEMS 2 (Mar. 29–31, 2004), http://esd.mit.edu/symposium/pdfs/papers/leveson-c.pdf (paper presented at the MIT Engineering Systems Symposium).

"Fly-Fix-Fly":[15] an airplane would be flown until an accident occurred. The reasons for the accident would then be investigated, and the defects that were discovered fixed. The lessons learned from the accident would be incorporated into the engineering rules and regulations for every aircraft of the relevant type. The airplanes would then resume flight—until the next accident. This safety method was based solely on learning from the experience of past mishaps, to repair the defects in the system so that the same accident would not recur. However, this system cannot protect against other, unknown defects in the airplane that could cause a different type of mishap in the future.[16] When the technology advanced and the cost of airplanes became increasingly higher, this approach no longer sufficed, therefore. The cost of learning from experience became too great. Moreover, the Fly-Fix-Fly method had never been accepted as a sufficient safety approach in certain fields, such as nuclear arms development programs and space travel exploration programs, which must necessarily be "First-Time-Safe."[17] Thus, already in the middle of the twentieth century, the approach shifted radically in the direction of modern safety.[18]

A tragic illustration of the great importance of safety is the fact that today, the very rare instances of civil airplane crashes primarily involve aircraft owned by small aviation companies that operate in states with limited safety controls.[19]

A fundamental safety principle in aviation is that safety must be integrated into the actual development and manufacture processes of the product: "Safety must be designed and built into airplanes, just as are performance, stability, and structural integrity. A safety group must be just as important a part of a manufacturer's organization as a stress, aerodynamics, or a weights group."[20] A second important principle is that "[t]he evaluation of safety work in positive terms is extremely difficult. When an accident does not occur, it is impossible to prove that some particular design feature prevented it."[21] Preventing accidents before they occur, while saving the high costs of learning from experience, thus became a primary objective in the safety field.[22] The "Fly-Fix-Fly" method was replaced by the "Identify-Analyze-Control"

---

[15] Boaz Sangero & Mordechai Halpert, *A Safety Doctrine for the Criminal Justice System*, 2011 MICH. ST. L. REV. 1293, 1296; HAROLD E. ROLAND & BRIAN MORIARTY, SYSTEM SAFETY ENGINEERING AND MANAGEMENT 8–9 (1990); PAUL S. RAY, *System Safety Engineering, in* HANDBOOK OF INDUSTRIAL AND SYSTEMS ENGINEERING 9-2 (Adedeji B. Badiru ed., 2005); RICHARD A. STEPHANS, SYSTEM SAFETY FOR THE 21ST CENTURY 3 (2004).

[16] Sangero & Halpert, *supra* note 15, at 1296–297.

[17] STEPHANS, *supra* note 15, at 3.

[18] Sangero & Halpert, *supra* note 15, at 1297.

[19] Miranda Anger, *International Aviation Safety: An Examination of the U.S., EU, and the Developing World*, 72 J. AIR L. & COMMERCE 141 (2007).

[20] Sangero & Halpert, *supra* note 15, at 1297; ROLAND & MORIARTY, *supra* note 15, at 10.

[21] Sangero & Halpert, *supra* note 15; USAF HANDBOOK, *supra* note 12, at 3.

[22] Sangero & Halpert, *supra* note 15; RAY, *supra* note 15, at 9-1.

approach:[23] systematic identification of future threats, analysis of the threats and the probability of their occurrence, and implementation of measures to eliminate the risk. Safety must be built into the product for its entire life span, from its inception until the consumer ceases to use it. The aim is "first-time-safe."[24]

Currently, it is understood to be imperative that any devices used in safety-critical systems be developed using safety methods that prevent, as much as possible, built-in defects in the devices.[25] The state supervises the manufacturers of such systems in order to ensure that they apply safety methods when they develop their products. A fundamental principle of safety engineering is that a product's safety cannot be verified solely by testing the performance of the finished product. That is to say, a product is not a "black box" where only its output is of interest and not how it executes that output.[26] Consequently, manufacturers must prove that their products are safe by adhering to standard safety practices, such as applying safety development systems. Similarly, in testing the safety of a product's software, it is not sufficient to look only at the completed software or execution of the end product. Rather, the software must be designed, from the outset, to prevent the incorporation of defects and to enable its testing for safety.[27]

Yet as we will see further on, the need for safety is not limited to devices. Rather, safety must be built into the system in its entirety, including in relation to the human decision-making processes within the system. To this end, federal regulatory agencies have been established, including: the Federal Aviation Administration (FAA), which regulates the various aspects of civil aviation and safety in aviation in general;[28] the National Highway Traffic Safety Administration (NHTSA);[29] the National Transportation Safety Board (NTSB), which is an autonomous federal agency responsible for investigating all civil aviation accidents and serious accidents in other areas of transportation, such as railway, highway, and marine accidents, and which makes safety recommendations accordingly;[30] and the Food and Drug

---

[23] Sangero & Halpert, *supra* note 15; USAF HANDBOOK, *supra* note 12, at 3.

[24] Sangero & Halpert, *supra* note 15.

[25] *Id.*

[26] See the FDA's policy on this matter in Medical Devices/Current Good Manufacturing Practice (CGMP)/ Final Rule, 61 Fed. Reg. 52601, 52606 (Oct. 7, 1996) (codified at 21 C.F.R. pts. 808, 812 and 820) [hereinafter FDA–CGMP]. *See also* Sangero & Halpert, *supra* note 15, at 1297–298.

[27] CENTER FOR DEVICES & RADIOLOGICAL HEALTH, FOOD & DRUG ADMIN., GENERAL PRINCIPLES OF SOFTWARE VALIDATION; FINAL GUIDANCE FOR INDUSTRY AND FDA STAFF (2002), *available at* www.fda.gov/downloads/RegulatoryInformation/Guidances/ucm126955.pdf (last visited July 4, 2014). *See also* Sangero & Halpert, *supra* note 15, at 1298.

[28] *See, e.g.,* Anger, *supra* note 19, at 142–47.

[29] *See, e.g.,* Jerry L. Mashaw, *Law and Engineering: In Search of the Law-Science Problem*, 66 LAW & CONTEMP. PROBS. 135, 136 (2003).

[30] *See, e.g.,* Squires, *supra* note 8, at 94.

Administration (FDA), which regulates food, drugs, medical devices, and medical diagnostic devices.[31] The workplace is another central area in which the need for advanced safety practices is well-recognized.[32]

In his book, Richard A. Stephans has suggested that the history of modern system-safety can be essentially broken down into the following six periods, and I have added a seventh:[33] The first period is the pre-1950s and the traditional "Trial-and-Error," or "Fly-Fix-Fly," approach. The second period is the 1960s, with the military standard MIL-STD-882 implemented by the U.S. Department of Defense and NASA. This central standard is updated every few years, with the most recent (MIL-STD-882E) issued in 2012.[34] This is a safety standard that manufacturers and suppliers that contract with the Defense Department are obligated to comply with. Third is the 1970s and the "Management Oversight and Risk Tree" (MORT) method, applied by the U.S. Department of Energy. MORT serves as both a specific analytical tool and a broad approach to system-safety. The program was developed for the Atomic Energy Commission.[35] Fourth, the 1980s saw the development of the facility system safety approach. Facility system-safety applies to military construction projects that require that the system-safety effort begin at the initial stages of the facility acquisition cycle.[36] In the fifth period, the 1990s, the risk-based process system safety approach emerged. The process safety regulation requires the assessment of any risk associated with a manufacturing or chemical-processing site with listed specified substances, and that to protect workers appropriate measures be taken to mitigate the consequences of an accident. Stephans's sixth period is the 2000s, where we saw a quest for intrinsic safety (safety designed and built into a system).[37] I suggest completing Stephans's list with a seventh period: the 2010s, in which the "Systems-Theoretic Accident Model and Processes" (STAMP) approach, based on constraints and controls, emerged.[38] In my estimation, this advanced model, which was developed by Professor Nancy Leveson, is very suited to the criminal justice system. Thus I will elaborate on it extensively further on and apply it to various mechanisms of the criminal justice system.

---

[31] *See, e.g.*, Strauss, *supra* note 7.

[32] *See, e.g.*, Brett R. Gordon, *Comment, Employee Involvement in the Enforcement of the Occupational Safety and the Health Laws of Canada and the United States*, 15 COMP. LABOR L.J. 527 (1993–1994); Brenda Barrett & Philip James, *Safe Systems: Past, Present—and Future?*, 17 INDUS. L.J. 26 (1988); AVI GRIFFEL, OCCUPATIONAL SAFETY AND HEALTH MANAGEMENT (2008) (in Hebrew).

[33] STEPHANS, *supra* note 15, at 3–9. Some of these will be described in detail further on.

[34] MIL-STD-882E, *supra* note 12.

[35] STEPHANS, *supra* note 15, at 39–42.

[36] *Id.* at 35.

[37] *Id.* at 3–9.

[38] NANCY G. LEVESON, ENGINEERING A SAFER WORLD: SYSTEMS THINKING APPLIED TO SAFETY (2011). I will present the fundamentals of this new approach to safety in Section XI below.

II. Basic Definitions

In this section, I will present the accepted definitions of seven fundamental concepts in the safety field. While generally drawing on the basic definitions that appear in the MIL-STD-882E standard, I have supplemented them with definitions from other sources when I felt the latter would better clarify the concepts.

1) "*Mishap*—An event or series of events resulting in unintentional death, injury, occupational illness, damage to or loss of equipment or property, or damage to the environment .... "[39]
(Alternatively: "*Accident*—An undesired and unplanned event that results in a loss [including loss of human life or injury, property damage, environmental pollution, and so on].")[40]

2) "*Risk*—A combination of the severity of the mishap and the probability that the mishap will occur."[41]
The basic calculation for risk is as follows:

Risk = Severity-of-the-Mishap x Probability.

3) "*Hazard*—A real or potential condition that could lead to" a mishap.[42]
(Alternatively: "*Hazard*—A system state or set of conditions that, together with a particular set of worst-case environment conditions, will lead to an accident [loss].")[43]

4) "*Safety*—Freedom from conditions that can cause" a mishap.[44]
(Alternatively: "*Safety*—Degree of freedom from hazard";[45] or "*Safety*—Freedom from harm. Safety is achieved by doing things right the first time, every time.";[46] or "*Safety*—Freedom from accidents [loss events].")[47]

5) "*Safety-critical*—A condition, event, operation, process, or item whose mishap severity consequence is either Catastrophic or Critical."[48]

---

[39] MIL-STD-882E, *supra* note 12, at 6.

[40] LEVESON, *supra* note 38, at 467. For reservations regarding use of the term "accident," which could wrongly lead to focus on guilt, and preference of the term "injury," see Michael Guarnieri, *Landmarks in the History of Safety*, 23 J. SAFETY RES. 151, 153–54, 157.

[41] MIL-STD-882E, *supra* note 12, at 7.

[42] *Id.* at 5.

[43] LEVESON, *supra* note 38, at 184, 467.

[44] MIL-STD-882E, *supra* note 12, at 7.

[45] Ray, *supra* note 15, at 9–3.

[46] STEPHANS, *supra* note 15, at 11.

[47] LEVESON, *supra* note 38, at 467.

[48] MIL-STD-882E, *supra* note 12, at 7.

6) *"System*—The organization of hardware, software, material, facilities, personnel, data, and services needed to perform a designated function within a stated environment with specified results."[49]

7) *"System safety*—The application of engineering and management principles, criteria, and techniques to achieve acceptable risk within the constraints of operational effectiveness and suitability, time, and cost throughout all phases of the system life-cycle."[50]

III. System-Safety Process: Identify, Analyze, Control

System safety is achieved through the "Identify-Analyze-Control" method. Under MIL-STD-882E, a system-safety process is comprised of eight stages:[51]

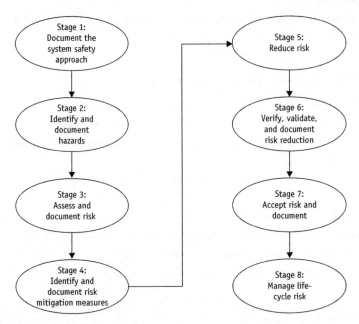

FIGURE 2.1 A System-Safety Process[52]

---

[49] *Id*. at 8.

[50] *Id*.

[51] *Id*. at 9.

[52] *Id*. The figure is taken from MIL-STD-882E

IV. Risk Assessment

Risk assessment, stage three of a system-safety process, is an integral part of modern safety. This aspect of the process can be best explained using three tables, presented below: a severity categories table (Table 2.1), a probability levels table (Table 2.2), and a risk assessment matrix (Table 2.3). For accuracy's sake, they are presented exactly

TABLE 2.1
SEVERITY CATEGORIES

Description	Severity Category	Mishap Result Criteria
Catastrophic	1	Could result in one or more of the following: death, permanent total disability, irreversible significant environmental impact, or monetary loss equal to or exceeding $10M.
Critical	2	Could result in one or more of the following: permanent partial disability, injuries or occupational illness that may result in hospitalization of at least three personnel, reversible significant environmental impact, or monetary loss equal to or exceeding $1M but less than $10M.
Marginal	3	Could result in one or more of the following: injury or occupational illness resulting in one or more lost work day(s), reversible moderate environmental impact, or monetary loss equal to or exceeding $100K but less than $1M.
Negligible	4	Could result in one or more of the following: injury or occupational illness not resulting in a lost work day, minimal environmental impact, or monetary loss less than $100K.

TABLE 2.2
PROBABILITY LEVELS

Description	Level	Specific Individual Item	Fleet or Inventory
Frequent	A	Likely to occur often in the life of an item.	Continuously experienced.
Probable	B	Will occur several times in the life of an item.	Will occur frequently.
Occasional	C	Likely to occur sometime in the life of an item.	Will occur several times.
Remote	D	Unlikely, but possible to occur in the life of an item.	Unlikely, but can reasonably be expected to occur.
Improbable	E	So unlikely, it can be assumed occurrence may not be experienced in the life of an item.	Unlikely to occur, but possible.
Eliminated	F	Incapable of occurrence. This level is used when potential hazards are identified and later eliminated.	Incapable of occurrence. This level is used when potential hazards are identified and later eliminated.

TABLE 2.3
RISK ASSESSMENT MATRIX

Probability	Severity	(1) Catastrophic	(2) Critical	(3) Marginal	(4) Negligible
(A) Frequent		High	High	Serious	Medium
(B) Probable		High	High	Serious	Medium
(C) Occasional		High	Serious	Medium	Low
(D) Remote		Serious	Medium	Medium	Low
(E) Improbable		Medium	Medium	Medium	Low
(F) Eliminated		Eliminated			

as they appear in military standard MIL-STD-882E,[53] but almost every safety text-book contains similar tables.

V. Fundamental Safety Concepts

In general, three basic features emerge from the fundamental concepts that recur in all descriptions of modern safety. The first is *safety culture*. The organizational and cultural perspective of safety is at complete odds with the classic paradigm that assumes that the majority of accidents are caused by defects in devices or due to human error.[54] The safety culture of an organization is composed of a set of behaviors, statements, beliefs, attitudes, and ethical conceptions of the workers at the different levels of the organization with regard to safety in the organization.[55]

Safety begins when all workers at all levels of an organization internalize the grave importance of ensuring safety. The central characteristics of safety culture in organizations are as follows:

1) Safety leadership that demonstrates a commitment to safety.[56]
2) Communication and feedback.[57]
3) Worker involvement and participation.[58]
4) A culture of learning (including best practices).[59]
5) A culture of accountability rather than blame.[60]

---

[53] *Id.* at 11–12.

[54] Squires, *supra* note 8, at 96; JAMES REASON, MANAGING THE RISKS OF ORGANIZATIONAL ACCIDENTS 195 (1997).

[55] Mark E. Meaney, *Error Reduction, Patient Safety and Institutional Ethics Committees*, 32 J.L. MED. & ETHICS 358 (2004); GRIFFEL, *supra* note 32, at 264–65.

[56] LEVESON, *supra* note 38, at 421.

[57] *Id.* at 421, 424; Reason, *supra* note 54, at 195; Squires, *supra* note 8, at 97.

[58] GRIFFEL, *supra* note 32, at 32–35.

[59] LEVESON, *supra* note 38, at 442.

[60] *Id.* at 426–33; Meaney, *supra* note 54.

6) A climate of safety, in which safety can be cultivated, in terms of the conceptions of the organization's members regarding maintaining safety in the organization.[61]

A slightly different way of describing safety culture is: "Safety starts with management leadership and commitment. Without these, the efforts of others in the organization are almost doomed to failure. Leadership creates culture, which drives behavior."[62]

The second feature of modern safety is the basic "Identify-Analyze-Control" method. Under this approach, future threats are systematically identified, the probability of their occurrence analyzed, and their risks neutralized or controlled.

The third fundamental component of modern safety is the never-ending process of Continual Improvement, with the objective being to achieve a state of "First-Time-Safe."[63] Because in many fields it is not possible to reach the ideal state of zero mishaps and zero accidents, it is necessary to apply a model that, once its safety targets have been met, sets new—higher—targets and strives to realize them. This process of ongoing improvement can be described schematically as follows:[64]

FIGURE 2.2 Continual Improvement

Stephans describes five fundamental safety concepts that feature in any safety effort:[65]

1. Safety is a line responsibility: "Line managers and supervisors are responsible for the safety of their organizational units and operations."[66]
2. Safety is productive: "Safety is achieved by doing things right the first time, every time."[67]

---

[61] GRIFFEL, *supra* note 32, at 32–35. *See also* REASON, *supra* note 54; Daniel R. Denison, *What Is the Difference between Organizational Culture and Organizational Climate? A Native's Point of View on a Decade of Paradigm Wars*, 21 ACAD. MGMT. REV. 619 (1996); Squires, *supra* note 8, at 97–105.

[62] LEVESON, *supra* note 38, at 177. *See also id.* at 416–43 (chapter 13: "Managing Safety and the Safety Culture").

[63] STEPHANS, *supra* note 15, at 51.

[64] Figure 2.2 is based on GRIFFEL, *supra* note 32, at 391.

[65] STEPHANS, *supra* note 15, at 11–15.

[66] *Id.* at 12.

[67] *Id.*

3. Safety requires an upstream effort. This can be schematically described in the context of the workplace as follows:[68]

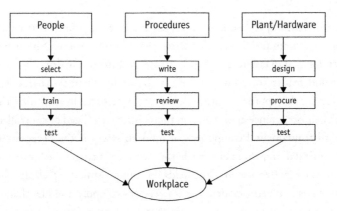

FIGURE 2.3 Upstream Effort of Safety in Workplace

4. Safety depends on the safety precedence sequence: "It is a prioritized list of controls that should be considered and applied, in sequence, to eliminate or control identified hazards.
    • Design for minimum hazard.
    • Provide safety devices.
    • Provide warning devices.
    • Control with procedures and training.
    • Accept remaining residual hazards."[69]
5. Systematic tools and techniques help in reducing error rates.

VI. Common Methods of System-Safety

In fields in which safety is standard practice, different methods have been developed for securing safety at the various stages of a system's operation, usually with governmental involvement.[70] It is the government that sets a project's objectives and specifications as well as the acceptable levels of risk.[71] This information regarding the safety requirements for a project is laid out in a document called the System Safety

---

[68] Figure 2.3 is taken from Stephans' book, *Id.* at 13.
[69] *Id.* at 14.
[70] *Id.* at 17.
[71] *Id.*

Management Plan (SSMP).[72] The SSMP serves as the road map for the project's safety program[73] and is presented to potential contractors during the contracting process.

The plan developed by contractors to meet the government's system-safety program requirements is generally entitled the System Safety Program Plan (SSPP).[74]

An additional important document, which the manufacturer must produce, is the Preliminary Hazard Analysis (PHA).[75] The PHA serves as the primary tool for hazard identification as well as initial hazard analysis. As a project is developed and more detailed design data become available, a System Hazard Analysis (SHA) and Sub-System Hazard Analyses (SSHA) may be conducted for more detailed, in-depth risk assessment information. The PHA and, especially, the SHA and SSHA are almost exclusively focused on hardware.[76] Another major type of analysis is the Operating Hazard Analysis (OHA), which factors in the people and procedures in the system analysis.[77]

The following are common analytical techniques in hazard analysis:[78]

1) Failure Modes and Effects Analysis (FMEA). The approach here is to break down the system into subsystems and then into the individual components, to identify the possible failure modes of each individual component and their potential impact on overall system safety.[79]

2) Fault Tree Analysis (FTA), qualitative or quantitative, with probability values. For this analysis, the undesirable event is listed in the top block and deductive logic is used to determine all subsequent events that could lead to the top event.[80] The fault tree is useful for identifying single-point failures.[81]

3) Energy Trace and Barrier Analysis (ETBA).[82]

4) Management Oversight and Risk Tree (MORT). This is a logic tree approach to identifying the risks of an operation, with management oversight requiring action to ensure safety.[83]

---

[72] *Id. See also* USAF HANDBOOK, *supra* note 12, at 110.

[73] USAF HANDBOOK, *supra* note 12, vii.

[74] STEPHANS, *supra* note 15, at 17–18. For details on the SSPP, see MIL-STD-882E, *supra* note 12, at 24–29.

[75] STEPHANS, *supra* note 15, at 18.

[76] *Id.*

[77] *Id.* at 18–19.

[78] *Id.*

[79] Ray, *supra* note 15, at 9–6; STEPHANS, *supra* note 15, at 155–59.

[80] Ray, *supra* note 15, at 9–7; STEPHANS, *supra* note 15, at 169–80.

[81] Ray, *supra* note 15, at 9–8.

[82] STEPHANS, *supra* note 15, at 149–54.

[83] Ray, *supra* note 15, at 9; STEPHANS, *supra* note 15, at 217–50.

5) Project Evaluation Tree (PET).[84]
6) Change Analysis.[85]
7) Common Cause Analysis.[86]

As Stephans describes, "[s]afety is achieved by continuing to use the safety precedence sequence to control hazards until all identified hazards are eliminated or controlled to an acceptable level and residual risks are formally accepted."[87] Under the heading "System Safety Tenets," he lists fifteen actions that are essential in performing the system-safety undertakings:[88]

1. Systematically identify, evaluate, and control hazards so as to prevent (or mitigate) accidents;
2. Set an order of precedence for controls dealing with hazards, starting with hazard elimination, that is, measures designed to prevent hazards, followed by administrative controls. Administrative controls include signs, warnings, precautionary practices, and training. Of lowest precedence are those controls that rely on people;
3. Act proactively rather than reactively to events. This begins with a program plan;
4. Design and build safety into a system rather than modifying the system at a later stage;
5. Develop and provide safety-related design guidance;
6. Use appropriate evaluation/analysis techniques;
7. Rely on factual information, engineering, and science in forming conclusions and formulating recommendations;
8. Quantify risk by multiplying the ranking of the undesired consequences of an event by the probability of its occurrence;
9. Design, when possible, to minimize or eliminate single-point failures that have undesired consequences. Design the system for at least 2-fault tolerance,[89] so that the system will be tolerant to multiple faults or system breakdowns that would have adverse safety consequences (i.e., redundancy, which will be explained below);

---

[84] STEPHANS, *supra* note 15, at 189–96.

[85] *Id.* at 211–16.

[86] *Id.* at 262.

[87] *Id.* at 19.

[88] *Id.* at 22–23.

[89] "Fault tolerant" means that in the presence of a hardware/software fault, the software will still provide continuous correct execution. *Id.* at 53.

10. Identify, evaluate, and control hazards throughout the system's life cycle and during the various operational phases for normal and abnormal environments;

11. After implementing controls to mitigate a hazard, recognize and accept the residual risk;

12. Recognize the quality assurance interface. Implement to continually improve the system;

13. Tabulate and disseminate lessons learned and incorporate those lessons for future safety enhancement;

14. Apply system-safety to systems to include processes, products, facilities, and services;

15. Recognize that near-miss conditions, if not corrected, most likely develop into accidents.

As we will see, the criminal justice system differs from most safety-critical systems in that the accidents that occur in the former—false convictions—are obscured and hidden from sight. Dr. Halpert and I have termed this the "Hidden Accidents Principle" in criminal law.[90] This principle underscores the tremendous importance of the final system-safety rule relating to near-miss conditions. I will therefore devote a separate, albeit brief, discussion to this rule further on. But first, I will consider the concept of "redundancy" noted above.

VII. Redundancy

Redundancy can be defined as "the ability to provide for the execution of a task if the primary unit fails or falters."[91] In a redundant system, there is the expectation that where one unit fails to function, the other units will compensate. High Reliability Organizations (HRO) "use technical redundancy, where parts are duplicated (e.g., backup computers) and personnel redundancy, where personnel functions are duplicated (e.g., more than one person is assigned to perform a given safety

[90] Sangero & Halpert, *supra* note 15, at 1314–16.

[91] *See* Nancy Leveson, Nicolas Dulac, Karen Marais & John Carroll, Moving beyond Normal Accidents and High Reliability Organizations: A Systems Approach to Safety in Complex Systems 5–6 (2009), *available at* http://sunnyday.mit.edu/papers.html (quoting Todd R. La Porte & Paula Consolini, *Working in Practice but Not in Theory: Theoretical Challenges of High-Reliability Organizations*, 1 J. Pub. Admin. Res. & Theory 19 (1991)).

check)."[92] Redundancy can reduce the probability of the entire system failing due to the failure of one of its components.[93] Thus, redundancy is a safety method, which must be planned carefully.[94]

System components can be organized as a series system, in the following manner:

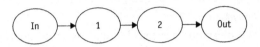

FIGURE 2.4   A Series System

In a series system, if either component 1 fails or component 2 fails, the entire system fails. As opposed to a series system, components can be connected in a parallel system, as follows:

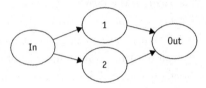

FIGURE 2.5   A Parallel System

Parallel systems are indicative of redundancy. In such systems, if component 1 fails, component 2 will not necessarily fail as well.

As will be shown at a further stage in the book, although the criminal justice system is considered a high-redundancy system, in fact, when one of its units fails (for example, a police investigator errs or acts deceptively), there is a high probability that this will be accompanied by the failure of other units as well (such as, the prosecutor and fact-finder, who believe the police investigator). Thus, redundancy in the criminal justice system must be planned so as to attain the desired safety.

---

[92] LEVESON ET AL., *supra* note 14 (quoting K.H. Roberts, *Some Characteristics of One Type of High Reliability Organization*, 1(2) ORG. SCI. 160 (1990)).

[93] Leveson, *supra* note 38, at 91.

[94] " The use of redundancy to provide protection against losses must include a detailed analysis of coverage and any potential gaps in the safety control provided by the redundancy." *Id.* at 471.

VIII. The Requirement to Report Accidents and Incidents (Near Accidents)

As described, prevailing safety theory ascribes considerable weight not to past experience but to preventing defects and problems before they arise. Consequently, in modern safety, which is not based solely on lessons from unfortunate experience through the investigation of accidents, there is a duty to report not only accidents but also "incidents,"[95] which are defined as situations in which there was potential for harm to be caused and it was averted by mere coincidence.[96] Modern safety has internalized the important understanding of the fact that "near-miss conditions, if not corrected, most likely develop into accidents."[97] Therefore, incident investigation is a critical element of safety. Indeed, serious accidents are usually preceded by a series of related incidents that did not end up in a critical mishap. Thus, near-miss incidents can be strongly indicative of an overall system failure with potentially serious outcomes.

In 1975, the FAA instituted a confidential near-misses reporting system, known as the Air Safety Reporting System (ASRS).[98] If a pilot, air traffic controller, or any other aviation employee reports on a dangerous situation, he or she will be exempt from liability. This system increased the incident reporting rate tremendously and created much better communication. The ASRS receives approximately five thousand reports a year, and analyses of these reports are published in pilot magazines.[99]

In the 1930s, Herbert William Heinrich[100] set what has come to be known as the "Heinrich Triangle" with regard to workplace industrial accidents. His claim was that for every workplace accident resulting in a major injury, approximately twenty-nine accidents causing minor injury and approximately three hundred accidents resulting in no injury occur.

It has been claimed that the risk factors in fatal and non-fatal incidents are identical to the risk factors in incidents that result in no injury. If we accept this premise,

---

[95] Int'l Civil Aviation Organization, Safety Management Manual § 4.3 (2006), *available at* http://www.icao.int/osg/isd/afi/Reference%20Material%5CSafety%20Oversight%20Manuals%5CSafety%20Management%20System%5CSMS%20Manual.pdf.

[96] *Id.*

[97] Stephans, *supra* note 15, at 23.

[98] Lucian L. Leape, *Error in Medicine*, 272 JAMA 1851, 1855 (1994).

[99] *Id.*

[100] H.W. Heinrich, Industrial Accident Prevention (1931); Griffel, *supra* note 32, at 71.

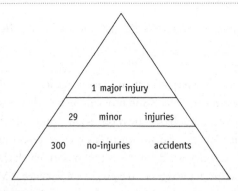

FIGURE 2.6 Heinrich Triangle

reducing the number of incidents at the bottom of the pyramid will lead to a parallel reduction in the number of serious accidents at the top of the pyramid.[101]

Although this 1:29:300[102] ratio is certainly not applicable in every field, it does reinforce the notion that we can see only the tip of the iceberg of accidents in general.

Eric Hollnagel had proposed a more advanced failure-types pyramid.[103] His model distinguishes among "accidents" (with the most serious outcomes), "incidents" (less serious outcomes), and "near misses."[104] What differentiates an accident from an incident is specific to each application and sphere,[105] but in general an accident is differentiated from an incident by the presence of a barrier in the latter, which prevents the former.[106]

The numbers may diverge significantly from this hypothetical model in reality. Hollangel explains that while we can be fairly certain regarding the number of accidents, failures with lesser consequences are reported with less consistency and reliability, near misses only rarely reported, and unsafe acts as a rule not reported at all.[107] We will see in Chapter 3 that even less is known or clear in the criminal justice system, due to the Hidden Accidents Principle that governs criminal law.

---

[101] GRIFFEL, *supra* note 32, at 71; ERIC HOLLANGEL, BARRIERS AND ACCIDENT PREVENTION 20–25 (2004).

[102] A ratio of 1:30:300 would form an exact triangle.

[103] HOLLANGEL, *supra* note 101.

[104] Hollangel's terminology is slightly different from that used above.

[105] HOLLANGEL, *supra* note 101, at 20.

[106] *Id.* at 21.

[107] *Id.* at 24–25.

FIGURE 2.7 The Failure-Types Pyramid[108]

Exemplifying the successful use of reporting and incident investigation is the FDA-supervised Medical Device Reporting (MDR) requirement in the medical field.[109] The FDA routinely releases "medical device safety alerts" and even orders product recalls based on reports deriving from the MDR.[110] In the criminal justice system, however, not only is there no mechanism for investigating incidents, even accidents are not always investigated. Instead, an incident in which an accused is prosecuted for a crime but revealed to be innocent at trial is lauded as the success of the criminal justice system rather than a "near miss."[111] In the aviation field, in contrast, avoidance of a near-crash between two planes would be regarded as mere luck and the incident would be exhaustively investigated.

A distinction is commonly made between a duty to report and voluntary reporting.[112] With regard to accidents—where actual damage is caused—a duty to report applies. For incidents, in contrast, voluntary reporting is at times deemed sufficient and likely to be accompanied by immunity from legal proceedings so as to encourage reporting and allay fears from criminal or disciplinary proceedings.[113] Thus, for example, in the National Academy of Sciences comprehensive report *To Err Is Human—Building a*

---

[108] Figure 2.7 is taken from Hollangel's book, *id.* at 24.

[109] FDA, HOW TO REPORT A PROBLEM (MEDICAL DEVICES), http://www.fda.gov/MedicalDevices/Safety/ReportaProblem/default.htm#1 (last visited July 5, 2014); Sangero & Halpert, *supra* note 15, at 1299.

[110] "**Medical device safety alert:** issued in situations where a medical device may present an unreasonable risk of substantial harm." FDA, BACKGROUND AND DEFINITIONS, http://www.fda.gov/Safety/Recalls/ucm165546.htm (last visited July 5, 2014); Sangero & Halpert, *supra* note 15, at 1299. There are three classes of recalls, based on severity: a firm-initiated recall, a recall requested by the FDA, and a recall ordered by the FDA under statutory authority. FDA, *supra.*

[111] Kansas v. Marsh, 548 U.S. 163, 193 (2006) (Scalia, J., concurring); Sangero & Halpert, *supra* note 15, at 1299. I wish to thank Prof. Alon Harel for this last idea.

[112] *See, e.g.,* FDA, *supra* note 109.

[113] *See, e.g.,* Strauss, *supra* note 7, at 363.

Better Health System, an entire chapter was devoted to error-reporting systems and another chapter to protecting voluntary reporting systems from legal discovery.[114]

IX. System-Safety Engineering Versus "Black-Box" Testing

The U.S. Air Force[115] has defined system-safety engineering as "an engineering discipline requiring specialized professional knowledge and skills in applying scientific and engineering principles, criteria, and techniques to identify and eliminate hazards, or reduce the associated risk."[116] System-safety, in addition, is intended "to achieve acceptable mishap risk through a systematic approach of hazard analysis, risk assessment, and risk management."[117] Accordingly, the fundamental objective of system-safety is to identify, evaluate, and eliminate or control hazards throughout a system's life cycle. Hazards can, of course, derive from the failure of certain components in the system, but other sources are also possible. One of the primary concerns of system-safety engineers, then, is "System Hazard Analysis,"[118] namely, the assessment of the interactions among a system's different components (including human resources, hardware, and software) as well as with the environment, and the effect of these interactions on potential systemic hazards.

From the earliest conceptual stages of a project through to its design, production, testing, operational use, and disposal, it is critical that system-safety measures be implemented.[119] System safety is distinguished from other safety approaches in its overriding emphasis on early identification and assessment of hazards,[120] which allows for quick action to eliminate or minimize risks before final design decisions are made.[121]

Safety engineering does not restrict itself to "black-box testing" of the final product's output, but, rather, entails a series of techniques applied throughout a product's life cycle, including its design, development, testing, manufacture, storage, delivery

---

[114] To Err Is Human: Building a Safer Health System 86–131 (Linda T. Kohn, Janet M. Corrigan & Molla S. Donaldson eds., 2000). *See also* Leveson, *supra* note 38, at 404–05.

[115] This section is based in part on an article I coauthored with Dr. Mordechai Halpert: Halpert & Sangero, *supra* note 11, at 74–76, 83–88.

[116] *See* USAF Handbook, *supra* note 12, vii; Halpert & Sangero, *supra* note 11, at 74–75.

[117] U.S. Dep't of Defense, Standard Practice for System Safety 3 (2000), *available at* http://www.faa.gov/library/manuals/aviation/risk_management/ss_handbook/media/app_h_1200.pdf; Halpert & Sangero, *supra* note 11, at 75.

[118] Leveson et al., *supra* note 14, at 3 (2004), http://esd.mit.edu/symposium/pdfs/papers/leveson-c.pdf (last visited July 5, 2014) (paper presented at the MIT Engineering Systems Symposium); Halpert & Sangero, *supra* note 11, at 75.

[119] Halpert & Sangero, *supra* note 11, at 75.

[120] *Id.*

[121] *Id.* Quality-system principles in line with this approach have been set in regulations. *See, e.g., Quality System Regulation,* 21 C.F.R. 820 (2008). *See also* Halpert & Sangero, *supra* note 11, at 75.

to the client, and maintenance. Accordingly, the FDA has stated in the context of medical devices, that it

> believes that because of the complexity of many components used in medical devices, their adequacy cannot always be assured through inspection and testing at the finished device manufacturer. This is especially true of software and software-related components, such as microprocessors and microcircuits. Quality must be designed and built into components through the application of proper quality systems.[122]

Similarly, in the context of software development and validation,[123] the approach of the FDA is that testing alone is not sufficient for determining whether software is "fit for its intended use":[124]

> Software quality assurance needs to focus on preventing the introduction of defects into the software development process and not on trying to "test quality into" the software code after it is written. Software testing is very limited in its ability to surface all latent defects in software code. For example, the complexity of most software prevents it from being exhaustively tested. *Software testing is a necessary activity. However, in most cases software testing by itself is not sufficient to establish confidence that the software is fit for its intended use.*[125]

These principles are standard practice in computer science. "[T]esting can only prove the existence of defects, not their absence.... If quality was not present in the requirements analysis, design, or implementation, testing cannot put it there."[126] Thus, software quality is ensured through proper design and by applying proper safety processes and not by "validating" and testing the product. Under this approach, there is a necessary connection between product quality and process.[127]

As I will show in Chapter 5, which deals with evidence, there is no awareness whatsoever in the field of forensic evidence regarding the need for safe development

---

[122] FDA–CGMP, *supra* note 26; Halpert & Sangero, *supra* note 11, at 76.

[123] Halpert & Sangero, *supra* note 11, at 76.

[124] *Id.* at 76.

[125] Center for Devices & Radiological Health, FDA, General Principles of Software Validation; Final Guidance for Industry and FDA Staff 11 (2002); Halpert & Sangero, *supra* note 11, at 76.

[126] Norman Hines, *The Problem with Testing, in* Crosstalk—The Journal of Defense Software Engineering 27, 27–28 (July 2001), *available at* http://www.stsc.hill. af.mil/crosstalk/2001/07/hines. html; Halpert & Sangero, *supra* note 11, at 76.

[127] Ron S. Kenett et al., Software Process Quality: Management and Control 17 (1999); Halpert & Sangero, *supra* note 11, at 76.

of the devices and kits used to produce forensic evidence. In fact, not even "black-box testing" is always conducted.

X. Safety in Medical Diagnostic Devices

In many areas of life, there is considerable awareness of safety and, consequently, general acceptance of modern safety methods.[128] Aviation is only one of many areas in which safety is practiced, including astronautics, transportation, engineering, and energy. In this section, I will take a brief look at the field of medical diagnostic devices, as the knowledge amassed there can be relatively easily applied in the context of forensic evidence devices and tests, such as DNA-testing kits, drug-testing kits, breathalyzers, and speed-measuring devices.

There is indisputable and unqualified need to prevent accidents in the context of medical devices, as exemplified by the case of the Dalkon Shield, an intrauterine contraceptive device first marketed in 1970. In *Medtronic, Inc. v. Lohr*,[129] the U.S. Supreme Court held that although the Shield had been "[t]outed as a safe and effective contraceptive," it had led to "a disturbingly high percentage of inadvertent pregnancies, serious infections, and even, in a few cases, death."[130] As the Shield was considered a medical device and not a drug, there was no need for FDA approval before it was put on the market.[131] The Court explained that "[i]n the early 1970's, several other devices, including catheters, artificial heart valves, defibrillators, and pacemakers ... attracted the attention of consumers, the [FDA], and Congress as possible health risks,"[132] but the FDA had only limited authority to prevent these risks from materializing. As a result, Congress enacted the Medical Device Amendments of 1976, which required FDA review of all medical devices before they could be marketed.[133]

United States' federal law and FDA regulations categorize medical devices intended for human use into three different classes according to level of hazard they pose to the public and the degree of control required.[134] Class I devices are subject to the least regulatory control, for they pose minimal potential harm to users and are

---

[128] This section is based on parts of the article I coauthored with Dr. Mordechai Halpert: Halpert & Sangero, *supra* note 11, at 72–74.

[129] *Id.*; 518 U.S. 470 (1996).

[130] 518 U.S. at 476.

[131] Carol T. Rieger, *The Judicial Councils Reform and Judicial Conduct and Disability Act: Will Judges Judge Judges?*, 37 EMORY L.J. 45, 62 (1988); Halpert & Sangero, *supra* note 11, at 72.

[132] 518 U.S. at 476.

[133] Halpert & Sangero, *supra* note 11, at 73.

[134] *See* 21 U.S.C. § 360c (2000); FDA, DEVICE CLASSES, http://www.fda.gov/medicaldevices/deviceregulationandguidance/overview/classifyyourdevice/default.htm (last visited July 3, 2014) (detailing the FDA device classes) [hereinafter FDA DEVICE CLASSES]; Halpert & Sangero, *supra* note 11.

generally simpler in design than Class II or Class III devices.[135] Some examples of Class I devices are elastic bandages and examination gloves.[136] The general controls for these medical devices include: registration of the manufacturers and distributors, listing the devices with the FDA prior to marketing, device labeling regulations, and premarket notification.[137] Class I devices must also comply with strict quality assurance requirements, such as good manufacturing practices (GMP).[138]

Class II devices pose a medium risk to users, and prominent examples of this category are the powered wheelchair and infusion pumps.[139] They do not fall under Class I devices because, on the one hand, the general controls are insufficient to contend with their risks while, on the other hand, there is sufficient information to establish special controls.[140] These special controls can range from special labeling requirements, to mandatory performance standards, to post-marketing surveillance review.

Finally, the most strictly regulated category is Class III medical devices,[141] about which there is insufficient information to ensure safety and effectiveness through general and/or special controls alone.[142] The devices in this category, such as the prosthetic heart valve, pose the most significant risk to human life, as they are generally used to support or sustain life and are vital to ensuring good health.[143] As a result, Class III medical devices are subject to premarket approval from the FDA.[144]

Forensic evidence devices, such as breathalyzers and DNA profiling software, are not, however, subject to the Class III stringent control system for medical devices, even though they, arguably, pose a threat to human life in that they can produce evidence sufficient for a murder conviction and death sentence. Moreover, they are not even subject to the minimal Class I requirements for devices such as examination gloves. The reality is that apparently, forensic equipment is not subject to any statutory requirements relating to their development, manufacture, or marketing.[145]

---

[135] FDA DEVICE CLASSES, *supra* note 134 ("Class I—General Controls").

[136] *Id.*

[137] *Id.*

[138] Good Manufacturing Practices (GMP)/Quality System (QS) Regulation, http://www.fda.gov/cdrh/devadvice/32.html (FDA website). *See also* FDA—CGMP, *supra* note 26; Halpert & Sangero, *supra* note 11, at 74.

[139] FDA DEVICE CLASSES, *supra* note 134 ("Class II—Special Controls").

[140] 21 U.S.C. § 360c(a)(1)(B) (2006); Halpert & Sangero, *supra* note 11, at 73.

[141] FDA DEVICE CLASSES, *supra* note 134 ("Class III—Premarket Approval").

[142] *Id.*

[143] *Id.*

[144] *Id.*

[145] Halpert & Sangero, *supra* note 11, at 74.

XI. "Stamp"—System-Theoretic Accident Model and Processes

Professor Nancy Leveson has developed a sophisticated safety model, best known by its acronym "STAMP"—System-Theoretic Accident Model and Processes. The model is based on a new systems theory, according to which traditional safety methods are not adequate for complex systems. Leveson proposes shifting the emphasis from the *reliability* of a system's components to system *control*.[146] To begin with, every system must be examined closely to determine what safety *constraints* are imperative for it to operate without mishap. For example, with regard to metro subway systems, one of the necessary constraints is that "[d]oors must be capable of opening only after train is stopped and properly aligned with platform unless emergency exists."[147] Similar constraints can—and should—be devised for the criminal justice system, so as to prevent false convictions.

The next stage in Leveson's model is the setting of hierarchical *control* structures that will ensure the enforcement of the safety constraints required for the system. Safety, Leveson explains, is a feature throughout the system, in its entirety, and not limited to any one component in the system. She eloquently summarizes her model in her recent book *Engineering a Safer World*:

> STAMP focuses particular attention on the role of constraints in safety management. Accidents are seen as resulting from inadequate control or enforcement of constraints on safety-related behavior at each level of the system development and system operations control structures. Accidents can be understood in terms of why the controls that were in place did not prevent or detect maladaptive changes.
>
> Accident causal analysis based on STAMP starts with identifying the safety constraints that were violated and then determines why the controls designed to enforce the safety constraints were inadequate or, if they were potentially adequate, why the system was unable to exert appropriate control over their enforcement.
>
> In this conception of safety, there is no "root cause." Instead, the accident "cause" consists of an inadequate safety control structure that under some circumstances leads to the violation of a behavioral safety constraint. Preventing

---

[146] LEVESON, DULAC, MARAIS & CARROLL, *supra* note 91. *See also* Leveson, *supra* note 38, at 7–14.
[147] This example is taken from LEVESON, *supra* note 38, at 192.

future accidents requires reengineering or designing the safety control structure to be more effective.[148]

As Leveson shows in *Engineering a Safer World*, STAMP has been tested with success—by her and, subsequently, by others—on different types of actual operating systems. Her model has proven to be both efficient and economic for the investigation of accidents as well as safety engineering, which aims to prevent accidents in advance. As she explains,

> The more one knows about an accident process, the more difficult it is to find one person or part of the system responsible, but the easier it is to find effective ways to prevent similar occurrences in the future.
>
> STAMP is useful not only in analyzing accidents that have occurred but in developing new and potentially more effective system engineering methodologies to prevent accidents. Hazard analysis can be thought of as investigating an accident before it occurs. Traditional hazard analysis techniques, such as fault tree analysis and various types of failure analysis techniques, do not work well for very complex systems, for software errors, human errors, and system design errors. Nor do they usually include organizational and management flaws.[149]

This final point is of particular relevance to our context, as the majority of failures in the criminal justice system are not technological errors but rather stem from human error and organizational and management flaws. Leveson clarifies that although system engineering was developed originally for technical systems, the STAMP approach is just as important and applicable to social systems:

> All systems are engineered in the sense that they are designed to achieve specific goals, namely to satisfy requirements and constraints. So ensuring hospital safety or pharmaceutical safety ... fall[s] within the broad definition of engineering.[150]

---

[148] LEVESON, *supra* note 38, at 100. Elsewhere, Leveson has formulated the STAMP "recipe" for safety more succinctly as "identifying the constraints required to maintain safety and then designing the system and operating conditions to ensure that the constraints are enforced." Nancy Leveson, *A New Accident Model for Engineering Safer Systems*, 42(4) SAFETY SCI. 237 (2004).

[149] LEVESON, *supra* note 38, at 101.

[150] *Id.* at 176. *See also id.* at 198–209 ("Safety Control Structures in Social Systems").

Accordingly, at later stages in this book I will propose applying and implementing the STAMP model in the criminal justice system.[151]

XII. Summary

This chapter has given a brief survey of modern system-safety. It is certainly not intended to serve as a substitute for the extensive professional literature in this field, which encompasses numerous regulations, books, and articles written by experts on the subject, to which they have devoted their professional lives. The modest purpose, instead, was to provide legalists and jurists a glance into the world of modern safety. To be sure, I have placed particular emphasis on those safety principles and methods that I believe suitable to the criminal justice system. Later on in the book, I will suggest ways to do this, noting that these are first steps on the way to more comprehensive reform. I of course do not purport to exhaust all of the safety methods that can and should be implemented in the criminal justice system, but to advance the general recommendation that modern safety be adopted in criminal law.[152] Moreover, if the key operative suggestion is adopted—to establish and fund an autonomous institute that will be charged with promoting safety in the criminal justice system similarly to what occurred a decade ago in the medical field[153] —then the hazard of wrongful conviction will significantly decrease.

---

[151] See Section V of Chapter 4 and Section III(C) of Chapter 6.

[152] Sangero & Halpert, *supra* note 15.

[153] See Section V of Chapter 1.

3 Safety in the Criminal Justice System—General Principles

I. General

In this and the next three chapters, I will lay out the foundations for developing a modern safety theory for the criminal justice system. This chapter will propose fundamental safety principles that, it emerges from my analysis, are vital for the criminal justice system. Chapter 4 will then present some basic modern safety methods that can, and should, be implemented in the criminal justice system. In Chapter 5, I will outline specific ways of practicing safety in relation to certain types of evidence, while Chapter 6 will address safety measures that can be implemented in various aspects of criminal procedure.

II. Defining Safety in the Criminal Justice System

In modern safety theory, very general definitions of safety, which are suited to many fields, are commonly accepted. Thus, for example, Nancy Leveson's most recent book includes the following generic definition: "**Safety**—Freedom from accidents (loss events)."[1] Into this definition, we must, of course, insert the general definition of "accident," which is as follows: "**Accident**—An undesired and unplanned event that results in a loss (including loss of human life or injury, property damage, environmental pollution, and so on)."[2] Another example of a general definition of safety is that found in the U.S. Air Force's *System Safety Handbook*: "**Safety**—Freedom from those conditions that can cause death, injury, occupational illness, or damage to or loss of equipment or property, or damage to the environment."[3]

In criminal justice, a false conviction is the central equivalent to an accident such as an airplane crash.[4] There are, of course, other types of accidents in criminal law besides false convictions, such as false arrest, an aggressive interrogation, or a humiliating search, which also cause significant harm to the innocent suspect. Yet generally, false conviction is the most significant accident in that it causes the greatest amount of harm. False convictions as a group can, of course, be distinguished and classified by the severity of the harm caused. For example, it is clear that short-term imprisonment is graver than a fine, long-term imprisonment is harsher than short-term imprisonment, and the death penalty is obviously the most severe punishment. Yet because all false convictions entail significant damage, including the stigma that attaches to the person who is falsely convicted and labeled a criminal, the suggested definition of accidents will cover all classes of false convictions (albeit not *only* false convictions). With regard to what defines a "false conviction," although all kinds of wrongful convictions should be prevented, including those marred by serious constitutional or other procedural or due process errors, the focus in this book is on convictions despite factual and actual innocence.[5]

It should be stressed that a false acquittal—a situation in which there was the evidence necessary to prove the defendant's guilt beyond a reasonable doubt but the fact-finder mistakenly acquitted him—does not constitute an accident. It can instead be regarded as the criminal justice system's failure to perform its function, just as when a plane fails to transport passengers to their intended destination.[6]

---

[1] Nancy G. Leveson, Engineering a Safer World: Systems Thinking Applied to Safety 468 (2011).

[2] *Id.*

[3] U.S. Air Force, System Safety Handbook, at vii (2000), *available at* http://www.system-safety. org/Documents/AF_System-Safety-HNDBK.pdf (last visited July 21, 2014); Boaz Sangero & Mordechai Halpert, *A Safety Doctrine for the Criminal Justice System*, 2011 Mich. St. L. Rev. 1293, 1300–01.

[4] Sangero & Halpert, *supra* note 3, at 1300. Others have also compared wrongful convictions to plane crashes. *See, e.g.,* Barry Scheck & Peter Neufeld, *Toward the Formation of "Innocence Commissions" in America*, 86 Judicature 98 (2002).

[5] Marvin Zalman, *An Integrated Justice Model of Wrongful Convictions*, 74 Alb. L. Rev. 1465, 1470 (2010–2011). *See also* Larry Laudan, Truth, Error, and Criminal Law 10 (2006).

[6] Mordechai Halpert & Boaz Sangero, *Towards Safety in the Criminal Justice System*, 36 Tel Aviv Univ. L. Rev. 363, 372 (2012) (in Hebrew).

Safety in the criminal justice system can be defined using an adapted form of the U.S. Air Force definition, as freedom from conditions that can cause harm to innocent people, particularly from being falsely convicted.[7] A more conservative definition could refer to the implementation of safety measures.[8] Under this definition, safety means the reduction of the risk of harm to the innocent through an ongoing process of risk identification and management in the criminal justice system.[9] Although it would not be realistic to attain a state of absolute safety, in which all innocent defendants are acquitted, resources should be invested in safety so as to diminish the rate of error in the system.[10]

In those fields in which there has traditionally been awareness of the need for modern safety—space, aviation, and transportation, for example—there is an ongoing attempt to improve safety, based on feedback that enables the determination of whether the previous safety goals have been attained and whether it is possible to move forward and set new goals. In the criminal justice system, however, there is no such feedback in general, due to what Dr. Mordechai Halpert and I dub the Hidden Accidents Principle in criminal law,[11] which considerably hinders any advancement in promoting safety. I will suggest ways to improve the criminal justice system despite this principle, such as implementing an incident-reporting duty and applying insights and experience from spheres of life in which accidents are discernible.[12]

III. The Hidden Accidents Principle in Criminal Law

As we will see in the subsequent chapters, modern safety measures are not implemented in the legal system. This is in contrast to the space, aviation, transportation, and engineering fields, where safety is common practice.[13] Why is this so? In other fields, an accident is both detected and detectable. A defect in a car can cause its observable crash, just as a defect in a bridge can cause its observable collapse.

---

[7] Sangero & Halpert, *supra* note 3, at 1300.

[8] "Safety is the state in which the risk of harm to persons or of property damage is reduced to, and maintained at or below, an acceptable level through a continuing process of hazard identification and risk management." INTERNATIONAL CIVIL AVIATION ORGANIZATION, SAFETY MANAGEMENT MANUAL 1.1 (2006), *available at* http://www.icao.int/fsix/_Library/SMM-9859_1ed_en.pdf. *See also* Sangero & Halpert, *supra* note 3, at 1300–01.

[9] Sangero & Halpert, *supra* note 3, at 1301.

[10] *Id.*

[11] *Id.* at 1314–16.

[12] See the discussion further on in Chapter 4.

[13] On this issue, see Mordechai Halpert & Boaz Sangero, *From a Plane Crash to the Conviction of an Innocent Person: Why Forensic Science Evidence Should Be Inadmissible unless It Has Been Developed as a Safety-Critical System*, 32 HAMLINE L. REV. 65 (2009).

Already by the 1940s, the fact that we are able to discern accidents and the damage they cause was an impetus in the development and institution of modern safety aimed at minimizing defects in products.[14]

Samuel Gross has noted in the context of false convictions, as follows:

> False convictions are not merely unobserved, but in most cases are also unobservable. The problem is not simply that we do not know for sure whether a particular prisoner is innocent. We also may not know for sure whether he is HIV positive, but we can test him, or the prison population as a whole, or a random sample. There is no general test for the accuracy of criminal convictions. If there were, we would use it at trial.[15]

Indeed, when a convicted defendant proclaims his innocence, this is usually met with complete disbelief due to people's confidence in a guilty verdict handed down at trial.[16] The general inability to detect false convictions is a prominent characteristic of criminal law, and these "accidents" typically "remain undetected." This inability "translates into optimism on the part of policymakers that false convictions only occur at a negligible rate."[17]

This reality means that the criminal justice system receives no feedback as to its inbuilt flaws and error rate. Due to the lack of external review, for example, forensic laboratory technicians have no conception of flaws in their practices and work.[18] Moreover, because of the Hidden Accidents Principle, effective system feedback is even theoretically implausible, and the quality of the system's functioning and safety practices can never be known. The only way to assess this is through comparison to other fields in which accidents are likely to cause serious harm.[19]

Post-conviction DNA testing has emerged in the last two decades as the leading technique for verifying a very narrow set of convictions, primarily rape convictions from the 1980s,[20] with the test results leading to a reopening of the case in some instances. In the framework of the groundbreaking Cardozo Innocence Project alone, over three-hundred wrongly convicted inmates have been exonerated and

---

[14] Sangero & Halpert, *supra* note 3, at 1314.

[15] Samuel R. Gross, *Convicting the Innocent*, 4 ANN. REV. L. SOC. SCI. 173, 175 (2008). See also Samuel R. Gross, *Pretrial Incentives, Post-Conviction Review, and Sorting Criminal Prosecutions by Guilt or Innocence*, 56 N.Y.L. SCH. L. REV. 1009, 1010 (2011–2012).

[16] Sangero & Halpert, *supra* note 3, at 1315.

[17] *Id.* at 1315. In the context of false confessions, this situation has been dubbed "the tip of the iceberg." GISLI H. GUDJONSSON, THE PSYCHOLOGY OF INTERROGATIONS AND CONFESSIONS: A HANDBOOK 173 (2003).

[18] Sangero & Halpert, *supra* note 3, at 1315. The case of the Houston Crime Lab is discussed in Section II of Chapter 5.

[19] *Id.* at 1315.

[20] *Id.*

released thus far,[21] but this is considerably less than the 5 to 10 percent false-conviction rate estimated in Chapter 1. Yet the exposure of these false convictions came as a shock to jurists no less than to the public at large, as the names and faces of some of the exonerees and the terrible suffering they experienced were publicized in the media.[22] Personal details such as that have a far stronger impact than abstract knowledge of the occurrence of false convictions.

On this background, clearly the Fly-Fix-Fly safety method is particularly unsuited to the criminal justice system, as the Hidden Accidents Principle makes it nearly impossible to learn from past accidents. Moreover, even modern safety methods such as the Identify-Analyze-Control and STAMP models discussed in Chapter 2 would not work well either due to the lack of meaningful feedback. Therefore, in addition to general modern safety methods, I will suggest safety principles and safety methods suited specifically to the criminal justice system.

IV. Why a Single Piece of Evidence Should not be Sufficient for a Conviction: Bayes' Theorem and Medical Diagnostics

A. GENERAL

Under the Hidden Accidents Principle in criminal law, the majority of false convictions go undetected. This means that the way to safety in the criminal justice system must be found by drawing on the insights and experience of other fields, where accidents are observable. The medical diagnostics field can be particularly enlightening as to how to contend with the challenge of hidden accidents and flaws in the system,[23] as it is prominently characterized by its efforts to find ways to diagnose rare diseases in low-risk populations, which are hard to detect.[24]

Indeed, using a single piece of evidence to determine the identity of the perpetrator of a crime can be analogized to using a single test to diagnose a rare disease. Just as a medical doctor should not base her diagnosis on a lone test without considering the statistical implications, law enforcement agents must be aware of the limitations of a single piece of evidence as an indicator of guilt.[25]

---

[21] Three-hundred-and-twenty-nine exonerees is the precise number. See the Innocence Project's website for this data, at www.innocenceproject.org (last visited April 15, 2015).

[22] Gross, *supra* note 15, at 174. *See also* Sangero & Halpert, *supra* note 3, at 1315–16.

[23] Boaz Sangero & Mordechai Halpert, *Why a Conviction Should Not Be Based on a Single Piece of Evidence: A Proposal for Reform*, 48 JURIMETRICS J. 43, 90–94 (2007).

[24] Klemens B. Meyer & Stephen G. Pauker, *Screening for HIV: Can We Afford the False Positive Rate?*, 317 NEW ENG. J. MED. 238 (1987); Sangero & Halpert, *supra* note 23.

[25] Illuminating in this respect is the *Allen* case, in which ignorance as to the limitations of a confession as the sole piece of evidence led to a false conviction. See a discussion of this case in Boaz Sangero & Mordechai Halpert, *Proposal to Reverse the View of a Confession: From Key Evidence Requiring Corroboration to Corroboration for Key Evidence*, 44 U. MICH. J.L. REFORM 511, 533–39 (2011).

B. BAYES' THEOREM AS ODDS

Before I describe the Bayes' Theorem and the medical diagnostic model, the following example[26] can illustrate why they are so critical. Assume that the manufacturer of a home HIV-testing kit reports an average 0.1 percent false positive rate. Thus, if 10,000 non-carriers test themselves with this kit, 10 false positive HIV results would obtain. Now, let us assume that John uses the kit to test himself and gets the positive result that he is an HIV-carrier. What is the probability that he is truly a carrier? The obvious answer seems to be 99.9 percent, with only 0.1 percent likelihood of a false positive. However, a crucial distinction should be made between conditional probability and inverse conditional probability: although the probability of a positive test result for a healthy person is, indeed, 0.1 percent, of relevance to us is the probability, given a positive test result, of the person tested actually being a carrier.

To illustrate, further assume that John is in a low-risk group for HIV: he practices safe sex; he does not use intravenous needles; he has never been given a blood transfusion. Say that the HIV-incidence rate for this group is 1-in-10,000, which, in medical statistical terms, is the base rate (incidence of the disease) for the group.[27] Thus, if 10,000 people in John's low-risk group were to test themselves using the home HIV-testing kit, 11 would get a positive result: 10 cases of error (false positives) for non-carriers (9999 x 0.1% ≅ 10), and 1 case of an actual HIV-carrier (because 1-in-10,000 members of this group is a carrier).[28] Consequently, contrary to what most intuitively presume, there is only a 1-in-11 (approximately 9 percent) likelihood that John is an HIV-carrier if he gets a positive test result, or in other words, there is a 10/11—about 91 percent—probability that this is a false positive.[29]

This demonstrates how test results analysis is no intuitive matter. A probabilistic analysis that takes into account the incidence of the disease within the tested population will tend to show that a test that, at first glance, appears to have precise results is in fact completely inconclusive on its own. This failure to factor in the incidence of a disease is a cognitive failure known in the psychological literature as the "base-rate fallacy"[30] or "base rate neglect"[31] and can be overcome through probabilistic analysis.[32]

---

[26] This is a modified version of an example—developed in Sangero & Halpert, *supra* note 23, at 47–50.

[27] *Id.* at 48.

[28] Assume that there is no possibility of a false negative, that is, that there will never be a negative test result for a carrier.

[29] Sangero & Halpert, *supra* note 23, at 48.

[30] Amos Tversky & Daniel Kahneman, *Evidential Impact of Base Rates, in* JUDGMENT UNDER UNCERTAINTY: HEURISTICS AND BIASES 153, 154 (Daniel Kahneman, Paul Slovic & Amos Tversky eds., 1982).

[31] Maya Bar-Hillel, *The Base-Rate Fallacy in Probability Judgments*, 44 ACTA PSYCHOLOGICA 211, 211 (1980); Tversky & Kahneman, *supra* note 30, at 153–60; Sangero & Halpert, *supra* note 23, at 50.

[32] Sangero & Halpert, *supra* note 23, at 48.

Bayes' Theorem, which originated in the eighteenth century,[33] is very significant in applied probability theory, and can be expressed in the form of odds:

Posterior Odds = Likelihood Ratio × Prior Odds [34]

This simple theorem holds that by updating our initial belief about something with objective new information, we arrive at a new and improved belief:[35]

> A simple statement of Bayes' Theorem uses three terms. One is the prior odds of a proposition—that is, the odds as assessed before receipt of the new evidence. The second is the posterior odds of the proposition—that is, the odds that the proposition is true as assessed after receipt of the new evidence. And the third is the likelihood ratio. Simply defined, the likelihood ratio of a given body of evidence with respect to a given proposition is the ratio of the probability that the evidence would arise given that the proposition is true to the probability that the evidence would arise given that the proposition is false.[36]

If we return to John in our example, the accuracy of the test (99.9 percent) is a component of the likelihood ratio. The likelihood ratio here is the quotient of two conditional probabilities: the numerator is the probability that the test result will be positive given that the person tested is a carrier, and the denominator is the probability that the test result will be positive given that the person tested is not a carrier. If we assume a zero-probability of a false negative (i.e., a negative test result for a carrier), the following likelihood ratio obtains:[37]

Likelihood Ratio = 1 / 0.001 = 1000

The Prior Odds here are the probability that a person is a carrier of the disease divided by the probability that he is not, *without* taking the test result into account.

---

[33] Thomas Bayes, *An Essay towards Solving a Problem in the Doctrine of Chances*, 53 PHIL. TRANSACTIONS ROYAL SOC'Y LONDON 370 (1763), *reprinted in* FACSIMILES OF TWO PAPERS BY BAYES (W. Edwards Deming ed., 1940); Sangero & Halpert, *supra* note 23, at 49–50.

[34] Sangero & Halpert, *supra* note 23. *See also, e.g.*, Stuart Spitalnic, *Test Properties 2: Likelihood Ratios, Bayes' Formula, and Receiver Operating Characteristic Curves*, HOSP. PHYSICIAN, Oct. 2004, at 53.

[35] SHARON B. MCGRAYNE, THE THEORY THAT WOULD NOT DIE, at xi (2012).

[36] Richard D. Friedman, *A Presumption of Innocence, Not of Even Odds*, 52 STAN. L. REV. 873, 875 (2000).

[37] Sangero & Halpert, *supra* note 23, at 49–50.

The Prior Odds for John, who is a member of a low-risk group with a base rate of 1/10,000, are as follows:

$$\text{Prior Odds} = 0.0001 / (1 - 0.0001) \cong 0.0001^{38}$$

The Posterior Odds are the probability that a person is a carrier divided by the probability that he is not, given a positive test result. If we now insert the figures we arrived at above into the Bayes' Theorem, the following obtains:

$$\text{Posterior Odds} = \text{Likelihood Ratio} \times \text{Prior Odds} = 1000 \times 0.0001 = 0.1$$

John's Posterior Odds, then, are 1/10: only 1 in 11 people who test positive from John's low-risk group will actually be a carrier, while 10 of the 11 positive test results will be false. This is the same result we arrived at above without using Bayes' Theorem directly but by applying its underlying rationale.[39]

As noted the mistaken intuition that if the home HIV test is 99.9 percent accurate, there is only a 0.1 percent probability that John is not a carrier if he tests positive (as opposed to the actual 91 percent probability of error) is the result of the base rate fallacy, which is also referred to as "the fallacy of the transposed conditional": rather than calculating the probability that a person is not a carrier given a positive test result ($10/11 \cong 91\%$), the probability of a non-carrier getting a positive test result is calculated ($1/1000 = 0.1\%$). From a Bayesian perspective, the source of this fallacy is that the Prior Odds are ignored and, consequently, the Posterior Odds are equated with the Likelihood Ratio. Daniel Kahneman and Amos Tversky have put this failure most succinctly as follows: "The failure to appreciate the relevance of prior probability in the presence of specific evidence is perhaps one of the most significant departures of intuition from the normative theory of prediction."[40]

C. APPLYING BAYES' THEOREM IN THE CRIMINAL JUSTICE SYSTEM

Lawyers, judges, and jurists are no less susceptible to these cognitive fallacies, for when they are relying on a single piece of evidence to convict a defendant, they are

---

[38] The denominator is supposed to complete the numerator to 1, because the probability that a person is a carrier and the probability that he is not a carrier are complementary probabilistic occurrences. Sangero & Halpert, *supra* note 23.

[39] *Id.*

[40] Daniel Kahneman & Amos Tversky, *On the Psychology of Prediction*, 80 PSYCHOL. REV. 237, 243 (1973); Sangero & Halpert, *supra* note 23.

ignoring the Prior Odds and the important distinction between conditional probability and inverse conditional probability.

In the criminal justice context, the given occurrence is a positive result yielded by scientific or other evidence. The probability of a person being a disease carrier in the medical diagnostic context is replaced by the probability of someone being guilty of a crime in the legal context; the probability of a person not being a carrier is replaced by the probability of a person being innocent. In medical diagnostics, the prior probability can be derived from the base rate; in criminal justice, the prior probability is the judge's (or the fact-finder's) assessment of the defendant's guilt or innocence based not on the main evidence but on other evidence.[41]

It is important to note here the debate as to whether Bayes' Theorem can and should be applied in criminal law, which began with the canonical exchange between Michael O. Finkelstein/William B. Fairley and Laurence H. Tribe.[42] I am not, however, proposing that judges (or fact-finders) apply the Theorem to make precise calculations to determine the cumulative weight of evidence. What I am suggesting, rather, is that the underlying logic of the formula be used to understand the risks of convicting a defendant based on one piece of evidence alone (of any type) and to persuade legislators to enact a safety rule that prohibits conviction on the basis of a single piece of evidence.

To illustrate, consider two hypotheses and one given event.[43] Under the first hypothesis, the suspect's Guilt (designated "G") is assumed, and under the second hypothesis, the suspect's Innocence (designated "I") is assumed. The given event is the specific piece of Evidence incriminating the suspect (designated "E"), which could be an eyewitness lineup identification or incriminating forensic lab test results. The basic odds formula is as follows:[44]

Likelihood Ratio × Prior Odds = Posterior Odds

The Likelihood Ratio (also known as the Bayes' Factor, which is used to update our prior beliefs with the evidence that we observe)[45] is the quotient of two conditional probabilities. The numerator is the probability of the existence of the evidence assuming the

---

[41] Sangero & Halpert, *supra* note 23.

[42] Michael O. Finkelstein & William B. Fairley, *A Bayesian Approach to Identification Evidence*, 83 HARV. L. REV. 489 (1970); Laurence H. Tribe, *Trial by Mathematics: Precision and Ritual in the Legal Process*, 84 HARV. L. REV. 1329 (1971). *See also* Alex Stein, *Judicial Fact-Finding and the Bayesian Method: The Case for Deeper Skepticism about Their Combination*, 1 INT'L J. EVIDENCE & PROOF 25 (1996); Sangero & Halpert, *supra* note 23, at 52 (2007); Edward K. Cheng, Essay: *Reconceptualizing the Burden of Proof*, 122 YALE L.J. 1254 (2013).

[43] Sangero & Halpert, *supra* note 25, at 539–41.

[44] *Id.* at 540.

[45] Cheng, *supra* note 42, at 1267.

suspect is guilty, and the denominator is the probability of the existence of the evidence assuming the suspect is innocent. This is the mathematical expression of the strength of the evidence. For example, if the incriminating evidence is an eyewitness identification in a police lineup, then a Likelihood Ratio of 10 means a 10 times greater likelihood the suspect was correctly identified as the guilty culprit than that the suspect is innocent and mistakenly identified. But the Likelihood Ratio is not, by itself, a sufficient indicator of a suspect's guilt or innocence, as it does not take into account any other evidence aside from one specific piece of evidence and, instead, presumes what is actually yet to be proven (the numerator assumes guilt and the denominator innocence).[46]

The Prior Odds are the probability of a suspect's guilt divided by the probability of his innocence without taking the identification into consideration and based on the other admissible evidence. These odds are called "Prior" because they reflect what we believe prior to observing the evidence.[47] Bayes' Theorem "updates" these prior beliefs by incorporating the evidence that we observe.[48] The Posterior Odds are then the product of the Likelihood Ratio times the Prior Odds. This represents the weight of the central specific piece of evidence combined with the other incriminating evidence against the suspect, expressed as follows:[49]

Posterior Odds = P (Guilt|Evidence) / P (Innocence|Evidence)

When the Posterior Odds is 1, the probability of guilt is identical to the probability of innocence (only 50 percent likelihood that the suspect is guilty). The greater the Posterior Odds, the greater the probability of guilt.[50]

Elsewhere, I have demonstrated with Dr. Mordechai Halpert the tremendous significance of not only the Likelihood Ratio but also the Prior Odds when a single piece of evidence is the basis for a conviction.[51] If we assume a Posterior Odds threshold of 90 as the minimum requirement for a conviction beyond a reasonable doubt, which is the criminal law standard of proof,[52] then about 5 percent of the convictions will be false. The following table further demonstrates the significance of the Prior Odds and the Likelihood Ratio, using different numerical values in applying Bayes' Theorem:[53]

---

46 Sangero & Halpert, *supra* note 25, at 540.
47 Cheng, *supra* note 42, at 1266.
48 *Id.* at 1267.
49 Sangero & Halpert, *supra* note 25, at 540–41.
50 *Id.* at 541.
51 Sangero & Halpert, *supra* note 23, at 54–55.
52 See the discussion of this threshold in Section II of Chapter 1.
53 This is a modified version of a table from Sangero & Halpert, *supra* note 23, at 54.

TABLE 3.1

PROBABILITIES OF GUILT UNDER BAYES' THEOREM

Prior Odds x	Likelihood Ratio =	Posterior Odds	Probability of Guilt Given the Evidence (rounded out)
("50:50") 1	10	10/1	91%
1/10	100	10/1	91%
1/100	1000	10/1	91%
1/1000	10,000	10/1	91%
1/10,000	100,000	10/1	91%
1/100,000	1,000,000	10/1	91%
1/1,000,000	10,000,000	10/1	91%
1/10,000	1000	0.1/1	9%

Table 3.1 demonstrates that even a slight possibility of error in a piece of evidence leads to the practical impossibility of showing guilt beyond a reasonable doubt only on the basis of that evidence (that is to say, in the absence of any other evidence that impacts the Prior Odds). For example, when the Prior Odds are 1/100,000 (or 1 in more than 100,000) only evidence that has an error rate below 1/1,000,000 will result in the desired Posterior Odds of 10. Yet in reality, no evidence has or can have such a low error rate and high level of accuracy. Moreover, the Prior Odds could be very low, 1 in millions, when there is exculpatory evidence, such as an alibi. In such circumstances, in order for a conviction to be based upon it, the accuracy of the (scientific) evidence should be an error rate of one error in several tens of millions of cases.[54]

Finally, the bottom row of Table 3.1 indicates the error rate that can be expected for realistic evidence, namely, 1 in 1000. Thus, if the Prior Odds of guilt are 1/10,000, the Posterior Odds will be a mere 0.1/1. In other words, 91 percent of convictions based on scientific evidence with a 1/1000 error rate and Prior Odds of 1/10,000 will be false.[55]

Chapter 5 will discuss the inherent limitations of the central accepted types of evidence in criminal law. It will demonstrate that as long as a given piece of evidence has not been shown to meet a certain (unrealistic) very high precision requirement, it should not constitute the sole grounds for convicting the defendant in question.

---

[54] *Id.* at 55.

[55] *Id.*

D. INSIGHTS AND LESSONS FROM THE FIELD OF MEDICAL DIAGNOSTICS

Table 3.2 sets out some fundamental definitions and formulas used in the medical diagnostic model:[56]

TABLE 3.2
THE GENERIC 2 X 2 TABLE:

	Has Condition	Does Not Have Condition	
Test Positive	A	B	Total Positive Tests (A + B)
Test Negative	C	D	Total Negative Tests (C + D)
	Number in Sample with Condition (A + C)	Number in Sample Without Condition (B + D)	Total Number of Subjects (A + B + C + D)

"Sensitivity" refers to the probability that a test will be positive for a patient who has the tested-for condition (e.g., HIV).
Sensitivity = A / (A+C)
"Specificity" refers to the probability that a test will be negative for a patient without the tested-for condition.
Specificity = D / (D+B)
"Positive Predictive Value" (PPV) refers to the probability that a patient has the condition given a positive test result.
PPV = A / (A+B)
"Negative Predictive Value" (NPV) refers to the probability that a patient does not have the condition given a negative test result.
NPV = D / (C+D)

Professionals in the testing diagnostics field and in measuring devices manufacturing commonly use these above concepts in describing a test's results. Because of the crucial importance of the data collected based on these concepts, FDA approval requires that manufacturers of medical devices provide not only data on a test's Specificity and Sensitivity but also the Positive and Negative Predictive Values for the various populations,[57] and the information is made public. This is a quintessential safety measure, for as demonstrated above in the HIV-test example, a test may be suitable for diagnosing high-risk populations but not (on its own at least) for diagnosing low-risk groups.

It is vital that those who will engage in safety in the legal field apply the error-prevention model developed and refined in the medical diagnostics field. The

---

[56] With some minor modifications, the definitions, formulas, and table are from Stuart Spitalnic's *Test Properties 2: Likelihood Ratios, Bayes' Formula, and Receiver Operating Characteristic Curves, supra* note 34. *See also* Stuart Spitalnic, *Test Properties 1: Sensitivity, Specificity and Predictive Values*, HOSP. PHYSICIAN, Sept. 2004, at 27.

[57] Sangero & Halpert, *supra* note 3, at 1298.

need for this is self-evident, first and foremost, with regard to forensic evidence, which should not, in essence, be any different from all other scientific tests. As we will see further on, the medical diagnostics model is suitable for weighing nonscientific evidence as well. Had even the most basic medical diagnostics model been adopted in the criminal justice system, it would have long arrived at the imperative safety rule that a conviction cannot be based on a single piece of evidence of any type. In Chapter 5, we will see that none of the types of evidence currently accepted in criminal law is suited to this function. The law's disregard for this problem is one of the central causes of the phenomenon of false convictions.

V. Adjusting the Beyond-A-Reasonable-Doubt Standard to a Safety Doctrine

The accepted standard of proof in American criminal law is guilt beyond a reasonable doubt,[58] and it is not unique to the U.S. criminal system.[59] While this standard seemingly guarantees a high degree of certainty of a conviction, it "does not mean beyond *any* doubt,"[60] for otherwise even the guilty could never be convicted: irrational and groundless doubts are always present. Thus, "the beyond a reasonable doubt standard is itself probabilistic,"[61] and there can be no absolute certainty in conviction.

Moreover, when a defendant is convicted based solely on his identification in a police lineup by a single eyewitness or on his confession, there is hardly a high degree of certainty regarding the conviction.[62] To contend with this, I have proposed with Dr. Mordechai Halpert the following safety-adapted version of the beyond-a-reasonable-doubt standard:

> Conviction in a criminal trial will be possible only where: (1) guilt has been proven beyond a reasonable doubt; and (additionally) (2) *all reasonable measures have been taken to ensure that false conviction does not occur.*[63]

---

[58] *In re* Winship, 397 U.S. 358, 361 (1970); Sangero & Halpert, *supra* note 3, at 1319–22.

[59] Alexander Volokh, *n Guilty Men*, 146 U. PA. L. REV. 173 (1997); Sangero & Halpert, *supra* note 3. This standard has been extensively discussed in the literature. *See, e.g.*, Note, *Reasonable Doubt: An Argument against Definition*, 108 HARV. L. REV. 1955 (1995); Note, Winship *on Rough Waters: The Erosion of the Reasonable Doubt Standard*, 106 HARV. L. REV. 1093 (1993); Robert C. Power, *Reasonable and Other Doubts: The Problem of Jury Instructions*, 67 TENN. L. REV. 45 (1999); Rinat Kitai, *Protecting the Guilty*, 6 BUF. CRIM. L. REV. 1163 (2003).

[60] Alex Stein, *Constitutional Evidence Law*, 61 VAND. L. REV. 65, 83 (2008); *see also* Sangero & Halpert, *supra* note 3.

[61] Victor v. Nebraska, 511 U.S. 1, 14 (1994); Sangero & Halpert, *supra* note 3 at 1320.

[62] *See also* Sangero & Halpert, *supra* note 23, at 90–94; Sangero & Halpert, *supra* note 25, at 533–39.

[63] Sangero & Halpert, *supra* note 3, at 1320.

The first condition will yield the current high level of certainty of guilt for convictions, but nothing near to absolute certainty. Thus, the second condition is aimed at ensuring adequate safety in arriving at a conviction. This means that the same probability threshold for a criminal conviction (such as the common 90 percent standard of proof)[64] cannot be applied uniformly in every case. Rather, under the safety-adjusted standard for proving guilt, if reasonable measures can be taken to increase the certainty of guilt beyond the "beyond a reasonable doubt" standard, they must be implemented.

Disregarding this second condition will lead to anomalies, as illustrated by the experience and practices of other safety-critical systems.[65] For example, in the fighter plane context, if the reasonable doubt standard (whether 90 percent or even 99 percent) were implemented, the planes would be considered safe to fly once the accident rate drops to 1 percent per flight. In the 1950s, however, a *0.01 percent* accident rate was found too costly despite the lower costs of manufacturing fighter planes at the time.[66] As a result, the industry instituted safety methods for reducing the rate of accidents. Indeed, it is inconceivable that the U.S. Air Force would settle for a 1 percent crash rate and not seek to minimize accidents.[67] In criminal law, however, the Hidden Accidents Principle misleads the system to suffice with the uniform beyond-reasonable-doubt certainty threshold, without any attempt at improving the system and reducing the occurrence of false convictions.

We can look to the criminal evidence context to further illustrate the possible anomalies that can arise from the failure to take safety measures to increase the certainty of convictions. Assume that significant incriminating evidence has been submitted in a murder trial, such as a fingerprint match and an eyewitness lineup identification of the defendant.[68] These two pieces of evidence combined or even on their own are sufficient to convict the defendant beyond a reasonable doubt under current practice and approaches.[69] Suppose, however, that there is a DNA sample from the crime scene that can be tested. Without a requirement that all possible safety measures be taken in convicting, and that proof beyond-a-reasonable-doubt not be relied on exclusively, the existing evidence would suffice for conviction and there would be no need to test the DNA, even though it could prove the defendant's

---

[64] *Id.* See also the discussion in Section II of Chapter 1.

[65] Sangero & Halpert, *supra* note 3, at 1321.

[66] AIR FORCE SYSTEM SAFETY HANDBOOK, *supra* note 3, at 2; Sangero & Halpert, *supra* note 3, at 1321.

[67] Sangero & Halpert, *supra* note 3.

[68] *Id.*

[69] As in the case of Stephen Cowans, for example, where evidence of this very kind was found sufficient to convict him for murder. Simon A. Cole, *More than Zero: Accounting for Error in Latent Fingerprint Identification*, 95 J. CRIM. L. & CRIMINOLOGY 985, 1034, 1014–16 (2005); Sangero & Halpert, *supra* note 3, at 1321.

innocence.[70] The proposed safety condition, in contrast, would require the examination of all reasonable potential evidence.[71] Cumulative evidence (fingerprint match and lineup identification) would be sufficient for proving guilt beyond a reasonable doubt *only* when there is no DNA sample available for testing.

A case that illustrates the tragic potential outcome of the failure to pursue and examine all possible exculpatory or incriminating evidence is the death-sentenced inmate who claimed he was innocent and requested DNA testing to prove this, but was refused and executed.[72] Given this, it is clear that the failure to examine potentially exculpatory evidence in itself creates reasonable doubt and mandates acquittal,[73] for any doubt as to guilt must weigh in a defendant's favor. But the logic question that arises, however, is whether it is reasonable that a certain set of evidence can be sufficient for convicting in one case but insufficient in another, simply because of the existence of reasonable potential evidence in the latter. Elsewhere, the imperative need for safety in the criminal justice system has been shown as justifying this distinction.[74] Moreover, the final result need not always be an acquittal: when possible, a court should order to do the requested test (such as DNA testing) and then decide according to the test results.

VI. Neutralizing the Conception of the Suspect's Guilt: Insights from Psychology

The wrongful conception of a suspect's guilt (known also as "tunnel vision," "presumption of guilt," and "making the defendant fit the crime"[75]) is common among police investigators, prosecutors, jurors, and even judges. It leads to many errors and underlies some of the central factors in false convictions, in the areas of both evidence and criminal procedure.

As Michel Foucault fascinatingly described in his book on the birth of the prison as an institution (surprisingly, imprisonment as punishment became common practice only about two centuries ago), at least in the past, there was a notion that all suspects—deriving simply from being a suspect—deserve some punishment, for it is (allegedly) implausible

---

[70] Cowans's conviction was overturned, after six years in prison, based on post-conviction DNA testing that exonerated him. Cole, *supra* note 69; Sangero & Halpert, *supra* note 3.

[71] Sangero & Halpert, *supra* note 3.

[72] GEORGE C. THOMAS III, THE SUPREME COURT ON TRIAL—HOW THE AMERICAN JUSTICE SYSTEM SACRIFICES INNOCENT DEFENDANTS 222 (2011).

[73] For a parallel approach in the tort context, see Ariel Porat & Alex Stein, *Liability for Uncertainty: Making Evidential Damage Actionable*, 18 CARDOZO L. REV. 1891, 1893 (1997); *see also* Sangero & Halpert, *supra* note 3, at 1321.

[74] Sangero & Halpert, *supra* note 3, at 1322.

[75] THOMAS, *supra* note 72, at 15.

for any suspect to be completely devoid of some guilt.[76] I maintain that to a certain extent, this perception persists to this day: the conception—at times very convenient for law-enforcement officers—that the suspect in custody is the perpetrator of the crime under investigation. In practice, then, the presumption of innocence that we uphold as a society[77] is replaced by a presumption of guilt.[78] This working premise is extremely convenient in that it is far easier to focus on one specific line of investigation than pursue a number of paths. It is convenient also because the present suspect is usually already in police custody. This premise is reinforced by the (inaccurate) estimation that the majority of suspects are guilty of what they have been accused. The conception of guilt gains momentum once the suspect is indicted and becomes the defendant. At this point, the well-known statistic that the overwhelming majority of defendants are convicted comes into play, supposedly supporting also the certainty of their guilt.[79] This final, dangerous assumption is likely to bias judges as well in their decision-making.

The conception of the suspect's guilt has a destructive effect on the work of police investigators.[80] Because they assume this guilt and see their sole task as proving it, their investigation focuses almost exclusively on the suspect and on the attempt to extract a confession. And once a confession has been obtained, the police investigation is usually closed. Other lines of investigation, which could have shed light on what truly happened, are never pursued. Moreover, even when later attempts are made to reopen the investigation, at times the evidence has already been lost. Any signs of inconsistency with the conception of guilt are either not acknowledged at all or else acknowledged but rejected as unreliable or insignificant. In the American legal literature, this phenomenon of focusing on the suspect based on the presumption of his guilt is referred to as "tunnel vision."[81] This is based on the fact that those

---

[76] M. FOUCAULT, DISCIPLINE AND PUNISH, THE BIRTH OF THE PRISON 42 (Alan Sheridan trans., 1977).

[77] Rinat Kitai, *Presuming Innocence*, 55 OKLA. L. REV. 257, 273–74 (2002).

[78] HERBERT L. PACKER, THE LIMITS OF THE CRIMINAL SANCTION 160 (1968); John Baldwin, *Police Interrogation: What Are the Rules of the Game? in* SUSPICION AND SILENCE: THE RIGHT TO SILENCE IN CRIMINAL INVESTIGATIONS 67 (David Morgan & Geoffrey M. Stephenson eds., 1994); Wayne T. Westling & Vicki Waye, *Videorecording Police Interrogations: Lessons from Australia*, 25 AM. J. CRIM. L. 493, 502 (1998); Saul M. Kassin, *Human Judges of Truth, Deception and Credibility: Confident but Erroneous*, 23 CARDOZO L. REV. 809, 814 (2002); Jonatan Simon, *Recovering the Craft of Policing: Wrongful Convictions, the War on Crime, and the Problem of Security, in* WHEN LAW FAILS: MAKING SENSE OF MISCARRIAGES OF JUSTICE 115, 120 (Charles J. Ogletree, Jr. & Austin Sarat eds., 2009).

[79] Kitai, *supra* note 77, at 266.

[80] *See, e.g.*, Boaz Sangero, Miranda *Is Not Enough: A New Justification for Demanding "Strong Corroboration" to a Confession*, 28 CARDOZO L. REV. 2791, 2815 (2007).

[81] Keith A. Findley & Michael S. Scott, *The Multiple Dimensions of Tunnel Vision in Criminal Cases*, 2006 WIS. L. REV. 291, 292 ("focus on a suspect, select and filter the evidence that will 'build a case' for conviction, while ignoring or suppressing evidence that points away from guilt"). *See also* Richard A. Leo, *False Confessions: Causes, Consequences, and Implications*, 37 J. AM. ACAD. PSYCHIATRY L. 332, 334 (2009) ("The Misclassification Error").

who are trapped in this conception behave as though they are in a tunnel that leads in only one particular direction, completely prevented from looking beyond the tunnel, in other directions. In a similar fashion to the influence of the combination of the conception and a confession, when the police have another piece of incriminating evidence against the suspect, such as a lineup identification, the combined force of the evidence and the conception of guilt work to lead investigators to regard the case as closed and refrain from investigating other possibilities.

In his article "Reverse Engineering," Danny Ciraco illustrates compellingly the impact of the conception of the suspect's guilt on the operation of law-enforcement agents. He compares the work of police investigators to how engineers take a finished product and try to copy the idea by taking the product apart and working backwards from end to start.[82] Similarly, law enforcement officers, trapped in the conception of the suspect's guilt, begin—conceptually, at least—from the finished product of a criminal conviction, which they assume to be the desired outcome (because the suspect is presumed to have committed the crime being investigated), and search solely for evidence supporting this assumption and outcome. This is unfortunately true of innumerable police investigations, prosecutorial work, and even some trial verdicts. As Karl Popper noted, it is easy to find confirmation or verification for any theory if that is what you are looking for.[83]

The need for the criminal justice system to learn from psychological research has been explained by Dan Simon as follows:

> One of the obvious features of the criminal justice process is that it is operationalized mostly through people: witnesses, detectives, suspects, lawyers, judges, and jurors. The wheels of the system are turned by the mental operations of these actors .... It thus seems sensible to examine the workings of the criminal justice process from a psychological perspective. Fortunately, a large body of experimental psychological research is at our disposal.[84]

In their expansive review of the psychological literature, Keith A. Findley and Michael Scott showed that "tunnel vision" is a human tendency that is explained by, among other things, a number of well-known cognitive biases, including hindsight bias, selective information processing, confirmation bias, and outcome bias.[85]

---

[82] Danny Ciraco, *Reverse Engineering*, 11 WINDSOR REV. LEGAL & SOC. ISSUES 41, 61 (2001).

[83] Karl R. Popper, *Science: Conjectures and Refutations, in* CONJECTURES AND REFUTATIONS 33 (1969).

[84] DAN SIMON, IN DOUBT—THE PSYCHOLOGY OF THE CRIMINAL JUSTICE PROCESS 2 (2012).

[85] Findley & Scott, *supra* note 81, at 307–22; SIMON, *supra* note 84, at 22–25. Simon also refers to five mechanisms of biased reasoning among interrogators: selective framing strategy, selective exposure, selective scrutiny, biased evaluation, and selective stopping. *Id.* at 36–39. *See also* Lucian L. Leape, *Error in Medicine*, 23 JAMA 1851 (2009).

Confirmation bias is "the tendency to seek or interpret evidence in ways that support existing beliefs, expectations, or hypotheses,"[86] rather than searching for or analyzing information regarding an alternative in an effort to refute the hypothesis.

"Hindsight bias" (or "knew-it-all-along-effect") is "a product of the fact that memory is a dynamic process of reconstruction,"[87] and it "might reinforce premature or unwarranted focus on an innocent suspect."[88] "Outcome bias" reflects "hindsight judgments about whether a decision was a good or bad one."[89] In the criminal justice system, there are forces (such as the public pressure on police investigators to solve crimes and catch criminals) and processes that greatly exacerbate the tunnel vision phenomenon.[90]

A quintessential example of the damaging effect of the misconception of suspects' guilt on police and prosecutorial work is the "Norfolk Four" case.[91] In this matter a woman was raped and murdered in her home,[92] and the police investigated her neighbor, Daniel Williams, who was a U.S. Navy sailor and had recently gotten married. At first, Williams vehemently denied any involvement in the crime. He was brought in for interrogation by a tough police detective, Robert Glenn Ford, who had a reputation for extracting confessions from suspects.[93] Under arrest and during the course of a very pressurized and extended interrogation, Williams confessed to the rape and murder.[94] However, the genetic comparison showed that the DNA taken from the crime scene was not his.[95] But Williams was not released, and instead, the person he shared an apartment with, Joseph Jesse Dick, who was a Navy sailor as well, was brought in for interrogation by Ford. After a long and intense interrogation, Dick also confessed to the rape and murder.[96] But his DNA did not match the semen sample taken from the crime scene either.[97] Yet even then neither man was released. The police returned to Dick and demanded that he tell them who else was present during the commission of the crime. After a grilling interrogation, Dick gave the names of two additional men: Eric and George. The police investigators tracked down Eric Cameron Wilson, who also confessed while interrogated

---

[86] Findley & Scott, *supra* note 81, at 309.
[87] *Id*. at 317.
[88] *Id*. at 318.
[89] *Id*. at 320.
[90] *Id*. at 322–33.
[91] Tom Wells & Richard A. Leo, The Wrong Guys—Murder, False Confessions, and the Norfolk Four (2008).
[92] *Id*. at 6.
[93] *Id*. at 29–30.
[94] *Id*. at 31–39.
[95] *Id*. at 54.
[96] *Id*. at 58–75.
[97] *Id*. at 95.

by Detective Ford.[98] But his DNA did not fit either,[99] and again, the police did not release him. The police could not find the man known as George.[100] On the basis of Dick's description of George, who perhaps did not even exist, the police apprehended another man: Derek Tice.[101] When shown photographs of suspects, Dick identified Tice as the so-called George.[102] In interrogation, Tice also confessed to the crime[103] and incriminated two additional men: Richard D. Pauley and Geoffrey A. Farris.[104] The police investigators then arrived at a seventh suspect: John Danser.[105] Four of the seven suspects did not hold up under interrogation and confessed to committing the crime: Williams, Dick, Wilson, and Tice. All seven underwent DNA testing, but none matched the DNA taken from the crime scene.

At this case, a miracle occurred: Omar Abdul Ballard, an inmate with prior convictions for rape and other violent crimes, wrote to his ex-girlfriend that he was the rapist and killer. The letter was handed over to the police,[106] and Ballard was brought in for interrogation. The police tested his DNA, and it was found to match the DNA sample from the crime scene.[107] Ballard confessed to the crime and told the police that he had acted alone.[108] No connection was found between him and the seven other suspects.[109] Were the seven original suspects finally released? Even in these circumstances, the conception of the suspect's guilt blinded the police and prosecution to the truth. The prosecution constructed a story according to which the seven sailors had allegedly gathered near the victim's house, planning to break in and rape her, but did not know how to break into the house. At this point, Ballard showed up, completely by coincidence, and offered to assist them in committing the crime. Thus, the misconception brought the police and the prosecution to *reduction ad absurdum*. The jurors also were apparently trapped in the wrongful conception of the accused's guilt, for they convicted the four sailors who had confessed and were put on trial, and sentenced them to long prison terms. Tice was even convicted a second time for the crime, when he was retried after his original conviction was vacated by the court.[110] Only after more than a decade were the details of this case exposed

---

[98] *Id.* at 114.
[99] *Id.* at 125.
[100] *Id.* at 129.
[101] *Id.* at 130.
[102] *Id.* at 130–31.
[103] *Id.* at 151.
[104] *Id.* at 152–53.
[105] *Id.* at 172.
[106] *Id.* at 187.
[107] *Id.* at 195.
[108] *Id.* at 197, 210.
[109] *Id.* at 196.
[110] *Id.* at 255.

in a book by Tom Wells and Richard A. Leo[111] and in an investigative documentary movie, *The Confessions,* directed by Ofra Bikel and broadcast on FRONTLINE.[112]

In Chapters 5 and 6, we will see how the conception of the accused's guilt is misleading and lies behind various factors in false convictions, both in criminal procedure (for example, in its impact on police investigative methods and their focus on the suspect) and in the realm of evidence.

How can we combat this harmful conception? As Findley and Scott have shown, rather than being aware of cognitive biases and seeking to prevent them, some of the common rules and practices in our adversarial criminal justice system actually reinforce these biases. One prominent example is the Reid interrogation technique. Under this method, a distinction is made between "interviews," in which the interrogation is conducted in an open manner with the aim of obtaining information and arriving at the truth, and "interrogations," where the investigator is certain of the suspect's guilt and is explicitly attempting to elicit a confession.[113] Were investigators indeed able to identify from the outset who did and did not commit a crime, this system could possibly work. However, to begin with, studies show that police investigators, prosecutors, jurors, judges, and, in fact, all of us are incapable of distinguishing truth from lies.[114] Furthermore, if we were to know that a person committed the crime he is suspected of, this knowledge would be the product of significant additional evidence to this effect, and there would then be no need for a confession.[115] Thus, the cognitive biases are built into the Reid technique itself. This system trains investigators to lock-onto a suspect based on gut feeling and unproven means and to pursue incriminating evidence against the suspect that will lead to conviction: his confession. Thus the presumption of innocence is knowingly replaced by a presumption of guilt.

In 1968, Herbert L. Packer wrote as follows about the presumption of guilt:[116]

The presumption of guilt is what makes it possible for the system to deal efficiently with large numbers, as the Crime Control Model demands. The supposition is

---

[111] WELLS & LEO, *supra* note 91.

[112] The movie *The Confessions* can be viewed at http://www.pbs.org/wgbh/pages/frontline/the-confessions (last visited July 28, 2014).

[113] Findley & Scott, *supra* note 81, at 334; SIMON, *supra* note 84, at 121–34. *See also* Brandon L. Garrett, *Interrogation Policies,* 49 U. RICH. L. REV. (forthcoming 2015).

[114] Saul M. Kassin & Christina T. Fong, *"I'm Innocent!": Effects of Training on Judgments of Truth and Deception in the Interrogation Room,* 23 LAW & HUM. BEHAV. 499 (1999); Saul M. Kassin, Christian A. Meissner & Rebecca J. Norwick, *"I'd Know a False Confession if I Saw One": A Comparative Study of College Students and Police Investigators,* 29 LAW & HUM. BEHAV. 211 (2005). For references to additional studies with similar results, *see id.* at 212, 222. *See also* Findley & Scott, *supra* note 81, at 336, and sources therein; Sangero, *supra* note 80, at 2820.

[115] For a more in-depth discussion, see Sangero & Halpert, *supra* note 25.

[116] PACKER, *supra* note 78. On the presumption of guilt, see Findley & Scott, *supra* note 81, at 340 n.327; Kitai, *supra* note 77.

that the screening processes operated by police and prosecutors are reliable indicators of probable guilt. Once a man has been arrested and investigated without being found to be probably innocent, or, to put it differently, once a determination has been made that there is enough evidence of guilt to permit holding him for further action, then all subsequent activity directed toward him is based on the view that he is probably guilty. The precise point at which this occurs will vary from case to case; in many cases it will occur as soon as the suspect is arrested, or even before, if the evidence of probable guilt that has come to the attention of the authorities is sufficiently strong. But in any case the presumption of guilt will begin to operate well before the "suspect" becomes a "defendant."

Findley and Scott have proposed a range of ways for contending with tunnel vision, covering substantial parts of criminal procedure and evidence law, because the many causes of this bias are deeply rooted in the prevailing system.[117] It appears that at least according to their analysis, combating this phenomenon mandates change to the very foundations of the system.

My aim is not to provide an exhaustive list of debiasing methods for the criminal justice system. An integral and vital component of my overall proposition for implementing safety in the system is the establishment of a central agency that will advance safety and, among other things, promote research on different issues and concerns, including debiasing techniques. The research should be focused on the investigation of accidents, principally by analyzing reports submitted under the accidents and incidents reporting duty, and on a comparison with diagnostic fields. Such research will need to examine police investigators training, common practices in the criminal justice field, and any possible alternatives. The recommended solutions will have to be verified through controlled studies, including simulations of legal cases in laboratory conditions, conducted by teams of experts from various disciplines, including psychology, safety professionals, and jurists.

The research, furthermore, could consider a variety of approaches and techniques. One would be developing awareness of the conception of the suspect's guilt and its ramifications. Second, police investigators, prosecutors, and judges should be trained about the misleading conception of a suspect's guilt, and its possible outcomes should be considered. Judges could also be required to warn jurors to this effect, and police investigators should be made aware that their job is not to solve cases at any cost but to assist the court in arriving at the truth and seeing that justice is done. Accordingly, if they are able to discover and expose exculpatory evidence, they should be duty-bound to do so. Third, police investigators could be encouraged to pursue a number of lines of investigation and

---

[117] Findley & Scott, *supra* note 81, at 354–96.

not focus solely on the suspect in custody. Thus, for example, it would be important to commend and promote not only an investigator who successfully finds incriminating evidence against a suspect but also one who exposes the truth and prevents an innocent person from being brought to trial. Fourth, police investigations should be supervised, and, if the need arises, investigators directed toward additional lines of investigation. Fifth, investigations should be made transparent through electronic recordings and preservation of all lineups, interviews, and interrogations in their entirety.[118] Six, it could also be beneficial to attach to every team investigating a serious crime an investigator whose purpose is to "go against the flow": to search for evidence of the suspect's innocence and thereby improve the investigation by making it richer and more comprehensive.[119]

George C. Thomas III has made the interesting suggestion to establish a pool of "criminal law specialists" who would work for the district attorney in some cases and for the chief public defender in others. "Hopefully, the time spent defending cases might move all lawyers to care less about convictions and more about getting the right outcome."[120] A similar arrangement already exists in the English system: "[T]he barrister who prosecutes one day may defend the next."[121] In addition to combating tunnel vision, this proposal could contend with both the problem of disparity of resources between the defense and prosecution and the ingrained loyalties that bind police, prosecutors, and judges.[122]

It is important to note that these are just a few ideas for consideration and in no way intended as an exhaustive list of possible solutions. I do not claim that these methods would achieve the desired goal, either. They must be examined thoroughly in controlled experiments, for example, and other means of reducing the problem must be explored as well by looking at areas of life in which accidents are not as undetectable as in criminal law.

VII. Pursuing the Ultimate Goal of Gathering and Submitting Accurate Evidence

As will be demonstrated in Chapter 5, all types of evidence presently admissible in criminal law are not perfectly accurate and can be subject to error. This includes both the traditional types of evidence (confessions and eyewitness testimony) as

---

[118] SIMON, *supra* note 84, at 47–48.

[119] *Id.* at 45–47. About two decades ago I have learned such an idea from my students while teaching them the seminar "Convicting the Innocent: Causes and Solutions".

[120] THOMAS, *supra* note 72, at 190–92 (the quotation is at *id.* at 191).

[121] *Id.* at 191–92.

[122] Susan A. Bandes, *Protecting the Innocent as the Primary Value of the Criminal Justice System*, 7 OHIO ST. J. CRIM. L. 413, 427 (2009).

well as the finest scientific evidence (DNA comparisons and fingerprint matching). The first central implication of this insight is the need to set a legal safety rule prohibiting convictions on the basis of a single piece of evidence.[123] A second central implication is demanding not only a proof of guilt beyond a reasonable doubt, but also that all reasonable measures have been taken to ensure that false conviction does not occur.[124] A third central implication is that it is crucial to strive to improve the accuracy of evidence used in criminal law.

The importance of such an approach was asserted extensively in the 2009 National Academy of Sciences report, which dealt at length with the need to improve forensic science.[125] The report described the current reality in which a scientific basis has been established only for DNA evidence, while all other types of scientific evidence suffer from a lack of data and scientific grounding. The authors of the report thus called for comprehensive studies to explore ways of improving forensic science and making it "true" science. Traditional types of evidence such as eyewitness identifications, which are not claimed to be scientific, are in similar need of ongoing improvement to increase their reliability and accuracy. In Chapter 5, I will address in greater detail the main types of evidence. Here, I seek only to propose a general guiding principle for increasing safety in the criminal justice system: pursuit of the ultimate goal of gathering and submitting accurate evidence. One possible means of advancing this idea and putting the theory into practice is through the proposed Safety in the Criminal Justice System Institute, which would invest the resources necessary for achieving this goal.

VIII. Starting with "Fly-Fix-Fly"

In the second chapter, we saw how modern safety theory has progressed far beyond the "Fly-Fix-Fly" safety method. Under this approach, an airplane flies until a mishap occurs. Following the discovery of the mishap, all airplanes of the relevant model are grounded, the defect fixed, and the airplanes then put back in the air—until the next mishap, when the process begins all over again. This method was the commonly accepted practice in the area of fighter airplanes until World War II, when it came to be viewed as too costly and outdated. As a result, modern safety began to develop, the essence of which is the "Identify-Analyze-Control" approach with

---

[123] See Section IV of Chapter 3.

[124] See Section V of Chapter 3.

[125] NAT'L ACADEMY OF SCIENCES ET AL., STRENGTHENING FORENSIC SCIENCE IN THE UNITED STATES: A PATH FORWARD (2009), *available at* http://www.nap.edu/catalog.php?record_id=12589 (last visited July 24, 2014).

its goal of "First-Time-Safe." In the criminal justice system, in contrast, even the obsolete Fly-Fix-Fly safety method is yet to be adopted, due to the lack of awareness of a need for safety to improve the system and prevent false convictions. Thus, even when a mishap is actually exposed in the criminal justice system, there is a tendency to regard it as a localized and lone occurrence or else as the fault of one "bad apple." No resources are invested in overall treatment of all incidents of the kind that arose. Moreover, there is even a tendency to present the fact that only a relatively few mishaps are detected as proof that the system works and that it uncovers mishaps and fixes them. Therefore, despite the fact that the Fly-Fix-Fly method has long been abandoned by modern safety theory, and despite the existence of far better and more advanced methods—which, in the next chapter, I recommend implementing in the criminal justice system—an outdated safety approach is certainly better than no safety approach at all. I thus recommend that as a first stage toward safety in the criminal justice system, the Fly-Fix-Fly method be systematically implemented throughout the system. In practice, there is no necessary contradiction between applying this method and modern safety approaches: the Fly-Fix-Fly method should be adopted initially as the necessary minimum to which modern safety methods are later added. Indeed, although the ideal option would be to plan the system in advance so as to ensure a negligible number of mishaps, when mishaps do emerge, it is inconceivable that they will not be investigated and the necessary systemic lessons learned.

One exceptional example of the proper application of the Fly-Fix-Fly method in criminal justice is in the context of the investigation of the serology division of the West Virginia state police crime laboratory.[126] After the exposure of the case on a television program, it emerged that over the years, laboratory workers, with the serology division chief, Fred Zain, at the forefront, had falsified lab test results so as to fabricate incriminating evidence against suspects. In an almost unprecedented move, retired judge James O. Holiday was appointed to carry out a comprehensive investigation into these occurrences and make far-reaching recommendations on the basis of his findings. The recommendations he made in his final report related to *all* the cases in which the serology division chief had been involved. Holiday recommended setting rules according to which any piece of evidence that Zain had handled was inadmissible and that, therefore, vacation of the relevant convictions could be applied for in a retrial; the court's determination would then be made according to the remaining evidence in the case. In addition, Holiday recommended setting rules also with regard to cases in which a conviction was obtained through a plea

---

[126]   438 S.E.2d 501 (W. Va. 1993) (in the matter of an investigation of the serology division of the West Virginia state police crime laboratory); JUSTIN BROOKS, WRONGFUL CONVICTIONS CASES AND MATERIALS 179–91 (2014).

bargain. Furthermore, it was decided that Judge Holiday's report be distributed to the relevant convicted inmates, so that they could file the appropriate applications. It was also recommended that proceedings against Zain be pursued. The West Virginia Supreme Court adopted all of the recommendations Holiday made in his report.[127]

This was a serious response to a very grave mishap in the criminal justice system that was uncharacteristically detected, and constituted a serious attempt at identifying all the cases that were impacted by the mishap and fixing the errors, similarly to how all airplanes of a type that crashes are grounded until the defect is fixed. Although this is still not the modern safety approach proposed in the next chapter, it is nonetheless significant progress relative to what is currently accepted in the criminal justice system. In the present state, then, this Fly-Fix-Fly approach should be adopted, and then at a later stage, the move be made toward more advanced safety methods.

In this chapter, I have proposed a number of general principles for attaining safety in the criminal justice system. The next chapter will suggest some modern safety methods from other fields that can be applied in the legal system. The two subsequent chapters will then suggest a way to safety with regard to specific kinds of evidence and criminal procedure.

---

[127] BROOKS, *supra* note 126, at 179–91.

4 Applying Modern Safety in the Criminal Justice System

I. General

In Chapter 2, the fundamentals of modern system-safety were presented.[1] I expanded on the safety methods that, in my estimation, can and should be implemented in the criminal justice system, which, in contrast to some of the other safety-critical systems, is based primarily on human decisions and actions and less on technology. In the third chapter, I presented general safety principles that I propose incorporating into the criminal justice system. These principles are drawn primarily from the research on the criminal justice system and less from modern safety. In this chapter, I will now propose specific modern safety principles and methods that can and should, in my view, be applied in the criminal justice system already at the first stage of integrating safety into the system. This is not an exhaustive list of principles and methods but, rather, merely the first step on the way to safety, which I hope will be taken further by others.

---

[1] I thank Dr. Daniel Hartmann and Professor Nancy Leveson for their helpful comments on this chapter.

II. The Establishment of a "Safety in the Criminal Justice System Institute" (SCJSI)

Introducing modern safety into systems lacking a culture of safety requires the establishment of a special institute to carry out this function, and the securing of resources necessary for the new institute to operate in a meaningful way. Thus, for example, in the field of aviation, the Federal Aviation Administration (FAA)[2] was established; in the field of transportation, the National Transportation Board (NTSB)[3] was founded; in the area of food and drugs, there is the Food and Drug Administration (FDA)[4]; the Occupational Safety and Health Administration (OSHA)[5] serves the occupational field; and various such bodies were established in the medical field, such as the National Center for Patient Safety (NCPS)[6] and the Center for Patient Safety Research and Practice.[7] In all of these fields, the recognition of safety issues and the need to improve performance led to national focus on safety leadership, the development of a knowledge base, and the distribution of information, an agenda to which substantial resources were devoted.[8]

It is certainly possible—at least theoretically—for safety to develop in any given field step by step, without the support of a central guiding institute. Yet an "evolutionary" process of this kind takes many years to reach completion, during which a heavy price will be paid in preventable accidents. In effect, from the moment the moral and economic justification for practicing safety in a particular field has been recognized—as in the criminal justice system, as I demonstrated in Chapter 1[9]—the failure to take decisive action to promote safety becomes negligence, for the harms that could have been prevented exceed immeasurably the means necessary for preventing them.[10]

For a variety of reasons, I seek to learn from the medical field how to best promote safety in the criminal justice system. First, the medical field, like the criminal justice system, is a safety-critical system where the majority of failures appear not

---

[2] *See, e.g.,* the FFA website at http://www.faa.gov/ (last visited May 17, 20014); COMM. ON QUALITY OF HEALTH CARE IN AM., INST. OF MED., NAT'L ACAD. OF SCI., TO ERR IS HUMAN: BUILDING A SAFER HEALTH SYSTEM 72 (Linda T. Kohn, Janet M. Corrigan & Molla S. Donaldson eds., 2000) [hereinafter TO ERR IS HUMAN].

[3] *See, e.g.,* TO ERR IS HUMAN, *supra* note 2, at 72.

[4] *See, e.g., id.* at 71.

[5] *See,* e.g., *id.* at 73.

[6] See the website http://www.patientsafety.gov (last visited May 17, 2014). The function of the Center is defined there as follows: "to develop and nurture a culture of safety .... Our goal is the nationwide reduction and prevention of inadvertent harm to patients as a result of their care."

[7] See the website http://www.patientsafetyresearch.org/index.htm (last visited May 17, 2014).

[8] TO ERR IS HUMAN, *supra* note 2, at 74–75.

[9] *See* Sections III and IV in Chapter 1.

[10] See Section IV in Chapter 1.

to be technological in nature but are rather the result of human error.[11] Second, in the medical field, too, there was insufficient awareness of the need to practice modern safety, and thus, up until a decade ago, a central safety institute had yet to be established. There, also, a significant conceptual change was required. Third, the National Academy of Sciences assisted the medical field in advancing the matter. Its detailed report from 2000, *To Err Is Human: Building a Safer Health System*,[12] analyzed the existing state of affairs and outlined the extent to which safety was lacking in the field. The report gave detailed recommendations for the establishment of an institute aimed at promoting safety in medicine. The fourth chapter of the report—"Building Leadership and Knowledge for Patient Safety"[13]—opened with the following recommendation: "Congress should create a Center for Patient Safety with the Agency for Healthcare Research and Quality."

And indeed, soon after the release of the report, Congress adopted its recommendation and passed legislation funding for the establishment of the Center for Patient Safety and Quality within the Agency for Healthcare Research and Quality.[14] Moreover, in 2005, the Patient Safety and Quality Improvement Act was enacted, providing for the establishment of patient safety organizations.[15]

The closest thing to this development in the legal field has been the National Academy of Sciences' 2009 report, *Strengthening Forensic Science in the United States*.[16] This extremely important report, which I will expand on in Chapter 5, deals with forensic evidence. However, in contrast to the report, which addresses only one important area requiring significant safety reform and improvement, I propose implementing modern safety throughout the entire criminal justice system, in all of its procedural and evidential components. It is noteworthy that even in relation to the relatively narrow context of forensic evidence, the National Academy of Sciences

---

[11] Lucian L. Leape, *Foreword: Preventing Medical Accidents: Is "Systems Analysis" the Answer?*, 27 AM. J. L. & MEDICINE 145, 147 (2001): "[C]learly, care of sick patients is immensely more complicated than flying aircraft. However, the challenge of systems design is the same; how to design our work patterns so that it is difficult to make mistakes, or at least, difficult to make mistakes that hurt patients."

[12] TO ERR IS HUMAN, *supra* note 2.

[13] *Id.* at 69–85.

[14] Leape, *supra* note 11, at 146–47. *See id.* also about the National Patient Safety Foundation and Institute of Medicine Committee on Quality of Health Care in America.

[15] 119 Stat. 424, Public Law 109-41-July 29, 2005. The Act provides for, among other things, funding for the advancement of the topic, a duty of confidentiality of disclosures regarding safety, reporter protection from adverse employment action and legal action, and certification of patient safety organizations. *Id. See also* Roy Itan & Robert Fowler, *Brief History of Patient Safety Culture and Science*, 20 J. CRITICAL CARE 2 (2005); Lucian L. Leape, *Error in Medicine*, 23 JAMA 1851 (2009).

[16] NATIONAL ACAD. OF SCI., COMM. ON IDENTIFYING THE NEEDS OF THE FORENSIC SCIENCES COMMUNITY, STRENGTHENING FORENSIC SCIENCE IN THE UNITED STATES: A PATH FORWARD (Feb. 18, 2009) [hereinafter NAS 2009].

recommended—as its very first recommendation in the report—that a new central institute be established to implement the required improvements:[17]

> Recommendation 1: To promote the development of forensic sciences into a mature field of multidisciplinary research and practice, founded on the systematic collection and analysis of relevant data, Congress should establish and appropriate funds for an independent federal entity, the National Institute of Forensic Science (NIFS).

If in forensic science, a relatively narrow field and one where even prior to the report, there were a number of institutes and organizations, a new central institute was necessary to significantly improve the field, then it is even more necessary for the implementation of safety throughout the criminal justice system.

What roles should be assigned to the Safety in the Criminal Justice System Institute (SCJSI), which will be responsible for incorporating modern safety into criminal justice? Again, I draw on other fields for guidance: in the medical field, the National Academy of Sciences recommended the following with regard to the establishment of the "Center of Patient Safety" (to demonstrate the extent to which this recommendation is relevant also to our context, I have replaced in square brackets the words "health care" with "the criminal justice system," and the word "patient" with the words "wrongfully accused persons" or, alternatively, "accused"):

This Center should

- set the national goals for patient [wrongfully accused persons] safety, track progress in meeting these goals, and issue an annual report to the President and Congress on patient [accused] safety; and
- develop knowledge and understanding of errors in health care [the criminal justice system] by developing a research agenda, funding Centers of Excellence, evaluating methods for identifying and preventing errors and funding dissemination and communication activities to improve patient [accused] safety.[18]

What are the more specific goals that should be set for the SCJSI? I propose a few central ones based on the experience of other fields in which modern safety is implemented, particularly the medical field,[19] and on my scholarly and practical

---

[17] *Id.* at S-14.
[18] To ERR IS HUMAN, *supra* note 2, at 69–70.
[19] *Id.* at 78–82.

knowledge of the criminal justice system. I do not claim these to be the only possible goals. Quite the contrary: this is only a starting point that others will surely
expand on.

First, in order to realize its central purpose—namely, the development of modern
safety in criminal justice so as to prevent errors and reduce, as much as possible, the
phenomenon of false convictions—the SCJSI will have to set for itself a number of
secondary goals: that is, intermediate goals to be pursued in its first years of activity,
that relate to the various components of the criminal justice system. These goals will
be determined by a forum of experts from the relevant research areas.

Second, the SCJSI will have to devise a sophisticated mechanism for mandatory
reporting of accidents and an incident reporting mechanism that is partly mandatory and partly voluntary (while allowing immunity from liability for the reporter).
In a separate section I will elaborate on the subject of reporting.

Third, the SCJSI will have to initiate and fund advanced research in all the relevant areas, such as eyewitness testimony, confessions, and forensic evidence. With
regard to forensic evidence, the detailed recommendations set forth in the NAS
2009 report can and should be adopted and integrated into the general effort to
increase safety in criminal justice.

Fourth, the SCJSI should foster a culture of safety among all those who work
in criminal justice, including the police investigators, laboratory experts, prosecutors, judges, and jury members. This will require the dissemination of information,
through research studies and publication as well as in workshops and training. It
would be best to incorporate this already into the basic professional training in the
relevant fields and in law studies.

Fifth, based on the research that the SCJSI will initiate and the reports that will
be received through the SCJSI's reporting mechanism, data should be gathered in
all the relevant areas. These data will be made fully accessible and released to the
public, and will be used for further research.

Sixth, the SCJSI must either include internal experts or else appoint external
teams of experts in each of the relevant areas, who, based on the collected data and
research findings, will formulate recommendations for improving every subsystem
in the criminal justice system, such as the police, prosecution, laboratory experts,
defense attorneys, jury members, and judges; moreover, a national code of ethics
will be formulated for each of these areas.[20] A team of experts must also be set up to
address the structure of the criminal justice system; this team will be able to make
recommendations for structural changes (such as removing administrative control of public forensic laboratories from the hands of law enforcement agencies or

---

[20] For a similar recommendation regarding the field of forensics, see NAS 2009, *supra* note 13, at S-19.

prosecution offices).[21] In addition, teams should be established to deal with each of the central types of evidence in criminal trials, with a separate team for each type of evidence. The teams will develop a "best practice" and suitable safety tools for their relevant field. Every team will include a safety professional, who will be qualified to propose the adoption of modern safety techniques that are implemented in other areas, such as aviation, transportation, engineering, and medicine.

Seventh, the SCJSI should publish the "best practices" and recommendations formulated by the various teams of experts and ensure that they are conveyed to the relevant position-holders, by way of training, continuing education programs, information campaigns, etc. Safety training should be made an integral part of the professional training, and periodical training workshops on safety should be a condition for professional promotion.

Eighth, the SCJSI should be allocated a significant budget that will not only be sufficient for the Institute's operations but also for encouraging other entities and researchers to engage in research with the potential of advancing safety in the criminal justice system. Thus, for example, it would be worthwhile to pursue collaborations with university researchers.

Ninth, the SCJSI should publish an annual report on what it has accomplished over the preceding year in promoting safety in criminal justice and what the Institute's goals will be for the forthcoming years. In this context, the principle of ongoing improvement, which I discuss further on in the chapter, is most relevant and noteworthy. Under this principle, once safety goals have been met, new goals must be set and pursued, in an ongoing, unending process. Accordingly, so long as there are false convictions (and it seems that this will always be the case, at least in the foreseeable future), there will be a need to continue on the path of ongoing improvement.

Last, of course, for any of the above to occur, Congress should pass legislation establishing the Institute and granting it a budget that will allow its effective operation. In the discussion of the economic justification for adopting safety measures in the criminal justice system,[22] I showed that as there is a significant rate of false convictions (at least 5 percent) and as considerable damage is caused by each false conviction, it is economically warranted to invest significant funds in the development of modern safety in criminal justice. The matter of how much should be left up to Congress, of course, but it is worthwhile noting that the National Academy of Sciences 2000 report proposed allocating $100 million annually to developing safety in the medical field.[23] As I have shown in Chapter 1(IV), such a sum would be appropriate in the criminal justice system as well.

---

[21] For such a recommendation, see NAS 2009, *supra* note 16, at S-17.

[22] *See* Section IV in Chapter 2.

[23] To Err Is Human, *supra* note 2, at 7–8.

III. Accident (False Conviction) and Incident Reporting Duties

We saw in Section IV of Chapter 2 the critical role modern safety theory attributes to accident and incident reporting. I will apply this insight here to the criminal justice system. First, of course, a thorough investigation is necessary into the causes of every false conviction that is revealed, so as to learn the necessary lessons. The Safety in the Criminal Justice System Institute, once it has been established, can be tasked with these investigations. It is vital that these investigations be carried out by an autonomous body that is not connected to the law enforcement authorities—namely, the police and prosecution—so that it can be expected to conduct thorough, objective, and effective investigations in terms of the conclusions it reaches, without any concern of attempted cover-ups. In this vein, Barry Scheck and Peter Neufeld have proposed forming "Innocence Commissions" in the United States to "investigate and monitor errors in the criminal justice system."[24]

This measure, however, is not sufficient in itself. To begin with, it will facilitate the implementation of only the outdated "Fly-Fix-Fly" safety method, in trial-and-error form, and will not advance the field toward modern safety methods based on "Identify-Analyze-Control" with the goal of "First Time Safe."[25] Second, due to the Hidden Accidents Principle of criminal law, we remain in the dark with regard to the overwhelming majority of false convictions; thus, a significant improvement of the system cannot be based only on the investigation of the minority of instances that are uncovered.

In this context, it should be stressed that the relatively few instances of false convictions that are exposed cannot form a representative sample of all cases of false conviction, nor can they inform us regarding the contributing factors in general. Thus, for example, the first (approximately) three hundred exonerations achieved by the Innocence Project were the result of post-conviction DNA testing and therefore paint a very specific picture only with regard to a very specific type of conviction: primarily instances of rape (for in these types of cases, the biological samples that are likely to aid in identifying the actual perpetrator are preserved) that occurred mainly in the 1980s (for from the 1990s onward, genetic testing was already being performed at the stage of the police investigation).[26] To illustrate that such a relatively small sample is not representative: the exonerations in the framework of the Innocence Project placed erroneous eyewitness identification

---

[24] Barry Scheck & Peter Neufeld, *Toward the Formation of "Innocence Commissions" in America*, 86 JUDICATURE 98, 99 (2002). "Thus, the key necessary features of an innocence commission will be subpoena power, access to first-rate investigative resources, and political independence." *Id.* at 100.

[25] See the discussion in Section II in Chapter 2.

[26] See the Innocence Project website at www.innocenceproject.org.

as the top cause of false convictions. In another study, in contrast, which examined approximately two thousand cases of exoneration (including approximately one thousand exonerations in the framework of group exonerations following the exposure of thirteen different cases of police corruption and mass incrimination of innocent citizens), police misconduct emerged as the chief cause of false convictions.[27]

This points to the necessity of instituting a sophisticated reporting mechanism for incidents—that is, near-accidents—which currently does not exist in any form. This SCJSI will bear responsibility for the operation of this mechanism as well. A database will be formed based on these reports, which, in turn, will provide the basis for improving the system. A distinction between mandatory reporting and voluntary reporting should be made. Mandatory reporting will apply not only to accidents—false convictions—but also to some types of incidents. The SCJSI should define which types of incidents are subject to a mandatory reporting duty (for example, perjury or falsification of evidence by a police investigator, forensic laboratory technician, or prosecutor) and who bears such a duty to report—certainly prosecutors, police investigators, and forensic laboratory staff, and perhaps also defense attorneys. It is crucial that the duty to report be accompanied by a mechanism for voluntary reporting, which should significantly augment the SCJSI database. To encourage such reporting, guaranteeing reporters immunity from criminal and civil liability, in the appropriate circumstances (such as lab sample contamination due to error) should be considered, as liability can deter reporting. This would be in line with the modern safety theory principle that a thorough investigation that will lead to the system's improvement should be preferred over an investigation aimed solely at imposing liability—in other words, the preference of accountability culture over blame culture.[28]

What types of incidents can and should be investigated? First of all, any case of a court acquittal should be thoroughly investigated so as to identify the system failures that led the police and prosecution astray.[29] There should be no concern that this would entail a vast number of cases to investigate, for the overwhelming

---

[27] Samuel R. Gross & Michael Shaffer, Exonerations in the United States, 1989–2012—Report by the National Registry of Exonerations (2013).

[28] *See* Section II (D) in Chapter 2.

[29] For a similar idea, see Jon B. Gould & Richard A. Leo, *One Hundred Years Later: Wrongful Convictions after a Century of Research*, 100 J. Crim. L. & Criminology 825, 863–64 (2010) ("What we want to know … [i]s which factors are uniquely present in the cases that lead the system to rightfully acquit or dismiss charges against the innocent that are not present in cases that lead the system to wrongfully convict the innocent. If we understand this, then it is a relatively short step to understanding what policy interventions can influence the justice system to get it right and acquit the innocent, thereby preventing future wrongful convictions.").

majority of criminal proceedings culminate in conviction. A distinction should be made between acquittals due to a reasonable doubt as to guilt and acquittals that assume the defendant's innocence, with only the latter requiring comprehensive investigation. Although it can be difficult to discern from a short jury verdict whether the acquittal was based solely on a reasonable doubt, it is possible to distill this from trial judge decisions and appeal decisions.

Second, it is possible and necessary to investigate cases in which the court found that an error in earlier proceedings led to conviction, but defines this as "harmless error" and, therefore, does not overturn the conviction. In Chapter 6, I discuss this doctrine, which, I maintain, facilitates the perpetuation of many false convictions. So long as the doctrine prevails and continues to be applied, there is a need to, at the very least, arrange a mechanism for reporting and collecting the data on all these cases, which should then be examined on two levels: first, each case should be scrutinized independently in an attempt to identify the source of the error and draw conclusions; second, studies about groups of cases should be conducted. Thus, for example, the latter type of investigation could expose that police oversight in documenting findings in the suspect's favor (or prosecutor oversight in disclosing potentially exonerating evidence to the defense) is not the exception but rather a common phenomenon or practice.

Third, cases in which the police and/or prosecution were wrongly convinced of the suspect's guilt can and should be investigated, even if the error emerged prior to indictment. For example, a National Institute of Justice report from 1996 stated that "every year since 1989, in about 25% of the sexual assault cases referred to the FBI where results could be obtained (primarily by State and local law enforcement), the primary suspect has been excluded by forensic DNA testing."[30] That is a veritable profusion of incidents crying out for in-depth investigation. Apparently, in about eight thousand of approximately ten thousand sexual assault cases between 1989 and 1996, the DNA revealed whether the suspect was the perpetrator of the crime, and in about one-quarter of these cases, the police had suspected the wrong person. And this was no ordinary suspicion but, rather, a strong suspicion based usually on a mistaken eyewitness identification, which led, among other things, to the expense of conducting genetic testing.[31] It can be assumed that without the DNA testing, the suspects would have been brought to trial and, in a significant number of cases, eventually convicted. Yet even if we put this assumption aside, there is still room to

---

[30] Peter Neufeld & Barry C. Scheck, *Commentary, in* EDWARD CONNORS, THOMAS LUNDREGAN, NEAL MILLER & TOM MCEWEN, CONVICTED BY JURIES, EXONERATED BY SCIENCE: CASE STUDIES IN THE USE OF DNA EVIDENCE TO ESTABLISH INNOCENCE AFTER TRIAL 10 (7th commentary) (1998), *available at* http://www.ipt-forensics.com/journal/volume10/j10_3_2.htm (last visited July 16, 2014).

[31] *Id.*

wonder why in one-quarter of the cases, the police suspected an innocent person. Thus, investigating incidents such as these is likely to improve the criminal justice system and make it less dangerous and much safer.

Along the same lines, James M. Doyle has proposed creating "clearinghouses for helpful errors." In his view, "[c]riminal justice journals could easily provide an analogous clearinghouse for the voluntary reporting of errors and the sharing of lessons distilled from those errors."[32]

There are a number of possible advantages to investigating incidents rather than accidents (false convictions): the availability of a greater number of cases for investigation; the fact that reported incidents occur in the recent past and are therefore easier to investigate; and the fact that actual damage has not been caused, which will reduce the resistance of law enforcement agents to investigating an incident and their motivation to hamper such an investigation. Another possible advantage is that an incident can be reported prior to the conclusion of the trial proceedings, making it possible to prevent a wrongful conviction in advance. Thus, for example, if a lab technician reports, in real time, the contamination of a sample during testing, and the incident is investigated, not only might the contaminated lab test results not be used as evidence in the trial but it could emerge that there is insufficient evidence to continue at trial without those results, or that knowledge of the results led the eyewitness to mistakenly identify the defendant (although optimally, of course, the test results should be withheld from the witness).

In sum, accident and incident reporting is a cornerstone of every modern safety model. Yet in the context of the criminal justice system, incident reporting (followed by an incident investigation in order to derive the necessary lessons) is the more crucial of the two, due to the Hidden Accidents Principle: as the majority of wrongful convictions are never exposed, it is obviously impossible to investigate them and draw conclusions.

IV. Safety Education and Training and a Culture of Safety

As we saw above in the review of modern safety theory, a culture of safety is regarded as the foundation on which all safety methods rest. Safety begins with the internalization of its tremendous importance. Central features of a safety culture in organizations include: safety leadership, two-way communication between management and workers, involvement and participation of workers, a learning culture

---

[32] James M. Doyle, *Learning from Error in American Criminal Justice*, 100 J. CRIM. L. & CRIMINOLOGY 109, 130 (2010).

(including best practices), and a culture of accountability rather than blame. Also vital is a safety climate in which safety can be cultivated.[33]

In contrast to other safety-critical systems, where there is consensus—at least at the declarative level—regarding the importance of safety (and the discussion will address shortly the question of the most effective ways of attaining maximum safety), the criminal justice system lacks any awareness of the need for modern safety practices. In fact, there is often no recognition of a need for any form of safety, and a safety discourse has yet to develop in the field. Given this state of affairs, the chances of a modern safety program succeeding are unlikely until a safety climate and culture of safety are created. Moreover, whereas in other fields, such as patient safety, the need for a shift from a culture of blame to a culture of safety is stressed,[34] I fear that in criminal justice, we have not even reached the less-developed stage of a culture of blame, due to the Hidden Accidents Principle in criminal law.

But who has the power to create a culture of safety? In other safety-critical systems, such as manufacturing, it is generally accepted that safety begins with management, which must demonstrate leadership and strong commitment to safety for a culture of safety to emerge in the organization.[35] In the criminal justice system, the counterpart to that leadership appears to be judges, district attorneys, and senior police investigating officers. Yet as the criminal justice leadership has yet to strive for a culture of safety to prevent false convictions, and seemingly has no awareness of a need to do so, there can be no optimism that this culture will arise out of nowhere. At least two measures are necessary to set the process in motion: First is the enactment of legislation declaring a commitment to safety and establishing the SCJSI and its scope of authority, tools, and budget. Second, the SCJSI must take a series of intensive actions in its first years of operation to induce the leadership in the criminal justice system to create a culture of safety.

Once the SCJSI has formulated detailed safety methods and best practices, the next stage will be the introduction of safety education and training for all workers who are part of the criminal justice system: police investigators, lab experts, prosecutors, defense attorneys, judges, and perhaps even jury members. The initial training will be integrated as a fundamental part of the training given to the various position-holders, including in law studies, and will be continued through periodic

---

[33] Avi Griffel, Occupational Safety and Health Management 32–35 (2008) (Hebrew); Nancy G. Leveson, Engineering a Safer World: Systems Thinking Applied to Safety 177 (2011).

[34] Mark E. Meaney, *Error Reduction, Patient Safety and Institutional Ethics Committees*, 32 J.L. Med. & Ethics 358 (2004).

[35] Leveson, *supra* note 33, at 177. *See also id.* at 415–43 (chapter 13: "Managing Safety and the Safety Culture").

training programs. All entities in the criminal justice system will be required to submit a periodic report to the SCJSI on the training and workshops they have completed. The training programs on safety will also be a condition for professional promotion; thus, a police investigator, lab expert, prosecutor, public defender, or judge will not be able to advance in position without such further training.

As can and should be understood from the field of modern safety, "[p]eople, both managers and operators, need to understand the risks they are taking in the decisions they make. Often bad decisions are made because the decision makers have an incorrect assessment of the risks being assumed, which has implications for training .... Training should not be a one-time event for employees but should be continual throughout their employment."[36] Moreover, "[i]f employees understand the intent of the safety program and commit to it, they are more likely to comply with that intention rather than simply follow rules when it is convenient to do so .... Everyone involved in controlling a potentially dangerous process needs to have safety training, not just the low-level controllers or operators .... One interesting option is to have managers serve as teachers."[37]

This, of course, is only a preliminary outline of what is necessary to create a culture of safety and institute education for safety and safety practices. In other areas of life, the subject is well developed.[38] One of the tasks of the SCJSI will be to study just how this is achieved in other areas, and to implement this as an integral part of the criminal justice system.

V. Identify-Analyze-Control in the Criminal Justice System

As we saw in Chapter 2, modern safety methods do not suffice with the trial-and-error approach of the outdated "Fly-Fix-Fly" model but are instead based on the advanced "Identify-Analyze-Control" model: systematic identification of the hazards, analysis and assessment of those hazards, and taking the necessary measures to control the hazards. In the criminal justice system, not even the outdated Fly-Fix-Fly method has been developed, among other things, because the accidents—wrongful convictions—are not discernible and are subject to the Hidden Accidents Principle in criminal law. Thus, there is a significant lack of feedback, which is critical for creating safety. One of the central functions of the Safety in the Criminal Justice System Institute will be to learn how this is attained in other areas and to develop an Identify-Analyze-Control model for the criminal justice system.

---

[36] LEVESON, *supra* note 33, at 410–11.

[37] *Id.* at 442–43.

[38] *Id.* at 459; RICHARD A. STEPHANS, SYSTEM SAFETY FOR THE 21ST CENTURY 48 (2004).

As the majority of false convictions are not discovered, the SCJSI will need to develop sophisticated methods for assessing hazards.[39] These methods could also be based on the data that will be gathered through the reporting duties the SCJSI will implement.

Assessing the existing hazards in the criminal justice system and determining the necessary measures to control them requires, of course, meticulous analysis of the system. In Chapter 5, I will demonstrate how the system can be improved in the evidentiary sphere and, in Chapter 6, in the procedural sphere. Here, however, I seek to illustrate, in brief, the overall picture, using as a basis the Bureau of Justice Statistics' Criminal Justice System Flowchart:[40]

By simplifying the chart by focusing on felonies while adding elements taken from evidence law, I created the following flowchart (Figure 2), which can and should form the basis for safety thinking. Under Leveson's advanced STAMP (System-Theoretic Accident Model and Processes) safety model,[41] for each stage in the chart below (that is to say, regarding every decision that brings the case closer to a possible conviction), it is necessary to define the safety constraints that are required in the criminal justice system to prevent the hazards that lead to wrongful convictions and, accordingly, to set the safety controls (and barriers) needed to enforce those safety constraints:

This will require a process of thorough safety thinking, which the SCJSI will embark on from the outset. As an example (only), I will focus on a decision to admit at trial a certain piece of evidence (E no. x) and assign it a certain weight. An imprecise piece of evidence that is admitted at trial and assigned significant probative weight as to the defendant's guilt is likely to lead to a false conviction. If we focus on a suspect's (or defendant's) confession as an example, using the detailed theoretical analysis of confessions,[42] it is possible to think of some hazards and the safety constraints necessary to prevent each hazard, as well as the controls (and barriers) needed to enforce these safety constraints, as analyzed in Table 4.1:

It is important to clarify that I do not claim Table 4.1 to exhaust all the safety constraints for confessions that are necessary to make the system safe from the hazard of false confessions, and it certainly does not represent all the controls (and barriers) needed for enforcing these safety constraints. This will all be determined following comprehensive groundwork by the SCJSI. My sole goal is to demonstrate

---

[39] For a general preliminary discussion of risk assessment in the criminal justice system, see the discussion of the false conviction rate in Chapter 1, Section II.

[40] The flowchart can be viewed at the Bureau of Justice Statistics Office of Justice Programs website at http://bjs.ojp.usdoj.gov/content/largechart.cfm (last visited Apr. 17, 2014).

[41] I discussed this in Chapter 2, Section VI.

[42] For a broad discussion of confessions, see Chapter 5, Section IV.

What is the sequence of events in the criminal justice system?

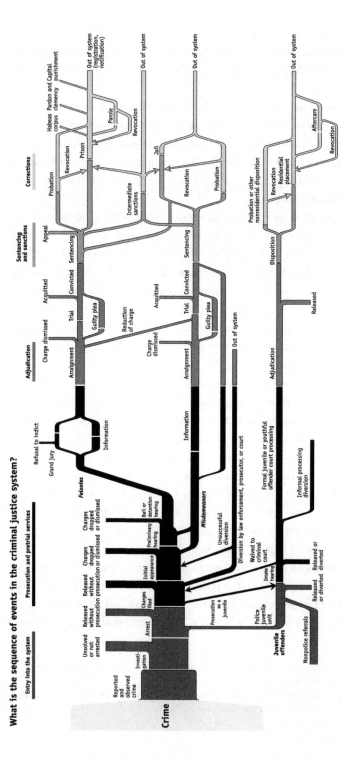

FIGURE 4.1 What Is the Sequence of Events in the Criminal Justice System?

Note: This chart gives a simplified view of caseflow through the criminal justice system. Procedures vary among jurisdictions. The weights of the lines are not intended to show actual size of caseloads.

Source: Adapted from *The Challenge of Crime in a Free Society,* President's Commission on Law Enforcement and Administration of Justice, 1967. This revision, a result of the Symposium on the 30th Anniversary of the President's Commission, was prepared by the Bureau of Justice Statistics in 1997.

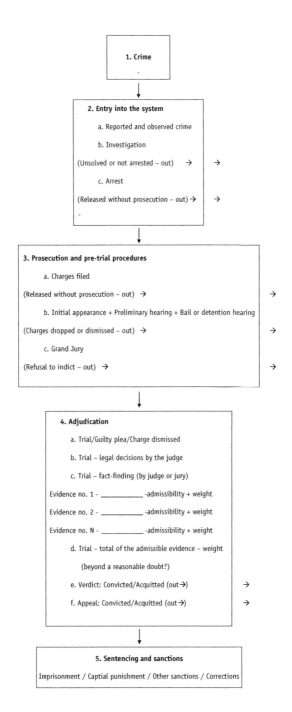

FIGURE 4.2 Criminal Justice System (Felonies)[43]

---

[43] The arrows pointing to the right indicate the case's exit from the criminal justice system.

what general direction systematic safety thinking should take in order to develop safety in the criminal justice system and reduce the risk of wrongfully convicting innocent defendants.

TABLE 4.1

ANALYZING CONFESSIONS ACCORDING TO THE STAMP MODEL

Hazards	Safety Constraints & Controls
1. An interrogation leads to a false confession.	**Safety Constraints:** a. A confession elicited during an interrogation must be voluntary. b. A confession elicited during an interrogation must be credible. c. Physical pressure of any type and significant psychological pressure must not be used to coerce a confession from a suspect (including: lying to the suspect about the existence of specific incriminating evidence against him, threatening the suspect, excessive duration of the interrogation). d. A great temptation to confess must not be created for the suspect, which is likely to lead an innocent person to falsely confess.
	Controls (and Barriers): e. A confession must not be obtained in violation of the *Miranda* rule (a suspect must be informed of his right to remain silent and right to legal counsel, retained or appointed, and that anything he says may be used against him in a court of law). f. The entire duration of the interrogation must be recorded on video (and not just the confession). g. A defense attorney must be allowed to be present as an observer during the interrogation. h. Police investigators and prosecutors must be instructed on the danger of violating guidelines (a)–(g). i. If a prosecutor supervises the police investigation, he must ensure that the police investigators act in accordance with guidelines (a)–(g). j. A prosecutor must not submit to the court a confession that was obtained in violation of guidelines (a)–(g).
2. Hazard: A plea-bargain leads to a false confession.	**Safety Constraints:** a. A confession in the framework of a plea-bargain must be voluntary. b. A confession in the framework of a plea-bargain must be credible. c. A temptation to confess must not be created by offering a considerably lighter sentence to a defendant if he confesses in the framework of a plea-bargain than the expected sentence if convicted at trial. d. The defendant must not be pressured to confess in the framework of a plea-bargain.
	Controls (and Barriers): e. A plea-bargain must not be made with a defendant if there is no significant evidence against him. f. A plea-bargain must not be made with someone prior to a decision to indict him.

Hazards	Safety Constraints & Controls
	g. A charge must not be included in the indictment as solely a negotiations tool. h. A plea-bargain must not be made with a defendant who has no legal representation.
	i. All of the evidence gathered by the prosecution must be disclosed to the defendant and his attorney, so that they can arrive at an informed decision. j. The various stages of the plea-bargain negotiations and agreement must be documented. k. Prosecutors must be instructed on the dangers of violating guidelines (a)–(j). l. A supervisory mechanism must be instituted to ensure that prosecutors act in accordance with Guidelines (a)–(j).
3. Hazard: A false confession is admitted as evidence at trial.	**Safety Constraints:** a. A confession must not be admitted as evidence if not proven to have been given voluntary and in line with the *Miranda* rule. b. A confession must not be admitted as evidence if there are significant signs that it is false.
	Controls (and Barriers): c. A confession must not be admitted as evidence if obtained in significant violation of any of the above guidelines directed at the police (1.a–g) or the guidelines directed at the prosecution (2.a–j). d. Judges must be instructed in training programs (and jury members by expert witnesses) on the dangers of violating guidelines (a), (b), and (c). e. In an appeal of a conviction, there must be close scrutiny of whether all the guidelines relating to all three above hazards were followed.
4. Hazard: A defendant is convicted based on a false confession.	**Safety Constraints:** a. A conviction must not be based on a confession if it is the sole piece of evidence (because a confession can be false and because the fact-finders have no way of discerning all false confessions). b. A conviction based on a confession must have strong corroboration (not only with respect to corpus delicti but also with regard to the identification of the accused as the perpetrator of the crime). c. A confession that is the basis of a conviction must include indications that the interrogee knew unrevealed details about the crime scene (that were unknown to the interrogators and, at the very least, had not been released to the public), accompanied by documentation that proves this.
	Controls (and Barriers): d. Judges must be instructed in training workshops (and jury members by expert witnesses) on the dangers of violating safety constraints a, b, and c.

Hazards	Safety Constraints & Controls
	e. In an appeal of a conviction, there must be close scrutiny of whether all the guidelines relating to all four above hazards were followed.
	f. Following conviction, a confession must not be viewed as a barrier to filing an appeal or moving for a retrial, and any new piece of evidence that is likely to show that the conviction was false must be examined.

VI. An Ongoing Process of Improvement

One of the central safety principles criminal justice should adopt from areas in which modern safety is accepted practice is the continuous pursuit of improvement and the perpetual process of increasing safety and decreasing the hazards and their probability. As we saw in Chapter 2, the following is generally accepted practice in other safety-critical systems:

(a) setting safety goals;
(b) pursuing those goals systematically;
(c) determining whether the goals have been met;
(d) if the goals have not been sufficiently met: returning to stage (b) and attempting to achieve those goals in other ways;
(e) if the goals have been met: returning to stage (a) and setting new, higher safety goals.

This is all conducted in an ongoing process of continual improvement.

This model of continual improvement should be "imported" into the criminal justice system and implemented by the Safety in the Criminal Justice System Institute. By the same token, the need for a perpetual process of ongoing improvement will serve as justification for the permanent operation of the SCJSI. The central difficulty will arise, in my estimation, with stage (c): determining whether the safety goals have been met. In other safety-critical systems, the feedback received from the system at the end of each safety-enhancement stage plays a very major role. This feedback makes it possible to know whether the safety goals were met, to draw conclusions, and to continue forward. The central feedback provided by the system is the accident rate. In very safe systems, such as aviation, the main feedback is the incident (almost-accident) rate, for accidents have been almost nonexistent in these areas since they adopted modern safety. In the criminal law system, however, there is no incident-reporting mechanism, and because the field is governed by the Hidden Accidents Principle, the majority of accidents in the criminal justice system—false convictions—are unknown. Thus, there is currently no feedback in the criminal justice system: the rate of false convictions is unknown, and those working in the system therefore do not know to what extent it is unsafe. And as shown in Chapter 1(II) regarding the false-conviction rate and to be shown in Chapters 5 and 6 regarding specific types of evidence and criminal procedures, the system is very unsafe.

So what can be done? As it is impossible to know whether a conviction is right or wrong, it is vital that safety mechanisms be instituted to contend with the typical causes behind false convictions. For example, as we know that a significant amount of police lineup identifications are faulty, the lineup procedure must be improved and upgraded so as to reduce the error rate; and so long as the error rate is not negligible, convicting a defendant based on eyewitness identification alone should be avoided. How can the lineup identification procedure be improved in the absence of feedback as to whether the right person was identified and convicted? Behavioral science studies in general can be of principal assistance in this respect, in particular lineup simulations. As will be shown further on in the book,[44] suggestions for certain improvements have already been made based on simulation studies, and some even adopted by the criminal justice system. Once some suggestions have been implemented, the relevant research in behavior science should be searched for additional recommendations, which should then be tested in the framework of the SCJSI and, if found suitable, introduced into the criminal justice system—as part of an unending process of constant improvement. That is to say: in the absence of system feedback on whether the convictions produced by the system are wrongful or rightful, there must be an ongoing process of improvement of every type of evidence and every procedure in the system. This will be necessary so long as the system remains in a state of imperfection, which seems likely to be its permanent condition.

VII. Redundancy

In the general review of modern system safety, we saw that redundancy is one of the fundamental elements of that safety. In the criminal justice system, there is a significant extent of inbuilt redundancy.[45] This is regarded as a sort of backup safety mechanism, the premise being that when one system unit fails (e.g., when an eyewitness makes a false identification), the other units will counteract this failure (e.g., the forensics laboratory, the prosecution in supervising the police investigation, the defense attorney by presenting or uncovering police error, or the fact-finders [judges

---

[44] See Chapter 5, Section V.

[45] William C. Thompson, *Beyond Bad Apples: Analyzing the Role of Forensic Science in Wrongful Convictions*, 37 Sw. U. L. Rev. 1027, 1032 n.32 and accompanying text (2008); Boaz Sangero & Mordechai Halpert, *A Safety Doctrine for the Criminal Justice System*, 2011 Mich. State L. Rev. 1293, 1310–11.

and jury members] and appellate courts). However, William C. Thompson has shown, in the context of the *Sutton* case, that the different components of the system are in fact interconnected and affect one another,[46] so that there is a significant risk of all parts collapsing at once and an overall system failure more likely than would be thought. In *Sutton,* the defendant was convicted based on eyewitness testimony and DNA testing.[47] Yet what were seen as two independent pieces of evidence were revealed to in fact be contingent on one another. The error began with an improper police lineup in which suggestive tactics were used. This was compounded by the fact that the lab technician who conducted the DNA testing knew that the suspect had been identified by an eyewitness, which led her and the prosecutor to ignore doubts regarding the DNA match. Finally, the eyewitness testified in court that she knew that the laboratory had confirmed her identification of the suspect, and therefore, she testified, she was confident in the identification.[48]

In fact, it has been shown that even fingerprint experts can be impacted by external information in making their determinations,[49] as exemplified by the investigation of a terrorist attack in Madrid and the wrongful identification of Brandon Mayfield, an American lawyer, as the prime suspect.[50] During the investigation, a similarity was found by an automatic fingerprint identification system between the fingerprints at the crime scene and Mayfield's fingerprints, which were in the computer database.[51] The fingerprints experts were told that Mayfield is a Muslim married to an Egyptian woman and that he had represented a terrorist in legal proceedings in the past. This later emerged as having impacted the fingerprint experts in considering possible error in the match between Mayfield's prints and those from the crime scene.[52]

Similarly, studies have shown how bias can shape nonscientific evidence as well. In one control study, it emerged that a significant proportion of eyewitnesses tend to retract or change their lineup identification when provided with information from the investigation—for example, when told that one of the lineup participants

---

[46] Thompson, *supra* note 45, at 1032. *See also* INNOCENCE PROJECT, Know the Cases: JOSIAH SUTTON, http://www.innocenceproject.org/Content/Josiah_Sutton.php (last visited Nov. 21, 2011); Michael Naughton & Gabe Tan, *The Need for Caution in the Use of DNA Evidence to Avoid Convicting the Innocent,* 15 INT. J. EVIDENCE & PROOF 245, 256 (2011).

[47] Thompson, *supra* note 45, at 1033. For the appeal of Sutton's conviction, see Sutton v. State, 2001 Tex. App. 337.

[48] Thompson, *supra* note 45, at 1034.

[49] Itiel E. Dror & David Charlton, *Why Experts Make Errors,* 56 J. FORENSIC IDENTIFICATION 600 (2006); Sangero & Halpert, *supra* note 45, at 1311.

[50] OFFICE OF THE INSPECTOR GEN., U.S. DEP'T OF JUSTICE, A REVIEW OF THE FBI's HANDLING OF THE BRANDON MAYFIELD CASE: UNCLASSIFIED AND REDACTED 12 (2006), *available at* http://www.usdoj.gov/oig/special/s0601/final.pdf.

[51] *Id.*; Sangero & Halpert, *supra* note 45, at 1311.

[52] *Id.* at 178.

confessed during interrogation.[53] There thus seems to be no safety policy in the criminal justice system designed to ensure the independence of different pieces of evidence.

One of the functions of the SCJSI, once established, will be to create redundancy and introduce efficient barriers that will prevent accidents in the criminal justice system. Thus, the Institute should seek to develop mechanisms that ensure evidentiary autonomy to the greatest extent possible. For example, with regard to scientific evidence, sequential unmasking protocols must be formulated to guarantee that bias-creating details from the investigation are kept from lab technicians working on evidence related to the case, such as the fact that the suspect was identified by a witness.[54] Redundancy is required in both evidence and criminal procedure, so that when one unit in the criminal justice system errs, the other units will rectify this failure, rather than the whole system falling like dominoes. This is vital in order to increase safety against wrongful convictions. In the coming chapters, I will present additional illustrations of the present lack of redundancy in the criminal justice system and of the possibility of enhancing safety by creating redundancy.

VIII. Summary

In this chapter and the preceding one, I proposed some general principles for safety in the criminal justice system, some of which are based on principles guiding other areas, where modern safety is common practice. In the two forthcoming chapters, I will examine closely some of the central types of evidence and procedures that are relied upon and applied in criminal law. With regard to each, I will show the current lack of safety and then propose some possible methods of hazard control. I again stress that my purpose is no more than to engage in some preliminary thinking about systematic modern safety in the context of the criminal justice system. The success of this process depends on others continuing this effort and on the establishment—hopefully—of the Safety in the Criminal Justice System Institute.

---

[53] Lisa E. Hasel & Saul M. Kassin, *On the Presumption of Evidentiary Independence: Can Confessions Corrupt Eyewitness Identifications?*, 20 PSYCHOL. SCI. 122 (2009); Sangero & Halpert, *supra* note 45, at 1311–12.

[54] Sangero & Halpert, *supra* note 45, at 1322–23.

5   Safety in Specific Types of Evidence

I. General

In Chapter 2, I presented the fundamentals of modern system-safety. In Chapter 3, I proposed general safety principles for the criminal justice system, and in Chapter 4, I demonstrated how it is possible to apply modern safety in the criminal justice system.

This chapter will now point the way to safety in the context of specific types of evidence. For each of the central kinds of evidence that will be discussed, I will begin by presenting the current lack of safety, which I term "unsafety," and then raise some possible safety measures to contend with this. My suggestions will be grounded on two bases: one, the specific analysis of each type of evidence in line with the most recent research on the subject; and two, modern safety theory and its application to the criminal justice system in accordance with the principles outlined in Chapters 2, 3, and 4. It is important to stress that what I propose represent only some of the possible safety measures that can be conceived of. Developing a comprehensive safety theory for the criminal justice system will require considerable additional cross-disciplinary research work, which I recommend be undertaken within the framework of the Safety in the Criminal Justice System Institute.[1]

II. Unsafety in Forensic Sciences Evidence

A. GENERAL

I have chosen, for my discussion purposes, to analyze the two central types of forensic sciences evidence currently predominating criminal law: DNA testing and fingerprint comparisons. For each of these, I will review the most up-to-date research on the topic. I will demonstrate why present use of these types of evidence is not error-free and fails to ensure safety from false convictions and, then, offer different ways of improving safety in these contexts. A general solution will be proposed with regard to all types of forensic evidence, based on an earlier proposition I developed with Dr. Mordechai Halpert, namely, that the legislator must enact a rule that precludes the admissibility of forensic evidence in court unless it has been developed as a "safety-critical system."[2] The knowledge and solution for developing safety-critical devices already exist in other engineering fields, such as medical devices or aviation devices. Thus, all that is needed is the willingness and reasonable resources to carry this out. Further on in this chapter, I will offer some additional general solutions.

This chapter will also address what is known as "junk science," which refers to evidence that is presented, inaccurately and misleadingly, as scientific evidence when it has, at best, a flimsy connection to science. Despite studies clearly pointing out this lack of scientific grounding, including the 2009 National Academy of Sciences report,[3] there are still courts that admit such evidence as scientific evidence. This is proof in itself of just how far the criminal justice system is from being a safe system. I will begin with a short background on the admissibility and weight of scientific evidence in criminal trials.

B. THE ADMISSIBILITY OF FORENSIC SCIENCES EVIDENCE: FROM *FRYE* TO *DAUBERT*

How can judges distinguish between "true" scientific evidence and inadmissible "junk" scientific evidence? In the past, the *Frye* standard, set in 1923, was

---

[1] See Section II of Chapter 4.

[2] Mordechai Halpert & Boaz Sangero, *From a Plane Crash to the Conviction of an Innocent Person: Why Forensic Science Evidence Should Be Inadmissible unless It Has Been Developed as a Safety-Critical System*, 32 HAMLINE L. REV. 65 (2009).

[3] NAT'L ACAD. SCI., COMM. ON IDENTIFYING THE NEEDS OF THE FORENSIC SCIENCES COMMUNITY, STRENGTHENING FORENSIC SCIENCE IN THE UNITED STATES: A PATH FORWARD (Feb. 18, 2009) [hereinafter NAS-2009 REPORT].

the prevailing rule in American law.[4] Under this rule, "general acceptance" of the method on which the evidence rests in the relevant scientific field is sufficient for it to be admissible in court. This rule predominated for seventy years, until it was supplanted by a more sophisticated rule, set in 1993 in *Daubert*.[5] Whereas the *Frye* rule enabled judges to refrain from a deep examination of the relevant scientific field and suffice with the fact that the method in question is generally accepted by the scientific community to which it belongs, the *Daubert* rule is designed to ensure greater caution: it made judges "gatekeepers," tasked with blocking the entry of nonscientific evidence fraudulently presented as scientific into the courtroom.

Daubert set four admissibility criteria for scientific evidence.[6] One, the scientific method on which the evidence is allegedly based must adhere to Karl Popper's principle of falsifiability: that is, the method must be empirically testable for falsifiability or refutability, and must have been successfully tested in order to be considered scientific methodology. Two, the error rate of the evidence must be known. Three, the scientific method must have been subject to peer review and published. And four, similar to the requirement under the *Frye* rule, the method must be accepted within the relevant scientific community. As Professor Alex Stein has compellingly explained, the fourth requirement is particularly crucial: admitting scientific evidence that does not meet the *Frye* standard would undermine the allocation of the risk of error, which cannot be contingent on a judicial prediction regarding the odds of the success of a particular scientific progress.[7]

The *Daubert* standard, along with certain refinements of the rule, thus requires judges to make an effort at delving into the relevant scientific field and to examine the reliability and validity of the scientific method (which is, in effect, a classification system) on which the evidence is grounded.[8] "Reliability" in this context refers to the consistency of the classification; for example, a test is reliable if the same result will be arrived at if performed by different experts and at different points in time. "Valid" means that the method (the classification system) is suited to the purposes it is used for. In the legal context, a test is valid if it suits the aim of distinguishing between who is guilty of committing the crime in question and who is innocent. A test can be reliable, but not valid. For example, a test that uses an arbitrary rule to

---

[4] Frye v. United States, 293 F. 1013 (D.C. Cir. 1923); BOAZ SANGERO, CONVICTING THE INNOCENT IN ISRAEL AND IN OTHER COUNTRIES—CAUSES AND SOLUTIONS 129 (2014) (in Hebrew).

[5] Daubert v. Merrell Dow Pharms., Inc., 509 U.S. 579 (1993).

[6] *Id.*; Boaz Sangero & Mordechai Halpert, *Scientific Evidence v. "Junk Science,"* 11 C.L.B. L. STUDIES 425, 430 (2014) (in Hebrew); Kristen Bolden, *DNA Fabrication, A Wake Up Call: The Need to Reevaluate the Admissibility and Reliability of DNA Evidence,* 27 GA. ST. U. L. REV. 409, 419–24 (2011).

[7] Alex Stein, *Against Free Proof,* 31 ISR. L. REV. 573, 587 (1997).

[8] Sangero & Halpert, *supra* note 6, at 431. On validity and reliability in the legal context, see Sandy A. Zabell, *Fingerprint Evidence,* 13 J.L. & POL. 143, 154 (2005).

distinguish between guilt and innocence according to skin color will be a reliable test, as different people will concur regarding the color of a defendant's skin, and as color will not alter over time. This method will not be valid, though: the color of a person's skin is immaterial to the question of his guilt or innocence. In contrast, reliability is a necessary condition for validity: if different experts can arrive at different outcomes, or if outcomes vary over time, then the test or method cannot be valid.

In effect, then, despite the fact that the *Daubert* rule takes precedence today, the two rules—*Daubert* and *Frye*—exist side by side in American case law.[9] Generally, emphasis on the criterion of acceptance by the relevant scientific community (the *Frye* test) will lead the court to relax the requirements for recognizing the scientificity of the given evidence, whereas a deeper examination of the scientific grounding and methodology of the evidence—in the spirit of the *Daubert* rule—will lead to a more rigorous approach.[10] Oftentimes, as judges struggle with the investigation of the scientific aspects that the *Daubert* rule is concerned with, they incorrectly classify methodological errors made by experts as relevant to the weight—and not to actual validity—of the evidence, and admit evidence as scientific when it is not deserving of the title, at times through resort to the *Frye* rule.[11]

One might wonder why should scientific evidence in particular be required to meet the criteria of reliability and validity when other types of evidence, such as witness testimony, are not. There are a number of possible interrelated, cumulative answers to this.[12] First, scientific evidence is purported to be science (expert testimony is an exception to the hearsay rule). Second, the "aura" of science can be expected to blind judges and jurors and lead them to overestimate the real probative strength of scientific evidence. Three, in the area of scientific evidence, it is more practical to require and examine reliability and validity. And finally, fourth, the path toward implementing appropriately rigorous standards for types of evidence that can determine people's fate must begin somewhere. The next step is to address the remaining types of evidence and apply similar rules and standards to them. Further on, I will propose such rules regarding confessions and eyewitness identifications.

---

[9] Bolden, *supra* note 6, at 419–24; Sangero & Halpert, *supra* note 6, at 431. The *Daubert* standard has been adopted in federal courts, where the federal rules of evidence also apply and set a similar arrangement. For a review of the various states that have adopted the *Daubert* rule as opposed to those that have continued to follow the *Frye* rule, see Edward K. Cheng & Albert H. Yoon, *Does Frye or Daubert Matter? A Study of Scientific Admissibility Standards*, 91 VA. L. REV. 471, 472–73 (2005).

[10] David L. Faigman, *Admissibility Regimes: The "Opinion Rule" and Other Oddities and Exceptions to Scientific Evidence, the Scientific Revolution, and Common Sense*, 36 SW. U. L. REV. 699 (2008).

[11] Jay P. Kesan, Note: *An Autopsy of Scientific Evidence in a Post-Daubert World*, 84 GEO. L.J. 1985, 2040 (1996).

[12] Sangero & Halpert, *supra* note 6, at 432.

C. THE WEIGHT OF FORENSIC SCIENCES EVIDENCE: FROM "UNIQUENESS," "INDIVIDUALIZATION," AND "PERFECTION" TO EMPIRICAL AND PROBABILISTIC FOUNDATION

Presumably, the different types of scientific evidence could have been expected to greatly advance and refine criminal law and make it more precise. There is no doubt that DNA testing and fingerprint comparisons—despite being what is termed "circumstantial" evidence—are far more accurate than the traditional types of evidence, referred to as "direct" evidence: eyewitness testimony and confessions. Yet in the framework of the work of the first Innocence Project, 185 of the first 250 wrongly convicted inmates who were exonerated—74 percent—had been convicted based on scientific evidence.[13] Moreover, to date, in the National Registry of Exonerations, 312 of the 1427 registered exonerations (22 percent) involved false or misleading forensic evidence.[14]

Why is it that the more accurate types of evidence are more misleading than other types of evidence? One possible explanation is that they blind judges and jury members. As one defense attorney remarked, "If you put God in the witness stand ... and God's testimony conflicted with the DNA evidence, everyone would automatically say, 'Why is God lying like this?'"[15] We all, justifiably, hold science in the highest esteem. However, judges and jurors are not scientists. Judges are trained legalists who are required to reach determinations on a wide variety of issues, from all spheres of life, some of which are from the scientific field. In present times, human knowledge is so vast that no one has the capacity to be an expert in a number of fields, to be a "Renaissance person." Accordingly, judges must rely on experts, who present them with the results of scientific tests they performed. As it is the judges and jurors—and not the experts—who are the triers of fact, judges can and should demand of experts not to suffice with testifying as to the results of the tests they performed but to describe in detail their methodology for judges and jurors to examine. This, of course, is contingent on proof of the validity and reliability of the scientific method used by the expert. Judges should require of experts scientific written support of their approaches, but not all judges do so. Many rely on the experts almost blindly, to the point where, in practice, they serve as no more than a rubber stamp.[16] In addition, as the law is based on legal precedents, if a court—especially a

---

[13] Brandon L. Garrett, Convicting the Innocent—Where Criminal Prosecutions Go Wrong 279 fig. A.5 (2011); Sangero, *supra* note 4, at 105.

[14] Nat'l Registry Exonerations, Exonerations by Contributing Factor, https://www.law. umich.edu/special/exoneration/Pages/ExonerationsContribFactorsByCrime.aspx (last visited Sept. 9, 2014).

[15] Laura Lafay, *Reasonable Doubt*, Style Wkly., July 6, 2005 (quoting defense attorney David Baugh), *cited in* J. Herbie DiFonzo, *The Crimes of Crime Labs*, 34 Hofstra L. Rev. 1 (2005).

[16] Sangero, *supra* note 4, at 105–06.

higher appellate court—makes the mistake of incorrectly admitting a specific type of evidence as "scientific," this is likely to set a precedent for other courts, who will follow it without re-examining the scientificity of the method. In this way, junk science, too, could be found admissible by one court, and other courts will follow suit without engaging in the necessary scrutiny; this is precisely what happened, over the course of many years, with microscopical hair comparisons, footprint comparisons, and voice comparisons. Furthermore, even when (genuine) scientists find in their research that certain allegedly "scientific" types of evidence are not grounded in science and are unreliable and invalid, many judges, who are used to basing convictions on such evidence, have difficulty accepting this, as it would mean conceding their own past mistakes.[17]

In practice, a "random match" is possible with every type of test (with the sole exception of DNA testing, where the probability of such a match is extremely slim). With all tests, moreover, there is a real possibility of a lab error or an error in the expert's interpretation of the results. In contrast to the prevailing conception of the objectivity of all determinations in expert testimony on scientific evidence, it has emerged that certain issues are in fact contingent on the expert's subjective interpretation of the findings.[18] And indeed, the chance of error, which always exists, combined with the fallacy of the transposed conditional, has been the underlying cause of many false convictions.[19]

In addition, forensic lab staff work very closely with the police and prosecution and are often even directly subordinate to them. Police investigators supply lab workers with investigation details that are completely irrelevant to the required lab testing but which strengthen the conception of the suspect's guilt, such as the fact that he confessed or was identified by a witness. Information of this sort is likely to bias the test results.[20]

The current situation has been well described as follows by Jennifer Mnookin:

> Forensic scientists have regularly testified in courts to matters that are, quite honestly, both less proven and less certain than they are claimed to be. They have overstated their degree of knowledge, underreported the chances of error, and suggested greater certainty than is warranted. More generally, many kinds

---

[17] D. Michael Risinger, *Whose Fault?—Daubert, the NAS Report, and the Notion of Error in Forensic Science*, 38 FORDHAM URBAN L.J. 519, 539 (2010); Sangero & Halpert, *supra* note 6, at 443.

[18] Sangero & Halpert, *supra* note 6, at 443.

[19] SANGERO, *supra* note 4, at 109.

[20] Jennifer L. Mnookin, *The Courts, the NAS, and the Future of Forensic Science*, 75 BROOK. L. REV. 1209, 1215 (2010); DiFonzo, *supra* note 15, at 4; William C. Thompson, *Beyond Bad Apples: Analyzing the Role of Forensic Science in Wrongful Convictions*, 37 SW. L. REV. 1027, 1034 (2008).

of forensic science are not entirely based on methods and approaches that we usually associate with validated research science. Their claims and the limits to their claims are not closely based on or constrained by the formal collection of data. Their empirical assertions are not grounded in careful research that has been subject to peer review and publication. There has been remarkably little formal validation of their methods. And there has been far too little study of how often forensic scientists might make mistakes, and when or why these possible errors are more likely to occur.[21]

From the perspective of the historical development of evidence law, every generation has realized that the weight once accorded to certain types of evidence was excessive.[22] Evidence that was formerly held to be very strong emerges, over the years, in both the research and in practice, as not as accurate as thought. Thus, for example, we know today that certain types of direct evidence once considered "classic" evidence—eyewitness testimony and confessions to the police[23]—are problematic and have led to many false convictions.[24] During the past century, scientific evidence has become the evidentiary "false messiah." To generalize, forensic scientists present scientific evidence in court as unequivocal evidence that reflects the uniqueness of every individual from all other human beings and produces perfect identification of every person. Yet this premise of uniqueness is nothing more than pure conjecture, with no data to support it; it is based on the assumption that nature (or God) never repeats itself. On the one hand, it exempts forensic scientists from the rigors of methodological research, data collection, and incidence calculation, and on the other hand, allows them to assert purportedly certain identification in court. As Michael J. Saks and Jonathan L. Koehler clarified in an article published in the leading journal *Science*, "the time is ripe for the traditional forensic sciences to replace antiquated assumptions of uniqueness and perfection with a more defensible empirical and probabilistic foundation."[25] Moreover, they further observed elsewhere, "[t]he concept of individualization, which lies at the core of numerous

---

[21] Mnookin, *supra* note 20, at 1210.

[22] SANGERO, *supra* note 4, at 47.

[23] The confession has even been deemed "the queen of evidence," rather than the "empress of false convictions" as it should be. *See* Boaz Sangero, Miranda *Is Not Enough: A New Justification for Demanding "Strong Corroboration" to a Confession*, 28 CARDOZO L. REV. 2791, 2800 (2007).

[24] Boaz Sangero & Mordechai Halpert, *Proposal to Reverse the View of a Confession: From Key Evidence Requiring Corroboration to Corroboration for Key Evidence*, 44 U. MICH. J.L. REFORM 511 (2011).

[25] Michael J. Saks & Jonathan J. Koehler, *The Coming Paradigm Shift in Forensic Identification Science*, 309 SCI. 892, 895 (2005). For a more detailed discussion, see Michael J. Saks & Jonathan J. Koehler, *The Individualization Fallacy in Forensic Science Evidence*, 61 VAND. L. REV. 199 (2008) [hereinafter Saks & Koehler, *The Individualization Fallacy*].

forensic science subfields, exists only in a metaphysical or rhetorical sense. There is no scientific basis for the individualization claims in forensic sciences."[26]

In a later article, Koehler and Saks summarized the issue as follows:

(1) the data necessary to achieve individualization have never been collected for any of the forensic science fields which aspire to individualize the source of crime scene evidence to its sole possible contributor;

(2) the best available—and perhaps the only scientifically defensible—approach to forensic identification is the use of random match probability estimates (which are not yet employed by any of the traditional forensic identification sciences);

(3) the argument that all objects are discernibly unique stands on little more than an oft-repeated maxim of forensic science legend and the illusory intuition that small frequencies imply uniqueness;

(4) probability estimates (by definition) cannot lead to uniqueness or individualization;

(5) assertions of individualization generally exaggerate what is known or can be accomplished by forensic examiners.[27]

Thus, it emerges that with the exception of the context of DNA comparisons, forensic experts tend to systematically violate the most basic scientific principle that probabilistic estimates (as well as verbal quantitative estimates) must be grounded in data.[28] As Koehler noted, "the specific language used in court by experts can be the difference between testimony that is truly helpful and testimony that is confusing or unhelpful."[29] Accordingly, he proposed that the forensic linguistic community should identify clear and consistent standards for reporting and testifying about test results, and that its members be trained in elementary statistics and probability.[30] In sum, Koehler and Saks pointedly asserted that forensic scientists should not be allowed "to say, in effect, 'trust me: that's the source.' Real scientists don't say 'trust me.' They provide data."[31]

---

[26] Saks & Koehler, *The Individualization Fallacy, supra* note 25, at 202.

[27] Jonathan J. Koehler & Michael J. Saks, *Individualization Claims in Forensic Science: Still Unwarranted*, 75 Brook. L. Rev. 1187, 1187 (2010). *But see* David H. Kaye, *Probability, Individualization and Uniqueness in Forensic Science Evidence: Listening to the Academies*, 75 Brook. L. Rev. 1163 (2010).

[28] Brandon L. Garrett & Peter J. Neufeld, *Invalid Forensic Science Testimony and Wrongful Convictions*, 95 Va. L. Rev. 1, 19 (2009); Sangero & Halpert, *supra* note 6, at 445; Mnookin, *supra* note 20, at 1210.

[29] Jonathan J. Koehler, *Linguistic Confusion in Court: Evidence from the Forensic Sciences*, 21 J.L. & Pol'y 515, 515 (2013).

[30] *Id.* at 537–38.

[31] Koehler & Saks, *supra* note 27, at 1208.

A scientific approach should be taken not only with regard to the random match probability, however, but also to the possibility of errors in lab testing. As noted, where the possibility of a random match is very rare (in genetic comparisons, for example, there is often a one-in-millions or even billions chance) and where the possibility of an error in the lab testing is far more common (at least one percentage rate in all likelihood), the courts and legislature must require that the prosecution provide also (and even principally) the latter figure as a condition for the admissibility of the evidence in court. This information is very important not only with respect to admissibility but also in terms of the correct weight to be attributed to the evidence. Currently, there is a tendency to ignore the possibility of error in the lab testing, and consequently, scientific evidence is accorded far greater weight than what is appropriate.[32] The possibility of a lab testing error is an inherent aspect of every scientific test. It appears that the law is perhaps the only sphere of life in which the tendency is to ignore this possibility. In the medical diagnostics field, for example, as we saw, the incidence of the disease in the risk group to which the testee belongs is vital to correctly calculate the positive predictive value of the test and not fall victim to the "base rate fallacy."[33] The FDA even requires of manufacturers of medical diagnostic devices to provide the positive predictive value of the test they manufacture with regard to different levels of the disease incidence among different risk-groups.[34]

In the past, a common erroneous claim (referred to in the literature as "case specific" or "false positive fallacy")[35] was that a court presumably has no need for statistics on laboratory-error rates as it allegedly has the ability to check that all necessary procedures were followed in the specific case before it and, thereby, ensure that no error could have occurred.[36] Today, it is generally understood that courts are incapable of making sure that no error occurred, and that even a negligible probability of lab error should, in certain circumstances, result in a significant diminishment of the weight of

---

[32] *See, e.g.*, Simon A. Cole, *More than Zero: Accounting for Error in Latent Print Identification*, 95 J. CRIM. L. & CRIMINOLOGY 985, 1034, 1073 (2005).

[33] See Section IV of Chapter 3.

[34] Steven Gutman, *Food and Drug Administration (FDA)'s Impact on Laboratory Performance: FDA's Perspective*, 42 CLINICAL CHEMISTRY 786, 787 (1996). *See also* FDA, STATISTICAL GUIDANCE ON REPORTING RESULTS FROM STUDIES EVALUATING DIAGNOSTIC TESTS (Mar. 13, 2007), *available at* http://www.fda.gov/MedicalDevices/DeviceRegulationandGuidance/GuidanceDocuments/ucm071148.htm (last visited Sept. 9, 2014); Sangero & Halpert, *supra* note 6, at 445–46.

[35] William C. Thompson et al., *How the Probability of a False Positive Affects the Value of DNA Evidence*, 48 J. FORENSIC SCI. 47, 51–52 (2003).

[36] NAT'L RESEARCH COUNCIL, THE EVALUATION OF FORENSIC DNA EVIDENCE 85 (1996) [hereinafter NRC-II REPORT].

the relevant evidence.[37] Errors occur even in the best of laboratories and even when the experts testify that all of the test protocols were followed.[38]

The foremost authority in the area of scientific evidence is the National Academy of Sciences' detailed and informative 2009 report, *Strengthening Forensic Science in the United States: A Path Forward*,[39] which was written by an interdisciplinary panel of distinguished scholars and practitioners. The report determined that the forensic science system does not function properly and that a significant improvement is required.[40] Despite the fact that forensic lab workers purport to engage in science, many lack the required training to do so, and there is an inadequate connection between their work and academic knowledge. This has led to significant knowledge gaps between scientists and forensic scientists.[41] For the forensic science field to be able to properly service the law, the organizational systems and structures must be significantly upgraded, training and qualifications improved, best practices adopted, and accreditation programs for laboratories made mandatory. The report emphasized that the most fundamental shortcoming emerged in the scientific knowledge of those who work in forensic science, and it called for genuine academic research in the area of forensic science to be conducted in the universities. Accordingly, the report recommended the establishment of an independent federal agency equipped with the necessary powers, authority, and resources to implement fundamental changes in the area of scientific evidence.[42] Obviously, such an agency would have very important ramifications for safety.

The report also recommended removing public forensic science laboratories from the administrative control of law enforcement agencies and prosecutor offices, standardizing laboratory reports, and instituting mandatory accreditation for all forensic laboratories, mandatory certification for all forensic workers, and a mandatory code of ethics.[43] Another very important recommendation was to conduct foundational research to assess the validity and reliability of methods used in the analysis of evidence, especially pattern evidence.[44]

---

[37] NAS-2009 REPORT, *supra* note 3, at 131: "However, even a very small (but nonzero) probability of false positive can affect the odds that a suspect is the source of a sample with a matching DNA profile." See also discussion of the fact that no distinction should be made between a lab error and a random match probability error at *id.* at 121.

[38] William C. Thompson, *Tarnish on the "Gold Standard": Understanding Recent Problems in Forensic DNA Testing*, 30 CHAMPION 10, 11–12, 13–14 (Jan.–Feb. 2006); Sangero & Halpert, *supra* note 6, at 446.

[39] NAS-2009 REPORT, *supra* note 3; Sangero & Halpert, *supra* note 6, at 446.

[40] NAS-2009 REPORT, *supra* note 3, at 14–19.

[41] *Id.* at 15. *See also* Saks & Koehler, *The Individualization Fallacy*, *supra* note 25, at 215.

[42] Sangero & Halpert, *supra* note 6, at 446–47.

[43] NAS-2009 REPORT, *supra* note 3, at 29.

[44] *Id.* at 22–23.

Of particular importance to our purposes are the report chapters that deal individually with each of the specific types of scientific evidence. Even putting aside any possible errors on the part of experts, it emerges that a considerable amount of "scientific evidence" is not grounded in science at all. The report estimated the scientific basis for each of the types of scientific evidence and types of pseudoscientific evidence, beginning with genetic comparisons, which is the most scientific type of evidence, and ending with "junk science," such as the microscopical hair comparisons. In what follows, in the individual discussions of some of these types of evidence, I will discard the "uniqueness," "individualization," and "perfection" myths and, instead, present their realistic weights in light of the NAS report's estimates.[45]

D. DNA TESTING

As described in the National Academy of Sciences' 2009 report, "[u]nlike many forensic techniques that were developed empirically within the forensic science community, with limited foundation in science theory or analysis, DNA analysis is a fortuitous by-product of cutting-edge science."[46] And certainly, DNA has strong probative value. But not even this type of evidence, considered the "Gold Standard" of forensic science, is error-free.

(1) Random Match Probability

The basic assumption in DNA testing is that with the exception of identical twins, every person's DNA is unique. However, for the purposes of DNA forensic evidence, not all the molecules in the two DNA samples are tested and compared.

Andrea Roth has provided a clear and detailed description of the DNA testing process as follows: In forensic testing, DNA is amplified and typed at several locations (loci) along the genetic strand.[47] A DNA profile consists of two genetic markers (alleles) at each locus, representing the two alleles he inherits from each of his two parents at that locus. The main iteration of DNA matching technology is called

---

[45] Sangero & Halpert, *supra* note 6, at 447.

[46] NAS-2009 REPORT, *supra* note 3, at 5–5.

[47] Andrea Roth, *Safety in Numbers? Deciding When DNA Alone Is Enough to Convict*, 85 N.Y.U. L. REV. 1130, 1135–36 (2010). For additional explanations of the scientific aspect of DNA testing, see David H. Kaye, *DNA Evidence: Probability, Population Genetics, and the Courts* 7 HARV. J.L. & TECH. 101, 101 (1993); FEDERAL JUDICIAL CENTER, REFERENCE MANUAL ON SCIENTIFIC EVIDENCE 485–76 (2d ed. 2000); NAT'L INST. JUSTICE, WHAT EVERY LAW ENFORCEMENT OFFICER SHOULD KNOW ABOUT DNA EVIDENCE (2004), at http://www.dna.gov/audiences/investigators/know (last visited Sept. 21, 2014); Boaz Sangero & Mordechai Halpert, *Why a Conviction Should Not Be Based on a Single Piece of Evidence: A Proposal for Reform*, 48 JURIMETRICS J. 43, 72 (2007).

Short Tandem Repeat (STR). The FBI and state laboratories use to test thirteen STR loci. The DNA analyst use a statistical table developed by the FBI based on sample groups of approximately two hundred people from each of four racial categories to estimate the chances of finding each particular allele at each particular locus in the different racial groups. Based on the assumption that the allelic frequencies among the loci are independent, the analyst multiplies the 26 (= 13x2) frequencies together to report for each group a "Random Match Probability" (RMP)—that a random person will have the 26-allele profile.[48]

It is important to recall that the court is not called upon to determine the random match probability, but rather the inverse conditional probability: namely, the probability that the two samples belong to the defendant and that, given a match, he is indeed guilty of the crime he is accused of.[49] To determine this probability, all the non-DNA-related evidence must be examined, either by applying the Bayes' Theorem rationale or any other accepted method.[50] The erroneous understanding that the random match probability represents the probability of the defendant's innocence is termed the "prosecutor's fallacy."[51]

The possibility of a random match in a DNA comparison is not particularly problematic in the context of a criminal trial, as it is well known that this probability must be taken into account.[52] Yet because the chances of a random match are at times expressed in astronomical terms (say, a one-in-a-billion probability of a match between the defendant's DNA and the crime scene DNA sample), there is a considerably greater risk of falsely convicting an innocent defendant based on a DNA comparison when the possibility of lab error is ignored (as, unfortunately, often is the case).[53] This was well illustrated by the HIV diagnosis example in Chapter 3,[54] where the initial intuition (of 99.9 percent being a carrier) radically shifted (to only 9 percent) when the possibility of a lab error and the specific incidence rate for the risk group to which the testee belongs were taken into account.

The danger of error is far greater when the police have no specific suspect whose DNA profile can be compared to the sample from the crime scene ("Verification"), and instead must look for a match to one of the (millions) of DNA profiles in the

[48] Roth, *supra* note 47, at 1135–36.
[49] Sangero & Halpert, *supra* note 47, at 72.
[50] *Id*.; Roth, *supra* note 47, at 1156.
[51] Koehler, *supra* note 29, at 521.
[52] Sangero & Halpert, *supra* note 47, at 73.
[53] People v. Reeves, 91 Cal. App. 4th 14, 46 (2001) ("[B]ecause appellant has not presented persuasive evidence of an ongoing controversy in the scientific community, we conclude that the NRC's recommendation is generally accepted, and DNA probability calculations need not be modified to account for a laboratory error rate."); Sangero & Halpert, *supra* note 47.
[54] See Section IV of Chapter 3.

DNA database ("Identification" or "database search"). This "cold hit" method can be expected to lead to false identifications,[55] and thus, I contend, the results of such a database search must not be admissible as evidence but, rather, serve only as a means for finding suspects. Once a suspect is found, other significant evidence should be searched for which connects him to the crime; in the absence of such evidence, the suspect should be acquitted if brought to trial.[56] An important question, beyond the scope of this book, is what boundaries should be imposed on such database searches under Fourth Amendment protections.[57]

The use of partial DNA profiles is another problem in this context. Although the current U.S. standard is that thirteen loci be tested to arrive at a twenty-six alleles profile, partial DNA profiles containing fewer alleles can also be searched against profiles in databases[58] (such as the FBI's CODIS).[59] Using such partial DNA evidence to support prosecuting someone the police have identified as a suspect, particularly when other evidence already points to his guilt, is, in itself, not objectionable. It is problematic, however, when the order of the police investigative methodology is reversed: when the partial genetic profile is screened against DNA-profiles data to "trawl" for potential suspects, rather than the partial DNA profile taken from the crime scene being matched against an already-identified suspect.[60] As Michael Naughton and Gabe Tan explain, three hazards arise. First, there is no way to estimate with sufficient certainty a match between the suspect's profile and the crime-scene profile if the latter is not complete. The authors illustrate this with the example of Raymond Easton, whose six STR markers matched the crime-scene profile, but later on, when four other loci were tested, none was a fit. Second, the match probability is significantly increased with a partial profile, and thus, speculative searches of partial crime-scene profiles against DNA profiles in databases often produce multiple "matches." Third, it makes innocent individuals

---

[55] *But see* Rick Visser, *When DNA Won't Work*, 49 IDAHO L. REV. 39 (2012).

[56] Sangero & Halpert, *supra* note 47, at 60. For another suggestion, see Roth, *supra* note 47. The author suggests a threshold of a 99.9 percent source probability (1:1:000) as satisfying the "beyond a reasonable doubt" requirement. I believe that this is not sufficient, as it relates only to the possibility of a random match and almost completely neglects the much greater possibility of a laboratory error.

[57] David H. Kaye, *A Fourth Amendment Theory of Arrestee DNA and Other Biometric Databases*, 15 U. PA. J. CONST. L. 1095 (2013); Catherine W. Kimel, *DNA Profiles, Computer Searches, and the Fourth Amendment*, 62 DUKE L.J. 993 (2013); David H. Kaye, *Why So Contrived? Fourth Amendment Balancing, Per Se Rules, and DNA Databases after* Maryland v. King, 104 CRIM. L. & CRIMINOLOGY 535 (2014); Maryland v. King, 133 S. Ct. 1958 (2013); Erin Murphy, *License, Registration, Cheek Swab: DNA Testing and the Divided Court*, 127 HARV. L. REV. 161 (2013–2014).

[58] Michael Naughton & Gabe Tan, *The Need for Caution in the Use of DNA Evidence to Avoid Convicting the Innocent*, 15 INT. J. EVIDENCE & PROOF 245, 251–53 (2011).

[59] On CODIS, see generally the NAS-2009 REPORT, *supra* note 3, at 5-3–5-4.

[60] Naughton & Tan, *supra* note 58, at 252.

whose DNA profiles are on the data more vulnerable to becoming suspects in a crime they did not commit and, accordingly, to being falsely convicted.[61]

In 2001, in an Arizona forensics laboratory, a nine-STR locus match was found between two unrelated individuals.[62] The random match probability for a match of nine-locus genotype in Arizona was 1 in 754 million Caucasians and 1 in 561 billion African Americans.[63] In 2005, during proceedings in an Arizona court in a case in which the state had only typed 9 loci, a DNA analyst testifying for the defense stated that she had found approximately 90(!) 9-locus, partial matches in a relatively small database with only 65,493 entries. These findings seem to contradict the usual court testimony of forensic experts, who tend to estimate the RMP as one in millions, billions, or trillions.[64] Keith Devlin, a mathematician at Stanford University, dismisses the extreme RMP numbers presented in courts as "nonsense" and "lies."[65] Moreover, some defense lawyers and researchers requested access to convicted-offender databases (such as the FBI's CODIS and the large national database NDIS) in order to test empirically the theoretical estimates. In response, the FBI threatened states that if they opened their databases to external scientists or defendants, the FBI would terminate their participation in the national database system.[66] In his article "Trawling DNA Databases for Partial Matches: What Is the FBI Afraid Of?," David Kaye observed as follows:

> [T]he release of the data, stripped of personal identifiers, for population-genetics research is permissible ... the FBI has nothing to fear and should reverse its policy of not researching the issue and maintaining the secrecy of the data ... the public and the legal community need to know that all reasonable efforts have been made to verify the accuracy of the numbers that are given to police, judges, and juries. Disclosure of the databases in anonymized form is the best policy.[67]

I agree with Kaye. A few researchers, including Bruce Weir and Laurence Mueller, have used simulations with databases in their research.[68] But the databases available to these researchers are relatively small. I contend that conducting expanded

---

[61] *Id.* at 252–53.
[62] David H. Kaye, *Trawling DNA Databases for Partial Matches: What Is the FBI Afraid Of?*, 19 CORNELL J. L. & PUB. POL'Y 145, 153–54 (2009).
[63] *Id.*
[64] *Id.*
[65] *Id.* at 148.
[66] *Id.* at 149.
[67] *Id.* at 150.
[68] *Id.* at 161.

simulations on the broadest national database (NDIS) would be an important safety tool for the criminal justice system. Indeed, people should not be judged and sentenced to jail on the basis of theory and calculations (of the RMP) alone, when we can verify (using strong computers) the exact RMP for each number of loci in a profile.

Last, another significant problem is that many crime-scene DNA samples contain a mixture of DNA from two or more people. This could also lead to the false identification of an innocent suspect as the perpetrator of the crime being investigated.[69] Indeed, the title of Naughton and Tan's article frames this concern in the very terms that underlie the objective of this book: "The Need for Caution in the Use of DNA Evidence to Avoid Convicting the Innocent."[70]

(2) Laboratory Error

There is a significant risk of false conviction with DNA evidence, due to the strong tendency to ignore the huge impact of a possible lab error in the DNA testing. The NAS 2009 report corrected this dangerous omission,[71] but as I will demonstrate, court verdicts have yet to reflect this.

The relatively recent use of genetic comparisons as scientific evidence in criminal trials emerged only in the 1980s.[72] When evidence from DNA testing first began to be submitted in court, forensic experts claimed a zero-probability of error in the test and absolute reliability.[73] Yet Koehler has rightly called for a distinction between a DNA match and a report of a DNA match, based on their differing probabilities of error.[74] Indeed, the National Academy of Sciences found that

> [a]lthough DNA laboratories are expected to conduct their examinations under stringent quality controlled environments, errors do occasionally occur. They usually involve situations in which interpretational ambiguities occur or in which samples were inappropriately processed and/or contaminated in the laboratory. Errors also can occur when there are limited amounts of DNA, which limits the amount of test information and increases the chance of misinterpretation. Casework reviews of mtDNA analysis suggest a wide range in

---

[69] Naughton & Tan, *supra* note 58, at 254–56.

[70] *Id.*

[71] *See supra* note 3.

[72] Kaye, *supra* note 47, at 101; Sangero & Halpert, *supra* note 47, at 72.

[73] Thompson et al., *supra* note 35, at 47–48.

[74] Jonathan J. Koehler, *On Conveying the Probative Value of DNA Evidence: Frequencies, Likelihood Ratios, and Error Rates*, 67 U. COLO. L. REV. 859, 868–69 (1996); Sangero & Halpert, *supra* note 47, at 73.

the quality of testing results that include contamination, inexperience in interpreting mixtures, and differences in how a test is conducted.[75]

Research has shown that a wide variety of factors can account for errors in DNA
testing.[76] For example, cross-contamination and sample mixups can be a chronic
occurrence at even the best DNA laboratories.[77] The hazards and risks increase with
Polymerase Chain Reaction (PCR)-based typing methods,[78] which entail the dupli-
cation of a small amount of DNA to produce a larger amount sufficient for conducting the DNA test.[79] Here, even minute contamination of the small sample is
likely to be dangerously amplified into a significant contamination of the enlarged
sample, which biases the test results. Errors can occur at any phase of the testing,
beginning with the sample-collecting stage and through to the actual test itself.[80] In
addition, the test involves subjective interpretation of lines that appear at its conclusion,[81] and an incorrect interpretation is likely to yield an erroneous result.[82] Even
the most human of errors, such as mislabeling samples, are possible, even in the
best of laboratories and even when the lab workers are certain that every precaution
against error has been taken.[83]

Some of the risks of scientific evidence are similar to those that arise with medical diagnostic tests,[84] but whereas the FDA fully regulates manufacturers of medical diagnostic devices, there is no such regulation of manufacturers of scientific
evidence equipment, including DNA testing equipment, despite the many risks

---

[75] NAS-2009 REPORT, *supra* note 3, at 5–4.

[76] Sangero & Halpert, *supra* note 47.

[77] Thompson, *supra* note 38, at 11–12, 13–14.

[78] Naughton & Tan, *supra* note 58, at 247; NRC-II REPORT, *supra* note 36, at 83, 84.

[79] The definition of PCR given in the FBI Standards for DNA (FBI, QUALITY ASSURANCE STANDARDS
FOR FORENSIC DNA TESTING LABORATORIES (2009), *available at* http://www.fbi.gov/about-us/
lab/biometric-analysis/codis/qas_testlabs (last visited Sept. 27, 2014) [hereinafter FBI STANDARDS FOR
DNA]) is as follows: "Polymerase Chain Reaction (PCR) is an enzymatic process by which a specific region
of DNA is replicated during repetitive cycles which consist of the following: . . . ."

[80] NRC-II REPORT, *supra* note 36, at 87.

[81] William C. Thompson et al., *Evaluating Forensic DNA Evidence: Essential Elements of a Competent Defense
Review: Part 1*, 27 CHAMPION, Apr. 2003, at 16, 21–24; NRC-II REPORT, *supra* note 36, at 84–85.

[82] *Id.*

[83] NATIONAL RESEARCH COUNCIL, DNA TECHNOLOGY IN FORENSIC SCIENCE 89 (1992) [hereinaf-
ter NRC-I REPORT]. For a deeper discussion of the causes of error, see Naughton & Tan, *supra* note 58;
Thompson, *supra* note 77; James Herbie DiFonzo, *In Praise of Statutes of Limitations in Sex Offense Cases*,
41 HOUS. L. REV. 1205, 1232–61 (2004).

[84] Boaz Sangero & Mordechai Halpert, *A Safety Doctrine for the Criminal Justice System*, 2011 MICH. ST.
L. REV. 1293, 1305.

entailed.[85] For example, there is no error-reporting duty for DNA testing equipment, which is accepted practice in safety-critical systems; this lack of duty leads to unsafety.[86]

An illustrative example is the user manual supplied by Applied Biosystems with DNA testing kits it manufactures,[87] which states as follows in bold lettering: "**For Research, Forensic and Paternity Use Only. Not for use in diagnostic procedures.**"[88] What this means is that the same, lone piece of evidence that is a sufficient basis for convicting and sentencing someone to an extended prison term or even death is insufficient foundation for a medical diagnosis.[89] Not surprisingly, problems with Applied Biosystems software have emerged,[90] and it seems that it was never approved by the FDA.

Accidents and incidents are not a rare phenomenon in DNA testing.[91] Exemplifying this is the widespread contamination discovered at the British Forensic Service. Researchers found that the DNA of twenty employees of the microfuge tubes manufacturer had contaminated the DNA evidence in scores of cases,[92] reporting that contamination had been found in "approximately 10% of scenes."[93] A similar case arose in Germany. In 2008, the German police offered a 100,000 Euro award for information leading to the arrest of a serial killer known as the "Phantom of Heilbronn."[94] Traces of her DNA had been found at some forty

---

[85] François Pompanon et al., *Genotyping Errors: Causes, Consequences and Solutions*, 6 NATURE REV. GENETICS 847, 852–53 (2005); Thompson, *supra* note 77, at 10, 14. The FBI's *Quality Assurance Standards for Forensic DNA Testing Laboratories* (*see* FBI STANDARDS FOR DNA, *supra* note 79) is important, but the only standard for DNA kits is imposed on laboratories and not the manufacturers ("standard 9.3—The laboratory shall identify critical reagents and evaluate them prior to use in casework. These critical reagents shall include but are not limited to the following: 9.3.1 Test kits or systems for performing quantitative PCR and genetic typing.").

[86] Sangero & Halpert, *supra* note 84, at 1305.

[87] *Id.* at 1306.

[88] APPLIED BIOSYSTEMS, AMPFLSTR SGM PLUS, PCR AMPLIFICATION KIT: USER'S MANUAL 2 (2011), *available at* http://www3.appliedbiosystems.com/cms/groups/applied_markets_support/documents/generaldocuments/cms_041049.pdf (last visited Sept. 24, 2014). The warning was recently slightly modified to "For Forensic or Paternity Use Only."

[89] Sangero & Halpert, *supra* note 84, at 1306.

[90] Jason R. Gilder et al., *Systematic Differences in Electropherogram Peak Heights Reported by Different Versions of the GeneScan Software*, 49 J. FORENSIC SCI. 92 (2004); Sangero & Halpert, *supra* note 84.

[91] Sangero & Halpert, *supra* note 84.

[92] Kevin Sullivan et al., *New Developments and Challenges in the Use of the UK DNA Database: Addressing the Issue of Contaminated Consumables*, 146 FORENSIC SCI. INT'L 175 (2004).

[93] *Id.* at 176; Sangero & Halpert, *supra* note 84, at 1306.

[94] Sangero & Halpert, *supra* note 84, at 1307; *Reward for "Phantom Killer" Reaches Record €300,000*, LOCAL, Jan. 13, 2009, http://www.thelocal.de/national/20090113-16739.html (last visited Sept. 24, 2014) [hereinafter *Reward for "Phantom Killer"*]; David H. Kaye, Commentary, *GINA's Genotypes*, 108 MICH. L. REV. FIRST IMPRESSIONS 51, 52 (2010).

crime scenes in Germany, Austria, and France, six of them murders.[95] In 2009, it was revealed that in fact there had never been a serial killer, and instead, the DNA found at all the crime scenes belonged to an innocent female worker at the Bavarian factory that manufactures the cotton swabs used in the DNA collection. The swabs had been contaminated with her DNA.[96]

Of course, optimists will maintain that the worst case scenario of such cases of contamination is that the actual perpetrator remains at large and not the false accusation of an innocent person.[97] But this is flawed thinking from the perspective of safety. First, safety in DNA testing could reduce the risk of false negatives, which are what allow the actual perpetrators to roam free. Second, safety in DNA testing would reduce also the risk of false positives that result from the relatively easy and undetectable contamination of samples. A primary hazard is cross-contamination between the genetic matter of an innocent suspect (or someone who becomes a suspect after the DNA test) and the DNA sample taken from a crime scene, which leads to the mistaken conclusion that the suspect committed the crime.[98]

In some cases, cross-contamination can lead to false conviction, as almost occurred in the Jaidyn Leskie murder investigation[99] and Russell John Gesah case[100] and actually occurred in the Farah Jama case.[101] A prominent case in which cross-contamination almost led to a false conviction is that of Jack Bellamy, a convicted sex offender, who was charged with the murder of Jane Durrua. In 2004, a DNA sample taken during the 1968 investigation of the murder was found to match

---

[95]   Kaye, *supra* note 94; Sangero & Halpert, *supra* note 84.

[96]   *Reward for "Phantom Killer", supra* note 94; Kaye, *supra* note 94; Sangero & Halpert, *supra* note 84.

[97]   Sangero & Halpert, *supra* note 84.

[98]   Thompson, *supra* note 85, at 10–12; Sangero & Halpert, *supra* note 84.

[99]   In the Jaidyn Leskie murder investigation, DNA samples taken from a young, "mentally challenged" girl matched the samples taken from the murder scene. INQUEST INTO THE DEATH OF JAIDYN RAYMOND LESKIE, CORONERS CASE NUMBER: 007/98 64-85, *available at* http://www.bioforensics.com/conference09/Workshop/Leskie_decision.pdf (last visited Sept. 24, 2014). It emerged in the coroner's inquiry that a sex crime committed against the girl had been investigated by the same laboratory that had tested the blood stains from the murder, which occurred around the same time. *Id* at 67–70. The coroner's final conclusion was that there had been cross-contamination between the girl's DNA and the DNA sample from the Leskie murder scene. *Id*. at 70–72, 85. The coroner noted that additional instances of contamination had been discovered at the same laboratory. *Id*. at 85; Sangero & Halpert, *supra* note 84, at 1307–08.

[100] In 2008, murder charges brought against Russell John Gesah based on DNA test results were dropped when it emerged that his DNA sample and the sample from the crime scene had been processed at the same time and by the same laboratory, raising cross-contamination concerns. Sangero & Halpert, *supra* note 84, at 1308.

[101] Farah Jama was convicted and sentenced to six years in prison. FRANK H.R. VINCENT, REPORT: INQUIRY INTO THE CIRCUMSTANCES THAT LED TO THE CONVICTION OF MR. FARAH ABDULKADIR JAMA (2010). Jama served about a year and a half until the prosecutor informed the court, in 2009, that the DNA sample had apparently been contaminated. The court vacated the conviction, and Jama was released from prison. *Id*.; Sangero & Halpert, *supra* note 84, at 1308.

Bellamy's DNA.[102] It later emerged, however, that Bellamy's original DNA sample and the sample from the Durrua investigation had been processed in the same laboratory and at the same time, giving serious reason to suspect cross-contamination[103] and leading the prosecutor to drop the charges against Bellamy. Finally, in 2008, different results were arrived at when the samples were tested by other laboratories, subsequent to which charges were filed against a new suspect, Robert Zarinsky, for the same murder.[104]

Not all DNA testing errors are ever detected. In the case of John Ruelas and Gary Lieterman, for examples, their DNA samples were found to match DNA found at a 1969 murder crime scene.[105] Ruelas, who had been a four-years-old at the time of the murder, was clearly not the perpetrator. Lieterman, in contrast, was convicted of the murder—despite the lack of a reasonable explanation for the match between Ruelas's DNA and the DNA at the crime scene, and in disregard of the fact that the sample from the victim and samples from the two suspects had been processed in the same laboratory at the same time. Given the Hidden Accidents Principle in criminal law, had Ruelas been an adult and not a child at the time of the murder, he would likely have been falsely convicted and the probability of cross-contamination never revealed.[106]

The media often reports on DNA testing mishaps, but does not always provide accurate information in doing so.[107] And as there is no reporting duty or duty to investigate DNA testing accidents—let alone incidents—the media is often the exclusive source of this information. Consequently, again, not only does the criminal justice system lack a safety approach for preventing accidents, but it makes no consistent attempt to learn from experience—that is, not even the outdated Fly-Fix-Fly method is applied in criminal law in a systematic fashion.[108]

William C. Thompson has reported on the considerable errors and problems in how DNA laboratories are managed, in the United States and elsewhere, in both confirmation cases and "cold hit" database searches.[109] His findings are based on

---

[102] Robert Hanley, *DNA Leads to Arrest in '68 Rape and Murder of Girl*, N.Y. Times, June 17, 2004, http://www.nytimes.com/2004/06/17/nyregion/dna-leads-to-arrest-in-68-rape-and-murder-of-girl-13.html?sec=&spon=&pagewanted=all (last visited Sept. 24, 2014); Sangero & Halpert, *supra* note 84, at 1308.

[103] WILLIAM C. THOMPSON, THE POTENTIAL FOR ERROR IN FORENSIC DNA TESTING (AND HOW THAT COMPLICATES THE USE OF DNA DATABASES FOR CRIMINAL IDENTIFICATION) 28–29 (2008).

[104] Sangero & Halpert, *supra* note 84, at 1308.

[105] Thompson, *supra* note 85, at 14; Sangero & Halpert, *supra* note 84, at 1308–09.

[106] Sangero & Halpert, *supra* note 84, at 1309.

[107] *Id.*

[108] *Id.*

[109] Thompson, *supra* note 77; Sangero & Halpert, *supra* note 47, at 75.

laboratory records and point to an unexpectedly high rate of detected cases of mislabeling and sample contamination.[110] Although the particular instances of laboratory contamination Thompson recorded were uncovered at early stages, he nonetheless noted that they raise grounds for concern, for cross-contamination is a regular occurrence even in the top-rated laboratories and "the same processes that cause detectable errors in some cases can cause undetectable errors in others."[111] Thompson noted that "[e]rrors that incriminate a suspect are unlikely to be detected as errors; they are likely to be treated as incriminating evidence."[112] He also considered the possibility of lab workers' falsifying test results to cover up contamination incidents, which can be the result of negligence and get a lab worker fired.[113]

Koehler, in turn, has reported on professional proficiency tests that were not blind.[114] The error rates in these tests were tremendous, varying between 1 and 4 percent.[115] Moreover, Koehler, Audrey Chia and Samuel Lindsey have claimed that when the probability of a laboratory error is much greater than the Random Match Probability, the latter probability is insignificant and the former probability is the relevant statistic.[116] To illustrate, an RMP of one in 100 millions creates a bias against the defendant, even if the probability of a laboratory error is 1 percent, because the RMP is the only statistic the jury hears. It is therefore preferable not to report the RMP to the jury. In a later article, Koehler made the recommendation—which I fully support—that the jury instructions on the possibility of an error in the testing include only one statistic, relating to both the random match probability and lab error combined.[117]

Another claim raised by Koehler is that the average error rate of all forensic laboratories should be taken into account in the absence of statistics regarding the error rate of the laboratory that performed the actual testing.[118] I take the further step, however, of maintaining that the absence of statistical data on the error rate of the relevant laboratory should render its test results inadmissible as criminal evidence given, among other things, the *Daubert* rule. Alternatively, if the court nonetheless

---

[110] Thompson, *supra* note 77; Sangero & Halpert, *supra* note 47, at 75.

[111] Thompson, *supra* note 77, at 12.

[112] *Id.*

[113] *Id. See also* Richard O. Lempert, *After the DNA Wars: A Mopping up Operation*, 31 ISR. L. REV. 536, 552–53 (1997); Sangero & Halpert, *supra* note 47, at 75.

[114] Jonathan J. Koehler, *Error and Exaggeration in the Presentation of DNA Evidence*, 34 JURIMETRICS J. 21, 26 (1993); Sangero & Halpert, *supra* note 47, at 75–76.

[115] Koehler, *supra* note 114, at 26.

[116] Jonathan J. Koehler et al., *The Random Match Probability in DNA Evidence: Irrelevant and Prejudicial?*, 35 JURIMETRICS J. 201, 210–11 (1995); Sangero & Halpert, *supra* note 47, at 76.

[117] Koehler, *supra* note 29, at 533.

[118] Jonathan J. Koehler, *Why DNA Likelihood Ratios Should Account for Error (Even When a National Research Council Report Says They Should Not)*, 37 JURIMETRICS J. 425, 433 (1997).

admits the results as evidence, safety considerations mandate that the error rate of the relevant laboratory be assumed to be at the highest level for laboratories of the same type.[119]

It has been claimed that retesting can reduce the error rate, particularly if it is performed by a different laboratory,[120] but this would not reduce the error rate to zero. First of all, the same cause of error in the first round of testing could quite possibly reoccur in the retesting at the second laboratory;[121] indeed, different laboratories have been known to make the same mistakes.[122] There is a variety of reasons for the same mistake to be repeated in different laboratories, including the erroneous analysis of the lines obtained in the test and contamination of the sample before the first test.[123] Another problem is that the first laboratory sometimes uses up all of the sample material, making retesting impossible.[124]

This notwithstanding, however, retesting could still prevent certain laboratory errors that lead to false convictions. Thus, as a necessary safety procedure, a legal rule should be passed requiring the retesting of DNA samples by an independent, objective expert as a condition for basing a conviction on DNA testing lab results.[125] However, DNA evidence should not suffice alone for convicting, because performing a second test will not neutralize altogether the significant risk of error.

Finally, the possibility of DNA fabrication was exposed as another source of concern by Israeli science researchers when they created artificial DNA that can fool current forensic testing procedures.[126] Following this, it was suggested that "the discovery of the ability to easily fabricate DNA evidence as well as a long history of DNA falsification and gross ineptness by crime laboratories demonstrate that DNA-based evidence's sterling reputation is undeserved."[127]

---

[119] Sangero & Halpert, *supra* note 47, at 76. A similar claim has been raised in Barry C. Scheck, *DNA and Daubert*, 15 CARDOZO L. Rev. 1959, 1981–85 (1994).

[120] NRC-II REPORT, *supra* note 36; Sangero & Halpert, *supra* note 47, at 78.

[121] David J. Balding, *Errors and Misunderstandings in the Second NRC Report*, 37 JURIMETRICS J. 469, 475–76 (1997).

[122] Koehler, *supra* note 118, at 437; Thompson et al., *supra* note 35, at 48.

[123] Thompson et al., *supra* note 35, at 48.

[124] This was common practice in the Houston police crime laboratory. DiFonzo, *supra* note 83, at 1242–49; Sangero & Halpert, *supra* note 47, at 78.

[125] Sangero & Halpert, *supra* note 47.

[126] D. Frumkin et al., *Authentication of Forensic DNA Samples*, 2009 FORENSIC SCI. INT. GENET. 1; Bolden, *supra* note 6.

[127] Bolden, *supra* note 6, at 440, 441 ("[C]ourts should evaluate DNA evidence on a case-by-case basis, evaluating the authenticity of the DNA evidence as well as the testing procedures used to obtain the results.").

(3) Summary and Recommendations

Although it is undisputed that DNA evidence is significant, weighty evidence that the courts must rely on, it must not be allowed to constitute the sole basis for a conviction in a criminal trial, for there is a very tangible danger that the conviction will be wrongful.[128]

Indeed, as discussed, the likelihood of a lab error in DNA testing tends to be considered in detachment from the other evidence in a case,[129] despite the fact that such errors are unavoidable and the court has no way of determining whether they occurred in the specific case before it. Not even retesting in another laboratory will fully contend with this problem. Moreover, although the probability of a lab error (which could amount to 1 in 100 cases) is much higher than the Random Match Probability, juries are not supplied with this statistic and instead hear only the impressive RMP statistic (which could amount to one-in-a-billion or even trillion cases).

As there are no adequate statistics on the error rates of different laboratories, the prosecution should bear the burden of establishing these rates regarding the specific laboratory that performed the testing it is relying on.[130] Above I suggested two alternative safety mechanisms when there is a lack of data on a specific laboratory: either the evidence must be found inadmissible or the evidence be admitted but ascribed the highest known rate of error for tests performed in laboratories of the relevant sort.

In 2009, the FBI released its *Quality Assurance Standards for Forensic DNA Testing Laboratories*.[131] These groundbreaking standards, based partially on the recommendations in the National Academy of Sciences reports,[132] include requirements for protocols regarding, among other things, the interpretation of DNA, mixed samples, and contamination. Also included are important standards relating to quality assurance programs, education and training of laboratory personnel, lab reports, lab review, proficiency testing, and corrective action when discrepancies are detected in proficiency tests and casework analysis.[133]

---

[128] Sangero & Halpert, *supra* note 47, at 79–80.

[129] *Id.*

[130] *Id.*

[131] FBI STANDARDS FOR DNA, *supra* note 79.

[132] *See* Standard 9.6, at *id.*: "The laboratory shall have and follow written guidelines for the interpretation of data. 9.6.2 For a given population(s), the statistical interpretation of autosomal loci shall be made following the recommendations 4.1, 4.2 or 4.3 as deemed applicable of the National Research Council report entitled 'The Evaluation of Forensic DNA Evidence' (1996) and/or court directed method."

[133] *Id.*

Although this is important progress, these are only the first steps forward, as these standards should be mandatory for each and every laboratory, federal and state. This has the potential to be an effective safety program, but in order to achieve this, the standards must not suffice with simply requiring that labs formulate their own protocols, but actually formulate in detail—and enforce—the necessary protocols.

In addition, a regulatory regime similar to the mandatory premarket approval process for medical diagnostic devices should be instituted for manufacturers of scientific evidence devices, including DNA kits.[134] This regime should impose an accident-reporting duty as well as a duty to report incidents that involve accuracy, similar to the arrangement for medical devices. This would supplement and support existing safety recommendations relating to accreditation of laboratories, as set forth in the NAS 2009 report.[135]

A final important way to safety in the context of DNA testing and evidence is the performance of extended simulations on the broadest database (NDIS). Using strong computers, researchers should verify and find out the exact Random Match Probability for each number of loci in a profile.

E. FINGERPRINT COMPARISONS

(1) The Possibility of Error

There are four stages to the basic approach of latent fingerprint experts, known as ACE-V: Analysis, Comparison, Evaluation, and Verification.[136] In the "Analysis" stage, the examiner examines closely the latent print associated with the crime being investigated and decides whether there is enough useful information contained in the image that it is "of value" for further examination. If there is, the examiner marks up the print and documents the minutiae he or she observes. In the "Comparison" stage, the analyst compares the latent print to a particular source print, noting observed similarities and differences. In the "Evaluation" stage, the expert reaches one of three possible conclusions: exclusion, identification, or inconclusive. If an identification conclusion is reached, then a second expert conducts the same process in the "Verification" stage.[137]

---

[134] This recommendation was originally made in Sangero & Halpert, *supra* note 84, at 1322.
[135] NAS-2009 REPORT, *supra* note 3.
[136] Mnookin, *supra* note 20, at 1217.
[137] *Id.*

Fingerprint evidence has long been considered very strong evidence.[138] Throughout the twentieth century, both courts and the general public regarded it as the epitome of reliable and certain evidence, and it served as a basis for many convictions.[139] Yet in recent years, this special status has become the subject of criticism for not being grounded in solid statistical theory and for being subject to error.[140]

As discussed above, there is general consensus as to the possibility of a random match in a DNA comparison so that all of the loci compared in a test will be identical for a number of people. For this reason, the test results are given in statistical form: in a population of X million people, on average, Y persons will share the same genetic profile. However, the prevailing assumption regarding fingerprint comparisons is that every fingerprint is unique and there is a zero-possibility of a random match.[141] Consequently, the courts tend not to require the adduction of random match data for fingerprints, and the prosecution therefore does not present any such data during trial. In effect, there are actually no data regarding this possibility,[142] but there is also no scientific proof that it is impossible for two people to have the same points of comparison in a fingerprint examined by an expert.[143] Forensic experts testifying in court present this evidence as unequivocal instead of making an effort to investigate and provide data about Random Match Probability. This leads to the perception of this evidence as far stronger than it actually is.[144]

---

[138] Id. at 1217 ("Fingerprint evidence is, in all likelihood, both more probative and less error-prone than some other kinds of forensic identification evidence, and it has a long and extremely substantial courtroom use.").

[139] Robert Epstein, Fingerprints Meet Daubert: The Myth of Fingerprint "Science" Is Revealed, 75 So. CAL. L. REV. 605, 605 n.3; Sangero & Halpert, supra note 6, at 63.

[140] Epstein, supra note 139; David A. Stoney, Measurement of Fingerprint Individuality, in ADVANCES IN FINGERPRINT TECHNOLOGY 327, 327–88 (Henry C. Lee & Robert E. Gaensslen eds., 2001); Sandy L. Zabell, Fingerprint Evidence, 13 J.L. & POL'Y 143, 152–55 (2005); Nathan Benedict, Fingerprints and the Daubert Standard for Admission of Scientific Evidence: Why Fingerprints Fail and a Proposed Remedy, 46 ARIZ. L. REV. 519, 526–33 (2004); Jennifer L. Mnookin, Fingerprint Evidence in the Age of DNA Profiling, 67 BROOK. L. REV. 13, 57–61 (2001); Sangero & Halpert, supra note 6, at 64; Mnookin, supra note 20; Elizabeth J. Reese, Techniques for Mitigating Cognitive Biases in Fingerprint Identification, 59 UCLA L. REV. 1252 (2012); Brandon Garrett & Gregory Mitchell, How Jurors Evaluate Fingerprint Evidence: The Relative Importance of Match Language, Method Information, and Error Acknowledgment, 10 J. EMPIRICAL LEGAL STUD. 484 (2013).

[141] David J. Balding & Peter Donnelly, Inferring Identity from DNA Profile Evidence, 92 PROC. NAT'L. ACAD. SCI. 11,741 (1995); Peter Donnelly & Richard D. Friedman, DNA Database Searches and the Legal Consumption of Scientific Evidence, 97 MICH. L. REV. 931 (1999); Thompson et al., supra note 35, at 49–51; William C. Thompson & Simon A. Cole, Psychological Aspects of Forensic Identification Evidence, in EXPERT PSYCHOLOGICAL TESTIMONY FOR THE COURTS 31, 44 (Mark Costanzo et al. eds., 2007); Sangero & Halpert, supra note 6, at 64.

[142] Mnookin, supra note 20, at 1221–26; Zabell, supra note 140, at 155–56.

[143] Mnookin, supra note 20, at 1225–26; Sharath Pankanti et al., On the Individuality of Fingerprints, 24 IEEE TRANSACTIONS ON PATTERN ANALYSIS & MACH. INTELLIGENCE 1010, 1010–11 (2002).

[144] Mnookin, supra note 20, at 1226; Saks & Koehler, supra note 25, at 893; Sangero & Halpert, supra note 6, at 64.

A 2002 study arrived at 6.10×10^{-8} probability of a fingerprint with 36 minutiae points sharing 12 minutiae points with another arbitrarily chosen fingerprint with 36 minutiae points.[145] Thus, some statistical theories have found a possibility of a random match between fingerprints, similar to cases with DNA comparisons.[146] The ramification of this is that it is possible for two different people to have fingerprints so similar that examiners are unable to distinguish between them.[147]

In the early 1990s, British researchers examined the sixteen-point standard for comparing fingerprints followed in England and Wales.[148] Their research findings showed the subjective nature of fingerprint analysis: different examiners arrived at entirely different points and numbers of comparison.[149] This outcome was reinforced by the results of proficiency tests for 156 fingerprint examiners, conducted in the United States under the auspices of the International Association for Identification and published in 1996.[150] The forensic science community was shocked by these results: of the 156 examiners tested, only 68 had both correctly identified the five latent print impressions that were supposed to be identified, and correctly noted the two elimination latent prints that were not supposed to be identified.[151] Forty-eight false matches were counted in total.[152] The combined results of these proficiency tests show that fingerprint examiners get erroneous results in an average of 0.8 percent of cases[153]—a significant error rate.

Errors in fingerprint analysis occur, of course, also in actual cases before the courts. Simon Cole reviewed twenty-two documented cases in the United States, England, and Scotland in which people were arrested and, at times, even served

[145] Pankanti et al., *supra* note 143, at 1021; Sangero & Halpert, *supra* note 6, at 64.

[146] Cedric Neumann et al., *Computation of Likelihood Ratios in Fingerprint Identification for Configurations of Three Minutiae*, 51 J. FORENSIC SCI. 1255, 1255 (2006).

[147] This was proven in the Brandon Mayfield case, discussed further on. *See* Sarah Kershaw et al., *Spain and U.S. at Odds on Mistaken Terror Arrest*, N.Y. TIMES, June 5, 2004, *available at* http://query.nytimes.com/gst/fullpage.html?res=9800EFDB1031F936A35755C0A9629C8B63 (last visited Sept. 10, 2014); Sangero & Halpert, *supra* note 6, at 65.

[148] Ian W. Evett & Richard L. Williams, *A Review of the Sixteen Points Fingerprint Standard in England and Wales*, 46 J. FORENSIC IDENTIFICATION 49 (1996); Sangero & Halpert, *supra* note 6, at 65.

[149] Evett & Williams, *supra* note 148; Sangero & Halpert, *supra* note 6, at 65. *See also* Mnookin, *supra* note 20, at 1221–22.

[150] David L. Grieve, *Possession of Truth*, 46 J. FORENSIC IDENTIFICATION 521, 523 (1996); Sangero & Halpert, *supra* note 6, at 65.

[151] Grieve, *supra* note 150, at 524.

[152] *Id.*

[153] Simon A. Cole, *More than Zero: Accounting for Error in Latent Print Identification*, 95 J. CRIM. L. & CRIMINOLOGY 985, 1034, 1073 (2005); Joseph L. Peterson & Penelope N. Markham, *Crime Laboratory Proficiency Testing Results, 1978–1991, II: Resolving Questions of Common Origin*, 40 J. FORENSIC SCI. 1009 (1995); Lyn Haber & Ralph N. Haber, *Error Rates for Human Fingerprint Examiners, in* AUTOMATIC FINGERPRINT RECOGNITION SYSTEMS 339, 349 (Nalini K. Ratha et al. eds., 2003); Sangero & Halpert, *supra* note 6, at 65.

prison sentences before the error was detected.[154] In light of the Hidden Accidents Principle in criminal law, this is likely only the tip of the iceberg of errors in fingerprint analysis, but the most errors have not been detected and the falsely convicted inmates remain in prison.

There are a number of causes for the frequency of laboratory errors in fingerprint analysis, including: the poor quality of fingerprints taken from the crime scene (as opposed to the good quality of prints calmly scanned by access control systems),[155] automated fingerprint identification systems,[156] substandard or unscientific practices among certain "experts,"[157] and the pressure exerted on laboratory staff by the police and/or prosecution to find a match.[158] In addition, latent images are often smaller in surface area than the full print, possibly distorted, and often contain artifacts resulting from the processes necessary to make a latent print visible. As a result, two impressions from two different sources could be mistaken as coming from the same source.[159]

Leading forensic science researchers have called[160] for the abandonment of "absolute conclusions" and, instead, for the recognition of the inherently probabilistic nature of fingerprint evidence. The key question is not the uniqueness of friction ridge skin but, rather, the fingerprint examiner's ability to derive sufficient information from very limited information. The researchers have suggested replacing experience and tradition (alone) with transparent and empirically based practice.[161] Yet, as the current situation is described by Mnookin,

> ACE-V's relationship to the scientific method is tenuous at best.... [L]atent fingerprint examination as a field lacks any formalized specifications about what is required in order to declare a match. There is no required minimum number of points of resemblance or minimum number of total print features, nor any required quantum of any specific kind of ridge detail .... Two fingerprint

---

[154] Cole, *supra* note 153, at 1001–16; Sangero & Halpert, *supra* note 6, at 65–66.

[155] Pankanti et al., *supra* note 143, at 1017; Sangero & Halpert, *supra* note 6, at 66.

[156] U.S. Dep't Justice, Office of the Inspector General, Oversight and Review Division, A Review of the FBI's Handling of the Brandon Mayfield Case (Unclassified and Redacted) 137 (Mar. 2006), http://www.justice.gov/oig/special/s0601/exec.pdf (last visited Sept. 12, 2014).

[157] Saks & Koehler, *supra* note 144, at 893.

[158] *Id.*; Sangero & Halpert, *supra* note 6, at 66.

[159] Jennifer L. Mnookin et al., *The Need for a Research Culture in the Forensic Sciences*, 58 UCLA L. Rev. 725, 751 (2011).

[160] Christopher Champod & Ian W. Evett, *A Probabilistic Approach to Fingerprint Evidence*, 51 J. Forensic Identification 101 (2001).

[161] *Id. See also* Mnookin et al., *supra* note 159, at 751.

analysts will often focus on different minutiae in their examination of the same print .... The judgment is fundamentally a subjective one, not based on any formalized measures of either quantity or sufficiency. Additionally, latent fingerprints examiners do not generally employ any statistical information or models in the ordinary ACE-V process .... [T]here simply is no well-accepted, fully-specified statistical model that is available for latent fingerprint examiners to employ .... [F]undamentally, fingerprint matching ought to be thought of as a probabilistic inquiry.[162]

(2) The Brandon Mayfield Case and the U.S. Department of Justice's Report

Following the 2004 terror attacks in Madrid, which led to 191 deaths and 2050 non-fatal injuries, the Spanish police found a fingerprint on a blue plastic bag near one of the attack sites; it contained detonators and explosives remnants.[163] The Spanish police requested assistance from the FBI,[164] which searched its fingerprint database using an Automated Fingerprint Identification System (AFIS). The search printout identified twenty potential suspects.[165] In analyzing the samples from the possible suspects, a fingerprint examiner found a match between the print taken from the attack site and that of a Portland, Oregon, attorney named Brandon Mayfield.[166] Mayfield told FBI interrogators that he had never been in Spain in his life, had been in the United States at the time of the attacks, and did not even have a passport.[167] Nonetheless, three senior FBI examiners verified the identification of Mayfield's fingerprints,[168] which was declared in the affidavit supporting an arrest warrant for Mayfield in the United States to be a "100% positive identification."[169] While Mayfield was in detention, the court appointed an independent fingerprint examiner to verify the identification made by FBI examiners.[170] Two weeks after Mayfield's arrest, the Spanish police located someone else, an Algerian named Ouhnane Daoud, whose fingerprints matched the prints found on the plastic bag at the scene of the attacks.[171] Thus, the 100 percent "certain" identification

---

[162] Mnookin, *supra* note 20, at 1219–26.
[163] U.S. Dep't Justice, *supra* note 156, at 29; Sangero & Halpert, *supra* note 6, at 66.
[164] *Id.* at 29–30.
[165] *Id.* at 30.
[166] *Id.* at 31.
[167] Mnookin, *supra* note 20, at 1228.
[168] U.S. Dep't Justice, *supra* note 156, at 29–33, 64.
[169] *Id.* at 64–65.
[170] *Id.* at 80–81; Sangero & Halpert, *supra* note 6, at 66.
[171] *Id.* at 81–82.

of Mayfield's fingerprints by four different examiners had been mistaken. Mayfield was released[172] and, subsequently, received $2 million in compensation.[173]

In 2006, the U.S. Justice Department released a comprehensive report on the Mayfield case.[174] The report stated that the main cause of the false identification was the very strong similarity between Mayfield's fingerprint and the print from the attack site, which, according to Spanish police, belonged to Ouhnane Daoud.[175] The report explained that it is possible for a great similarity between fingerprints to arise in an AFIS search, as the system scans millions of prints and compares each to the prints found at the scene of the crime.[176] The system produces a list of twenty candidates who it has found to have the most similar fingerprints to the crime scene fingerprints.[177] Consequently, the fingerprint examiners had to analyze fingerprints that were very similar to those of Daoud. The report cautioned that the risk of error with "cold hit" database searches is far greater than when suspects are identified by way of a regular police investigation,[178] and the constantly growing size of the databases increases the risk of misidentification.[179]

Peer pressure and "expectation bias" also played a role in the misidentification: once the first expert has declared a match between prints, the verifying experts naturally expect to find the same match.[180] And indeed, the Justice Department report determined that the second, verifying examiner knew that the first examiner had found a match between Mayfield's print and the fingerprints from the scene of the crime.[181] Thus, the report recommended that such information be withheld from verifying examiners.[182]

Another factor in the match found in the misidentification of Mayfield's prints is cognitive bias. Mayfield had converted to Islam sometime earlier, his wife was Egyptian, and he had once represented a known terrorist in a child custody dispute. The report determined that this background information did not influence

---

[172] Robert B. Stacey, *Report on Erroneous Fingerprint Individualization in the Madrid Train Bombing Case*, 54 J. FORENSIC IDENTIFICATION 706 (2004); William C. Thompson & Simon A. Cole, *Lessons from the Brandon Mayfield Case*, 29 CHAMPION, Apr. 2005, at 42; Steven T. Wax & Christopher J. Schatz, *A Multitude of Errors: The Brandon Mayfield Case*, 28 CHAMPION, Sept.–Oct. 2004, at 6; Sangero & Halpert, *supra* note 6, at 66–67; Mnookin, *supra* note 20, at 1228–30.

[173] Mnookin, *supra* note 20, at 1229.

[174] U.S. DEP'T JUSTICE, *supra* note 156.

[175] *Id.* at 130.

[176] *Id.* at 137.

[177] *Id.*

[178] *Id.* at 137.

[179] Mnookin, *supra* note 20, at 1229.

[180] *Id.* at 1230.

[181] U.S. DEP'T JUSTICE, *supra* note 156, 175–77.

[182] *Id.* at 204.

the initial identification of a match, as it was unknown to police investigators at the time, but did impact the verification stage when examiners had this data.[183] Forensic examiners often have access to or are provided with external information about the case that is irrelevant to the analysis,[184] and research has shown that this impacts the analysis. Itiel E. Dror et al. used the Mayfield case to prove "contextual bias" in these circumstances: Five experts were each given a (different) pair of latent print and potential source print and told that they were the prints from the well-known Mayfield case, when in fact each expert received a pair of prints which the same expert had analyzed and identified in the past as a 100 percent match and on which he had testified in court. In the Dror et al. experiment, three of the experts arrived at the opposite conclusion of no match, likely due to bias; one expert found the prints to be "inconclusive"; and only one was consistent and again identified a match between the prints.[185] Other experiments conducted by Dror et al., with different experts, also found a bias.[186]

Whereas in the medical diagnostics field and other scientific fields, a formalized effort is made to shield researchers from "contextual information," no such procedures generally exist in the forensic sciences field.[187] Thus, to prevent some of the biases, I suggest giving fingerprint examiners not just the suspect's print to compare against the latent print from the crime scene, but several "filler" prints as well from other people. This will prevent the examiner from knowing at the outset which print belongs to the suspect.[188]

As we see then, errors in fingerprint analysis can and do (as in the Mayfield case) actually occur in reality and are not a mere theoretical probability. Given the Hidden Accidents Principle, moreover, there are likely many more cases in which these errors remain undetected.[189] Compounding this is the fact that some fingerprints are so similar to one another that examiners are incapable of distinguishing

---

[183] *Id.* at 179.

[184] Mnookin, *supra* note 20, at 1230.

[185] Itiel E. Dror, David Charlton & Ailsa E. Péron, *Contextual Information Renders Experts Vulnerable to Making Erroneous Identifications*, 156 FORENSIC SCI. INT'L 74 (2006). *See also* Mnookin, *supra* note 20, at 1231–32.

[186] Itiel E. Dror & D. Charlton, *Why Experts Make Errors*, 56 J. FORENSIC IDENTIFICATION 600 (2006); Itiel E. Dror & Robert Rosenthal, *Meta-analytically Quantifying the Reliability and Biasability of Forensic Experts*, 53 J. FORENSIC SCI. 900 (2008). *See also* Mnookin, *supra* note 20, at 1231–32.

[187] Mnookin, *supra* note 20, at 1230–31.

[188] For a similar recommendation, see Gary L. Wells et al., *Forensic Science Testing: The Forensic Filler-Control Method for Controlling Contextual Bias, Estimating Error Rates, and Calibrating Analysts' Reports*, 2 J. APPLIED RES. MEMORY & COGNITION 53 (2013). *See also* William C. Thompson, *What Role Should Investigative Facts Play in the Evaluation of Scientific Evidence*, 43 AUSTRALIAN J. FORENSIC SCI. 123 (2011).

[189] Sangero & Halpert, *supra* note 6, at 68.

between them. Thus, the general error rate in fingerprint analysis is unknown.[190] It is commonly estimated to be low, but proficiency tests given to examiners belie this.

(2) The Case Law

Fingerprint analysis evidence is generally sufficient as the sole basis for a conviction in American courts.[191] Over the last decade, courts have begun to indicate skepticism with regard to this type of evidence,[192] with some explicitly holding errors to be possible in fingerprint comparisons.[193] However, the problematic report referred to by the FBI as the "50K Study" gave undeserving support to fingerprint evidence.[194] Although the findings of this so-called study were never published in a scientific journal or subject to peer review (as the *Daubert* standard requires),[195] judges have nonetheless relied on them in their rulings.[196]

The study was, in fact, conducted to find support for the claim relied on by prosecutors that every fingerprint is unique, and false positive errors are not possible in fingerprint comparisons.[197] FBI examiners used an automated fingerprint identification system with a computerized database of 50,000 fingerprints, to compare each fingerprint against itself and against the 49,999 other fingerprints in the database.[198] This process yielded 2.5 billion comparisons (50,000 × 50,000),[199] which was considered by some courts as evidence that false positives cannot occur in fingerprint comparison.[200]

The main methodological flaw in the FBI study was the comparison of the fingerprint images against *themselves*.[201] For the study to be scientifically valid, the 50,000

---

[190] Mnookin, *supra* note 20, at 1227; Mnookin, *supra* note 140, at 60.

[191] *See, e.g.*, People v. Ford, 606 N.E.2d 690, 693 (Ill. App. Ct. 1992); People v. Rhodes, 422 N.E.2d 605, 608 (Ill. 1981). *See also* Sangero & Halpert, *supra* note 6, at 69.

[192] *See* United States v. Llera Plaza, 188 F. Supp. 2d 549, 565 (E.D. Pa. 2002). *See also* Epstein, *supra* note 139; Simon A. Cole, *Grandfathering Evidence: Fingerprint Admissibility Rulings from* Jennings *to* Llera Plaza *and Back Again*, 41 AM. CRIM. L. REV. 1189, 1196–97 (2004); David H. Kaye, *The Nonscience of Fingerprinting:* United States v. Llera-Plaza, 21 QUINNIPIAC L. REV. 1073 (2003); Michael Lynch & Simon A. Cole, *Science and Technology Studies on Trial: Dilemmas of Expertise*, 35 SOC. STUD. SCI. 269 (2005); Jennifer L. Mnookin, *Fingerprints: Not a Gold Standard*, 20 ISSUES IN SCI. & TECH. 47 (2003); Sangero & Halpert, *supra* note 6, at 69.

[193] State v. Quintana, 103 P.3d 168, 171 (Utah Ct. App. 2004); United States v. Crisp, 324 F.3d 261, 273–74 (4th Cir. 2003) (Michael, J., dissenting); Sangero & Halpert, *supra* note 6.

[194] Epstein, *supra* note 139, at 629–32; Cole, *supra* note 153, at 1046–48 n. 334.

[195] Daubert v. Merrel Dow Pharm. Inc., 509 U.S. 579, 593 (1993).

[196] *See, e.g.*, United States v. Mitchell, 365 F.3d 215, 239–41 (3d Cir. 2004); United States v. Sanchez–Birruetta, 128 Fed. App'x 571 (9th Cir. 2005).

[197] *Sanchez-Birruetta*, 128 Fed. App'x. at 573; Sangero & Halpert, *supra* note 6, at 70–71.

[198] *Mitchell*, 365 F.3d at 225; Sangero & Halpert, *supra* note 6, at 70.

[199] *Mitchell*, 365 F.3d at 225. In a second experiment, they compared partial prints. *Id.* at 226.

[200] *Sanchez-Birruetta*, 128 Fed. App'x 571.

[201] Sangero & Halpert, *supra* note 6, at 70.

images had to have been compared with 50,000 *other* images of the same finger-prints (there should have been two different images of each fingerprint). When 50,000 images are compared against themselves, there is of course no possibility of error. The image is stored on the computer as a digital file, which is a collection of digits. When two images are identical, the digits that represent them will also be identical. Two different digital images, however, even of the same fingerprint, will be represented in the computer's memory by different digits, and in this case, an error *is* possible. If we take what occurs in the reality of a forensic fingerprint com-parison, two different images are in fact compared: the one from the crime scene and the image of the suspect's fingerprint. Given this grave analytical mistake, this study has not surprisingly drawn harsh criticism from experts in the field.[202]

Mnookin has described three approaches in American case law to fingerprint evidence.[203] The first is to simply ignore the problem: courts hold that fingerprint evidence easily passes the *Daubert* tests and disregard all the above-mentioned dif-ficulties with this evidence—the lack of scientific testing, of a meaningful error rate, and of a statistical foundation or validated, objective criteria for determining a match.[204] The second approach is to seemingly apply the *Daubert* tests to the fin-gerprint evidence but too easily conclude its admissibility: "these courts, though squirming a bit and acknowledging some of the legitimate concerns regarding the research basis for this evidence, find that, on balance, the evidence still warrants admission in its traditional form, though without fully explaining what justifies this conclusion."[205] The third approach taken by courts is to allow the fingerprints expert to testify on the similarities and differences in the patterns at issue, while prohibiting or limiting her from presenting conclusions regarding the meaning of the similarities.[206]

Based on the 2009 National Academy of Sciences Report, discussed in detail below, Mnookin offers another approach, namely "exclusion (for now)":[207]

At present, pattern identification evidence does not have the empiri-cal data to back up the claims made in court. Moreover, just as with DNA

---

[202] Christophe Champod & Ian W. Evett, *A Probabilistic Approach to Fingerprint Evidence*, 51 J. FORENSIC IDENT. 101, 112 (2001); David H. Kaye, *Questioning a Courtroom Proof of the Uniqueness of Fingerprints*, 71 INT'L STAT. REV. 521 (2003); Pankanti et al., *supra* note 143, at 1015; Sangero & Halpert, *supra* note 6.

[203] Mnookin, *supra* note 20, at 1241–65.

[204] *Id*. at 1243–47. The example is the verdict in United States v. Havvard, 117 F. Supp. 2d 848 (S.D. Ind. 2000).

[205] Mnookin, *supra* note 20, at 1248–52. The example is the verdict in United States v. Sullivan, 246 F. Supp. 2d 700 (E.D. Ky. 2003).

[206] Mnookin, *supra* note 20, at 1252–64. The example is the verdict in *Llera Plaza* (I), 179 F. Supp. 2d 492, 516 (E.D. Pa. 2002) (Judge Pollak).

[207] Mnookin, *supra* note 20, at 1265–74.

evidence—which, after an initial honeymoon period, was excluded by a number of jurisdictions for a short period of time because of concerns about the subjectivity of standards for determining a match; insufficient research into the underlying questions of population genetics; and general technical sloppiness—exclusion would be a great motivator for pursuing the research necessary to justify admissibility .... Good proficiency tests, which show the extent to which examiners make errors in a variety of different levels of difficulty, should suffice to support a finding of adequate validity, presuming that the error rates discovered through this testing process are tolerably low, and the match between what was tested and the "task at hand" in the particular case is sufficiently close .... [T]he courts should care less about the details of the method ... and more about what evidence there is to support the conclusion that the methods actually work ... how accurate are examiners when matching latent prints to a particular source; latent prints which are often partial, frequently smudged, and perhaps even distorted?[208]

Mnookin estimates that if judges require that experts provide the error rate of their work as a prerequisite for the admissibility of fingerprint evidence, research will be conducted and this very important knowledge produced. Experts should not be able to simply claim an error rate of zero, and they must give up the claim that they are able to individualize.[209] I find this view convincing and an important step on the way to safety in fingerprints evidence. In fact, in a promising decision from 2007, a court excluded fingerprint evidence, describing it as "a subjective, untested, unverifiable identification procedure that purports to be infallible."[210]

(3) The 2009 National Academy of Sciences Report

As opposed to the "50K study," the most informative document on the accuracy of fingerprint comparison is the 2009 Academy of Sciences report on forensic science in the United States.[211] The report deals with fingerprints under the category of "friction ridge analysis": palm prints and sole prints.[212] The report found that the training of personnel to perform latent print identifications varies from agency to agency and can amount to only a one-week-long course. Not all agencies

208 *Id.* at 1265–67.
209 *Id.* at 1275.
210 Maryland v. Rose, No. K06-0545 (Balt. County Cir. Ct. 2007). The decision was overturned by a federal judge in United States v. Rose, No. CCB-08-0149, 2009 WL 4691612 (D. Md. Dec. 8, 2009).
211 NAS-2009 REPORT, *supra* note 3.
212 *Id.* at 5-7–5-14.

require that their staff acquire and maintain certification.[213] The technique used to examine prints is Analysis-Comparison-Evaluation-Verification (ACE-V).[214] In the Analysis stage, the examiner considers the following features: condition of the skin; type of residue, mechanics of touch, nature of the surface touched, development technique, capture technique, and size of the latent print. In the next stage, a visual comparison is made between the latent print and the known print (from the suspect). The examiner then performs an evaluation as to whether there is identification (source determination). Last, there is verification of the first examiner's findings by another qualified examiner, who repeats the observations and comes to a conclusion, although he or she may be aware of the conclusion arrived at by the first examiner. The NAS report describes the process and its problematic subjective aspects as follows:

> Note that the ACE-V method does not specify particular measurements or a standard test protocol, and examiners must make subjective assessments throughout. In the United States, the threshold for making a source identification is deliberately kept subjective, so that the examiner can take into account both the quantity and quality of comparable details. As a result, the outcome of a friction ridge analysis is not necessarily repeatable from examiner to examiner. In fact, recent research by Dror has shown that experienced examiners do not necessarily agree with even their own past conclusions when the examination is presented in a different context some time later.[215]

It is important to stress again in this context that the experts usually work with the police and have knowledge of details of the investigation, such as the fact that the suspect was identified by the victim. This extraneous knowledge is likely to influence the experts' subjective evaluations as to a match between the prints. The report notes further on this issue of subjectivity, that it

> is intrinsic to friction ridge analysis, as can be seen when comparing it with DNA analysis .... By contrast, before examining two fingerprints, one cannot say a priori which features should be compared .... For these reasons, population statistics for fingerprints have not been developed, and friction ridge analysis relies on subjective judgments by the examiner. Little research has

---

[213] *Id.* at 5–8.

[214] *Id.* at 5-8–5-10.

[215] *Id.* at 5-9–5-10. The report refers to Dror & Charlton, *supra* note 186, at 600–16.

been directed toward developing population statistics, although more would be feasible.[216]

A safety approach, however, would lead to this much-needed research, which should lead in turn to the design and implementation of objective standards.

On the matter of "methods of interpretation," the report found that

> [t]he clarity of the prints being compared is a major underlying factor .... Clearly, the reliability of the ACE-V process could be improved if specific measurement criteria were defined. Those criteria become increasingly important when working with latent prints that are smudged and incomplete, or when comparing impressions from two individuals whose prints are unusually similar.[217]

The report also referred to the reporting of results: "the friction ridge community actively discourages its members from testifying in terms of the probability of a match."

The report concurred[218] with Mnookin's observations, which she stated as follows:

> Experts therefore make only what they term "positive" or "absolute" identifications—essentially making the claim that they have matched the latent print to the one and only person in the entire world whose fingerprint could have produced it .... [S]uch claims ... are unjustified / .... Therefore, in order to pass scrutiny under Daubert, fingerprint identification experts should exhibit a greater degree of epistemological humility. Claims of "absolute" and "positive" identification should be replaced by more modest claims about the meaning and significance of a "match."[219]

In its "summary assessment," the report referred to Lyn Haber and Ralph Norman Haber's work,[220] where they showed that there is no scientific evidence of the validity of the ACE-V method. Examiners differ at each stage of the method in their conclusions, and no single protocol has been officially accepted by the profession;

---

[216] NAS-2009 REPORT, *supra* note 3, at 5–10.

[217] *Id.*

[218] *Id.* at 5-11–5-12.

[219] Jennifer L. Mnookin, *The Validity of Latent Fingerprint Identification: Confessions of a Fingerprinting Moderate*, 7 L. PROBABILITY & RISK 127 (2008).

[220] L. Haber & R.N. Haber, *Scientific Validation of Fingerprints Evidence under* Daubert, 7 LAW PROBABILITY & RISK 87 (2008).

therefore the validity of the ACE-V method cannot be tested. The report also noted that two legal decisions have highlighted the crucial issues of the lack of documentation and lack of data as to the error rate.[221] Another justified criticism of the latent print community is that examiners can too easily explain a "difference" as an "acceptable distortion" in order to make an identification.[222]

Finally, the report made a very important recommendation: the establishment of an independent federal agency to regulate, supervise, and improve forensic sciences, to be known as the National Institute for Forensic Science (NIFS).[223]

(4) The 2012 Expert Working Group Report

Perhaps the most significant development in this field of late is the 2012 National Institute of Standards and Technology report, entitled *Latent Print Examination and Human Factors: Improving the Practice through a Systems Approach—The Report of the Expert Working Group on Human Factors in Latent Print Analysis.*[224] The report's most noteworthy recommendation, consistent with the recommendations in the 2009 NAS report, is as follows:

> Because empirical evidence and statistical reasoning do not support a source attribution to the exclusion of all other individuals in the world, latent print examiners should not report or testify, directly or by implication, to a source attribution to the exclusion of all others in the world.[225]

Another important recommendation relates to the problematic and flawed use of automated fingerprint identification system (AFIS) search, as illustrated by the Brandon Mayfield case:

> When comparing latent prints to exemplars generated through AFIS searches, examiners must recognize the possibility and dangers of incidental similarity. Adjustments such as a higher decision threshold, stricter tolerances for differences in appearance, and explicit feature weighting need to be considered. Modified quality assurance practices for this scenario also should be considered.[226]

---

[221] New Hampshire v. Longill, 157 N.H. 77, 945 A.2d 1 (N.H. Apr. 4, 2008); Maryland v. Rose, No. K06-0545 (Md. Cir. Ct. Oct. 19, 2007).
[222] NAS-2009 REPORT, *supra* note 3, at 5–14.
[223] *Id.* at 5–14.
[224] Available at http://www.nist.gov/oles/upload/latent.pdf (last visited Sept. 13, 2014).
[225] *Id.* at 197.
[226] *Id.* at 199.

Other important recommendations in the report relate to reporting, documentation, and testimony, including the adoption of codes of ethics.[227] There is also a set of recommendations that stem from a safety approach, as proposed in this book. As explained in the report,

> Supervision of the staff members and management of the facilities are essential to risk reduction and quality assurance and control. Effective management requires good information about the incidence and sources of errors. Making the information available requires a culture in which both management and stuff understand that openness about errors is not necessarily a path to punitive sanctions ....[228]

Also in line with the safety approach I advocate adopting is the report's recommendations to improve staff training and education,[229] to provide proper facilities and equipment,[230] and to channel federal support to research efforts.[231]

(5) Summary and Recommendations

It is important to stress that I do not advocate generally ruling out the admissibility of fingerprint evidence.[232] Such a sweeping move, in my view,[233] would be decidedly misguided. This is indisputably significant and weighty evidence[234] that the courts should be allowed to continue to rely on. What is necessary, however, is that this type of evidence be improved and upgraded, and it must not be allowed to constitute the sole basis of a conviction.

In the current state of affairs, as described, there is essentially a lack of scientific grounding for fingerprint comparisons, and the possibility of a random match has never been refuted; more significant, courts are not presented with the error rates

---

[227] *Id.* at 200–01.

[228] *Id.* at 201.

[229] *Id.* at 202–03.

[230] *Id.* at 203.

[231] *Id.* at 203–06.

[232] I have stressed this as well elsewhere, with Dr. Halpert, in Sangero & Halpert, *supra* note 47, at 71.

[233] See, for example, claims that fingerprint evidence does not meet the criteria of the *Daubert* ruling, in Epstein, *supra* note 139.

[234] Computerized models have been developed in the field of pattern recognition, for the computerized comparison of fingerprints. *See* Joaquin Gonzalez-Rodriguez et al., *Bayesian Analysis of Fingerprint, Face and Signature Evidences with Automatic Biometric Systems,* 155 FORENSIC SCI. INT'L 126, 132–34 (2005). These models provide data on the error rate in various categories of test conditions for different systems. *Id.* Thus, computerized fingerprint evidence has an identification capability and enables the determination of an identification error rate. *See* Sangero & Halpert, *supra* note 47, at 71. There is still much to be done in this field, however.

of experts testifying before them. It is therefore almost shocking that this evidence plays such a main role in criminal trials and convictions. Even if the Random Mach Probability were proven to be very low (or even zero) and the error rate to be very low (but non-zero), a conviction beyond a reasonable doubt would still be impossible to establish based solely on this evidence.[235] Moreover, under the modern safety approach proposed in this book, it is necessary to strive to gather and present the most accurate evidence possible in a criminal investigation. Thus, there should be a rule requiring that examiners work for an independent federal agency and not under the authority of the law enforcement agencies. As I will explain below, forensic science evidence, including fingerprint comparisons, should not be admissible in court unless it has been developed as a safety-critical system. A substantial leap in this direction would be to adopt the recommendations made in the National Academy of Sciences 2009 report and the 2012 Expert Working Group report, including conducting research that will establish probabilities, rather than absolute results, and research on error rates and developing and implementing appropriate protocols for fingerprints comparison.[236]

Finally, we should also recall the possibility of transferring fingerprints of an innocent person to a crime scene by the wrongdoer or by a police officer in an effort to frame the innocent person. This possibility contributes to the lack of safety regarding fingerprint evidence.[237]

F. "JUNK SCIENCE" AS EVIDENCE

During the early modern period of history, from 1450 to 1750, the infamous "Satanic witch trials" were conducted in England, in which women were accused of witch-craft and worshipping the Devil. In order to prove the guilt of the accused, so-called experts were called upon, who searched—and often found—the "Devil's mark" on the women's bodies. In particular, they searched for the remains of what was known as the "witches' teat" by which the women purportedly nourished the Devil. These experts developed special methods for examining the women's bodies for these marks. The English courts admitted their testimony as evidence that proved guilt. Moreover,

---

[235] As Dr. Halpert and I have shown elsewhere, in Sangero & Halpert, *supra* note 47, at 71.

[236] NAS-2009 REPORT, *supra* note 3, at 5-7–5-14. *See also id.* s-23:

> Recommendation 12: Congress should authorize and appropriate funds for the National Institute of Forensic Science (NIFS) to launch a new broad-based effort to achieve nationwide fingerprint data interoperability. To that end, NIFS should convene a task force comprising relevant experts from the National Institute of Standards and Technology and the major law enforcement agencies …. And industry, as appropriate, to develop….

[237] For a discussion of such an Israeli case of transfering a fingerprint of the suspect to the crime scene by a police officer see SANGERO, *supra* note 4, at 190–91.

even when the Devil's mark could not be found on a woman's body, this was not regarded as a sign of innocence. The convicted women were punished by death.[238] The question that arises is: How far have we advanced since then? For it emerges that to this very day, certain types of evidence—such as microscopical hair comparisons, shoeprint comparisons, and voiceprint identification—which are deserving of the title "junk science"[239] unfortunately continue to be admitted by courts as evidence.[240]

The 2009 National Academy of Sciences report, which, as noted, is the leading authority in this field, reviewed in detail the various areas of microscopical comparison and comparisons based on an expert's subjective impression, and determined that none of these fields is currently grounded in science,[241] with the sole exception of DNA comparisons.[242]

The law is not a science—certainly not an exact one. In the law, crucial decisions are made in conditions of uncertainty. In scientific research, there is no need to reach a conclusion at a particular given moment, and the research can be continued until it reaches an advanced stage in which precise conclusions can be made. In the law, there is a need to arrive at a determination within a reasonable period of time, and it is not possible to wait interminably for more data and information. Science is considered to be precise, and therefore, it is no wonder that legal practitioners tend to go in pursuit of it. When police investigators, prosecutors, and judges base a defendant's guilt on scientific evidence, they feel more secure and convinced. When a piece of evidence is truly scientific—that is, well grounded in valid and reliable scientific research—their reliance on this evidence should be commended, so long as they are not blinded into putting everything else aside and according this evidence more weight that it warrants. As we saw, even the strongest scientific evidence

---

[238] ORNA ALYAGON DARR, MARKS OF AN ABSOLUTE WITCH (2011); SANGERO, *supra* note 4, at 125.

[239] Even though the expression "junk science" was in use already in the 1980s, it only achieved wider recognition in the legal world following the release of Peter W. Huber's book, GALILEO'S REVENGE: JUNK SCIENCE IN THE COURTROOM (1991), and his similarly entitled article, Peter W. Huber, *Junk Science in the Courtroom*, 26 VAL. U. L. REV. 723 (1992). At a certain point, the term came to be used also to describe forensic science that leads to many false convictions. *See, e.g.*, Paul C. Giannelli, *Junk Science: The Criminal Cases*, 84 J. CRIM. L. & CRIMINOLOGY 105 (1993); David Bernstein, *Junk Science in the United States and the Commonwealth*, 21 YALE J. INT'L L. 123 (1996); Thomas R. May, *Fire Pattern Analysis, Junk Science, Old Wives Tales, and Ipse Dixit: Emerging Forensic 3D Imaging Technologies to the Rescue?*, 16 RICH. J.L. & TECH. 13 (2010); Sangero & Halpert, *supra* note 6, at 427.

[240] Garrett & Neufeld, *supra* note 28; BARRY SCHECK ET AL., ACTUAL INNOCENCE: FIVE DAYS TO EXECUTION AND OTHER DISPATCHES FROM THE WRONGLY CONVICTED 158–71 (2000); Erica Beecher-Monas, *Blinded by Science: How Judges Avoid the Science in Scientific Evidence*, 71 TEMP. L. REV. 55 (1998); Saks & Koehler, *supra* note 25; GARRETT, *supra* note 13, at 84–117 (ch. 4: Flawed Forensics).

[241] NAS-2009 REPORT, *supra* note 3, at 161; SANGERO, *supra* note 4, at 127.

[242] NAS-2009 REPORT, *supra* note 3, at 7. "With the exception of nuclear DNA analysis, however, no forensic method has been rigorously shown to have the capacity to consistently, and with a high degree of certainty, demonstrate a connection between evidence and a specific individual or source."

today—DNA genetic comparisons and fingerprint comparisons—are not suffi-ciently strong to serve as the sole basis for proving guilt beyond a reasonable doubt (almost certainty). This is somewhat due to the possibility of a random match, but mostly to do with the far more probable likelihood of a lab error or error in an expert's analysis.[243]

This subsection is devoted to those types of evidence that are deceptively pre-sented as "scientific" when they in fact lack a sufficient scientific basis, and when, moreover, courts sometimes refer to them in their decisions as "scientific." Junk sci-ence disguised as true science is likely to mislead judges and jurors into thinking that this is actually scientific evidence and result in false convictions.[244]

The background to the present discussion is the two preceding discussions in this chapter on the admissibility and weight of forensic science evidence. I will consider an additional factor that contributes to courts' misguided admission of junk sci-ence as evidence, namely, the "Sherlock Holmes myth" and "CSI effect," and the misleading or erroneous presentation of evidence by police and prosecution experts.

An additional characterization of the forensic sciences field is necessary here, which is relevant also to evidence that is grounded in science, such as DNA com-parisons, but the development of fields of junk science constitutes the peak of the process. As there is no symmetry in criminal law and there is an uneven balance of power between the prosecution and defense, almost all the scientific evidence submitted in court is presented by the prosecution.[245] Even on the few occasions on which the defense counsel submits expert testimony, judges tend to prefer the testimony of the prosecution's expert witness.[246]

Crime laboratories, which engage in what is called "forensic science" and produce scientific evidence, are usually not autonomous but, rather, operate under the direct authority of the police and prosecution.[247] The laboratory personnel work closely and routinely with the police investigators and, at times, also with prosecutors, making it hard to expect them to be completely objective in performing their jobs. It is reasonable to assume that police investigators bring pressure to bear on lab staff to find evidence that supports the suspect's guilt. In addition, the police investigators

[243] SANGERO, *supra* note 4, at 128; Sangero & Halpert, *supra* note 47.

[244] SANGERO, *supra* note 4, at 129.

[245] An empirical study conducted in the United States found that court-appointed defense attorneys hire experts in only 2 percent of their criminal cases and in only 17 percent of their manslaughter cases. *See* Keith A. Findley & Michael S. Scott, *The Multiple Dimensions of Tunnel Vision in Criminal Cases*, 2006 WIS. L. REV. 291, 292, who refer to Michael McConville & Chestler L. Mirsky, *Criminal Defense of the Poor in New York City*, 15 N.Y.U. REV. L. & SOC. CHANGE 581, 764 (1986–1987). *See also* Sangero & Halpert, *supra* note 232, at 434.

[246] Garrett & Neufeld, *supra* note 28, at 90–91.

[247] *Id.* at 33; Difonzo, *supra* note 15, at 4–5.

feed the lab workers details of the investigation that are completely irrelevant to the tests they perform, but that reinforce the conception of the suspect's guilt, such as the fact that the suspect confessed or was identified by the victim.[248] Here, too, the misconception of the suspect's guilt plays a vital role: many in the law enforcement system tend to assume that the suspect is guilty and that they need simply find evidence that proves this.[249] At times, the job lab workers are requested to do, by very definition, is to conduct only tests that are likely to incriminate the suspect, without performing any other tests that could prove his innocence or even incriminate someone else.[250] At a later stage, the testimony of the expert is also likely to be misleading. Thus, for example, experts tend to testify to a significantly higher level of precision in the test that they performed than the real degree of precision according to the most up-to-date scientific research.[251]

Many judges are unaware of the possibility—which always exists—of a lab testing error and do not question the experts on this; the experts, for their part, often do not bother to volunteer such information. Moreover, with regard to the majority of the branches of "forensic science," even if the experts wanted to provide the court with information about the precision of the tests and their estimated error rate, they would not be able to do so due to the lack of research and data.[252]

In addition, the majority of the "forensic sciences" branches—particularly those in which experts testify on the comparisons they perform between marks at the crime scene and marks made by an object or limb belonging to the defendant—have been developed especially for the purpose of solving crimes: they were not developed by scientists. These branches are not, therefore, based on methodical scientific research with an adequate database but, rather, on experience gathered by "experts" through their use of the very system to solve crimes.[253]

It has been suggested that a distinction be drawn between "scientists" and "technicians."[254] To guarantee objectivity, scientists use "blind tests" to determine whether a particular result is correct or the product of contamination. In contrast, technicians usually know "how" but not "why." Many forensic fields fall into the sphere of technicians' work and not scientific work. Technicians, even when they are

---

[248] Thompson, *supra* note 20, at 1034.

[249] Findley & Scott, *supra* note 245, at 292 ("[F]ocus on a suspect, select and filter the evidence that will 'build a case' for conviction, while ignoring or suppressing evidence that points away from guilt."). See a more detailed discussion in Section VI of Chapter 3.

[250] Garrett & Neufeld, *supra* note 28, at 81–83.

[251] *Id.* at 84.

[252] SANGERO, *supra* note 4, at 106.

[253] *Id.* at 107. See also the details at the Innocence Project Website, www.innocenceproject.org.

[254] Craig M. Cooley, *Forensic Science or Forgettable Science?*, 80 INDIANA. L.J. 80, 81–82 (2005); SANGERO, *supra* note 4, at 107.

doing their job properly, lack the necessary scientific training to plan experiments that will turn their work into science. In addition, they lack the necessary databases for basing statistic calculations. In fact, many forensic areas were developed by law-enforcement agents, who, in their attempt to solve crimes and, often, to find incriminating evidence against the suspect, tended to turn unfounded premises of the individualization of certain crime scene marks into so-called science. Allegedly, if a mark found at the crime scene resembles the mark left by an object or limb belonging to the defendant, this necessitates the conclusion that the defendant's object or limb left the mark found at the crime scene. This is the case with regard to microscopical comparisons of hair, fibers, tool marks, weapon marks, shoeprints, teeth prints, and even ear prints.[255] The possibilities are limitless.

On the list of those responsible for this current state of shoddiness we should also include the great detective Sherlock Holmes, as D. Michael Risinger has suggested.[256] What do we all love about Sherlock Holmes? Among other things, he has contributed to the great faith we all have in the brain's ability to perpetually and precisely deduce the criminal's identity and how he acted from the evidence found at the crime scene. And, moreover, apparently not only the public at large but also forensic practitioners have been raised on the Sherlock Holmes myth. Similarly, many wrongly think that work of forensic labs is as perfect as it appears on the popular *CSI* television series, whose influence on jurors and other entities in the criminal justice system has been significant and harmful.[257]

Studies have uncovered the development of a nonscientific subculture in laboratories, out of an eagerness to please police investigators and "deliver the goods" rather than adhere to science, even if the results are not unequivocal and likely to disappoint those who believe that the suspect committed the crime and seek a way to convince the court of this.[258] This was the case in the infamous Houston crime lab scandal: the lab was closed down after it emerged that for many years, it had been systematically providing erroneous lab results, which had served as the basis for many convictions. The exposure of the scandal in 2002 on a television program left authorities no choice but to make a sweeping investigation of the matter. After many partial reports, a comprehensive report was finally released in 2007

---

[255] Beatrice Schiffer & Christophe Champod, *Judicial Error and Forensic Science: Pondering the Contribution of DNA Evidence, in* Wrongful Conviction: International Perspectives on Miscarriages of Justice 33–34, 37–38 (C. Ronald Huff & Martin Killias eds., 2008); Sangero, *supra* note 4, at 107.

[256] D. Michael Risinger, *Whose Fault?*—Daubert, *the NAS Report, and the Notion of Error in Forensic Science,* 38 Fordham Urban L.J. 519 (2010); Sangero, *supra* note 4, at 108.

[257] Difonzo, *supra* note 15, at 2–3 ("'CSI Effect,' popularly defined as 'the perception of the near-infallibility of forensic science in response to the TV show.'"); Mnookin, *supra* note 20, at 1209; Bolden, *supra* note 6, at 425; NAS-2009 Report, *supra* note 3, at 1-10-1-11.

[258] Saks & Koehler, *supra* note 25, at 892–95; Sangero, *supra* note 4, at 108.

regarding the laboratory's operation.[259] The investigation, which reviewed over a thousand cases, uncovered wrongdoing by nine different crime lab workers.[260] The investigation report pointed to a long list of malfunctions in the police lab's work, including: failure to perform appropriate control experiments in DNA testing, systematically misleading reporting regarding the statistical significance of DNA matches that were found, failure to report possibly exculpatory findings in suspects' favor, experts' misrepresentation and exaggeration of their credentials and training in court, misleading representation of findings, and even fabrication of findings. It was found that these practices had continued for an entire decade, until exposed on the television program.[261] Similar such malfunctioning was exposed at the Illinois state police crime lab and in the work of Texas forensic pathologist Ralph Erdmann, whose testimony contributed to at least twenty death-penalty convictions, and who was convicted of falsifying autopsies.[262]

One central problem is that some of the types of evidence submitted in the past to the court—and, in some cases, that continue to be presented—are based on forensic methods and techniques that are entirely unreliable, such as microscopical comparisons of hair, bite marks on the skin, shoeprints, and voiceprints. As clarified in the 2009 NAS report, and as many scientists have cautioned in their work, these identification methods have no scientific grounding, are not based on data, and are unreliable.[263]

A second central problem is that it emerged from the data collected in the framework of the Innocence Project that the majority (61 percent) of expert testimonies for the prosecution in the cases of false conviction were invalid and faulty; the experts had presented the findings of the tests that they had performed misleadingly and erroneously and had arriving at conclusions in an unscientific manner. This was the case with regard to both the unreliable types of evidence discussed above as well as reliable scientific evidence, such as DNA comparisons and serological blood-type tests. Common to the experts' errors in their testimonies was their biased presentation of the forensic evidence as stronger than it truly was in reality.[264]

Allegedly, due to the *Daubert* rule, judges should have become "gatekeepers," preventing the entry into the courtroom of evidence that is not scientifically reliable or

[259] MICHAEL BROMWICH ET AL., FINAL REPORT OF THE INDEPENDENT INVESTIGATOR FOR THE HOUSTON POLICE DEPARTMENT CRIME LABORATORY AND PROPERTY ROOM (June 13, 2007), *available at* http://www.hpdlabinvestigation.org/reports/070613report.pdf (last visited Sept. 15, 2014). *See also* SANGERO, *supra* note 4, at 108.

[260] Bolden, *supra* note 6, at 418.

[261] Thompson, *supra* note 20.

[262] Bolden, *supra* note 6.

[263] NAS-2009 REPORT, *supra* note 3; SANGERO, *supra* note 4, at 135.

[264] GARRETT, *supra* note 13, at 84–117; *see especially id.* at 90. *See also* Garrett & Neufeld, *supra* note 28; SANGERO, *supra* note 4, at 135–36.

valid. However, in reality, usually only the prosecution succeeds in submitting an expert opinion, which is usually incriminating, for defendants lack the necessary resources to submit expert opinions in their favor. As judges do not have expertise in all of the scientific or pseudoscientific fields presented to them, they are often misled by the prosecution's biased expert opinion, while the defense attorney lacks the tools for refuting it. It is interesting to note that in civil trials, especially tort lawsuits—which never involve capital cases or human liberty and tend to revolve solely around matters of money—judges delve far more deeply into the evidence presented as scientific, and here, in practice, function as gatekeepers and prevent junk science from being admitted at trial. How does this happen? In civil law, expert opinions are often submitted by both parties to the litigation—the plaintiff and the defendant—which allows the judge to compare and confront the evidence and make a far deeper investigation into its reliability and validity.[265] In criminal law, judges tend to rely on the prosecution's experts that they perform their work in line with precise scientific standards, and tend to rely on the defense attorneys to expose any imprecision in that work. Both of these assumptions are misplaced.[266]

An additional problem is that the professional expertise in the fields examined in crime laboratories is acquired in the framework of entities associated with the police and prosecution. The experts who testify at criminal trials are almost always prosecution witnesses and almost always work for the police. In effect, they see themselves as part of the law-enforcement system and consider their job to be to assist in finding evidence pointing to the suspect's guilt. Here, again, we witness the destructive effect of the conception of the suspect's guilt.[267]

An extreme example of such an "accomplished" expert was Fred Zain, the head of the West Virginian state crime lab. In the framework of the Innocence Project's work, it emerged that Zain would often falsify the results of tests to fabricate supposedly scientific evidence that would incriminate suspects. An investigation revealed that he had shamelessly lied in his testimonies as an expert before courts in thirteen different states in the United States and had manipulated test results in 134 different cases.[268] Moreover, Zain would often testify in court that he himself had performed the tests when in fact others had conducted them.[269]

---

[265] Beecher-Monas, *supra* note 240, at 56; David L. Faigman, *Admissibility Regimes: The "Opinion Rule" and Other Oddities and Exceptions to Scientific Evidence, the Scientific Revolution, and Common Sense*, 36 Sw. U. L. Rev. 699, 722 (2008); GARRETT, *supra* note 13, at 91; Kesan, *supra* note 11, at 2040.

[266] Garrett & Neufeld, *supra* note 28, at 97; SANGERO, *supra* note 4, at 136.

[267] See Section VI of Chapter 3, and SANGERO, *supra* note 4, at 136.

[268] Bolden, *supra* note 6, at 418.

[269] For a more detailed description of the Fred Zain case, see SCHECK, NEUFELD & DWYER, *supra* note 240, at 107–25. *See also* Paul C. Giannelli & Kevin C. McMunigal, *Prosecutors, Ethics, and Expert Witnesses*, 76 FORDHAM L. REV. 1494 1497–98 (2008); SANGERO, *supra* note 4, at 136–37.

Forensic experts do not perform their examinations as "blind tests"—that is, without knowledge of additional information about the investigation—and in fact often have been informed by police investigators on the details of the investigation. It is only natural, as human beings, that they are influenced by the knowledge that additional evidence exists supporting the suspect's guilt, such as his identification by the victim or confession to the police or even an additional piece of scientific evidence. All tests have the subjective component of the expert's assessment and interpretation of the findings. The knowledge that there are other pieces of evidence against the suspect is likely to bias the expert toward an incriminating interpretation of findings that are not unequivocal.[270] Moreover, in many cases, experts have been prevented from performing tests that are likely to rule out the suspect's involvement in the crime, and in other cases, the prosecution withheld from the defense findings pointing to the defendant's innocence. In their summations at trial, prosecutors often present the lab findings in a misleading and erroneous manner, so that they will be perceived as incriminating.[271]

Another phenomenon that has emerged is that those experts who give misleading and erroneous testimony are not merely a few "rotten apples" but rather are quite many in number. According to the findings of the Innocence Project, from among the 250 first exonerations obtained in the framework of the Project, 81 different experts, working in 54 different laboratories, in 28 different states across the United States, were found to have given faulty expert testimony.[272] This gives pause to think about the thousands of other trials at which these same experts testified but the convicted defendants have not been retried and, in all likelihood, will never be retried because, among other reasons, there are no genetic samples that can be tested in these cases.[273] Here, again, we feel the effect of the Hidden Accidents Principle in criminal law.

Even when (genuine) scientists indicate in their research that certain methods are in no way scientific and call for an improvement of laboratory work practices even with methods that are grounded in science (particularly genetic comparisons), forensic scientists tend to resist the recommendations for improvement. They are very used to the practices they learned in their training, have accepted them as

---

[270] GARRETT, *supra* note 13, at 92. On experts' biases, see also Itiel E. Dror et al., *Contextual Information Renders Experts Vulnerable to Making Erroneous Identifications*, 156 FORENSIC SCI. INT'L 74 (2006); Itiel E. Dror et al., *When Emotions Get the Better of Us: The Effect of Contextual Top-Down Processing on Matching Fingerprints*, 19 APPLIED COGNITIVE PSYCH. 799 (2005).

[271] GARRETT, *supra* note 13, at 108–09, 110–13. *See also* Garrett & Neufeld, *supra* note 28, at 34; SANGERO, *supra* note 4, at 138.

[272] GARRETT, *supra* note 13, at 93. For more detail, see Garrett &Neufeld, *supra* note 28, at 24.

[273] GARRETT, *supra* note 13, at 93; SANGERO, *supra* note 4, at 138–39.

correct, and followed them for many years; therefore they see these suggestions for change as a personal attack that they almost instinctively attempt to fight.[274]

Yet to reduce the number of false convictions that stem from faulty expert testimony, there is an urgent need for fundamental changes in this field. This includes: separating the forensics lab work from the police work, to enable forensic testing to be conducted in autonomous, objective labs; instituting "blind" expert checks, where the experts do not know that their work is being checked; requiring that experts base their work on data and provide the courts with precise data regarding tests' error rates; and adopting additional changes recommended in the National Academy of Sciences 2009 report.[275]

Finally, a technique that is particularly illustrative of "junk science" is microscopical hair comparison.[276] Herman Douglas May was seventeen years old in 1988 and had been involved in a few minor offenses, such as stealing a guitar from the truck of a man whom May alleged owed him money but refused to pay.[277] Around the time when May stole the guitar, a burglary was committed, during which a woman was raped. May was identified by the woman as the rapist in what was described as an unfairly suggestive identification procedure.[278] At trial, moreover, the forensic expert gave testimony against May, according to which hair found at the scene of the crime resembled May's hair, based on the expert's microscopic examination of the hair samples, and May could thus be the source of the hair at the crime scene.[279] May was convicted, and only twelve years later, after mitochondrial DNA testing was performed on both the sperm and hair found at the crime scene was it determined that he was not the rapist.[280] A similar, infamous case is the false conviction of Gary Dotson for a rape that had never occurred, based on the microscopical comparison of pieces of hair.[281]

---

[274] Risinger, *supra* note 256, at 535; Sangero & Halpert, *supra* note 6, at 442; Mnookin et al., *supra* note 159, at 744–60.

[275] NAS-2009 REPORT, *supra* note 3; SANGERO, *supra* note 4, at 139.

[276] Beth Albright & Debbie Davis, *Guilty until Proven Innocent: The Case of Herman Douglas May*, 30 N. KY. L. REV. 585, 586 (2003); Sangero & Halpert, *supra* note 6, at 447.

[277] Albright & Davis, *supra* note 276, at 586–87.

[278] *Id.* at 589. On the Supreme Court's lenient approach to suggestive identification and for criticism of this case law, see Gary L. Wells & Deah S. Quinlivan, *Suggestive Eyewitness Identification Procedures and the Supreme Court's Reliability Test in Light of Eyewitness Science: 30 Years Later*, 33 LAW HUM. BEHAV. 1 (2009).

[279] Albright & Davis, *supra* note 276, at 592.

[280] *Id.* at 599; Sangero & Halpert, *supra* note 6, at 447.

[281] At a later stage, the young woman confessed to having fabricated the rape and falsely accused Dotson, in an attempt to hide from her parents that she had had consensual sexual relations with her boyfriend (who was not Dotson). She also described the events in a book she wrote, CATHLEEN C. WEBB & MARIE CHAPIAN, FORGIVE ME (1985). For a detailed description of the case, including references, see GARRETT, *supra* note 13, at 84–89.

In twenty-one of the first seventy exonerations in which the Innocence Project was involved, erroneous testimony on the microscopical comparison of hair had been given.[282] In a later study, it emerged that in 75 of the Project's first 250 exonerations, the convictions had also been based on microscopic comparisons of hair,[283] and in 29 of these cases, erroneous expert testimony had been given. In eighteen of the cases, moreover, the experts had grounded their testimony on an individualization claim, that is to say, that the hair found at the scene of the crime was unique to the defendant.[284] In six of the exoneration cases, mitochondrial DNA testing ruled out the expert's assessment of a match between the hair at the scene of the crime and the defendant's hair.[285]

The method by which hair is microscopically compared has not changed much over the last century.[286] Hair (at times only a sole strand) found at the crime scene is compared to hair taken from the suspect. Routine practice is to take fifty strands of hair from the suspect when comparing head hair, and twenty-five pieces of hair when comparing to the hair from another part of the body.[287] In the first stage of the process, the expert makes a number of determinations with regard to the hair found at the crime scene:[288] whether it is, indeed, hair and not some other fiber; whether it is human hair or animal hair; the part of the body from which the hair comes from; the race of the person to whom the hair belongs; whether the hair has been dyed; whether the hair fell out naturally at the crime scene or was forcibly torn out; and whether the hair was cut. In the second stage, the expert examines the hair without using any instrument, to determine its color and structure (straight, wavy, or curly). The third stage is when the expert examines the hair with a microscope and determines a set of characteristics, which are then compared to the same characteristics of the suspect's hair. These characteristics relate to hair color, structure, the structure of the hair follicle, and acquired features, such as cosmetic treatments or flaws in the hair.[289]

However, these characteristics are not the same for all of a person's hair. And as they can vary on one person, there is a broad overlap in the characteristics of the hair of different people. Therefore, this type of comparison between pieces of hair

---

[282]   Albright & Davis, *supra* note 276, at 592; Sangero & Halpert, *supra* note 6, at 447–48.

[283]   GARRETT, *supra* note 13, at 95.

[284]   *Id.* at 47.

[285]   *Id.* at 51.

[286]   Walter F. Rowe, *The Current Status of Microscopical Hair Comparisons*, 1 SCIENTIFIC WORLD 867, 868 (2001); Sangero & Halpert, *supra* note 6, at 448.

[287]   NAS-2009 REPORT, *supra* note 3, at 157.

[288]   Paul C. Giannelli, *Microscopic Hair Comparisons: A Cautionary Tale*, 46 CRIM. L. BULL. 531(2010).

[289]   Rowe, *supra* note 286, at 867. For more details, see SCIENTIFIC WORKING GROUP ON MATERIALS ANALYSIS (SWGMAT), FORENSIC HUMAN HAIR EXAMINATION GUIDELINES 10.1–10.5 (2005) [hereinafter SWGMAT]; Sangero & Halpert, *supra* note 6, at 448.

from two different people often points to an—alleged—match. In addition, as this comparison entails subjective determinations, different experts are likely to arrive (and do arrive) at conflicting conclusions.[290] There is no possibility of determining individuality on the basis of a microscopic comparison of pieces of hair, and the probabilistic strength of such evidence is unknown. On this subject, the National Academy of Sciences stated as follows[291]:

> No scientifically accepted statistics exist about the frequency with which particular characteristics of hair are distributed in the population. There appear to be no uniform standards on the number of features on which hairs must agree before an examiner may declare a "match."

It further stated in the same report:[292]

> In cases where there seems to be a morphological match (based on microscopic examination), it must be confirmed using mtDNA analysis, microscopic studies alone are of limited probative value. The committee found no scientific support for the use of hair comparisons for individualization in the absence of nuclear DNA.

Today, a genetic comparison of hair can be performed, which is very precise and can be used to test the (weak) strength of the microscopic comparisons conducted in the past. There are two types of genetic tests. The first tests the DNA found in the cell in the root of the hair.[293] This test is the preferred one as, aside from identical twins, no two people share the same DNA. However, often, the hair root is not available for testing. In such circumstances, the second type of test can be performed: mitochondrial DNA testing. The working hypothesis is that mitochondrial DNA is maternally inherited.[294] Were it not for the occurrence of mutations, everyone would have identical mitochondrial DNA; but mutations have led to differentiations across population groups. Thus, mitochondrial testing can rule out the possibility that the suspect committed the crime, but cannot determine the identity of the actual perpetrator, as many people share the same mitochondrial DNA, passed on to them through a shared matrilineal line.

---

[290] GARRETT, *supra* note 13, at 49; Sangero & Halpert, *supra* note 6, at 448.

[291] NAS-2009 REPORT, *supra* note 3, at 160.

[292] *Id.* at 161.

[293] SWGMAT, *supra* note 289; Sangero & Halpert, *supra* note 6, at 449.

[294] Alice R. Isenberg & Jodi M. Moore, *Mitochondrial DNA Analysis at the FBI Laboratory*, 1 FORENSIC SCI. COMM. (1999); Richard E. Giles et al., *Maternal Inheritance of Human Mitochondrial DNA*, 77 PROC. NATI. ACAD. SCI. USA 6715 (1980); Sangero & Halpert, *supra* note 6.

The only circumstances in which some probative strength can be accorded to microscopical hair comparisons is when a suspect can be ruled out as the perpetrator of the crime.[295] The National Academy of Sciences 2009 report stated the following regarding this possibility:[296]

> The results of analyses from hair comparisons typically are accepted as class associations; that is, a conclusion of a "match" means only that the hair could have come from any person whose hair exhibited—within some levels of measurement uncertainties—the same microscopic characteristics, but it cannot uniquely identify one person. However, this information might be sufficiently useful to "narrow the pool" by excluding certain persons as sources of the hair.

A general consensus has been reached that microscopical hair comparisons are junk science.[297] This realization was possible due to the development of genetic comparisons, which proved conclusively that microscopical comparisons are far from being scientific. One of the lessons that should be learned from this development is the definite possibility that courts will admit nonscientific evidence as scientific evidence and even convict on the basis of that evidence. The problem is that there are still areas in which the courts treat junk science like true science, and there is no possibility of providing compelling proof (through DNA testing or any other strong, concurred-upon technique) that the method is not scientific and must not be relied upon in a criminal trial. This is the case with voice comparisons and shoe-print comparisons.[298]

I have discussed the critical problems with junk science and elaborated on some of the changes necessary to make forensic evidence a more precise and scientific field, so as to improve the factual determinations in criminal trials and prevent judges from being misled. As an intermediate remedy—until the necessary fundamental changes are implemented—the courts must be more rigorous in examining "scientific evidence" brought before them and not admit dubious evidence warranting the label "junk science." In line with the *Daubert* rule, for a given type of evidence to be admissible, it must meet accepted scientific standards and be reliable, valid, and testable but, of course, unrefuted. In addition, in light of past experience, the courts must regard experts testifying before them with measured suspicion and not put blind faith in their testimony.

---

[295] Giannelli, *supra* note 288 ("There is also agreement that, with sufficient exemplars, a person may be excluded as a suspect."); Sangero & Halpert, *supra* note 6, at 451.

[296] NAS-2009 REPORT, *supra* note 3, at 156.

[297] *See, e.g.*, Scheck, Neufeld & Dweyer, *supra* note 240, at 161–63; Sangero & Halpert, *supra* note 6, at 451–52.

[298] I have elaborated on this at length in a coauthored article with Dr. Mordechai Halpert, at Sangero & Halpert, *supra* note 6.

To conclude this discussion of the phenomenon of "junk science" and its hazards, I would like to propose a simple test that will assist judges in distinguishing between an area that is most certainly not scientific and one that could be scientific but must be more deeply examined in line with the *Daubert* rule. I call this test the "MIT test" (Massachusetts Institute of Technology). I came up with this test recently, while giving a lecture on "Scientific Evidence versus 'Junk Science'" to Israeli judges at a workshop. At the end of the lecture, the judge who had organized the workshop thanked me and recounted that because I "go against the flow," he had deliberated whether to schedule my lecture at the beginning of the week-long workshop or at the end. I responded by telling the judges that this was not the important issue, and what is actually far more relevant is that almost all of the workshop lecturers were from the police forensic lab practitioners. I suggested to the judges that they learn about scientific evidence not from police lab technicians but from members of the academia: professors from the Weizmann Science Institute or from the *Technion*, which are the Israeli counterparts of MIT.

The judge who had organized the workshop regretfully noted that research work is not being conducted in the universities on each and every one of the forensic fields. I immediately proposed the following to the audience of judges: "This, then, is an easily applied selection-test, which can assist you judges in preventing junk science from entering your courts: when a piece of so-called 'scientific evidence' is submitted to you but is not researched at the Weizmann Institute or *Technion*, this is proof that it is not science!"

I propose that American judges can apply the same test, simply substituting in MIT for the Weizmann Institute and *Technion*. Of course, this does not mean that any alleged expertise based on a field in which there is meaningful academic work should be automatically admitted as scientific evidence. But in the absence of academic interest and work, we can be certain that this is not science. This "MIT test" is an easy selection test relative to the *Daubert* rule, for it avoids both the complicated application of the *Daubert* standard and the embarrassment of the incorrect application of the tests by judges.[299] If the courts were to apply such test, they would never admit as scientific evidence opinions submitted by charlatan

---

[299] On the incorrect application of the *Daubert* rule by the courts, see Mnookin et al., *supra* note 159, at 758–59:

> [E]ven after Daubert ... emphasized the need for judicial gatekeeping to assure the validity of expert evidence in court, most judges confronted with pattern identification evidence have continued to admit it without restriction. If courts are not going to insist upon better evidence of validity, if they are instead going to continue to permit forensic scientists to reach extremely strong conclusions about their own abilities to make identifications, and if legal challenges remain both relatively rare and generally unsuccessful, then why should the forensic science community consider changing its practices?

experts with regard to microscopical hair comparisons, shoeprint comparisons, and voice comparisons, nor would they convict and send to prison defendants based on other "junk science" evidence.

III. Safety Measures

A. DEVELOPING FORENSIC SCIENCE EVIDENCE AS A SAFETY-CRITICAL SYSTEM

Based on a single piece of DNA evidence that was obtained when a sample was run through a database, Daryl Mack was convicted of murder and sentence to death;[300] he was executed on April 26, 2006.[301] Yet there is a possibility, even if low, of erroneous findings being produced by the computer software used in the DNA comparison, just as a lab testing error is possible.[302] This is only one context in which forensic evidence can put the life of an innocent person at risk. As Dr. Halpert and I have shown elsewhere, any device used to produce forensic evidence is fundamentally a "safety-critical system" in that it endangers human life.[303] Studies have demonstrated how erroneous scientific evidence occasionally leads to false convictions,[304] and this is no less catastrophic than a car brakes failure. Yet no mandatory regulation is in place—with regard to any forensic evidence whatsoever—to supervise forensic software or device development in accordance with safety-critical standards, despite the broad implementation of such regulations in other fields involving life-and-death.[305]

In previous chapters, we have seen that the outdated "Fly-Fix-Fly" method[306] is not a sufficient safety system, and that "black box" testing[307] does not suffice either. Thus, it is mandatory that devices producing forensic science evidence be developed using safety methods that are suited to their nature as safety-critical systems.[308] However, the greater hazard is that not even the Fly-Fix-Fly method has been implemented in the criminal justice system.[309] When the manufacturer of a forensic evidence equipment (such as a breathalyzer) markets a device that occasionally produces erroneous results due to a design or software defect, the chances that a court will detect the error are slim. In contrast, an airplane with a safety

---

[300] Mack v. State, 75 P.3d 803 (Nev. 2003); Halpert & Sangero, *supra* note 2, at 83.

[301] Halpert & Sangero, *supra* note 2, at 83.

[302] See Section II(D) in Chapter 5.

[303] Halpert & Sangero, *supra* note 2, at 83.

[304] See Section II in Chapter 5.

[305] Halpert & Sangero, *supra* note 2, at 83.

[306] See Section I in Chapter 2.

[307] See Section IX in Chapter 2

[308] Halpert & Sangero, *supra* note 2.

[309] *Id.* at 85.

defect will necessarily be involved in an accident or incident (a "near miss") at some point in time, and the defect will be exposed. This is not the case with flaws in forensic-evidence-producing devices. If an innocent defendant is convicted based on erroneous scientific evidence (assuming that the law allows a conviction to be based on a single piece of evidence[310]), his claim of innocence will not be considered a refutation of the reliability of the forensic device, and the chances of proving a testing error are low. In addition, many view a conviction to be in itself confirmation of the device's reliability. Therefore, to prevent or minimize the possibility of errors in forensic equipment, great precautions must be taken in the design and manufacturing processes. Due to the Hidden Accidents Principle, these are the only stages at which there is a reasonable possibility of discovering and avoiding defects.[311]

A forensic device developed in accordance with safety-critical standards can be expected to produce more precise and reliable scientific evidence.[312] To begin with, there will be fewer false positives—that is, fewer cases in which an innocent suspect or defendant is implicated by erroneous test results in a crime she did not commit. In addition, there will be fewer false negatives as well, in which a test or device erroneously rules out the actual perpetrator of the crime being investigated. This, of course, would lead to more efficient criminal law enforcement, making the safety-improvement of forensic devices a win-win situation.

Finally, legislators should enact regulation of the development process of forensic equipment designed to be used by the criminal justice system.[313] An approval requirement should be set for manufacturers of forensic devices similar to what is required of manufacturers of medical diagnostic devices.[314] Legislators should also set a rule for the admissibility of evidence produced by a forensic device in criminal proceedings requiring that the device be developed and supervised as a safety-critical system.[315]

B. OTHER SAFETY CHANGES IN SCIENTIFIC EVIDENCE

What changes and reforms must the forensic sciences undergo in order to contribute to the legal field without misleading it? A number of recommendations to this end were made in the National Academy of Sciences (NAS) 2009 report,[316] the

---

[310] See Section IV in Chapter 3.
[311] As Dr. Halpert and I have shown in Halpert & Sangero, *supra* note 2, at 77–82, the special legal proceedings in *Chun* concerning the breathalyzer exemplify this well.
[312] *Id.* at 89.
[313] *Id.* at 93.
[314] See Section X in Chapter 2.
[315] Halpert & Sangero, *supra* note 2, at 93–94.
[316] NAS-2009 REPORT, *supra* note 3.

National Association of Criminal Defense Lawyers (NACDL) report from 2010,[317] and various research studies.[318]

(1) The NAS 2009 report recommended establishing a National Institute of Forensic Science (NIFS),[319] with a similar recommendation made also in the 2010 NACDL report.[320] This Institute could be easily integrated into the Safety in the Criminal Justice System Institute (SCJSI) when established.[321]

Whether in the guise of the NIFS or the general SCJI, such a federal agency should be tasked with the following: to set and enforce best practices for forensic science, to set standards for mandatory accreditation of forensic laboratories and mandatory certification for forensic examiners, to improve research and educational programs, to establish a standard terminology to be used in reporting and testing and model laboratories reports, and so on.[322]

(2) A very important recommendation made in the NAS 2009 report was achieving autonomy and objectivity by removing all public forensic laboratories from the administrative control of law enforcement agencies.[323] In this context, it is crucial to ensure that all laboratory personnel receive only the minimal information required for performing the testing and that they be given no additional details about the suspect (optimally, they should not even know that the sample has been taken from a suspect) or about the case that are likely to bias them in performing the test.[324]

(3) Some of the more important recommendations in the NAS 2009 report related to research development: the promotion of scholarly, competitive peer-reviewed research regarding the validity of forensic methods and accuracy of forensic analyses and data collection, as well as research on human observer bias and sources of human error in forensic testing.[325] In the wake of this report, thirteen different experts, from both sides of

---

[317] Nat'l Ass'n of Criminal Defense Lawyers (NACDL), Principles and Recommendations to Strengthen Forensic Evidence and Its Presentation in the Courtroom (Austin, Texas, 2010) [hereinafter NACDL-2010 Report], *available at* www.nacdl.org/WorkArea/DownloadAsset. aspx?id=17775 (last visited Sept. 18, 2014).

[318] Halpert & Sangero, *supra* note 2; Sangero & Halpert, *supra* note 84.

[319] NAS-2009 Report, *supra* note 3, S-14 (Recommendation 1).

[320] NACDL-2010 Report, *supra* note 318, at 3–4.

[321] Sangero & Halpert, *supra* note 318, at 1324.

[322] NAS-2009 Report, *supra* note 3, S-14–S-17 (Recommendations 1–3).

[323] *Id.* at S-17.

[324] *See supra* text accompanying notes 182–188.

[325] NAS-2009 Report, *supra* note 3, S-14–S-18 (Recommendations 1, 3, 5).

the fence—forensic science professionals and academic scholars—joined together to write an article aimed at setting a framework for research culture in the forensic sciences.[326] Their conclusion was as follows:

> We all believe that many forms of forensic science today stand on an insufficiently developed empirical research foundation. We all believe that forensic science does not yet have a well-developed research culture. These disciplines, in our view, need to increase their commitment to empirical evidence as the basis for their claims. Sound research, rather than experience and training, must become the central method by which assertions are justified.[327]

In response to the question, "What is a research culture?," the experts explained that it is

> a culture in which the question of the relationship between research-based knowledge and laboratory practices is both foregrounded and central. We mean a culture in which the following questions are primary: What do we know? How do we know that? How sure are we about that? We mean a culture in which these questions are answered by reference to data, to published studies, and to publicly accessible materials, rather than primarily by reference to experience or craft knowledge, or simply assumed to be true because they have long been assumed to be true.[328]

To this important explanation, I would add that the need for a culture of research in forensic science would be clear to all if there were a culture of safety in the criminal justice system.

(4) Accreditation and certification: There should be mandatory laboratory accreditation and individual certification of forensic science professionals.[329]

(5) A code of ethics: The NAS 2009 report recommended that the NIFS establish a national code of ethics for forensic science and mechanisms for its enforcement.[330]

---

[326] Jennifer L. Mnookin, Simon A. Cole, Itiel E. Dror, Barry A. J. Fisher, Max M. Houck, Keith Inman, David H. Kaye, Jonathan J. Koehler, Glenn Langenburg, D. Michael Risinger, Norah Rudin, Jay Siegel, and David A. Stoney, *The Need for a Research Culture in the Forensic Sciences*, 58 UCLA L. REV. 725 (2011).

[327] *Id.* at 778.

[328] *Id.* at 740.

[329] NAS-2009 REPORT, *supra* note 3, S-19 (Recommendation 8).

[330] *Id.* at S-19 (Recommendation 9).

(6) Education and training: The NAS 2009 report also recommended taking measures to attract students in the physical and life sciences to pursuing graduate studies in multidisciplinary fields critical to the practice of forensic science. Moreover, law students, law practitioners, and judges should be encouraged to acquire basic knowledge in these fields.[331]

The 2010 report of the National Association of Criminal Defense Lawyers (NACDL), which is based on the 2009 NAS report, offered more specific and detailed recommendations, as well as adding some new crucial recommendations. These recommendations can be divided into seven major areas:

(1) The establishment and funding of a central, science-based federal agency: The primary and central reform suggested is that Congress establish and allocate funds for a science-based federal agency, for the purpose of promoting "the development of forensic science into a field of multidisciplinary research and practice founded on the systematic creation, collection, and analysis of relevant data." Validated and reliable forensic evidence is an important and vital component of the criminal justice system, and its development should be encouraged. Moreover, "the results of any forensic theory or technique whose validity, limitations, and measures of uncertainty have not been established should not be admitted into evidence" in a criminal trial, and prior admissibility or use of the results of a forensic discipline, technique, or theory is not conclusive proof of their validity or reliability. Accordingly, one of the agency's central and immediate priorities should be generating research programs for determining the validity, limitations, and measures of uncertainty of forensic theories or techniques, particularly with regard to forensic evidence that supposedly identifies any specific individual as being involved in a crime scene. This was followed by detailed recommendations regarding staffing, scope of responsibilities, board of accreditation and certification, and a proficiency testing program.[332]

(2) Establishing a culture of science. The principle here is that "a culture of science that encourages independence, openness, objectivity, error management, and critical review should be promoted in forensic science practitioners and facilities." This culture already exists among many forensic science practitioners and facilities, but a fundamental commitment to a culture of science should exist among *all* facilities and *all* practitioners.

---

[331]   *Id.* at S-20 (Recommendation 10).
[332]   NACDL-2010 Report, *supra* note 317, at 3–4.

This was accompanied with detailed recommendations regarding autonomy, openness, objectivity, error management, and critical review.[333]

(3) Setting a national code of ethics: The report expressed the principle that "all forensic science practitioners and supervisors should be required to adhere to a professional code of ethics that clearly articulates ethical obligations and contains a meaningful enforcement mechanism." The detailed recommendations in this context relate to continuing education, acknowledgment of subjectivity, disclosure obligations, and enforcement.[334]

(4) The institution of a prerequisite of research: The report recommended establishing and fully funding research programs relating to the accuracy, reliability, and validity of forensic theories and techniques and their limitations and measures of uncertainty where calculable, to be led and conducted principally by credentialed and qualified scientists at national research institutions with forensic science practitioners, particularly "those guided by a culture-of-science mindset and with histories of independence from law enforcement," as active research participants and partners. Detailed recommendations were further given relating to determination of probability associations, relationship between research studies and case work, critical review, errors rates, automated techniques, minimizing bias, and documentation.[335]

(5) Improvement of education: The report noted that legal professionals generally lack the necessary scientific expertise and knowledge to understand and assess forensic evidence in an informed way. Thus, legal practitioners and judges must receive meaningful education and training "in the fundamentals of science, statistics, and common forensic practices and in the limitations of and potential forms and scope of error associated with those practices." The detailed recommendations related to law students, lawyers, and judges, as well as educational resources.[336]

(6) The principle of transparency and disclosure: Transparency is vital to a fair and effective criminal justice system and "the hallmark of good science." An attorney's ability to evaluate, investigate, present, and confront forensic evidence at trial is contingent on complete and timely disclosure of information about the forensic examination, the conclusions of the forensic science practitioner, and the facility where the examination was conducted. "In every case involving forensic evidence, regardless of the current state of the science and/or advancements made, both the prosecution

---

[333] *Id.* at 4–6.
[334] *Id.* at 6–7.
[335] *Id.* at 7–10.
[336] *Id.* at 10–11.

and the defense will require full access to the forensic evidence and underlying data related to a particular case." The detailed recommendations here related to transparency of forensic facility operations, ethical requirements, disclosure obligations, access to research and litigants, minimum disclosure requirements, reports, and databases.[337]

(7) Allocating defense resources, particularly for indigent defense services:

The principle articulated in this context is that "forensic reform must be viewed within the framework of the fundamental constitutional protections established to ensure fair and accurate verdicts based on trustworthy evidence and to prevent wrongful convictions." The prosecution tends to be the "primary proponent of forensic evidence," but defense attorneys also sometimes use forensic evidence at trial. The report noted that many exonerations of innocently convicted defendants have been based on forensic evidence submitted by defense counsel. Defense counsel should, thus, be able to consult with forensic experts and experts in related scientific fields to present in court the scientific limits of the evidence, the results of independent testing, and the testimony of independent experts when appropriate. It was therefore recommended that the defense be ensured the necessary resources for obtaining such assistance from forensic and scientific experts and for the use of forensic facilities for independent, confidential testing. Indigent defendants, like defendants with financial means, moreover, should be ensured access to assistance from appropriate experts. The detailed recommendations addressed the topics of indigent defense, experts, consultation, and confidential testing.[338]

To the important and detailed recommendations made in the reports of the NAS and NACDL, I would add two general recommendations that implement two fundamental safety rules, on which I have elaborated at great length in this book and elsewhere with Dr. Mordechai Halpert, and a third, unique recommendation, which I raised here for the first time.

The first safety recommendation is that a legal rule must be set that precludes convicting on the basis of any single piece of evidence.[339] The rationale for this rule is that errors arise in every scientific test and that the possibility of an error, which is not negligible, prevents proof of guilt beyond a reasonable doubt on the basis of a single piece of evidence.

---

[337] *Id.* at 11–14.
[338] *Id.* at 14–16.
[339] Sangero & Halpert, *supra* note 47. See also Section IV of Chapter 3.

The second safety recommendation relates to regulation: manufacturers of forensic scientific equipment and forensic labs must be subject to safety regulation similar to the FDA's regulation of manufacturers of medical equipment and medical laboratories. The role of regulating scientific evidence must be shifted from judges to professional regulators with expertise in the relevant scientific fields,[340] which is standard practice in other areas with regard to safety-critical systems.

The third safety recommendation is the adoption of the "MIT test" I proposed above in discussing the distinction between scientific evidence and junk science. Under this selection-test, which would precede the *Daubert* examination of evidence presented as scientific, if there is no systematic scientific academic work in the relevant field, then the evidence is not scientific.

Finally, further recommendations for improving forensic evidence should be developed by the proposed Safety in the Criminal Justice System Institute.

In line with the principles of safety, these recommendations must not, of course, be assumed to be exhaustive or necessarily well-suited to their goals. Rather there is a need to revisit and check them after they have been implemented, to verify whether each one attains its objective, all in an attempt for unending improvement, as is accepted practice in the area of modern safety.

IV. Confessions

A. CURRENT UNSAFETY

(1) The Hazard of False Confessions

In the past, courts tended to view a defendant's confession, even when extracted by police interrogators, as very strong evidence that is (and should be) sufficient to attain a conviction.[341] The rationale was that a voluntary confession is the product of an overwhelming sense of guilt.[342] Moreover, a confession is viewed as superior to any other type of evidence as direct evidence of guilt.[343] Thus, the confession has been crowned the "queen of evidence."[344]

---

[340] Halpert & Sangero, *supra* note 2, at 83.

[341] Boaz Sangero, Miranda *Is Not Enough: A New Justification for Demanding "Strong Corroboration" to a Confession*, 28 CARDOZO L. REV. 2791, 2794–800 (2007); Stephen C. Thaman, Miranda *in Comparative Law*, 45 ST. LOUIS U. L.J. 581, 581 (2001) ("Historically, confessions of guilt have been the 'best evidence in the whole world.'"); Talia Fischer & Issachar Rosen-Zvi, *The Confessional Penalty*, 30 CARDOZO L. REV. 871, 872 (2008).

[342] King v. Warickshall, (1783) 168 Eng. Rep. 234 (K.B.); Sparf v. United States, 156 U.S. 51, 55 (1895).

[343] Paul G. Cassell, Miranda's *Social Costs: An Empirical Reassessment*, 90 Nw. U. L. REV. 387, 441 (1996).

[344] Significant support for the belief that the confession is the "queen of evidence" can be attributed to Andrey Vyshinsky, Prosecutor General of the Soviet Union and the legal mastermind behind Stalin's Great Purge during the late 1930s. *See* Harold J. Berman, *Introduction*, SOVIET CRIMINAL LAW AND

Yet many studies have pointed to the phenomenon of false confessions.[345] According to the findings of studies conducted by the Innocence Project, of the first 225 cases in which DNA testing proved a conviction to be false, about one-quarter of those convictions had been based on a (presumably false) confession (23 percent of the exonerations).[346] Moreover, the National Registry of Exonerations includes 178 exonerations in cases in which the defendant had confessed.[347] Thus, on this background, skeptics can no longer continue to call into doubt the occurrence of false confessions.[348]

Other researchers have revealed the significant extent to which wrongful convictions based on false confessions occur.[349] Indeed, in only a small proportion of cases in which a claim of wrongful conviction is made do the necessary physical conditions exist to enable DNA testing. Accordingly, it can be inferred from those cases in which DNA testing has proven a false conviction that there are in fact many more such cases of wrongful conviction,[350] which go undetected due to the Hidden Accidents Principle in criminal law. Given this unequivocal evidence of numerous false convictions based on wrongful confessions given during police interrogations, I have suggested crowning this type of confession the "empress of wrongful convictions."[351]

PROCEDURE: THE RSFSR CODES 92 (Harold J. Berman & James W. Spindler trans., 1966); IDEAS AND FORCES IN SOVIET LEGAL HISTORY: A READER ON THE SOVIET STATE AND LAW 288 (Zigurds L. Zile ed., 1992).

[345]   Sangero, *supra* note 341, at 2795.

[346]   See http://www.innocenceproject.org (last visited Aug. 1, 2014); SCHECK, NEUFELD & DWYER, *supra* note 240; Keith A. Findley, *Learning from Our Mistakes: A Criminal Justice Commission to Study Wrongful Convictions*, 38 CAL. W. L. REV. 333 (2002); Brandon L. Garrett, *Judging Innocence*, 108 COLUM. L. REV. 55, 76 (2008).

[347]   THE NATIONAL REGISTRY OF EXONERATIONS, EXONERATIONS BY CONTRIBUTING FACTOR, https://www.law.umich.edu/special/exoneration/Pages/ExonerationsContribFactorsByCrime.aspx (last visited Sept. 1, 2014).

[348]   Richard J. Ofshe & Richard A. Leo, *The Decision to Confess Falsely: Rational Choice and Irrational Action*, 74 DENV. U. L. REV. 979, 983 (1997); Steven A. Drizin & Marissa J. Reich, *Heeding the Lessons of History: The Need for Mandatory Recording of Police Interrogations to Accurately Assess the Reliability and Voluntariness of Confessions*, 52 DRAKE L. REV. 619, 634 (2004); Marcy Strauss, *The Sounds of Silence: Reconsidering the Invocation of the Right to Remain Silent under Miranda*, 17 WM. & MARY BILL RTS. J. 773, 809 (2009).

[349]   Hugo Adam Bedau & Michael L. Radelet, *Miscarriages of Justice in Potentially Capital Cases*, 40 STAN. L. REV. 21, 56–63 (1987); Richard A. Leo & Richard J. Ofshe, *The Consequences of False Confessions: Deprivations of Liberty and Miscarriages of Justice in the Age of Psychological Interrogation*, 88 J. CRIM. L. & CRIMINOLOGY 429 (1998); Stephen A. Drizin & Richard A. Leo, *The Problem of False Confessions in the Post-DNA World*, 82 N.C. L. REV. 891, 911 (2004).

[350]   Leo & Ofshe, *supra* note 349, at 431–32; Steven B. Duke, *Does Miranda Protect the Innocent or the Guilty?*, 10 CHAP. L. REV. 551, 566 (2007); Sangero, *supra* note 341, at 2797; Fischer & Rosen-Zvi, *supra* note 341, at 875.

[351]   Sangero, *supra* note 341, at 2800.

A confession of guilt is, in itself, an unusual phenomenon. A confession is prima facie suspicious evidence, for it works against the confessor's interests in exposing him to conviction and punishment. The premise is that a rational suspect will only confess if faced by overwhelming evidence against him or offered promises from the police or prosecution of a lenient punishment, or out of a belief that confessing is in fact to his benefit.[352] In contrast, confession should normally be considered suspicious and irrational when there is no significant evidence against the confessor, and no apparent reward was offered for confessing.[353]

Three different classifications of false confessions have been proposed in the psychology literature: voluntary confessions, coerced-internalized confessions, and coerced-compliant confessions.[354] The voluntary category refers to cases in which an individual turns herself into the police of her own initiative and incriminates herself in a crime she did not commit.[355] This phenomenon is most prominent in high-profile cases, such as the Lindbergh baby kidnapping in 1938, when two hundred people voluntarily confessed to the crime,[356] and the 1947 Elizabeth Short murder, to which over fifty people confessed voluntarily.[357] Various reasons have been offered to explain this type of confession, such as a pathological need for attention or self-punishment, a sense of guilt or delusions, a perception of tangible gain from confessing, or the aim to protect someone else.[358] This category of voluntary confessors also includes people who cannot differentiate between fantasy and reality; who wish to atone for past, prohibited behavior (real or imagined); or who have self-destructive tendencies.[359]

---

[352] Daniel J. Seidmann & Alex Stein, *The Right to Silence Helps the Innocent: A Game-Theoretic Analysis of the Fifth Amendment Privilege*, 114 HARV. L. REV. 430, 464 (2000); Lawrence Rosenthal, *Against Orthodoxy: Miranda Is Not Prophylactic and the Constitution Is Not Perfect*, 10 CHAP. L. REV. 579, 587 (2007); Boaz Sangero & Mordechai Halpert, *Proposal to Reverse the View of a Confession: From Key Evidence Requiring Corroboration to Corroboration for Key Evidence* 44 U. MICH. J. L. REFORM 511 (2011); Sangero, *supra* note 341, at 2800; Rinat Kitai-Sangero, *Detention for the Purpose of Interrogation as Modern "Torture,"* 85 U. DET. MERCY L. REV. 137, 148 (2008); Rinat Kitai-Sangero, *Respecting the Privilege against Self-Incrimination: A Call for Providing Miranda Warnings in Non-custodial Interrogations*, 42 N.M. L. REV. 203, 213–14 (2012).

[353] Sangero & Halpert, *supra* note 352, at 516; Sangero, *supra* note 341, at 2800; Kitai-Sangero, *supra* note 352, at 214.

[354] SAUL KASSIN & LAWRENCE WRIGHTSMAN, THE PSYCHOLOGY OF EVIDENCE AND TRIAL PROCEDURE 67–94 (1985); Saul Kassin, *The Psychology of Confessions*, 4 ANN. REV. L. SOC. SCI. 193, 195 (2008). *See also* Sangero & Halpert, *supra* note 352, at 518–19; Sangero, *supra* note 341, at 2798–800.

[355] Kassin, *supra* note 354, at 195.

[356] *Id.*

[357] *Id.*

[358] *Id.*

[359] Sangero, *supra* note 341, at 2798–800 (based on the Israeli Justice Goldberg Commission report, REPORT OF THE COMMISSION REGARDING CONVICTIONS BASED SOLELY ON CONFESSIONS AND REGARDING THE GROUNDS FOR RETRIALS (1994) [hereinafter GOLDBERG COMMISSION REPORT]; Duke, *supra* note 350, at 565.

The suspect's personality can also be a factor in false confessions. Some people are more vulnerable to external pressure than others and, thus, at a higher risk of falsely confessing,[360] particularly those who tend toward compliance in social situations because of their eagerness to please others and avoid confrontation, especially with authority figures.[361] People who suffer from a high level of anxiety, fear, or depression; delusions; and other psychological disorders are also more vulnerable than others,[362] as are the intellectually disabled or mentally impaired.[363] Juveniles, moreover, are at the highest risk of confessing to something they did not commit.[364] As Maimonides recognized "The court shall not put a man to death or flog him on his own admission ... perhaps he was one of those who are in misery, bitter in soul, who long for death ... perhaps this was the reason that prompted him to confess to a crime he had not committed, in order that he be put to death."[365]

Studies conducted in recent decades have shown that the varied reasons for voluntary false confessions can even border on the bizarre.[366] People have falsely confessed so as to avoid the burden of a trial (for minor offenses), out of a fear of the death penalty, to cover up for friends, or due to promised financial reward from a criminal organization. Some have falsely confessed in the hope that this would prevent their names from being published in the newspapers, and others in order to make it in time for a university exam or important chess tournament. There are those who have confessed fearing they would be exposed as adulterers or because they were too drunk to remember what happened. Some have even given a false confession as a joke or to impress a girlfriend. In one case, an inmate confessed to a murder he did not commit to prove that a wrongful conviction is possible—and he succeeded. Reality, therefore, is often stranger than fiction.[367]

---

[360] Kassin, *supra* note 354, at 203. *See also* Sangero & Halpert, *supra* note 352, at 522–23; Sangero, *supra* note 341, at 2798.

[361] Kassin, *supra* note 354.

[362] *Id.*

[363] *Id.* at 206; Paul G. Cassell, *The Guilty and the "Innocent": An Examination of Alleged Cases of Wrongful Conviction from False Confessions*, 22 HARV. J.L. & PUB. POL'Y 523, 583 (1999); Sangero, *supra* note 341, at 2809; Drizin & Leo, *supra* note 349, at 919.

[364] Kassin, *supra* note 354, at 203–05.

[365] MAIMONIDES, MISHNEH TORAH [CODE OF JEWISH LAW], Book of Judges, *Hilchot Sanhedrin* [*Laws of the Sanhedrin*] 18:6 (author's translation).

[366] Sangero, *supra* note 341, at 2799–800.

[367] *See* Bedau & Radelet, *supra* note 349, at 58–63; ROYAL COMMISSION ON CRIMINAL JUSTICE: REPORT PRESENTED TO PARLIAMENT (July 1993) (Viscount Runciman of Doxford, Chairman); GOLDBERG COMMISSION REPORT, *supra* note 359; ARYE RATTNER, CONVICTING THE INNOCENT, WHEN JUSTICE GOES WRONG (1983) (unpublished PhD dissertation, Ohio State University) (on file with author); Arye Rattner, *Convicted but Innocent: Wrongful Conviction and the Criminal Justice System*, 12 LAW & HUM. BEHAV. 283 (1988). Another central factor in false confessions is suspects' misguided conviction that after making a confession that was elicited by police interrogators through improper methods,

Coerced-internalized false confessions is the second category of false confession. It refers to instances in which an innocent person becomes convinced during the course of the police interrogation that he is actually guilty of what he is being accused of.[368] This can occur with a suspect who was under the influence of drugs or alcohol during the event in question and does not recall clearly what occurred; in such circumstances, he may be convinced to believe the police's version of events.[369] In other cases, even an innocent suspect who was not under the influence of drugs or alcohol may be led, due to police interrogation techniques, to believe that he is guilty and simply repressing the painful event.[370] In one such case, a fourteen-year-old confessed to the stabbing and murder of his sister after police interrogators misled him into believing that they had physical evidence of his guilt and that he had committed the crime. The charges were eventually dropped only after the police found the victim's blood on a neighbor's clothing.[371] Even when not subject to stressful conditions, people are quite easily manipulated into believing that their perception of reality is wrong.[372]

The third, and central, category of confessions, coerced-compliant confessions, is connected to the second one, as the suspect's certainty of his guilt usually is the result of the pressure of being interrogated by the police.[373] In this type of instance, a suspect will falsely confess for short-term benefits, such as being allowed to sleep, left alone, or even released.[374]

---

additional confessions have no weight. At times, a suspect may be deceived into believing this and then make a subsequent confession that is facially valid as it was not extracted using improper methods. *See* Peter Mirfield, *Successive Confessions and the Poisonous Tree*, 1996 CRIM. L. REV. 554. However, contrast this to the ruling on this matter in Missouri v. Seibert, 542 U.S. 600 (2004). *See also* Charles J. Ogletree, Commentary, *Are Confessions Really Good for the Soul?: A Proposal to Mirandize Miranda*, 100 HARV. L. REV. 1826, 1840 (1987); Sangero, *supra* note 341, at 2800.

[368] Kassin, *supra* note 354, at 195–96; Gail Johnson, *False Confessions and Fundamental Fairness: The Need for Electronic Recording of Custodial Interrogations*, 6 B.U. PUB. INT. L.J. 719, 719 (1997); Duke, *supra* note 350, at 566; Sangero & Halpert, *supra* note 352, at 519; Sangero, *supra* note 341, at 2798.

[369] Deborah Young, *Unnecessary Evil: Police Lying in Interrogations*, 28 CONN. L. REV. 425, 462 (1996).

[370] DAVID WOLCHOVER & HEATON ARMSTRONG, ON CONFESSION EVIDENCE 95 (1996); Welsh S. White, *False Confessions and the Constitution: Safeguards against Untrustworthy Confessions*, 32 HARV. C.R.–C.L. L. REV. 105, 128 (1997).

[371] Kassin, *supra* note 354, at 195–96.

[372] Patrick A. Malone, *"You Have the Right to Remain Silent": Miranda after Twenty Years* (1986), *reprinted in* THE MIRANDA DEBATE: LAW, JUSTICE AND POLICING 75, 82 (Richard A. Leo & George C. Thomas III eds., 1998) [hereinafter THE MIRANDA DEBATE].

[373] Sangero & Halpert, *supra* note 352, at 518–19; Sangero, *supra* note 341, at 2798–99.

[374] Kassin, *supra* note 354, at 195. A prominent illustration of such cases is the Norfolk Four affair, in which four young navy soldiers falsely confessed to a rape and murder. The details of this astonishing case were discussed in the concept of the misperception ("tunnel vision") regarding the suspect's guilt, in Chapter 3, Section VI.

The central doctrine on confessions in American law was set in *Miranda v. Arizona*,[375] in which the Supreme Court ruled that, in principle, a custodial interrogation constitutes a violation of Fifth Amendment privilege against self-incrimination. Recognizing that coercive pressure is inherent to custodial interrogations, the Court concluded that "without proper safeguards the process of in-custody interrogation of persons suspected or accused of crime contains inherently compelling pressures which work to undermine the individual's will to resist and to compel him to speak where he would not otherwise do so freely."[376] The Court further stressed that "the modern practice of in-custody interrogation is psychologically rather than physically oriented,"[377] and that "[u]nless adequate protective devices are employed to dispel the compulsion inherent in custodial surroundings, no statement obtained from the defendant can truly be the product of his free choice."[378] Accordingly, since the *Miranda* ruling, custodial police interrogators must advise suspects of their rights upon arrest: the right to remain silent, as anything they say can be used against them in court; the right to consult with a lawyer and have a lawyer present during interrogation; and the right to an appointed attorney, prior to any questioning, if they cannot afford one. Under the *Miranda* rule, therefore, a confession obtained during the infringement of these rights is a violation of the Fifth Amendment and, therefore, inadmissible in court.[379]

The *Miranda* ruling was a serious attempt at addressing the problem of involuntary confessions. The *Miranda* rule diminishes the risk of police interrogators exerting physical and psychological pressure on suspects that can prompt them to involuntarily confess. However, even after *Miranda*, there remains a significant incidence of false confessions and wrongful convictions based on such confessions. Apparently, although police practice has (generally) shifted from coercive interrogation to what scholars term more sophisticated "psychological" interrogation techniques, the number of false confessions is still considerable.[380]

---

[375] 384 U.S. 436 (1966); *see also* RONALD N. BOYCE & ROLLIN M. PERKINS, CRIMINAL LAW AND PROCEDURE—CASES AND MATERIALS (8TH ED., 1999), at 218–26. The *Miranda* ruling was confirmed in Dickerson v. United States, 530 U.S. 428 (2000). For a detailed critique of the *Miranda* rules and a proposal to nullify them, see JOSEPH D. GRANO, CONFESSIONS, TRUTH, AND THE LAW (1993). For a collection of two dozen articles dealing with the *Miranda* ruling, see THE *MIRANDA* DEBATE, *supra* note 372.

[376] *Miranda*, 384 U.S at 467.

[377] *Id.* at 448.

[378] *Id.* at 458.

[379] Furthermore, there are other rules that, in rare cases, may lead to the exclusion of involuntary confessions that have been obtained in violation of the Constitution. *See* MCCORMICK ON EVIDENCE 226–42 (JOHN W. STRONG ed., 5th ed. 1999).

[380] *See* Leo & Ofshe, *supra* note 349. *See also* Laurie Magid, *The* Miranda *Debate: Questions Past, Present and Future*, 36 HOUS. L. REV. 1251 (1999) (book review).

To begin with, detention in itself is a risk factor for eliciting false confessions. Despite the presumption of innocence, conditions in detention are extremely harsh, at times even worse than prison conditions.[381] In her article on conditions of confinement, Rinat Kitai-Sangero noted,

> Conditions of pretrial detainees in custody are harsh all over the world ... in some places also deplorable and humiliating.... Many detainees are housed in old facilities that are inadequate for their needs.... Detainees may suffer from poor ventilation and lighting, a lack of direct sunlight, defects in food, and lack of sanitary facilities. Many jails suffer from severe overcrowding and often operate beyond their capacity ... a small space with almost no privacy. The fact that the number of detainees occasionally exceeds the bed capacity, forces detainees to "sleep on mattresses spread on floors in hallways and next to urinals."[382]

In such harsh conditions—even before pressure (legitimate or illegitimate) is applied by police interrogators—it would not be so unlikely for some people to confess to a crime that they did not commit, if this would lead to immediate release from police custody and spare them the anguish of being separated from family and friends in degrading physical conditions. In addition, informing a suspect of his or her rights does not counteract, in and of itself, the coercive atmosphere created by custodial interrogation.[383]

Studies analyzing interrogation tapes and conducting surveys among police interrogators have found that over 80 percent of suspects waive their right to remain silent and to consult with counsel.[384] In a lab simulation of a police interrogation, moreover, 81 percent of the subjects designated "innocent" waived their right to remain silent, whereas only 36 percent of the "guilty" subjects did the same.[385] This has been

---

[381] Rinat Kitai-Sangero, *Conditions of Confinement—The Duty to Grant the Greatest Possible Liberty for Pretrial Detainees*, 43 CRIM. L. BULL. 250 (2007); Richard S. Frase, *Comparative Criminal Justice as a Guide to American Law Reform: How Do the French Do It, How Can We Find Out, and Why Should We Care?*, 78 CAL. L. REV. 542, 594 (1990); David C. Gorlin, Note: *Evaluating Punishment in Purgatory: The Need to Separate Pretrial Detainees' Conditions-of-Confinement Claims from Inadequate Eighth Amendment Analysis*, 108 MICH. L. REV. 417, 419 (2009).

[382] Kitai-Sangero, *supra* note 381 (citing Rhodes v. Chapman, 452 U.S. 337, 355 (1981)).

[383] Alfredo Garcia, *Is* Miranda *Dead, Was It Overruled, Or Is It Irrelevant?*, 10 ST. THOMAS L. REV. 461, 473 (1998); Duke, *supra* note 350, at 566.

[384] Kassin, *supra* note 354, at 200. *See also* Sangero & Halpert, *supra* note 352, at 517; Strauss, *supra* note 348, at 774; Gordon Van Kessel, *The Suspect as a Source of Testimonial Evidence: A Comparison of the English and American Approaches*, 38 HASTINGS L.J. 1, 110 (1986); Raymond J. Toney, *English Criminal Procedure under Article 6 of the European Convention on Human Rights: Implications for Custodial Interrogation Practices*, 24 HOUS. J. INT'L L. 411, 427 (2002).

[385] Kassin, *supra* note 354; Sangero & Halpert, *supra* note 352.

termed the "innocence-confession paradox,"[386] in that the *Miranda* warnings do not sufficiently protect the innocent, who are most in need of the intended protection.[387] Innocent suspects waive their right to remain silent as they believe that, having done no wrong and having nothing to hide,[388] they will persuade the police interrogator of their innocence;[389] this exposes them to the risk of making a false confession. In particular, someone with no criminal record will have a greater tendency to waive his or her right to remain silent.[390]

Many suspects are motivated to talk, as they want to persuade the police of their innocence and believe in their ability to do so[391]—even guilty suspects, who believe they will be able to successfully lie.[392] Suspects talk so that the police will not think they are guilty,[393] some in an attempt to discover what the police know about them.[394] It has been contended that the conclusion in *Miranda* that a custodial interrogation is inherently coercive cannot be reconciled with the assertion that the coercion disappears as soon as the suspect is advised of his or her rights.[395] The *Miranda* ruling suffers, it is claimed, from an internal contradiction.[396] Suspects who are exposed to the coercion inherent to custodial interrogations are unable to make an autonomous decision as to whether to waive their rights.[397]

In American case law, the use of deceit by police interrogators, even during the course of interrogation, is not regarded as prohibited and, in any event, does not render the confession elicited through its use inadmissible.[398] Yet presenting fabricated

---

[386] Kassin, *supra* note 354, at 206.

[387] *Id.* at 207.

[388] *Id.*

[389] *Id.* at 200.

[390] *Id.*; Richard L. Leo, Miranda's *Revenge: Police Interrogation as a Confidence Game*, 30 LAW & SOC'Y REV. 259 (1996). For a compelling argument that the right to remain silent is desirable in that it increases the likelihood that fact-finders will believe the innocent and thus be able to distinguish between the innocent (who will tend to talk) and guilty (who will tend to remain silent), see Daniel J. Seidmann & Alex Stein, *The Right to Silence Helps the Innocent: A Game Theoretic Analysis of the Fifth Amendment Privilege*, 114 HARV. L. REV. 430 (2000); Alex Stein, *The Right to Silence Helps the Innocent: A Response to Critics*, 30 CARDOZO L. REV. 1115 (2008). *See also* Sangero & Halpert, *supra* note 352, at 518.

[391] George C. Thomas III, Miranda's *Illusion: Telling Stories in the Police Interrogation Room*, 81 TEX. L. REV. 1091, 1095 (2003) (book review of WELSH S. WHITE, MIRANDA'S WANING PROTECTIONS (2001)); Paul Shechtman, *An Essay on* Miranda's *Fortieth Birthday*, 10 CHAP. L. REV. 655, 656 (2007).

[392] Thomas, *id.*, at 1110; Shechtman, *supra* note 391.

[393] Shechtman, *supra* note 391.

[394] *Id.*

[395] Steven Penney, *Theories of Confession Admissibility: A Historical View*, 25 AM. J. CRIM. L. 309, 311 (1998).

[396] Louis Michael Seidman, Brown *and* Miranda, 80 CAL. L. REV. 673, 740 (1992).

[397] Penney, *supra* note 395, at 371.

[398] *See* Amanda L. Prebble, *Manipulated by* Miranda: *A Critical Analysis of Bright Lines and Voluntary Confessions under* United States v. Dickerson, 68 U. CIN. L. REV. 555, 583 (1999). *See also* White, *supra* note 370, at 105; Richard A. Leo, *From Coercion to Deception: The Changing Nature of Police Interrogation in America*, 18 CRIME L. & SOC. CHANGE 35 (1992).

incriminating evidence to a suspect, such as a supposed fingerprint or DNA match, creates a significant risk of eliciting a false confession,[399] which has been shown both in actual cases and psychological experiments.[400] Four hazards arise when the police show a suspect forensic evidence supposedly pointing to his guilt:[401] The first is that the suspect could become persuaded that he actually committed the crime he is accused of.[402] The second risk is that he may come to believe that it is pointless to continue denying guilt even if he is innocent.[403] A third danger is that the suspect might be traumatized into thinking that the police are purposely incriminating him.[404] Fourth, the suspect could get trapped in a web of lies, which confirms for the police their mistaken presumption that he is guilty.[405] In light of these risks, the English Court of Appeals ruled that although the police bear no obligation to disclose to suspects all of the investigative evidence they have against them, a suspect must not be actively misled.[406]

"Maximization" and "minimization" tactics are powerful tools for extracting false confessions.[407] Minimization techniques include downplaying the severity of the offense in question, faking sympathy for the suspect, blaming the victim, and suggesting reasonable explanations for the crime.[408] Maximization tactics include showing confidence in the suspect's guilt despite a lack of strong incriminating evidence,[409] expressing disappointment in the suspect's responses in the interrogation,[410] accusing the suspect of a more serious offense than is actually being investigated,[411] and humiliating the suspect.[412]

---

[399] Kassin, *supra* note 354, at 202–03; Brandon L. Garrett, *The Substance of False Confessions,* 62 STAN. L. REV. 1051, 1054 (2010). *See also* Sangero & Halpert, *supra* note 352, at 520–21.

[400] Kassin, *supra* note 354, at 202–03.

[401] Boaz Sangero, *Using Tricks and Cover Agents for Extracting Confessions,* 9 C.L.B. L. STUDIES 399, 415 (2011) (in Hebrew).

[402] *Id.*

[403] R. v. Oickle [2000] 2 S.C.R. 3, section 43; Sangero & Halpert, *supra* note 352, at 520; Thomas, *supra* note 391, at 1118.

[404] Young, *supra* note 369, at 469.

[405] Sangero & Halpert, *supra* note 352, at 520.

[406] R. v. Imran & Hussain, 1997 Crim. L. Rev. 754.

[407] Alan Hirsch, *Threats, Promises, and False Confessions: Lessons of Slavery,* 49 HOW. L.J. 31, 33–35 (2005); GISLI H. GUDJONSSON, THE PSYCHOLOGY OF INTERROGATIONS AND CONFESSIONS: A HANDBOOK 203–04 (2003). *See also* Halpert & Sangero, *supra* note 352, at 521.

[408] Magid, *supra* note 380, at 1307; Malone, *supra* note 372, at 80; WOLCHOVER & ARMSTRONG, *supra* note 370, at 70; GRANO, *supra* note 375; Young, *supra* note 369, at 430–31.

[409] WOLCHOVER & ARMSTRONG, *supra* note 370, at 69; White, *supra* note 370, at 151.

[410] WOLCHOVER & ARMSTRONG, *supra* note 370, at 77.

[411] *Id.* at 73.

[412] *Id.* at 79; Yale Kamisar, *On the Fortieth Anniversary of the* Miranda *Case: Why We Needed It, How We Got It—And What Happened to It,* 5 OHIO ST. J. CRIM. L. 163, 187 (2007).

An empirical study conducted by Richard Leo found a strong correlation between the number of different tactics used by an interrogator and the likelihood of extracting a confession. Moreover, the longer the interrogation, the greater the chances of obtaining a confession.[413] These findings were confirmed by an experiment that simulated realistic conditions, which showed the extent to which certain interrogation tactics increase the likelihood of a confession, particularly a false one: whereas the probability that a guilty interrogee will confess doubles, the likelihood of an innocent person confessing increases sevenfold.[414].

I contend that a fundamental error lies at the foundation of police interrogative tactics.[415] As will be shown further on, confessions should be accorded relatively little weight as proof of guilt given the fact that false confessions are not a rare occurrence and fact-finders cannot distinguish them from true confessions. Regardless, however, a confession is still wrongly taken to be compelling evidence of guilt, leading police interrogators to go to great lengths to extract one.[416] The irony, however, is that the greater the effort made to get a confession by any means, even through questionable tactics (such as jailhouse snitches or falsifying incriminating evidence), the less reliable the confession. In addition, the measures police interrogators take to get a confession might not only lead a suspect to falsely confess but also prevent fact-finders from identifying a false confession. This could occur, for example, if interrogators were to contaminate a confession by giving the suspect details of the crime, and this knowledge later on reinforces the reliability of his confession as evidence in court.[417]

Chapter 3 discussed how the Reid Technique of Interviewing and Interrogation, a prevalent practice in American police departments,[418] reinforces police's "tunnel vision" as to a suspect's guilt and leads to false confessions. The typical interrogation is intensely confrontational.[419] The Reid protocol directs interrogators to hamper any attempt by the suspect to deny his guilt and provide an alternative version.[420] Police are advised to employ both *minimization* techniques as well as *maximization*

---

[413] Richard A. Leo, *Criminal Law: Inside the Interrogation Room*, 86 J. Crim. L. & Criminology 266, 292–93 (1996); Kassin, *supra* note 354, at 201–02; Garrett, *supra* note 399; Leo & Ofshe, *supra* note 349; Sangero & Halpert, *supra* note 352, at 520.

[414] Melissa B. Russano et al., *Investigating True and False Confessions within a Novel Experimental Paradigm*, 16 Psychol. Sci. 481 (2005). *See also* Sangero & Halpert, *supra* note 352, at 521.

[415] Sangero, *supra* note 401, at 409–10; Sangero & Halpert, *supra* note 352, at 522.

[416] Alberto B. Lopez, *$10 and a Denim Jacket? A Model Statute for Compensating the Wrongfully Convicted*, 36 Ga. L. Rev. 665, 682 (2002).

[417] Sangero, *supra* note 401; Sangero & Halpert, *supra* note 352.

[418] Dan Simon, In Doubt—The Psychology of the Criminal Justice Process 121–22 (2012); Brandon L. Garrett, *Interrogation Policies*, 49 U. Richmond L. Rev. __ (forthcoming 2015).

[419] Simon, *supra* note 418, at 132.

[420] Simon, *supra* note 418, at 133; Garrett, *supra* note 418.

tactics when interrogating the suspect. Psychological experimental studies have found that suspects usually understand minimizing themes as an implicit promise of leniency and maximizing themes as an implicit threat of severe punishment, while the use of a combination of the techniques considerably increases false confessions.[421] Indeed, there is no indication that applying the Reid model tends to induce confessions from only the guilty.[422] The use of the Reid method in police interrogations is a clear example of how a criminal justice system lacking awareness as to the importance of safety is likely to employ practices that undermine safety. In contrast, the English PEACE method is a good example of an attempt to implement safety in police interrogations, and will be described further on.

(2) Convicting the Innocent Based on a False Confession

We know today that despite the Hidden Accidents Principle,[423] false confessions are not a rare occurrence, and many are submitted as evidence in court. How can the legal system effectively contend with this phenomenon?[424]

The Insufficiency of the Corroboration Requirement
As explained above, many suspects give a confession due to psychological pressures exerted on them during police interrogation. Yet despite being coerced, such confessions are often viewed as voluntary because the suspects were advised of their *Miranda* rights. Moreover, a considerable number of false confessions were given voluntarily, without any illegitimate pressure on the part of the police interrogators.[425] As I will demonstrate below, such cases illustrate that it is not sufficient to address (in legislation and the case law) the external factors causing false confessions (illegitimate pressure from interrogators); rather, the internal factors that impel an individual to make a false confession must also be considered. American law, it will be shown, does not make a serious attempt at contending with the risk of a false confession that is voluntarily given.

In *Escobedo v. Illinois*, Justice Arthur Goldberg commented,

> We have also learned the companion lesson of history, ancient and modern, that a system of criminal law which comes to depend on the confession will, in the long run, be less reliable and more subject to abuses than a system

---

[421] SIMON, *supra* note 418, at 137.

[422] SIMON, *supra* note 418, at 139. *See also* Brandon L. Garrett, *Contaminated Confessions Revisited*, 101 VA. L. REV. (forthcoming 2015).

[423] See Section III of Chapter 3.

[424] *See* Sangero & Halpert, *supra* note 352, at 523.

[425] Bedau & Radelet, *supra* note 349, at 56–63.

which depends on extrinsic evidence independently secured through skillful investigation.[426]

American law only appears to provide a rule that copes adequately with the possibility that a confession, even if voluntary, might be false. Under this rule, for a person to be convicted on the basis of his out-of-court confession, it must be corroborated by other evidence at trial. Such a rule is applied in many American state jurisdictions, through either legislation or the case law.[427] It would seem, then, that American law has a satisfactory requirement for ensuring that a confession is not false. However, upon closer examination, the contents of the corroboration requirement emerge as not serving the purpose for which the rule is intended.

Below I propose an enhanced requirement for *strong* corroboration of a confession at trial, with two central objectives. The first is the reduction of the fear that a confession could be false even when voluntary, and the second is to ensure that police investigators do not limit themselves to interrogating a suspect and attempting to extract a confession, but rather employ sophisticated investigative techniques and make an relentless effort to uncover objective, tangible evidence that is extrinsic to the suspect, aiming at pursuing the truth.

The traditional formulation of this requirement in American law mandates that there be some evidence other than the confession that tends to establish the corpus delicti.[428] Only "slight" corroborative evidence is required, not evidence that proves the corpus delicti beyond a reasonable doubt.[429]

"Corpus delicti" literally means "the body of the crime." The current American corroborative evidence requirement relates therefore only to the actual commission of the offense in question and not to whether the accused is the person who actually committed it. In a criminal trial, there are three main elements that the prosecution must usually prove: (1) that an injury or harm occurred constituting the crime, (2) that this injury or harm was caused in a criminal manner, and (3) that the accused was the person who inflicted this injury or harm.[430] Whereas Wigmore maintains that corpus delicti relates only to the first of these three elements, most U.S. courts have defined it as including both the first and second elements. Accordingly, the

---

[426] 378 U.S. 478, 490 (1964).

[427] *See, e.g.*, the survey in McCormick, *supra* note 379, at 212. *See also* Corey J. Ayling, Comment, *Corroborating Confessions: An Empirical Analysis of Legal Safeguards against False Confessions*, 1984 Wis. L. Rev. 1121.

[428] Opper v. United States, 384 U.S. 84, 93 (1954); Sangero, *supra* note 341, at 2803; Fischer & Rosen-Zvi, *supra* note 341, at 885–86. In offenses with no tangible corpus delicti, the corroboration must implicate the accused; Smith v. United States, 348 U.S. 147, 154 (1954).

[429] McCormick, *supra* note 379, at 214.

[430] *Id.*

corroborating evidence must tend to point to the existence of the harm or injury constituting the offense and indicate that this harm or injury was the result of a criminal activity. There is not, however, a need to show that the accused is the guilty perpetrator.[431]

Yet a requirement for evidence of the actual commission of the crime, in addition to the accused's confession, could counteract some false confessions and prevent wrongful convictions. It would also save the legal system the tremendous embarrassment of convicting someone for a crime that subsequently emerges as never having been committed, such as when a person is convicted of murder and the alleged "victim" is later found to be alive.[432] Such circumstances account for only a small minority of the cases of false confessions and wrongful convictions, however. In the overwhelming majority of cases, the police have strong evidence that a crime was in fact committed, and the central question relating to a confession is whether the suspect is the actual perpetrator of the crime. It is precisely this question that the American corroboration requirement fails to address and, thereby, facilitates the conviction of innocent suspects who confess. The question of whether a crime was actually committed is meaningless, then, if deliberated in respect to a person who was not involved in the incident. When the wrong person is charged, proof that a crime was committed indicates nothing as to the involvement or guilt of this person in relation to the crime.

The misguided notion of limiting the corroboration requirement to proof of the corpus delicti prevails also in the literature. Thus, for example, Wigmore held the corroboration requirement to be unnecessary, while McCormick has maintained that, in light of various doctrines, particularly those based on the Fifth Amendment, the *Miranda* rules, and the voluntariness requirement for confessions, there is no need for additional rules to guide police investigators (including the corroboration requirement).[433] This approach is clearly mistaken. Although the *Miranda* rules and its like do, indeed, alleviate the risk of physical pressure being exerted on suspects by police interrogators, which will induce suspects to make involuntary confessions, methods of psychological interrogation are also liable to result in involuntary confessions. The *Miranda* rules are presumably designed to also contend with the latter hazard, but, as explained, merely informing a suspect of his rights is not sufficient to eliminate the risk. Furthermore, as also explained, studies show that even a voluntary confession can be false. Last, if the goal is not just to prevent investigators

---

[431] *Id.*

[432] Leo & Ofshe, *supra* note 349, at 450–51. In 1990, in Texas, a suspect confessed to the murder of his ex-girlfriend after failing a polygraph test. She was later found alive and well in Arizona.

[433] McCormick, *supra* note 379, at 213–14 (for the positions of both Wigmore and McCormick on this issue).

from abusing interrogated suspects (which is certainly an important, albeit narrow, objective) but also to direct them toward sophisticated techniques and persisting at a proper investigation aimed at finding objective, tangible evidence extrinsic to the suspect (such as forensic evidence), then the corroboration requirement is not only desirable but essential.[434]

Elsewhere, I have recommended instituting a statutory strong corroboration requirement for convicting based on a confession. This mandatory condition would require strong, autonomous corroboration of the allegation that the defendant is the perpetrator of the crime.[435] Yet even this stronger requirement would not always suffice to prevent a false conviction, due to the light evidentiary weight that should be accorded to a confession.

Fact-Finders (In)ability to Discern True from False Confessions
In a world in which the law-enforcement system could distinguish between what is true and what is false, it can be assumed that false confessions would be filtered out. Yet contrary to what is commonly believed, research has shown that police investigators, prosecutors, judges, and juries are unable to distinguish between a true confession and a false one. [436] An interesting experimental study uncovered two perhaps counterintuitive findings. The first is that police investigators do not identify false confessions any better than students. The only differences are that investigators are very sure of themselves, even when they are wrong, and operate under a misguided conception of the suspect's guilt; they are therefore biased and inclined to believe false confessions, and tend not to believe denials. Second, both police investigators and students are unable to discern true confessions from false confessions to the point that when there is an equal number of true and false confessions, the same results would be reached with a simple flip of a coin.[437]

---

[434] It is important to also note that the Supreme Court decision in Opper v. United States, 348 U.S. 84 (1954) offered an alternative approach to the corroboration requirement, whereby rather than evidence supporting the corpus delicti, it is necessary to present "substantial independent evidence which would tend to establish the trustworthiness of the statement." *Id.* at 93. *See also* McCORMICK, *supra* note 379, at 215. As explained by McCormick, *id.* at 215–16, this requirement is even weaker than the weak requirement that a confession be corroborated in regard to the corpus delicti. For further discussion, see Sangero, *supra* note 341, at 2805–06.

[435] Sangero, *supra* note 341, at 2818–26. *See also* Sangero & Halpert, *supra* note 352, at 526.

[436] Danny Ciraco, *Reverse Engineering*, 11 W.R.L.S.I. 41, 51–52 (2001); Saul M. Kassin, *Human Judges of Truth, Deception, and Credibility: Confident but Erroneous*, 23 CARDOZO L. REV. 809, 812 (2002).

[437] Saul M. Kassin, Christian A. Meissner & Rebecca J. Norwick, *"I'd Know a False Confession if I Saw One": A Comparative Study of College Students and Police Investigators*, 29 LAW & HUM. BEHAV. 211 (2005). See also the references to additional studies with similar findings in *id.* at 212, 222; Ciraco, *supra* note 436.

The interrogation process is usually triggered by a baseless assumption that the suspect is lying.[438] To supposedly assist police investigators in discerning whether a confession is true or false, the Reid protocol sets out what is known as the Behavioral Analysis Interview (BAI) method, listing supposed indicators of lying, such as gaze aversion. However, not only is there is no scientific support for these indicators, but research has shown that such physical cues are in no way informative for distinguishing between deceit and truth-telling.[439] As Dan Simon concludes, "[T]he BAI protocol amounts to a cacophony of commonly held but poorly diagnostic intuitions. Its validity is hardly reinforced by its conjectural propositions and folksy aphorisms. Yet the protocol continues to be the leading interrogation tool used by law enforcement agencies across North America."[440]

In the context of the trial proceedings, moreover, Richard A. Leo and Richard J. Ofshe showed, in a study of sixty false confessions, that 73 percent led to wrongful convictions.[441] A more comprehensive study by Stephen A. Drizin and Leo similarly found that 86 percent of the 120 false confessions that went to trial led to wrongful convictions.[442] In addition, the work of the Innocence Project has exposed the fact that false confessions lead to wrongful convictions, and that fact-finders, be they judges or jurors, fail to recognize the falsity of these confessions.[443]

A central reason behind fact-finders' inability to identify false confessions is that police investigators contaminate the confessions by feeding "inside information" to the confessing suspect, which is then included in the confession. Brandon Garrett conducted two sweeping studies on this matter that encompassed sixty-three rape and murder convictions based on false confessions. The one study examined forty Innocence Project cases, and the second study looked at twenty-three additional such cases.

In all of the sixty-three cases, post-conviction DNA testing assisted in exposing the confessions as false. In seventeen of the sixty-three cases, DNA testing had excluded the defendants already at the time of their trials, but they were nevertheless found guilty. As described by Garrett, confessions "trump[] DNA."[444]

---

[438] SIMON, *supra* note 418, at 207.

[439] *Id.* at 122–32.

[440] *Id.* at 131.

[441] Leo & Ofshe, *supra* note 349.

[442] Drizin & Leo, *supra* note 349, at 993. *See also* Sangero & Halpert, *supra* note 352, at 526.

[443] *See* Garrett, *supra* note 346, at 76; Garrett, *supra* note 399. *See also* Richard A. Leo & Deborah Davis, *From False Confession to Wrongful Conviction: Seven Psychological Processes*, 32 J. PSYCHIATRY & L. 9, 19–20 (2010).

[444] Garrett, *supra* note 422.

Of the sixty-three confessions, fifty-nine were not simple admissions of "I did it" but detailed statements precisely describing the commission of the crime.[445] And in many of these cases, the prosecution argued at trial that these were details that only the true perpetrator could have known, and claimed that they had not been revealed to the defendant, either inadvertently or intentionally, by the police investigators.[446] A great number of the fifty-nine false confessions in those studies had to have been contaminated by the police, despite police testimony to the contrary in court. Because of such contamination and its subsequent denial, it is nearly impossible for judges and jurors to discern false confessions. A confession, especially one that includes "inside information," blinds fact-finders to the point that they tend to ignore contradictory evidence, such as an alibi and even DNA evidence.[447] Furthermore, the tainting of a confession also has an impact on the appeal and post-conviction review processes.[448]

There are, then, a number of reasons that fact-finders fail to identify false confessions.[449] To begin with, the mistaken belief that a person would not confess to a crime he did not commit continues to persist among both judges and jurors, to the extent that some may even completely ignore the possibility that a confession could be false.[450] Second, as studies have shown, police investigators, prosecutors, judges, and jurors are simply unable to discern a true confession from a false one.[451] Third, the tainting of confessions by police investigators[452] seriously impedes the ability of judges and jurors to identify a false confession. Fourth, judges and jurors, like the police and prosecutors, often also hold a distorted perception of the defendant's guilt.[453] This misconception is reinforced by the presence of correct details of the crime (especially "inside information") in the defendant's confession, which are interpreted as supporting the validity of the confession. When there are inaccurate details in a confession or the investigation protocol is faulty, the tendency is to minimize their value relevance.[454] Moreover, in contrast to the decisive weight

---

[445] Garrett, *supra* note 399, at 1054; Garrett, *supra* note 422. *See also* Sangero & Halpert, *supra* note 352, at 519.
[446] Garrett, *supra* note 422.
[447] *Id.*
[448] *Id.*
[449] Sangero & Halpert, *supra* note 352, at 526–28; White, *supra* note 370, at 108; Drizin & Leo, *supra* note 349, at 910; Hirsch, *supra* note 67, at 33; Drizin & Reich, *supra* note 348, at 637; Fischer & Rosen-Zvi, *supra* note 341, at 881.
[450] Richard A. Leo, *False Confessions: Causes, Consequences, and Implications*, 37 J. AM. ACAD. PSYCHIATRY L. 332, 341 (2009); Sangero & Halpert, *supra* note 352, at 526.
[451] Kassin, Meissner & Norwick, *supra* note 97, and accompanying text; Sangero & Halpert, *supra* note 352, at 527.
[452] Garrett, *supra* note 399, at 1090–92; Sangero & Halpert, *supra* note 352.
[453] See Section VI of Chapter 3; Sangero & Halpert, *supra* note 352, at 519.
[454] Garrett, *supra* note 399, at 1088; Sangero & Halpert, *supra* note 352.

accorded to a confession, no significance is usually attributed to a denial, either during the police interrogation or the court proceedings.[455] Last, police investigators tend to rely on prosecutors and judges to filter out later on police errors—that is, any false confessions they may have extracted during interrogations. Prosecutors, in turn, tend to rely both on police (in carrying out their investigations) and on judges (in conducting the trial proceedings) to prevent wrongful convictions. Judges and juries, for their part, tend to rely on the law-enforcement agents—the police and prosecution—to bring only the guilty to trial, while appellate judges similarly rely on trial judges. Consequently, as soon as a critical error occurs (e.g., an innocent person is targeted as a suspect and gives a false confession),[456] these interdependent elements of the system of checks and balances fall like dominoes, eventually resulting in a wrongful conviction. As false confessions occur at a significant rate, measures must be applied to attain safety in the system, including the use of probability theory to determine the appropriate weight to be attributed to confessions.[457]

B. POSSIBLE SAFETY MEASURES

(1) Bayesian Logic and Confessions

Up to this point, I have sought to show that a confession should always be treated with suspicion as evidence and its reliability as questionable.[458] Moreover, even those who consider confessions to be reliable evidence must be wary of convicting solely based on a defendant's confession, without any other significant corroborative evidence, for this cannot be reconciled with a concept of safety. Indeed, from a probabilistic perspective,[459] the concern with wrongfully convicting an innocent person arises not only when a confession is the sole piece of evidence, but also given the fact that even strong corroborative evidence might not suffice to ensure a safe conviction given the weak weight that should be attributed to confessions in general.

Before turning to a detailed mathematical calculation of this proposition, it is helpful to illustrate this with an intuitive numerical example. Assume that a crime was committed and that the person interrogated for committing the crime—not due to any evidence linking her to the specific crime but because she was already in

---

[455] A. Farkas & E. Ro'th, *The Constitutional Limits of the Efficiency of Criminal Justice*, 37 ACTA JURIDICA HUNGARICA 139, 145 (1995–1997); Sangero & Halpert, *supra* note 352.

[456] Leo, *supra* note 110, at 334–38; Sangero & Halpert, *supra* note 352, at 528.

[457] Sangero & Halpert, *supra* note 352.

[458] *Id.* at 539; Sangero, *supra* note 341, at 2800.

[459] Sangero & Halpert, *supra* note 352, at 539–50.

police custody and being investigated for a different crime—has confessed.[460] In her confession, the suspect did not provide any information not already known to the police or the public, and the police have not found any additional evidence tying her to the crime. The person who confessed resides in a city in which there are two million adults, each of whom is as likely as she to have committed the crime. (Recall that no other evidence apart from the confession links the suspect to the crime). Now assume corroborated data showing that one out of ten confessions is false and a 50 percent probability that a court will erroneously believe a false confession.[461] If all the residents of the suspect's city were to be interrogated,[462] then, two hundred thousand false confessions (and one true confession if the actual perpetrator were to confess) would likely be given, and a court could be expected to believe 100,001 of those confessions. Thus, while there is a one-in-two-million likelihood that the person in custody is the actual culprit in the absence of any evidence linking her to the crime prior to her confession, once she has given a confession the likelihood increases, but remains slim, to 1 in 100,001. Even if the story moves to a small city of only 100,000 adults, a confession lacking corroboration would increase the probability of actual culpability from 1:100,000 to only 1:5001. Similarly, in a village of only 1000 adults, instead of a ratio of 1:1000, a non-corroborated confession would lead to a ratio of 1:51, that is, approximately, 2 percent, which does not even meet the 51 percent threshold of a balance of probabilities, nor, of course, the beyond-a-reasonable- doubt requirement of 90 percent.[463]

Bayes' Theorem

In the following probabilistic calculation, which I have made elsewhere with Dr. Mordechai Halpert,[464] the case of an interrogated suspect who has confessed to a certain crime is analyzed using two hypotheses and one given event. The first hypothesis is that the suspect is guilty ("G"), and the second that he is innocent ("I"). The given event is the suspect's confession to this specific crime during his interrogation ("E" signifying evidence).

---

[460] This example was adapted from Mordechai Halpert & Boaz Sangero, *From the Fallacy of the Transposed Conditional to Wrongful Convictions Based on Confessions*, 26 BAR-ILAN L. STUDIES 733, 772–73 (2010) (in Hebrew). Responsibility for any error is solely mine.

[461] This is a conservative, optimistic assumption; the research discussed above supports a much more pessimistic estimate.

[462] Assume that there are two million investigating teams, and none of them is aware of the existence of the other teams. Each team operates under the conception of the suspect's guilt and goes to great lengths to extract a confession.

[463] Although it is common to suffice with 90 percent, I maintain that safety requires 99 percent.

[464] Sangero & Halpert, *supra* note 352, at 539–41.

Presented in an odds form, Bayes' Theorem dictates that[465]

Likelihood Ratio × Prior Odds = Posterior Odds

The Likelihood Ratio is the probability ("P") of an interrogated suspect confessing if he is guilty divided by the probability of his confessing if he is innocent.[466]

$$\text{Likelihood Ratio} \equiv \frac{P(E \,|\, G)}{P(E \,|\, I)}$$

This expresses mathematically the strength of the evidence—that is, his confession. To illustrate, a likelihood ratio of 5 means that the probability of a guilty suspect confessing when interrogated is 5 times greater than the probability of an innocent suspect confessing during interrogation. The Likelihood Ratio in itself, however, is an insufficient measure of a suspect's guilt or innocence, for it fails to take into account any other evidence apart from the confession and assumes what in fact we are trying to prove: the numerator of the Likelihood Ratio assumes guilt and the denominator assumes innocence.[467]

Prior Odds, in contrast, equal the probability of guilt divided by the probability of innocence *without* taking the suspect's confession into account and, instead, based on other admissible evidence:[468]

$$\text{Prior Odds} \equiv \frac{P(G)}{P(I)}$$

These odds are "Prior" because they are what we believe to obtain prior to observing the evidence of guilt.[469] Through Bayes' Theorem, we "refine" our prior estimates by incorporating the evidence observed,[470] which, in the given example, is the suspect's confession.

If we multiply the Likelihood Ratio by the Prior Odds, we arrive at the Posterior Odds, which is what we are seeking in a criminal trial. The Posterior Odds represent the weight of a confession combined with other evidence:[471]

$$\text{Posterior Odds} \equiv \frac{P(G \,|\, E)}{P(I \,|\, E)}$$

---

[465] See Section IV(B) of Chapter 3.
[466] Sangero & Halpert, *supra* note 352, at 540.
[467] *Id.*
[468] *Id.*
[469] Edward K. Cheng, *Essay: Reconceptualizing the Burden of Proof*, 122 YALE L.J. 1254, 1266 (2013).
[470] *Id.* at 1267.
[471] Sangero & Halpert, *supra* note 352, at 540–41.

When the Posterior Odds = 1, the probability of a suspect's guilt given his confession is equal to the probability of his innocence given his confession. When the Posterior Odds are >1, the probability of the confessing suspect's guilt is greater than the probability of his innocence. Accordingly, the greater the Posterior Odds, the stronger the likelihood of guilt. When the Posterior Odds are <1, the probability of the suspect's innocence given (and despite) his confession is greater than the probability of his guilt. Accordingly, the lower the Posterior Odds, the greater the probability of innocence.[472]

From a Bayesian perspective, in order to reach a verdict in a criminal trial, the Posterior Odds of guilt must be calculated. Bayes' Theorem demonstrates the huge significance of Prior Odds, which are determined by evidence other than the suspect's confession. To illustrate, we can return to our above example of a person who is interrogated by the police for committing a crime without any solid evidence tying her to that crime and, in the end, there is no incriminating evidence other than her confession. If we assume that all other residents of the city in which she lives are equally likely to have committed the crime she is suspected of, the Prior Odds of her guilt would be very low (in our numeric example above, as low as 1 in 2 million).[473]

Determining the Likelihood Ratio of a Confession: The Bayes' Factor

The research shows that many suspects actually confess during interrogation to crimes they did not commit. Moreover, as I have discussed, the numerous instances of false confessions that have been uncovered can be reasonably assumed to be only the tip of the iceberg of this phenomenon, given the Hidden Accidents Principle.[474] Indeed, there are no hard statistics on false confessions, nor can any be compiled.[475] However, based on the research and the false confessions that have been exposed, and taking into account the proven impact of interrogation and detention conditions on suspects, *at least* one out of every ten innocent suspects has been estimated to give a false confession during interrogation.[476]

Yet, as also discussed above, the courts and juries are incapable of discerning false confessions. The Likelihood Ratio of a confession is impacted by both the

---

[472] *Id.* at 541.

[473] *Id.*

[474] Gudjonsson, *supra* note 67, at 173; Sangero & Halpert, *supra* note 352, at 541.

[475] Leo & Ofshe, supra note 349, at 431–32; Duke, *supra* note 350, at 566; Sangero, *supra* note 341, at 2797; Fischer & Rosen-Zvi, *supra* note 341, at 875; Garrett, *supra* note 422 ("Researchers cannot ethically test coercive interrogation techniques in a laboratory setting, and in actual cases there often may not be evidence like DNA that can confirm whether the confession is true or false").

[476] Sangero & Halpert, *supra* note 352, at 542.

possibility of a false confession and the possibility of a court fact-finder error when assessing the reliability of a confession.[477] As a quantitative illustration, assume that it has been proven statistically that there is a 10 percent probability of an innocent person giving a false confession and a 50 percent probability of the court successfully discerning a false confession.[478] This means that the probability of a confession that is false and not being identified as such by the court is 5 percent (0.05), which is the denominator in the Likelihood Ratio. The numerator in the Likelihood Ratio is the probability that a guilty person would confess. As the lack of a confession (i.e., the presence of a denial) is not viewed as evidence of innocence (the guilty often deny their guilt), this probability can be no greater than 50 percent (0.5).[479] When we set this as the numerator in the Likelihood Ratio, we get the following equation:[480]

$$\text{Likelihood Ratio} = \frac{P(E\,|\,G)}{P(E\,|\,I)} = \frac{0.5}{0.05} = 10$$

Posterior Odds Required for a Criminal Conviction
American law seems to accept the (unsafe) threshold of 10 (90 percent) for Posterior Odds as meeting the beyond-a-reasonable-doubt requirement for a criminal conviction.[481]

Prior Odds Required for Convicting Based on a Confession
When Posterior Odds of 10 and a Likelihood Ratio of 10 are inserted into the first equation set out above, the outcome is that the Prior Odds necessary to convict someone based on his confession must be at least 1:[482]

$$\text{Prior Odds} = \frac{\text{Posterior Odds}}{\text{Likelihood Ratio}} \geq \frac{10}{10} = 1$$

---

[477] *Id.*

[478] Given the research discussed earlier on, including studies conducted by Leo and Ofshe, this is an optimistic and conservative estimate. *Id.*

[479] Namely, the probability of a false negative for confessions is less than 50 percent. *Id.* at 543.

[480] *Id.*

[481] A threshold of 100 for Posterior Odds, which means proving guilt at a level of 99 percent, should be preferred, but this is not accepted in American law. See the discussion in Section V of Chapter 3.

[482] Sangero & Halpert, *supra* note 352, at 548.

From this, the following requirement follows:[483]

$$\text{Prior Odds} = \frac{P(G)}{P(I)} \geq 1 \Rightarrow P(G) \geq 1 \times P(I)$$

Thus, the probability of guilt based on incriminating evidence but *without* a confession must be at least 51 percent to satisfy the standard of proof of guilt beyond a reasonable doubt (i.e., a Posterior Odds threshold of 10) given a confession.[484] We can derive from this that a confession should be treated like corroboration for other substantial incriminating evidence (if such exists) and not as the primary evidence of guilt, which can ground a conviction with corroboration. This shift will entail a significant reversal in how the role of the confession is conceived in criminal law.[485]

Elsewhere, Dr. Mordechai Halpert and I have illustrated this conclusion with the case of George Allen, convicted in 1983 of rape and murder.[486] Allen was taken into police custody for questioning after being stopped by police and being unable to produce a photo ID to prove he was not another individual who was wanted for the murder. In the course of his interrogation, Allen confessed to the crime; he was subsequently convicted at trial and sentenced to life imprisonment.[487] Were the serious hazards of convicting someone based solely on his confession taken into account, the court likely would have determined a very high probability of Allen's innocence. Indeed, the Prior Odds of Allen's guilt were very low, for without his confession, there was no significant evidence linking him to the crime as opposed to any other resident of the city in which it occurred. To counteract such low Prior Odds, the key piece of evidence (the confession in this case) would (based on the laws of probability) have had to be far more reliable than it was and can ever be as evidence, as research in the field shows.[488] Only in 2012, after thirty years in jail, was Allen exonerated and released based on post-conviction DNA testing that led to the reopening of the case and a renewed police investigation.[489]

Given the very real hazard of convicting innocent defendants, the police should not set eliciting a confession as their prime goal when interrogating a suspect against whom there is no well-grounded evidence of his or her guilt.[490] In addition,

---

[483] *Id.*

[484] *Id.*

[485] *Id.* at 548–49.

[486] *Id.* at 533–539; *State v. Allen*, 684 S.W.2d 417 (Mo. App. E.D. 1984).

[487] Sangero & Halpert, *supra* note 352, at 514.

[488] *Id.* at 554–55.

[489] See the Innocence Project website at http://www.innocenceproject.org (Last visited May 2, 2015).

[490] Sangero & Halpert, *supra* note 352, at 515.

legislators should amend current law to preclude confessions from being the sole, or key, piece of evidence for a conviction, and to assign them only corroborative weight, to support other key evidence in a case. For the time being, however, at the very least, there must be a requirement for "strong corroboration" of confessions, namely, objective, independent (unrelated to the confession) and significant evidence that the defendant committed the crime.[491]

(2) Additional Recommendations

I have made two main recommendations here: for disallowance of conviction on the basis of a confession alone, and for the police to refrain from interrogations aimed at extracting a confession in the absence of a well-grounded suspicion against the interrogated suspect.

It is important and useful to consider, in addition, some of the recommendations that have been raised in the legal literature. First, it has been suggested that safety considerations require that all police interrogations be documented in video, from beginning to end, and not just confessions.[492] Second, police interrogators, prosecutors, jurors, and judges should be taught and advised on the dangers of false confessions. Third, the length of interrogations should be limited.[493] Fourth, the police should be prohibited from lying to and deceiving suspects, especially with regard to evidence (especially scientific evidence) of their guilt.[494] And fifth, jurors should hear expert testimony on the recent research on false confessions, their causes, and so on.[495] Obviously, all of these recommendations, as well as others, should be assessed carefully both before and after their implementation.

(3) The English PEACE Protocol

Last, an additional source for increasing safety in confessions is the UK Home Office's instructions for investigative interviewing, known as PEACE (Planning and preparation; Engage and explain; Account clarification and challenge; Closure;

---

[491] Sangero, *supra* note 341.

[492] For a detailed explanation of the importance of recording interrogations and an explanation as to why this will not suffice, see Sangero, *supra* note 341, at 2825–27. *See also* Garrett, *supra* note 422.

[493] Mark Costanzo & Richard A. Leo, *Research and Expert Testimony on Interrogations and Confessions, in* EXPERT PSYCHOLOGICAL TESTIMONY FOR THE COURTS 88 (Mark Costanzo, Daniel Krauss & Kathy Pezdek eds., 2007).

[494] White, *supra* note 370, at 148; GEORGE C. THOMAS III, THE SUPREME COURT ON TRIAL: HOW THE AMERICAN JUSTICE SYSTEM SACRIFICES INNOCENT DEFENDANTS 195 (2008); Young, *supra* note 369, at 426 (generally opposing lying to the suspect during interrogation).

[495] Garrett, *supra* note 422. Other recommendations were elaborated on in Chapter 4, in the context of the discussion of applying the STAMP model to confessions.

Evaluation), which it published in 1993.[496] The main principles set forth in this protocol are as follows: First, it states that the purpose of a police interview is to obtain full, accurate, and reliable accounts on matters being investigated by the police. Second, investigators must act fairly and without prejudice in interviewing and dealing with suspects, and they must "not assume that all suspects are going to lie, say nothing or provide a self-serving version of events." Third, Principle 2 of the protocol requires that people "with clear or perceived vulnerabilities" be treated "with particular care, and extra safeguards should be put in place."

Simon has described this method as follows:

> In sharp contrast to accusatory protocols that instruct interrogators to silence and shut down the suspect from stating anything but an admission, the Conversation Management method encourages the suspect to provide an abundance of information. This approach both offers the suspect a fair opportunity to make his case and provides the interrogator material for challenging that account. Importantly, the Conversation Management approach discourages aggressive treatment of the suspect, and it forbids resorting to minimization, maximization, intimidation, or any other technique that might be coercive.[497]

The contrast with the Reid protocol is clear: as Simon notes, the PEACE method is grounded on a sophisticated use of information, with the purpose of exposing lies and contradictions, as opposed to the Reid method, which points to confrontation, accusation, or even coercion of suspects being interrogated. Given the inherent risks of the Reid approach, discussed above, it is vital that a new interrogative approach, such as the PEACE method, be explored, as New Zealand, Norway, Sweden, and Denmark have all done.[498]

(4) Applying the Safety STAMP Model to Confessions

Finally, based on the research regarding confessions that was described here, I recommend applying Leveson's Systems-Theoretic Accident Model and Processes (STAMP),

---

[496] COLLEGE OF POLICING, INVESTIGATIVE INTERVIEWING (2013), http://www.app.college.police.uk/app-content/investigations/investigative-interviewing/ (last visited Oct. 9, 2014). *See also* SIMON, *supra* note 418, at 140–42. I have certain reservations about the seventh principle of the PEACE method, which is as follows: "Principle 7—Even when a suspect exercises the right to silence, investigators have a responsibility to put questions to them [*sic*]." In my opinion, greater respect should have been accorded to the right to silence, and police investigators should not have been instructed to undermine it. *See* in this regard Michigan v. Mosley, 423 U.S. 96, 104–07 (1975).

[497] SIMON, *supra* note 418, at 141.

[498] *Id.* at 142.

based on constraints and controls, to confessions. My detailed suggestion was presented above in Chapter 4. It could be properly developed in the framework of the proposed Safety in the Criminal Justice System Institute (SCJSI).

V. Eyewitness Identification

A. CURRENT UNSAFETY

(1) Studies on Mistaken Identification

In many criminal law systems, eyewitness identification of a suspect is sufficient to estab-lish that he is the perpetrator of the crime in question, without any need for additional corroborating evidence.[499] But this lofty legal status stands in contrast to the undisputed assertion in the professional literature that an erroneous eyewitness identification is far from rare,[500] with many scholars holding this to be the most common cause of false convictions. In 1932, Edwin M. Borchard already had found mistaken eyewitness iden-tification to be the chief cause of false convictions of innocent people—in twenty-nine of the sixty-five cases he had examined.[501] Similar findings have continued to emerge in the research in the decades that followed his trailblazing research. In a study of wrongful convictions conducted by Arye Rattner, mistaken eyewitness identification was found to be the main cause: it appeared in 52 percent of the cases he examined.[502] Hugo Adam Bedau and Michael L. Radelet arrived at a similar finding in their study,[503] while an even higher error rate, of 77 percent, emerged in the framework of Innocence Project exonerations.[504] The findings in Samuel L. Gross and Michael Shaffer's study of

---

[499] MCCORMICK, *supra* note 379, at 722. The leading English case is R. v. Turnbull, [1977] Q.B. 224 (CA Crim. Div.) (it suffices for the judge to warn the jury about the danger of relying on eyewitness testi-mony as the sole evidence of guilt). *See also* COLIN TAPPER, CROSS & TAPPER ON EVIDENCE 234–35, 670–87 (9th ed. 1999); IAN H. DENNIS, THE LAW OF EVIDENCE 203 (1999). The leading Israeli case is Cr.A. 347/88, Demanjuk v. State of Israel, 47(4) P.D. 221, 392, 429 (in Hebrew). *See also* DENNIS, *supra*, at 196–228; Boaz Sangero & Mordechai Halpert, Why a Conviction Should Not Be Based on a Single Piece of Evidence: A proposal for Reform, 48 JURIMETRICS J. 43, 90–94 (2007).

[500] Margery Malkin Koosed, *The Proposed Innocence Protection Act Won't—Unless It Also Curbs Mistaken Identifications*, 63 OHIO ST. L.J. 263 (2002); Gabriel W. Gorenstein & Phoebe Ellsworth, *Effect of Choosing an Incorrect Photograph on a Later Identification by an Eyewitness*, 65 J. APPLIED PSYCHOL. 616 (1980); BRIAN L. CUTLER & STEVEN D. PENROD, MISTAKEN IDENTIFICATION—THE EYEWITNESS, PSYCHOLOGY AND THE LAW (1995); Sangero & Halpert, *supra* note 499, at 90.

[501] E.M. BORCHARD, CONVICTING THE INNOCENT: ERRORS OF CRIMINAL JUSTICE (1932).

[502] Rattner, *supra* note 367.

[503] Bedau & Radelet, *supra* note 349 (out of the 350 miscarriages of justice uncovered by the study, 193 (55 per-cent) were caused by the mistakes of witnesses).

[504] According to the findings of the Innocence Project, of the first 225 cases in which genetic testing proved the falsity of the conviction, 173 (77 percent) of the convictions were based on eyewitness misidentifica-tion. See the Innocence Project website www.innocenceproject.org for the table "Contributing Causes of Wrongful Convictions" (last visited Sept. 1, 2014). *See also* GARRETT, supra note 13, at 279 fig. A.5 (2011) (190 of the first 250 exonerations, amounting to 76 percent, achieved by the Innocence Project).

891 exonerations of innocently convicted inmates echoed the Innocence Project findings: in 76 percent of the cases, the false conviction was found to have been based also (and, at times, only) on a mistaken eyewitness identification. In approximately half of these cases, the eyewitnesses had actually erred in identifying the defendant, while in the other half of the cases, they had in fact lied either with regard to the perpetrator's identity or regarding the very occurrence of the crime.[505] Moreover, of the 1438 exonerations recorded in the National Registry of Exonerations, 507 involved mistaken witness identification (35 percent).[506] Indeed, the English Criminal Law Revision Commission declared in its report on the matter, "We regard mistaken identification as by far the greatest cause of actual or possible wrong convictions."[507]

Two facts are informative as to the extent of false eyewitness identifications. The first is that the data suggest that, on average, eyewitnesses pick known innocent fillers in police lineups 30 percent of the time. Second, more than seventy-five thousand suspects are identified annually by eyewitnesses in the United States.[508] Indeed, eyewitness identification has been shown to be inaccurate. "Overall, data from real-life cases show that just under 45% of witnesses pick the suspect, about 35% decline to make a choice, and about 20% pick innocent fillers."[509] The experimental data pertain to lineups in which the suspect is present. In target-absent lineups, 48 percent of witnesses pick an innocent filler.[510]

Research has demonstrated that, contrary to what is commonly believed—by judges and jurors as well—the accuracy of an eyewitness identification and the quality of the description of the perpetrator given by an eyewitness to the police do not correlate.[511] Furthermore, the degree of a witness's certainty in the identification, which

---

[505] Samuel R. Gross & Michael Shaffer, Exonerations in the United States, 1989–2012, Report by the National Registry of Exonerations 52 tbl. 14 (2012), *available at* http://globalwrong.files.wordpress.com/2012/05/exonerations_us_1989_2012_full_report.pdf (last visited Oct. 10, 2014).

[506] Nat'l Registry of Exonerations, Exonerations by Contributing Factor (2014), https://www.law.umich.edu/special/exoneration/Pages/ExonerationsContribFactorsByCrime.aspx (last visited Oct. 10, 2014).

[507] Criminal Law Revision Comm'n, Eleventh Report of the Criminal Law Revision Commission, at para. 196 (1972); *See also* Patrick Devlin, Report to the Secretary of State for the Home Department of the Departmental Committee on Evidence of Identification in Criminal Cases, at para. 8.1 (1976); Dennis, *supra* note 499, at 197–202; Sangero & Halpert, *supra* note 499, at 91.

[508] Garrett, *supra* note 13, at 50.

[509] Simon, *supra* note 418, at 53. See *id.* n.5 for a list of relevant studies.

[510] *Id.*

[511] Melissa Pigott, John Brigham & Robert Bothwell, *A Field Study of the Relationship between Quality of Eyewitnesses' Description and Identification Accuracy*, 17 J. Police Sci. & Admin. 84 (1990); Sangero & Halpert, *supra* note 499, at 91.

reflects social and environmental factors and variables and the witness's personality and traits,[512] bears no relation to the accuracy of that identification.[513] Cognitive psychology studies have shown that human memory is prone to errors and bias and, thus, cannot be trusted, particularly with remembering faces.[514] There are incomplete memories, and there are false memories, and research shows that it is hard to distinguish these from true memories.[515] The process of remembering faces is commonly divided into three stages,[516] and any of these stages can account for an eyewitness's mistaken identification. The first stage of the process is the "acquisition," or "encoding," stage, when the witness first perceives the incident and acquires information: his eyes and ears are exposed to a profusion of visual details and auditory effects, but he can focus on only some of this information. With terrifying or traumatic circumstances or brief occurrences, which usually characterize a criminal incident, a witness can absorb only a small proportion of what is transpiring. Thus, an imperfect and perhaps even distorted, picture of what happened forms in his mind.[517] This is reinforced by what psychological research has shown to be people's difficulty with recognizing the faces of people who are from a different race.[518] In the framework of the Innocent Project cases, for example, the majority of the mistaken identifications had been cross-racial, where a white victim misidentified a black suspect.[519]

The second stage in remembering faces is the "retention" stage. This refers to what happens between the occurrence of the event being remembered and the point at which a witness reconstructs what he saw and/or heard.[520] In the final stage of the process, the "retrieval" stage, the witness "retrieves" the information he acquired and retained in his memory and conveys it to others.[521] His reconstruction of events

---

[512] Evan Brown, Kenneth Deffenbacher & William Sturgill, *Memory for Faces and the Circumstances of Encounter*, 62 J. APPLIED PSYCHOL. 311 (1977).

[513] Gary L. Wells et al., *Eyewitness Identification Procedures: Recommendations for Lineups and Photospreads*, 22 LAW & HUM. BEHAV. 603, 622–27 (1998); ELIZABETH F. LOFTUS, EYEWITNESS TESTIMONY, 100–01 (1979); Keith A. Findley, *Guilt v. Guiltiness: Innocents at Risk: Adversary Imbalance, Forensic Science, and the Search for Truth*, 38 SETON HALL L. REV. 893, 917 (2008).

[514] Robert Buckhout, *Eyewitness Testimony*, SCI. AM., Dec. 1974, at 23; Sangero & Halpert, *supra* note 499, at 91.

[515] SIMON, *supra* note 418, at 97–106.

[516] LOFTUS, *supra* note 513, at 20–109.

[517] Steven I. Friedland, *On Common Sense and the Evaluation of Witness Credibility*, 40 CASE W. RES. L. REV. 165, 181 (1989/1990). *See also* LOFTUS, *supra* note 513, at 20–51; Sangero & Halpert, *supra* note 499, at 91.

[518] LOFTUS, *supra* note 513, at 136–42; Gary L. Wells & Elizabeth F. Loftus, *Eyewitness Memory for People and Events, in* 11 HANDBOOK OF PSYCHOLOGY 156 (R.K. Otto & I. B. Weiner eds., 2013) (ch. 9); SIMON, *supra* note 418, at 63.

[519] GARRETT, *supra* note 13, at 51, 72–74.

[520] LOFTUS, *supra* note 513, at 52–87; Sangero & Halpert, *supra* note 499, at 91.

[521] LOFTUS, *supra* note 513, at 88–109; Sangero & Halpert, *supra* note 499, at 92.

is impacted by the actual information he absorbed during the original event as well as what he experienced during the retention stage and the circumstances surrounding the request that he recall what he saw and heard.[522]

In any one of these stages, distortion that leads to error is a reasonable possibility.[523] This could be due to individual variables or circumstances, including a witness's individual abilities and capacities, the duration of his exposure to the event in question, and whether he was experiencing any trauma or distress when witnessing the event (e.g., because he was the actual victim or simply has a strong reaction to the event). Cultural and social variables can also account for distortions, as can systemic factors, such as how the police investigation and the identification lineup are conducted, including the number of fillers and how the suspect is identified.[524] Studies have shown that police behavior during the procedure can be critical in mistaken identifications, such as suggestive remarks and hints and the directions they give to the eyewitness.[525] Moreover, the identification procedure can also have a significant impact on the likelihood of error, with studies showing the preferability of a sequential live lineup procedure over a simultaneous procedure[526] and that the error rate for a photo lineup is considerably greater than for a live lineup.[527] The unsafety of this situation has been succinctly described by Elizabeth F. Loftus and Gary Wells, the leading researchers in this field, as follows: "Eyewitness evidence ... is typically collected by nonspecialists who have little or no training in human memory. Police protocols for collecting, preserving, and interpreting eyewitness evidence have not integrated

---

[522] Loftus, *supra* note 513. Witnesses also have an over-inclination to pick someone from the lineup. In experimental studies that gave witnesses a second chance to choose after being informed that they were wrong in their first attempt, 60 percent then picked someone else. SIMON, *supra* note 418, at 56.

[523] Friedland, *supra* note 517, at 178–80; Sangero & Halpert, *supra* note 499, at 92.

[524] GARY L. WELLS, EYEWITNESS IDENTIFICATION 13–25 (1988); Wells & Loftus, *supra* note 518, at 156–57. See especially table 9.1 in Wells & Loftus, *id.*, which maps "eyewitness identification variables and their categories": sex of witness, intelligence, age, face recognition skills, personality, alcohol, prior exposure/source confusion/bystander, view, disguise of perpetrator, exposure time, same versus other-race identification, stress, weapon, retention interval, interpolated mugshots, overheard descriptions, prelineup instructions, structure of lineup/fillers, simultaneous/sequential procedure, suggestive behaviors during lineup, postidentification feedback. The three categories noted are: chronological, system versus estimator, general impairment versus suspect-bias. See also SIMON, *supra* note 418, at 58–76.

[525] GARRETT, *supra* note 13, at 48–50. According to the Innocence Project findings, "in 78% of these trials (125 of 161 cases), there was evidence that police contaminated the eyewitness identifications." *Id.* at 49. See also figure A.9, *id.* at 281: "Eyewitness misidentification": Discrepancy in description—63 percent, Initial non-i.d.—40 percent, Suggestive lineup—34 percent, Showup—34 percent, Suggestive remarks—28 percent, Initially uncertain—21 percent, Did not see face—9 percent, and Hypnotized—3 percent.

[526] R.C.L. Lindsay & Gary L. Wells, *Improving Eyewitness Identifications from Lineups: Simultaneous versus Sequential Lineup Presentation*, 70 J. APPLIED PSYCHOL. 556 (1985).

[527] Gary L. Wells & R.C.L. Lindsay, *Methodological Notes on the Accuracy-Confidence Relation in Eyewitness Identification*, 70 J. APPLIED. PSYCHOL. 413, 414 (1985) (arguing that no evidentiary weight should be given to the identification of a suspect from a photo array in an album when there is no suspect to begin with); Sangero & Halpert, *supra* note 499, at 92.

the results of research conducted by memory experts."[528] Simon further notes the inherently problematic nature of eyewitness identifications and police lineups:

> Absent national standards of best practices, the nation's almost 20,000 law enforcement departments are largely free to conduct lineups as they see fit. Many departments appear to have no standing policies or procedures, and the training of the officers who conduct the procedures is haphazard and nonuniform, at best. A recent survey of more than 500 police officers reveals an inadequate and inconsistent knowledge of the factors that influence the accuracy of identifications....[529]

Thus, when an eyewitness identification is the evidence on which fact-finders must decide whether to convict, it is vital that they weigh the very reasonable likelihood of error as well as of false testimony.[530] Yet whereas the courts tend to accord very strong weight to eyewitness identification of the suspect as the perpetrator of the crime, they tend not to give much evidentiary weight to a failure to do so, that is to say, a witness's failure to identify the suspect or her identification of a filler in the lineup as the perpetrator.[531] The tendency, rather, is to attribute the failure to identify the suspect to the witness's short memory span or fear, for example. Thus, courts do not regard a witness's failure to identify the suspect as indicative of the suspect's innocence. In fact, a very plausible explanation for this tendency is the impact of the common misperception of the suspect's guilt.[532] Yet the very same factors believed to account for a failure to identify (such as short memory span) are, of course, likely to also lead to a misidentification of an innocent suspect. Thus, there is no way to logically reconcile according incriminating weight to an eyewitness identification with the rejection of exculpatory weight to a failure to identify.

B. POSSIBLE SAFETY MEASURES

(1) Negation of a Conviction Based Only on Eyewitness Testimony

The general principle proposed to implement in the criminal justice system is that a conviction must not be based on a sole piece of evidence.[533] Above, I showed the proposal's relevance in the context of a confession,[534] and it seems no less relevant in

---

[528] Wells & Loftus, *supra* note 518, at 149.

[529] SIMON, *supra* note 418, at 76.

[530] Sangero & Halpert, *supra* note 499, at 92.

[531] Gary L. Wells & Rod C. L. Lindsay, *On Estimating the Diagnosticity of Eyewitness Non-identifications*, 88 PSYCHOL. BULL. 776, 777 (1980).

[532] See Section VI of Chapter 3.

[533] See Section IV of Chapter 3.

[534] See Section IV of Chapter 5.

the context of an eyewitness identification[535] when it is the only evidence of a defendant's guilt. Indeed, a similar question arises as in the context of confessions: had the witness been able to see, say, ten thousand, rather than ten, people in the police lineup, how many would have resembled the person he saw committing the crime? What if, moreover, every resident of the relevant state were to participate in the lineup?[536]

As discussed above, studies show the erroneous identification of an innocent suspect to be a prevalent phenomenon.[537] It is quite possible that an eyewitness will even give a detailed description of an innocent suspect prior to making the identification and have great confidence in the (nonetheless) wrong identification. Yet significant evidentiary weight is given to eyewitness confidence[538] and the ability to give a detailed description of the offender.[539] The Hidden Accidents Principle makes it likely, moreover, that there are many more instances of mistaken eyewitness identification than have been exposed. We can assume, based on the available data and research, at least one out of ten cases of eyewitness identification to be mistaken, but the courts—and police investigators and prosecutors—seem incapable or unequipped to detect these errors.[540] Most people, including judges, intuitively assume a connection between the extent of a witness's confidence in his identification of the suspect and the accuracy of that identification, as well as between the quality of the eyewitness description of the suspect and the accuracy of the subsequent identification. Yet studies show that no such correlation exists,[541] and thus investigators, prosecutors, judges, and juries cannot use these factors—eyewitness confidence and descriptions—as the basis for determining the accuracy of an eyewitness identification. Based on the relevant research, courts' error rate with regard to mistaken identification testimony can be estimated to stand at approximately 50 percent, meaning that eyewitness testimony would yield similar results as confessions in the numeric hypothetical example analyzed in the latter context.[542]

Moreover, in most cases of a conviction based solely on eyewitness identification, an error will be made.[543] Studies have shown that in a significant number of cases of wrongful conviction based on eyewitness testimony, there was no other significant

---

[535] Sangero & Halpert, *supra* note 499, at 92.

[536] *Id.* at 92–93.

[537] *Id.* at 93.

[538] Garrett, *supra* note 346, at 63–68; Manson v. Brathwaite, 432 U.S. 98 (1977).

[539] Garrett, *supra* note 346, at 68–70; 432 U.S. 98.

[540] Sangero & Halpert, *supra* note 499, at 93.

[541] *Id.*

[542] *Id.* See also Section IV of Chapter 5.

[543] This is not to say that most eyewitness testimony is erroneous. Rather, I am focusing specifically on cases in which the eyewitness testimony stands on its own and there is no other evidence connecting the defendant to the crime. Sangero & Halpert, *supra* note 499, at 93.

evidence that tied the defendant to the crime. As I have showed elsewhere with Dr. Mordechai Halpert, this possibility of error in eyewitness identification and the wrongful conviction it can lead to mandates not only close scrutiny of any additional evidence—incriminating and exculpatory—by the court but also a legal rule prohibiting conviction based solely on eyewitness testimony—that is, when there is no additional significant evidence of guilt.[544] Similar to the case of confessions, there must be a requirement for "strong corroboration": independent, significant evidence that the defendant committed the offense he is accused of. [545] In addition, conducting a police lineup should be permitted only when there is reasonable suspicion that the suspect committed the crime in question.[546]

(2) Proper Protocols for Police Lineup Identifications

In both the research and the Innocence Project cases, mistaken eyewitness testimony has emerged as the primary cause of wrongful conviction.[547] Although this was a revelation in the legal field, it is well known in the psychological literature, which has documented and examined the problematic nature of eyewitness testimony since the 1970s.[548] For example, researchers found that informing an eyewitness that the suspect might not be in the lineup reduces the rate of false identification significantly but the rate at which actual perpetrators are identified only slightly,[549] thereby neutralizing "relative judgment conceptualization."[550] However, even when eyewitnesses are thus advised, the rate of mistaken lineup identification remains high,[551] not only in the laboratory but also in reality.[552]

Several protocols have been proposed for police lineup procedures, based on psychological studies on the subject. These protocols are aimed at decreasing the risk of erroneous identification but without impacting, to as great an extent as possible, the likelihood of identifying the actual perpetrator in the lineup.[553] One of these proposals, formulated by Wells, includes seven recommendations in conducting

---

[544] *Id.*

[545] *Id.*, at 93–94.

[546] *See infra* note 556 and accompanying text.

[547] See the Innocence Project Home Page at http://www.innocenceproject.org (last visited May 3, 2015).

[548] Gary Wells, *Eyewitness Identification: Systemic Reforms*, 2006 WIS. L. REV. 615, 615–16; Mordechai Halpert & Boaz Sangero, *Towards Safety in the Criminal Justice System*, 36 TEL AVIV U. L. REV. 363, 389–91 (2013) (in Hebrew).

[549] Wells, *supra* note 548, at 625.

[550] Wells & Loftus, *supra* note 518, at 157–58.

[551] *Id.* at 619.

[552] Gary L. Wells et al., *Eyewitness Evidence Improving Its Probative Value*, 7 PSYCHOL. SCI. PUB. INT. 45, 50–51 (2006).

[553] Halpert & Sangero, *supra* note 548, at 390.

lineups:[554] First, no more than one suspect should be included in a lineup. Second, a suspect should not "stand out" and be conspicuous relative to the other lineup participants. Third, eyewitnesses should be told that the suspect might not be in the lineup. Fourth, instead of the customary simultaneous lineup procedure, which is known to lead to mistaken identification by elimination,[555] a sequential procedure should be used, with only one lineup participant paraded before the eyewitness at a time. Fifth, a "double blind test" should be implemented in lineups, so that not only the eyewitness but also whoever is administering the lineup does not know who the actual suspect is and which participants are just fillers. Sixth, the lineup administer should take the eyewitness's confidence statement without giving any feedback regarding the accuracy of the identification. And finally, seventh, given the Bayes Theorem probability calculations, a lineup should be allowed only when there is a reasonable suspicion that the suspect committed the crime.[556]

(3) Other Safety Measures

Others have also recommended that lineups be recorded on video,[557] and preferably, all police investigative work should be video documented, so that there will be direct, full documentation for the court of what transpires. In line with this, it has also been recommended that eyewitness descriptions of suspects be recorded by a police officer not involved in the investigation, before any identification procedure is conducted.[558] Simon has offered a more detailed protocol, with eighteen instructions for the police, aimed at maximizing both the accuracy of identifications and the transparency of the procedures used to elicit them.[559] He has also formulated recommendations for reform of the trial proceedings in this context: eyewitness identifications emanating from flawed lineup procedures should be ruled inadmissible, and in-court identifications[560] should not be allowed as a first identification or following any suggestive identification procedure.[561]

---

[554] Wells, *supra* note 548, at 623–41.

[555] Wells & Loftus, *supra* note 518, at 158; SIMON, *supra* note 418, at 71.

[556] Wells & Loftus, *supra* note 518.

[557] VIRGINIA STATE CRIME COMM'N, MISTAKEN EYEWITNESS IDENTIFICATION 32, 33, 38, 39 (2005), *available at* http://leg2.state.va.us/dls/h&sdocs.nsf/By+Year/HD402005/$file/HD40.pdf. *See also* Halpert & Sangero, *supra* note 548, at 390.

[558] THOMAS, *supra* note 494.

[559] SIMON, *supra* note 418, at 80–86. Alongside these recommendations for improving the lineup identification procedure, Simon recommended adopting the Cognitive Interview Protocol, developed by Ron Fisher and Edward Geiselman, for police interviews of witnesses. This Protocol has been adopted in the United Kingdom. *Id.* at 118 and n.204.

[560] On in-court identifications, see *infra* note 574 and accompanying text.

[561] SIMON, *supra* note 418, at 178.

Instituting computerized lineups could be the most substantial measure toward increasing accuracy in lineup identifications. This would entail compiling a large database with video clips of fillers. A suspect would be filmed, and the computer program would then choose video clips of fillers who resemble her and resemble the eyewitness's description of the suspect. This procedure, which would be conducted without the direct involvement of law enforcement personnel, would neutralize most biases. It would also be easier to find many suitable fillers, and the lineup would be conducted as a sequential procedure and recorded.[562]

All of these recommended measures to prevent mistaken identifications would entail low costs relative to the potential harm involved.[563] New Jersey became the first state, in 2001, to initiate reforms of police lineups, later followed by several other states.[564] One notable and important step forward was the 1998 publication of the Scientific Review Paper of the American Psychology-Law Association,[565] which led to the drafting of the Guide for Law Enforcement by the National Institute of Justice.[566] This Guide provides detailed instructions on a number of procedures relating to witness interviews and identifications: obtaining information from the witness, instructing the witness prior to viewing the lineup, conducting the identification procedure, recording identification results, establishing mug books and composites procedures, setting up procedures for interviewing the witness by the follow-up investigator; and establishing field identification procedure (showup).[567]

The issue of eyewitness identification illustrates prominently how the criminal justice system can learn from the psychological field and adopt simple safety measures that have been developed and long recognized in the psychology literature. However, for some reason, despite these insights and the high price many people pay, the criminal justice system has remained disturbingly safety "unaware" in this context, and not every state or police department has engaged in the necessary reforms to make lineup procedures safe.[568] In practice, police fail to follow or even

---

[562] *Id.* at 86–89.

[563] Wells, *supra* note 548, at 632. *See also* Halpert & Sangero, *supra* note 548, at 391.

[564] Wells, *supra* note 548, at 641–43; Garrett, *supra* note 346, at 123–24.

[565] Wells et al., *supra* note 513; Marvin Zalman, *An Integrated Justice Model of Wrongful Convictions*, 74 ALB. L. REV. 1465, 1490 (2011).

[566] NAT'L INST. JUSTICE, TECHNICAL WORKING GROUP FOR EYEWITNESS EVIDENCE: TRAINING TEAMS, *available at* https://www.ncjrs.gov/nij/eyewitness/tech_working_group.html (last visited Oct. 10, 2014); U.S. DEP'T JUSTICE, OFFICE OF JUSTICE PROGRAMS, NAT'L INST. JUSTICE, EYEWITNESS EVIDENCE: A GUIDE FOR LAW ENFORCEMENT (1999), *available at* https://www.ncjrs.gov/pdffiles1/nij/178240.pdf (last visited Sept. 23, 2014).

[567] *Id.*

[568] Wells, *supra* note 548, at 641–43. *See also* Halpert & Sangero, *supra* note 548, at 391.

to have proper lineup protocols,[569] and they at times resort to stacked lineups[570] and suggestive remarks.[571] Even worse, instead of live lineups, they sometimes use extremely unreliable and suggestive methods of identification, such as "showups" (where the witness is shown a single suspect or photo to identify)[572] or an array of photos.[573] In addition, courts allow "in-court identifications" even though this procedure is known to be highly suggestive; the witness need only point to the person seated at the defense table, next to the defense attorney. Despite the fact that research has shown the weak probative weight of such poor diagnostic and misleading identifications, they have a strong impact on fact-finders on the premise that "seeing is believing."[574]

Another area in which improvement is vital is ensuring the presence of the suspect's lawyer during the police lineup procedure. In *Wade*,[575] the Supreme Court recognized that this is a critical stage at which the suspect is entitled to have the aid of counsel, which can prevent unfairness in the composition of the lineup and reduce the chances of suggestiveness.[576] In later decisions, however, the Court held that the right to counsel is applicable only after adversary judicial criminal proceedings have begun, that is, only after the suspect has been indicted. Thus, in many cases, police do not ensure that the suspect's counsel is present during the lineup.[577] This must be changed, for the very reasons pointed to in *Wade*.[578]

It is important to stress that improving the accuracy of police lineups is crucial not only to ensure more accurate verdicts, but also—and perhaps even more so—to ensure more accurate eyewitness identifications in cases that never go to court and end up in conviction in the framework of a plea bargain. In these cases,

---

[569] GARRETT, *supra* note 13, at 60.

[570] *Id.* at 57–59.

[571] *Id.* at 59–62.

[572] SIMON, *supra* note 418, at 69 ("[S]howup procedures are the wild card of identification procedures: they are the most widely used, the least studied, and probably the most error prone.").

[573] GARRETT, *supra* note 13, at 54–57.

[574] SIMON, *supra* note 418, at 154–57. A few defense attorneys have challenged this practice of in-court identification, by seating someone other than the defendant next to them. The witnesses have at times picked out the innocent substitutes. Unfortunately, judges tend to respond angrily to this tactic and cite the defense attorneys for contempt. *Id.* at 157.

[575] United States v. Wade, 388 U.S. 218 (1967).

[576] LOFTUS, *supra* note 513, at 181–82.

[577] *Id.* at 184–85. *See also* Kirby v. Illinois, 406 U.S. 682 (1972); GARRETT, *supra* note 13, at 54; Craig M. Bradley, *United States, in* CRIMINAL PROCEDURE—A WORLDWIDE STUDY 532 (Craig M. Bradley ed., 2007).

[578] Barry C. Feld, *Criminalizing Juvenile Justice: Rules of Procedure for the Juvenile Court*, 69 MINN. L. REV. 141, 210–14 (1984); Wefing & Frase, *supra* note 381, at 586; John B. Wefing, *Wishful Thinking by Ronald J. Tabak: Why DNA Evidence Will Not Lead to the Abolition of the Death Penalty*, 33 CON. L. REV. 861, 881, 884 (2001).

the eyewitness identification cannot be challenged in cross-examination and cannot be revealed as false.[579]

As Wells and Loftus have noted, "[T]here remains a large gap between what psychological science advises for collecting eyewitness evidence and actual practices of criminal investigators. Future research needs to address this gap."[580] Loftus has suggested that judges be more liberal in allowing the defense to present to the jury expert psychological testimony about the factors that affect the reliability of eyewitness accounts. Such testimony could help to safeguard against mistaken identifications.[581] Moreover, more detailed safety recommendations could and should be formulated by the proposed Safety in the Criminal Justice System Institute (SCJSI) and implemented on a trial basis, for ongoing assessment and refinement over time.

(4) New Developments: The 2014 National Academy of Sciences Report

After I had completed writing this book, in October 2014, the National Academy of Sciences (NAS) released a very important report, entitled *Identify the Culprit—Assessing Eyewitness Identification.*[582] The title of the NAS committee that prepared the report is no less interesting from the perspective of safety: the Committee on Scientific Approaches to Understanding and Maximizing the Validity and Reliability of Eyewitness Identification in Law Enforcement and the Courts. This shows that it is possible—and necessary—to scientifically assess not only forensic evidence, as the NAS did in its important 2009 report, but all evidence that serves as the basis for criminal convictions. A proper safety approach should lead the NAS to issue, first, a similar report that takes a scientific approach to confessions, which are a central cause of false convictions, and then additional reports that deal with each type of evidence used in criminal law, starting with the most central types.

The latest 2014 report began with the following important observation:

Eyewitnesses play an important role in criminal cases when they can identify culprits. Yet it is well known that eyewitnesses make mistakes, and their memories can be affected by various factors including the very law enforcement procedures

---

[579] LOFTUS, *supra* note 513, at 180.
[580] Wells & Loftus, *supra* note 518, at 158.
[581] Loftus, *supra* note 513, at 191–203. *See also* THOMAS, *supra* note 494, at 196–97.
[582] NAT'L ACAD. SCIENCES, COMMITTEE ON SCIENTIFIC APPROACHES TO UNDERSTANDING AND MAXIMIZING THE VALIDITY AND RELIABILITY OF EYEWITNESS IDENTIFICATION IN LAW ENFORCEMENT AND THE COURTS, A REPORT: IDENTIFY THE CULPRIT—ASSESSING EYEWITNESS IDENTIFICATION (2014), *available at* http://public.psych.iastate.edu/glwells/NAS_Eyewitness_ID_Report.pdf (prepublication copy—unedited proofs) (last visited Oct. 14, 2014).

designed to test their memories. For several decades, scientists have conducted research on the factors that affect the accuracy of eyewitness identification procedures. Basic research on the processes that underlie human visual perception and memory have given us an increasingly clear picture of how eyewitness identifications are made and, more important, an improved understanding of the principled limits on vision and memory that may lead to failures of identification.[583]

Among its other functions, the committee was charged with drafting a *"consensus report with appropriate findings and recommendations."*[584] Due to the conservative approach taken by the committee, it made recommendations on which there is broad consensus among researchers in the field, which, in my view, justifies the immediate and unequivocal adoption of each one. I will first present the eleven crucial recommendations made in the report, some of which may be familiar from the studies and recommendations discussed in this chapter. I will then note what I view to still be lacking in this important report from a safety perspective.

In the first group of recommendations, five recommendations call for the establishment of best practices for the law enforcement community:[585]

1. Train all law enforcement officers in eyewitness identification;
2. Implement double-blind lineup and photo array procedures;
3. Develop and use standardized witness instructions;
4. Document witness confidence judgments;
5. Videotape the Witness Identification Process.

The second group of recommendations includes four recommendations for strengthening the value of eyewitness identification evidence in court. In the preface to these recommendations, the following insightful comment illustrates the tremendous gap between the commonly applied legal rules and scientific method in particular and safety in general:

The *Manson v. Brathwaite* test under the Due Process Clause of the U.S. Constitution for assessing eyewitness identification evidence was established in 1977, before much applied research on eyewitness identification had been conducted. This test evaluates the "reliability" of eyewitness identifications using factors derived from prior rulings and not from empirically validated sources. As critics have pointed out, the *Manson v. Brathwaite* test includes

---

[583] *Id.* at 1.
[584] *Id.* (emphasis added).
[585] *Id.* at 72–74.

factors that are not diagnostic of reliability. Moreover, the test treats factors such as the confidence of a witness as independent markers of reliability when, in fact, it is now well established that confidence judgments may vary over time and can be powerfully swayed by many factors.[586]

The relevant recommendations are as follows:[587]

6. Conduct pretrial judicial inquiry (the committee recommends that a judge make basic inquiries when eyewitness identification evidence is offered);
7. Make juries aware of prior identifications;
8. Use scientific framework expert testimony;
9. Use jury instructions as an alternative means to convey information.

In the third and final group of recommendations, two recommendations are made for improving the scientific foundation underpinning eyewitness identification research:[588]

10. Establish a national research initiative on eyewitness identification;
11. Conduct additional research on system and estimator variables.

There is no doubt that these are very important recommendations from a safety perspective, especially as they are issued by the leading authority in the scientific field. But what is nonetheless missing here? First of all, the report sufficed with recommending establishing standardized protocols for lineup identifications but without providing a detailed "model" protocol. Thus, for example, it lacks even the most basic recommendation, on which all researchers in the field concur, that before eyewitnesses make a lineup identification, they should be informed that the criminal they saw at the scene of the crime might not be among the lineup participants.

Second, as the NAS committee sufficed with making recommendations that fall within the bounds of the consensus in the field, it refrained[589] from important near-consensus recommendations. Exemplifying this is the failure to recommend shifting from simultaneous lineups to sequential lineups, even though it is broadly recognized that simultaneous lineups lead witnesses to identify the suspect through a process of elimination, by comparing him or her to the rest of the lineup participants. The common denominator (in this context, among researchers in the field) is,

---

[586] *Id.* at 4, 74–75.
[587] *Id.* at 74–77.
[588] *Id.* at 77–81.
[589] *Id.* at 2.

by nature, low. It is a mistake to suffice with recommendations that meet only this high threshold. Identification lineups continue to be conducted, and if a method that is almost consensus or even supported by the majority of researchers in the field (such as sequential lineups) is not adopted, then we will be "stuck" with a method that the majority of researchers caution against (such as simultaneous lineups).

Third and finally, the NAS report lacks what I consider to be the central safety rule, namely, that a defendant cannot be convicted solely on the basis of an eyewitness identification, and that additional evidence connecting him to the commission of the crime is required. The generalized version of this rule is that a conviction cannot be based on a sole piece of evidence of any type. In the area of eyewitness testimony, the NAS report makes no such recommendation, despite the fact that the research and insights presented in the report strongly support adopting this important rule.

6 Safety in Criminal Procedures

I. General

Chapter 2 outlined the fundamentals of modern system-safety. Chapter 3 suggested general safety principles for the criminal justice system. Chapter 4 demonstrated how modern safety can be applied in the criminal justice system. In this chapter, I will now point the way to safety in criminal procedures similarly to how the analysis was constructed in Chapter 5 with regard to evidence: for each of the central procedures chosen for discussion, I will first describe the present state of a lack of safety ("unsafety") and then propose some possible safety measures. The latter suggestions will be based both on an analysis of each specific procedure according to recent research on the subject, as well as on modern safety theory and its application in the criminal justice system under the principles outlined in Chapters 2, 3, and 4. It is important to stress that I will offer only *examples* of possible safety measures. Developing a comprehensive safety theory for criminal law requires substantial cross-disciplinary work by researchers, which, I propose, should be conducted within the framework of a Safety in the Criminal Justice System Institute (SCJSI).

In previous chapters, I already noted two central causes of false convictions that originate in criminal procedure: the conception of the suspect's guilt, or the "tunnel vision" phenomenon, and organizational failures in general and, in particular, a lack of redundancy in criminal procedure.[1] These two factors will not be explored here in detail, but will be mentioned in the discussion. Indeed, in this chapter, I do not attempt to review all of the central phenomena in criminal procedure that lead to false convictions, as this is beyond the scope of the discussion. This includes, for example, the contention held by many (including myself) that the adversarial system does not adequately defend the innocent; thus, inquisitorial elements should be incorporated into the system so that judges do not simply listen to the adversaries' arguments but also take positive action to investigate the truth, for instance, by summoning court witnesses.[2] Other central factors of false convictions deriving from criminal procedure that will not be discussed in this chapter for reasons of brevity are inadequate legal representation at trial,[3] racial bias,[4] judicial error, and the lack of a general right to open-file discovery for defendants.[5]

---

[1] These are discussed in Chapters 3 (section VI) and 4 (section VII), respectively.

[2] GEORGE C. THOMAS III, THE SUPREME COURT ON TRIAL: HOW THE AMERICAN JUSTICE SYSTEM SACRIFICES INNOCENT DEFENDANTS, ch. 9 (2008); Marvin Zalman, *The Adversary System and Wrongful Conviction, in* WRONGFUL CONVICTION: INTERNATIONAL PERSPECTIVES ON MISCARRIAGES OF JUSTICE 79 (C. Ronald Huff & Martin Killias eds., 2008); D. Michael Risinger, *Unsafe Verdicts: The Need for Reformed Standards for the Trial and Review of Factual Innocence Claims*, 41 HOUS. L. REV. 1281 (2004) (suggesting that the adversarial system is not suited to cases with a claim of innocence). For an example of the function of an inquisitorial criminal justice system, see Thomas Weigend & Jenia Lontcheva Turner, *The Constitutionality of Negotiated Criminal Judgments in Germany*, 15 GERMAN L.J. 81 (2014).

[3] *See, e.g.*, BARRY SCHECK, PETER NEUFELD & JIM DWYER, ACTUAL INNOCENCE: FIVE DAYS TO EXECUTION AND OTHER DISPATCHES FROM THE WRONGLY CONVICTED 183–92 (2000).

[4] *See, e.g.*, DAVID COLE, NO EQUAL JUSTICE (1999); RANDALL KENNEDY, RACE, CRIME AND THE LAW (1997); MICHEL TONRY, MALIGN NEGLECT: RACE CRIME AND PUNISHMENT IN AMERICA (1995); Karen Parker et al., *Race, the Death Penalty, and Wrongful Convictions*, 2003 CRIM. JUST 49; THOMAS, *supra* note 2, at 4, 117–38.

[5] Under *Brady v. Maryland*, 373 U.S. 83 (1963), which compelled the prosecution to disclose only exculpatory evidence to the defense and only evidence that is material to guilt or punishment, defendants in criminal trials are granted very limited access to the prosecution's documents in the case file and have no general right to evidence discovery. *See* Roger J. Traynor, *Ground Lost and Found in Criminal Discovery*, 39 N.Y.U. L. REV. 228, 233 (1964); Rodney Uphoff, *Convicting the Innocent: Aberration or Systemic Problem?*, 2006 WIS. L. REV. 739, 835; Mary Prosser, *Reforming Criminal Discovery: Why Old Objections May Yield to New Realities*, 2006 WIS. L. REV. 541, 557–58; Keith A. Findley, *Guilt v. Guiltiness: Innocents at Risk: Adversary Imbalance, Forensic Science, and the Search for Truth*, 38 SETON HALL L. REV. 893, 901 (2008). The Supreme Court has, accordingly, held: "We know of no constitutional requirement that the prosecution make a complete and detailed accounting to the defense of all police investigatory work on a case." Moore v. Illinois, 408 U.S. 786, 795 (1972). The *Brady* rule does not, therefore, enable defense counsel to assess the potential of quasi-neutral evidence for its case, and indeed, defendants could benefit not only from quasi-neutral evidence but even from unfavorable evidence. *See* Comment, *The Prosecutor's Constitutional Duty to Reveal Evidence to the Defendant*, 74 YALE L.J. 136, 147 (1964); Victor Bass, Brady v. Maryland *and the Prosecutor's Duty to Disclose*, 40 U. CHI. L. REV. 112, 135 (1972). This limited access makes it difficult for innocent defendants

II. Police and Prosecution Negligence and Misconduct

A. CURRENT UNSAFETY

(1) General

Herbert Packer observed that police and prosecutors must be required to abide by due process norms regardless of the guilt or innocence of suspects or defendants, so as to prevent the emergence of a culture of misconduct that will impact both the guilty and innocent.[6] A central cause of false convictions is negligence or misconduct by police investigators, lab technicians, and prosecutors.[7] Misconduct can refer to any of the following, among other things: deliberate suggestiveness in identification procedures; fabrication of evidence; withholding of evidence from the defense by the prosecution or from the prosecution by the police; deliberate mishandling, mistreatment, or destruction of evidence; coercion of a false confession; deliberate contamination of confessions; and conscious reliance on unreliable government informants or snitches.[8]

Over two decades (until 2005), the number of documented cases of prosecutorial misconduct has tripled.[9] In 1999, a study conducted in the framework of the Innocence Project already found that in 42 percent of false convictions there had been prosecutorial misconduct, and police misconduct in 50 percent of the cases.[10] The most recent empiric study on this issue, conducted by Samuel R. Gross and Michael Shaffer, examined 2043 formal exonerations, between the years 1989 and 2012, of falsely convicted defendants.[11] Of these cases, 1170 were part of the group

---

to expose the truth and be exonerated. *See* Uphoff, *supra*, at 835. My recommendation is that prosecution authorities turn over to the defense not only exculpatory evidence but the entirety of the evidence gathered in the police investigation that is not privileged, so as to prevent the conviction of innocent defendants. *See* Bass, *supra*, at 113; William J. Brennan, Jr., *The Criminal Prosecution: Sporting Event or Quest for Truth?*, 1963 WASH. U. L.Q. 279, 287; Comment, *supra*, at 147; Prosser, *supra*, at 600; United States v. Bagley, 473 U.S. 667, 695–96 (Marshall, Brennan, JJ., dissenting).

[6] HERBERT PACKER, THE LIMITS OF CRIMINAL SANCTION 168 (1968); Susan A. Bandes, *Protecting the Innocent as the Primary Value of the Criminal Justice System*, 7 OHIO ST. J. CRIM. L. 413, 437 (2009).

[7] INNOCENCE PROJECT, GOVERNMENT MISCONDUCT, http://www.innocenceproject.org/understand/ Government-Misconduct.php (last visited July 10, 2013).

[8] *Id.* For additional examples of misconduct, see Andrew M. Hetherington, *Thirty-First Annual Review of Criminal Procedure: III. Trial: Prosecutorial Misconduct*, 90 GEO. L.J. 1679, 1679–90 (2002). *See also* Brandon L. Garrett, *Innocence, Harmless Error, and Federal Wrongful Conviction Law*, 2005 WIS. L. REV. 35, 78–87 (on suggestive eyewitness identification procedures); *id.* at 87–92 (on coerced confessions); *id.* at 93–97 (on fabrication of evidence).

[9] Alexandra White Dunahoe, *Revisiting the Cost-Benefit Calculus of the Misbehaving Prosecutor: Deterrence Economics and Transitory Prosecutors*, 61 N.Y.U. ANN. SURV. AM. L. 45, 46 (2005); *see also* Natasha Minsker, *Prosecutorial Misconduct in Death Penalty Cases*, 45 CAL. W. L. REV. 373, 374–76 (2009).

[10] JIM DWYER ET AL., ACTUAL INNOCENCE: WHEN JUSTICE GOES WRONG AND HOW TO MAKE IT RIGHT 246 (2003).

[11] Samuel R. Gross & Michael Shaffer, EXONERATIONS IN THE UNITED STATES, 1989–2012—REPORT BY THE NATIONAL REGISTRY OF EXONERATIONS (2012), *available at* http://globalwrong.files.wordpress. com/2012/05/exonerations_us_1989_2012_full_report.pdf (last visited Oct. 5, 2014).

exonerations of falsely convicted individuals that resulted from the exposure of thirteen cases of police corruption in recent years. In 368 of the 873 individual exonerations (i.e., that were not in the framework of the group exonerations), the false convictions had also been due to police or prosecutorial misconduct. Misconduct, therefore, accounted for the wrongful convictions in 42 percent of the individual exonerations and 75 percent of all the exonerations. This outcome puts misconduct at the top of the list of causes of false convictions, surpassing even mistaken or false eyewitness testimony. And as the researchers clarified, they did not have all the data. As usual, in investigating false convictions, then, this is only the tip of the iceberg, due to the Hidden Accidents Principle in criminal law, which keeps the majority of instances hidden from sight. Moreover, even when misconduct is uncovered in post-conviction proceedings, courts tend to find this only "harmless error" and to uphold the original conviction.[12]

A central factor in police and prosecutorial negligence and misconduct is "tunnel vision" in presuming the suspect's guilt. As I demonstrated in Chapter 3, in order to develop a safer model the criminal law-enforcement system must look to the psychological research on biases of this type.

(2) Police Misconduct

Police misconduct accounts for many cases of false conviction.[13] Two types of criminal conduct on the part of the police can be distinguished.[14] The first is corruption, as in the notorious Rampart[15] and Tulia[16] scandals and Newsome case,[17] in which

---

[12] Garrett, *supra* note 8, at 109, 59–62, 78–97; Michael T. Fisher, *Harmless Error, Prosecutorial Misconduct, and Due Process: There's More to Due Process than the Bottom Line*, 88 COLUM. L. REV. 1298 (1988). I will discuss the doctrine of "harmless error" further in Section IV of this chapter.

[13] Garrett, *supra* note 8, at 42.

[14] Similar to the distinction I make between two categories of police misconduct, it has been suggested that "if the prosecutorial misconduct occurs to frame an innocent person, it is corrupt. It is still inexcusable if it is instead designed to facilitate the conviction of a person the prosecutor believes is guilty." Peter A. Joy, *The Relationship between Prosecutorial Misconduct and Wrongful Convictions: Shaping Remedies for a Broken System*, 2006 WIS. L. REV. 399, 407.

[15] Samuel R. Gross et al., *Exonerations in the United States, 1989 through 2003*, 95 J. CRIM. L. & CRIMINOLOGY 523, 534–36 (2005). In the LAPD Rampart scandal, a corrupt police officer who was awaiting trial for dealing in cocaine revealed how he and his colleagues in the unit had incriminated defendants by fabricating evidence, false testimony, and more. *Id.* At least a hundred defendants were similarly incriminated and convicted, with most pleading guilty to the charges against them. *Id.*

[16] In the Tulia scandal, thirty-nine defendants were brought to trial for drug offenses as a result of a single piece of false testimony given by an undercover police detective. *Id.* at 534. Most of the defendants pleaded guilty and were convicted. *Id.* at 534–36.

[17] Garrett, *supra* note 8, at 47. Ten years after Newsome's conviction for murder, the court ordered the Chicago Police Department to run unidentified fingerprints taken from objects found at the crime scene. A police officer who discovered that the prints matched those of a prisoner who had been sentenced to death for another murder lied that no match to the prints had been found.

the police incriminated suspects despite being aware of their actual innocence. The second type of criminal conduct arises when the police are certain of the suspect's guilt but fear that he will be acquitted due to insufficient evidence. To prevent this outcome, police investigators either withhold evidence that would prove the suspect's innocence or "enhance" or fabricate incriminating evidence. They justify this as serving the "noble cause" of upholding the law and public safety.[18] This latter type of criminal misconduct is more pervasive and, therefore, the more dangerous kind. Police investigators' distorted perception that their role is to ensure conviction is very likely to motivate this behavior. This conduct, in turn, misleads the fact-finders in exercising their discretion at trial.

Laurie Levenson has suggested a systematic diagnosis for police corruption.[19] In investigating the "police culture" that leads to misconduct, based, among other things, on findings in many commission reports, Levenson identified the following factors as common predictors of police misconduct and corruption: an insulated police department; a strong code of silence; the prevalence of a "professional" model as opposed to "community policing"; an ineffective or unfair professional disciplinary system; and inadequate screening, training, and supervision of police personnel.[20] Levenson elaborated on how the traditional legal avenues for contending with police misconduct—namely, the exclusionary rule, civil rights claims, administrative discipline, and commission inquiries and reports—all fail to bring about long-term, meaningful change in police practices.[21] In particular, the exceptions to the exclusionary rule that have developed over time have stripped it of its effectiveness in deterring police misconduct.[22] Moreover, the Supreme Court's *Herring* decision further weakened the rule's deterrent effect.[23] Last, even federal civil rights actions face significant obstacles, such as the qualified immunity defense and collateral estoppel defense.[24]

To be an effective deterrent of police or prosecutorial misconduct, a criminal sanction must be implemented swiftly and consistently. Yet criminal prosecutions

---

[18] Randall Grometstein & Jennifer Balboni, *Backing out of a Constitutional Ditch: Constitutional Remedies for Gross Prosecutorial Misconduct Post* Thompson, 75 ALB. L. REV. 1243, 1273–74 (2011/2012).

[19] Laurie L. Levenson, *Police Corruption and New Models for Reform*, 35 SUFFOLK U. L. REV. 1 (2001).

[20] *Id.* at 13–16.

[21] *Id.* at 18–25; *see also* Matthew V. Hess, *Good Cop—Bad Cop: Reassessing the Legal Remedies for Police Misconduct*, 1993 UTAH L. REV. 149.

[22] Levenson, *supra* note 19, at 18–19.

[23] Herring v. United States, 555 U.S. 135 (2009). For the weakening of the deterrent effect in general since *Herring*, see Claire Angelique Nolasco, Rolando V. del Carmen & Michael S. Vaughn, *What* Herring *Hath Wrought: An Analysis of Post-*Herring *Cases in the Federal Courts*, 38 AM. J. CRIM. L. 221, 253 (2011).

[24] Hess, *supra* note 21, at 158–62; Christopher L. McIlwain, *The Qualified Immunity Defense in the Eleventh Circuit and Its Application to Excessive Force Claims*, 49 ALA. L. REV. 941, 941–42 (1998) (regarding qualified immunity).

of police officers are rare.[25] The nature of the criminal justice system is that prosecutors and police investigators must work in close collaboration, leading prosecutors to be naturally averse to bringing criminal charges against investigators. Independent and impartial investigations of police wrongdoing may be an unrealistic expectation.[26] In federal prosecutions of police misconduct, moreover, the specific intent requirement, in conjunction with the beyond-a-reasonable-doubt standard and jurors' law-and-order bias, makes obtaining a conviction very difficult.[27]

In many cases, the wrongly accused have no civil remedy to resort to when they have been the victims of gross negligence or indifference that amounts to police misconduct. The rule that releases the police from a constitutional obligation to investigate exculpatory evidence they uncover after establishing probable cause for arrest[28] inflicts intolerable harm on the innocent. There are countless examples of such circumstances. Paul Romero, who was implicated in a murder, was held in jail for about three months until his case was dismissed.[29] Romero claimed from the outset of his interrogation that he had been in his apartment the night of the murder and that three people could corroborate his alibi. He also gave the police investigator the name of someone who had threatened the victim about two hours prior to the murder.[30] The police, however, did not act to verify this information in any way. The court entered a summary judgment in favor of the defendants and denied Romero a remedy, ruling that a police officer who finds probable cause to arrest does not violate a constitutional obligation "by failing to investigate the defendant's alleged alibi witnesses."[31]

In another case, Allen Wade Simmons was held in jail for approximately eight months for armed robbery and shooting based on eyewitness identification, and released only when the actual perpetrator was found.[32] Police failed to inform the district attorney's office that Simmons's fingerprints did not match the fingerprints found on the cigarette packet the robber had inadvertently dropped at the crime scene. Moreover, even when the police received, after Simmons had been indicted, information implicating another person (who eventually emerged to be the true culprit), the latter's fingerprints were not compared with those found on the cigarette

---

[25] Hess, *supra* note 21, at 184.

[26] *Id.*

[27] *Id.* at 185.

[28] Adele Bernhard, *When Justice Fails: Indemnification for Unjust Conviction*, 6 U. CHI. L. SCH. ROUNDTABLE 73, 86–88 (1999); Michael Avery, *Paying for Silence: The Liability of Police Officers under Section 1983 for Suppressing Exculpatory Evidence*, 13 TEMPLE POL. & CIVIL RTS. L. REV. 1, 13 (2003).

[29] Romero v. Fay, 45 F.3d 1472 (10th Cir. 1995).

[30] *Id.* at 1473.

[31] *Id.* at 1476.

[32] Simmons v. McElveen, 846 F.2d 337 (5th Cir. 1988).

packet. Deeming the police officers' conduct "mere negligence,"[33] the court ruled in favor of the defendants, and Simmons was denied any remedy.

Similarly, John Kelly was held in jail for one year before the charges against him, including cocaine possession, were dropped.[34] A week after his arrest, the state crime laboratory released its report according to which the substance found in Kelly's home was not a prohibited drug.[35] The report was sent to both the district attorney and the police investigators, but for some undetermined reason, it reached the district attorney's office only months later.[36] Moreover, the police detective did not bring the contents of the report to the district attorney's attention. In its decision on the claim brought by Kelly against the police, the court held that the police had no reason to suspect that the district attorney's office had never received the report and, therefore, was under no affirmative duty to inform the district attorney about the report.[37] However, the court held, the police detective had not mentioned the exculpatory report in the affidavit in support of the arrest warrant for cocaine possession. Only on this last issue did the court hold that the detective is not immune against Kelly's claim.[38]

The crucial importance of compensating someone who suffered harm due to the system's negligence is obvious. However, the examples I presented above were not intended as illustrations of this point, but rather, to demonstrate the extent to which the system lacks safety mechanisms for preventing such harms from occurring from the outset, including false suspicions or extended false detention. A safety system would prevent a suspect from being held in custody for a year simply because the prosecution did not receive a lab report determining that the substance in question is not a prohibited drug. Nor would a person be imprisoned for months simply because a police detective failed to inform the prosecutor that the suspect's fingerprints do not match the fingerprints found at the scene of the crime. Proposals for amending this situation as raised in the literature should be assessed and considered, such as: close supervision of the police investigators by prosecutors;[39] creating an external unit to investigate suspicions of police misconduct; and implementing a mechanism that will inform prosecutors of instances of police misconduct, such as fabrication of evidence.[40] Judges must strictly scrutinize the credibility of police

---

[33] *Id.* at 339.
[34] Kelly v. Curtis, 21 F.3d 1544 (11th Cir. 1994). For a detailed analysis of this case, see Boaz Sangero & Mordechai Halpert, *A Safety Doctrine for the Criminal Justice System*, MICH. STATE L. REV. 1293 (2012).
[35] *Kelly*, 21 F.3d at 1547.
[36] *Id.* at 1548.
[37] *Id.* at 1552.
[38] *Id.* at 1548, 1554.
[39] Levenson, *supra* note 19, at 33–37.
[40] *Id.* at 37–39.

reports, for the knowledge that the courts almost automatically give greater credence to the police's version of the facts fosters misconduct and even corruption.[41] Judges must inform prosecutors or the external supervisory unit of any instance of police misconduct exposed at trial. Defense attorneys should have access to databanks on police misconduct during the course of investigations or trials. Effective methods of educating police officers to place emphasis on uncovering the truth and not on "winning" should be developed.

(3) Prosecutorial Misconduct

Every stage of the criminal process is susceptible to prosecutorial misconduct, from the decision to indict, through the trial proceedings, and up to the post-conviction proceedings. Misconduct during trial can include concealment of exculpatory evidence, improper opening or closing statements, improper questioning of witnesses, and submission of false or misleading evidence.[42] Prosecutorial misconduct is no rare occurrence, and criminal defense attorneys give accounts of many such instances.[43]

The general causes of prosecutorial misconduct tend to be overzealousness, an excessive determination to get a conviction, and tunnel vision in presuming the accused's guilt.[44] It has been suggested that prosecutorial misconduct is not generally a matter of "isolated instances of unprincipled choices or the failure of character on the part of some prosecutors,"[45] but, rather, "largely the result of three institutional conditions: vague ethics rules that provide ambiguous guidance to prosecutors; vast discretionary authority with little or no transparency; and inadequate remedies for prosecutorial misconduct."[46] The ethics rules do, indeed, send a mixed signal to prosecutors in directing them to be both adversarial and neutral. The result is ambiguous norms, with the rules failing to provide prosecutors with a comprehensive and clear list of what amounts to prosecutorial misconduct.[47]

---

[41] *Id.* at 39–42.

[42] Michael D. Cicchini, *Prosecutorial Misconduct at Trial: A New Perspective Rooted in Confrontation Clause Jurisprudence*, 37 SETON HALL L. REV. 335, 335 (2007); Alisha L. McKay, *Let the Master Answer: Why the Doctrine of Respondent Superior Should Be Used to Address Egregious Prosecutorial Misconduct Resulting in Wrongful Convictions*, 2012 WIS. L. REV. 1215, 1222; THOMAS, *supra* note 2, at 189.

[43] Prentice L. White, *Absolute Immunity: A License to Rape Justice at Will*, 17 WASH. & LEE J. CIVIL RTS. & SOC. JUST. 333, 344 (2011).

[44] McKay, *supra* note 42, at 1223.

[45] Joy, *supra* note 14, at 400.

[46] *Id.*

[47] *Id.* at 416.

George Thomas has described the problematic nature of "the job we ask prosecutors to do" as follows:

The goals of serving justice and being an advocate are in tension, if not downright contradictory. ... The career incentives for prosecutors are also in tension with protecting innocence. Prosecutors typically have ambitions that transcend their current position—to advance in the ranks of prosecutors, to become a judge, to run for political office. The current system rewards conviction rates and either ignores or penalizes dismissals and acquittals. In short, we have failed to develop an incentive structure for prosecutors that rewards the pursuit of justice rather the pursuit of competitive advantage.[48]

What, then, is the proper function of a prosecutor in the criminal law? Is he allowed to conceal from the accused, the defense attorney, and the court materials gathered in the police investigation that are likely to aid the defense? Is it his job to get a conviction at any cost? The answer to all of these questions is a definitive no. The role of the prosecutor is to aid the court in arriving at the truth, which is the foundation of doing justice. The prosecutor represents the whole public, the public interest, for he is an apparatus of the elected government. Thus, he bears a particularly rigorous duty of fairness and must act with absolute fairness. Accordingly, as defined by Justice George Sutherland in *Berger*, prosecutorial misconduct is "overstepping the bounds of that propriety and fairness which should characterize the conduct of such an officer in the prosecution of a criminal offense."[49] Therefore, if a prosecutor is aware of possibly exculpatory evidence that emerged in the course of the police investigation, disclosing it to the defense is not a matter of discretion, as an act of "benevolence," but, rather, an obligation.[50] The adversarial system, however, cultivates a dynamic of competition that is likely to cause prosecutors to seek to win at all costs; moreover, they are also likely to misconceive their role when their success is measured by their conviction rate,[51] which can mislead them to thinking that their responsibility to win supersedes their duty to do justice.[52]

---

[48] Thomas, *supra* note 2, at 25.
[49] Berger v. United States, 295 U.S. 78, 84 (1935).
[50] Daniel J. Capra, *Access to Exculpatory Evidence: Avoiding the* Agurs *Problems of Prosecutorial Discretion and Retrospective Review*, 53 Fordham. L. Rev. 391, 394 (1984); John J. Douglass, *Fatal Attraction? The Uneasy Courtship of* Brady *and Plea Bargaining*, 50 Emory L.J. 437, 437–38 (2001).
[51] Keith A. Findley & Michael S. Scott, *The Multiple Dimensions of Tunnel Vision in Criminal Cases*, 2006 Wis. L. Rev. 291, 328; Bandes, *supra* note 6, at 415. Bandes agrees with Thomas, *supra* note 2, ch. 1, who wrote about the prosecutorial culture that emphasizes conviction rates.
[52] Thomas, *supra* note 2, at 170–71.

Prosecutors are the most powerful actors in the criminal justice system,[53] and their decisions have far-reaching consequences for individuals' life and liberty.[54] This enormous power must be kept in check, but unfortunately, the current legal remedies for prosecutorial misconduct are ineffective. Rarely do courts find unethical or unprofessional prosecutorial conduct to constitute misconduct.[55] Even in cases of misconduct, a main problem is prosecutors' immunity from civil actions. Two types of such immunity are provided for in the central federal civil rights statute:[56] the doctrine of absolute immunity that shields prosecutors from personal liability, even if they acted maliciously, when they act as advocates, in their quasi-judicial capacity;[57] and qualified immunity that applies when they function as investigators or administrators.[58] Following the Supreme Court's interpretation of this provision in *Connick v. Thompson*[59] in 2011, commentators concluded that prosecutorial immunity was now so broad as to render civil actions completely ineffectual.[60] This civil immunity is compounded by a lack of effective disciplinary sanctions and criminal actions.[61] Judges tend not to bring instances of prosecutorial misconduct to the attention of the relevant professional associations.[62] Criminal sanctions are not applied to discourage prosecutorial misconduct.[63] Few prosecutors who have committed misconduct have faced disciplinary charges;[64] some have even been promoted.[65] In the absence of an effective remedy for prosecutorial misconduct, neither the prosecutors as individuals nor the system as a whole has any incentive to alter this conduct.[66]

---

[53] Adam M. Gershowitz, *Prosecutorial Shaming: Naming Attorneys to Reduce Prosecutorial Misconduct*, 42 U.C. DAVIS L. REV. 1059, 1061 (2009).

[54] White, *supra* note 43, at 357.

[55] *Id.* at 339.

[56] 42 U.S.C. § 1983 (1974); Margaret Z. Johns, *Reconsidering Absolute Prosecutorial Immunity*, 2005 B.Y.U.L. REV. 53, 53–54.

[57] Imbler v. Pachtman, 424 U.S. 409, 422–23, 427 (1976).

[58] *Id.* at 430–31.

[59] 131 S. Ct. 1350 (2011).

[60] McKay, *supra* note 42; David Keenan et al., *The Myth of Prosecutorial Accountability after* Connick v. Thompson: *Why Existing Professional Responsibility Measures Cannot Protect against Prosecutorial Misconduct*, 121 YALE L.J. ONLINE 203 (2011).

[61] McKay, *supra* note 42, at 1227–31.

[62] *Id.* at 1228.

[63] *Id.* at 1230–31; Johns, *supra* note 56, at 71.

[64] Grometstein & Balboni, *supra* note 18, at 1269.

[65] *Id.* at 1270.

[66] White, *supra* note 43, at 358; Grometstein & Balboni, *supra* note 18, at 1274–75.

B. POSSIBLE SAFETY MEASURES

In order to reduce the risk of false convictions deriving from police and prosecutorial negligence and misconduct, first and foremost, this hazard must be acknowledged. This must then be followed by measures to reduce this risk, accompanied by research to determine whether they are attaining their goals. These measures would include: educating and informing law-enforcement personnel as to the hazards of this conduct; instituting and enforcing sanctions against law-enforcement officers who break the law; imposing organizational liability for prosecutorial misconduct;[67] stricter judicial rulings when instances of negligence or misconduct are exposed in court, including the exclusion of illegally obtained evidence (which is an already-existing sanction but subject to the court's discretion[68]) and acquitting defendants when exculpatory evidence was concealed; firm judicial rulings that convey clearly the high standards citizens are entitled to demand of the law-enforcement officials who represent them; and increasing redundancy in the system, so that a person's fate is not determined by a sole individual as in the cases described above. Of course, as required by the principles of safety, these recommended measures must be assessed and fine-tuned for effectivity before they can be viewed as proven safety techniques.

An interesting recommendation is that made by the ABA Prosecution Function Standards, that every prosecutor office adopt a "prosecutor's handbook" with "a statement of (i) general policies to guide the exercise of prosecutorial discretion and (ii) procedures of the office." This handbook, the Standards recommend, should be made available to the public "except for subject matters declared 'confidential.'"[69] The National District Attorneys Association (NDAA) makes a similar recommendation.[70] In accordance with the general safety principles I outlined in Chapter 11, such a step is crucial, yet this recommendation has been adopted only in the federal system and a few states.[71]

Internal controls are not, however, sufficient. Other recommended measures include extending the prosecutor's discovery obligation (for example, instituting an open-file discovery duty) and narrowing the prosecutor's discretion in using informants (for example, requiring prosecutors to file a pretrial notice detailing the agreement with the informant) and other cooperating witnesses who receive something of value from the prosecutor.[72] Moreover, abolishing prosecutors' absolute immunity

---

[67] Grometstein & Balboni, *supra* note 18, at 1267–68.

[68] Herring v. United States, 555 U.S. 135 (2009).

[69] Joy, *supra* note 14, at 421–22.

[70] *Id.* at 422.

[71] *Id.* at 422–23.

[72] *Id.* at 425; Garrett, *supra* note 8, at 73–74, 105.

from civil liability would enhance their accountability and serve to more effectively deter prosecutorial misconduct.[73] Indeed, this immunity not only protects dishonest prosecutors at the expense of the innocently accused, it also undermines deterrence of misconduct.[74] Thus, prosecutors who obstruct justice should be subject to the very same sanctions faced by defense attorneys, for example.[75] It has also been suggested that judges not be allowed discretion on how to sanction prosecutorial misconduct. A finding of prosecutorial misconduct should lead to an automatic mistrial without any judicial determination as to whether the defendant would have been found guilty absent the misconduct. Moreover, in cases of intentional prosecutorial misconduct, a retrial should be barred under the double-jeopardy doctrine.[76] Relatedly, it has been proposed that the harmless error doctrine not be applied in instances of prosecutorial misconduct.[77]

Another interesting proposal put forth is that sentence reduction could serve as a remedy for prosecutorial misconduct.[78] The remedies for violations of defendants' procedural rights are usually "all or nothing," and the existing remedies for prosecutorial misconduct are ineffective because of the courts' reluctance to resort to them given their high costs, particularly the possibility of a guilty defendant going free. Thus, it could be effective to include sentence reduction in the courts' remedial arsenal as "an intermediate remedy" for prosecutorial misconduct. This would advance the "corrective, expressive and deterrent" goals.[79]

An additional possible means of reducing prosecutorial misconduct is to make public prosecutorial misconduct[80] and implement a "prosecutorial shaming" policy.[81] When appellate courts reverse convictions due to serious prosecutorial misconduct at trial, the offending prosecutors are often not named in the opinions,[82] possibly because the judges themselves were often prosecutors in the past and do not wish to censure former colleagues.[83] Without any public shaming for their improper actions, prosecutors are subject to neither internal pressure from the criminal justice system nor external pressure from the public to refrain from misconduct.[84] If prosecutorial misconduct has been serious enough to lead to the reversal of a criminal

---

[73] Joy, *supra* note 14, at 425; Grometstein & Balboni, *supra* note 18, at 1280.
[74] *Id.* at 56.
[75] White, *supra* note 43, at 367–68.
[76] Cicchini, *supra* note 42, at 336.
[77] White, *supra* note 43, at 371–72.
[78] Sonja B. Starr, *Sentence Reduction as a Remedy for Prosecutorial Misconduct*, 97 GEO. L.J. 1509 (2009).
[79] *Id.* at 1511.
[80] White, *supra* note 43, at 363.
[81] Gershowitz, *supra* note 53.
[82] *Id.* at 1062.
[83] *Id.* at 1105.
[84] *Id.* at 1063.

conviction, trial judges, defense lawyers, and all prosecutors should be apprised of the identity of the offending prosecutor. It has been suggested that "Prosecutorial Misconduct Projects" (similar to the Innocence Project) be established to identify currently unnamed prosecutors who have been found guilty of misconduct, and compile and release a regularly updated list of offenders and their acts of misconduct. Such projects "would shame bad actors, educate younger prosecutors, and enable judges to keep a closer watch on prior offenders so as to avoid misconduct in future cases."[85] In my opinion, such an important database should not be limited only to those rare instances in which criminal convictions are overturned due to prosecutorial misconduct. Rather it should include each and every instance in which a court has determined prosecutorial misconduct occurred even if it deemed it "harmless error." A proposal along similar lines suggested establishing an external committee to examine cases of improper prosecutorial conduct.[86] Last, more detailed recommendations could be drafted by the proposed Safety in the Criminal Justice System Institute. There is no reason, of course, to assume that each one of the proposals recommended in the literature would necessarily lead to a reduction in police and prosecutorial misconduct. Thus, as required by general safety principles, following the implementation of any given recommendation, it is vital that follow-up and research be conducted to assess its contribution to diminishing the phenomenon.

III. Plea-Bargains

A. CURRENT UNSAFETY

In a plea-bargain arrangement, the defendant agrees to admit to the facts that constitute a particular offense, and in exchange, the prosecution agrees not to charge the defendant with a more serious offense, or agrees to a lighter sentence than could be expected following conviction at trial.[87] Advocates of plea-bargains[88] stress efficiency considerations,[89] claiming that the state in this way saves the resources it

---

[85] *Id.* at 1105.

[86] White, *supra* note 43, at 380.

[87] For different definitions of "plea bargain," see William F. McDonald, *From Plea Negotiation to Coercive Justice: Notes on the Respecification of a Concept*, 13 Law & Soc'y Rev. 385 (1979). On the history and development of plea bargains, see Albert W. Alschuler, *Plea Bargaining and Its History*, 79 Colum. L. Rev. 1 (1979); John H. Langbein, *Understanding the Short History of Plea Bargaining*, 13 Law & Soc'y Rev. 261 (1979).

[88] *See, e.g.*, Robert E. Scott & William J. Stuntz, *Plea Bargaining as Contract*, 101 Yale L.J. 1909 (1992); Allen Wertheimer, *The Prosecutor and the Gunman*, 89 Ethics 269 (1979); Frank H. Easterbrook, *Plea Bargaining as Compromise*, 101 Yale L.J. 1969 (1992).

[89] For an economic analysis of plea-bargains, see William M. Landes, *An Economic Analysis of the Courts, in* Essays in the Economics of Crime and Punishment 164 (Gary S. Becker & William M. Landes eds., 1974).

would spend on conducting a full trial, which can be channeled to law enforcement, thereby increasing deterrence. They further argue that defendants also derive utility from this: under the (not clear-cut) assumption that they act rationally, defendants multiply their chances of conviction by the expected sentence at the end of a trial, compare the result to the offer made by the prosecution, and decide whether it is worthwhile for them to confess in a plea-bargain or go to trial. Under this argument, the plea-bargain system gives the defendant an additional option and, thereby, works in her favor. In addition, defendants are spared the tension of a trial and the uncertainty as to their future, as well as saving heavy legal representation costs. The premise guiding some of the proponents of plea-bargains is that they are made in "the shadow of the trial" and, therefore, very closely approximate the anticipated outcome at trial, while saving the resources necessary to arrive at that outcome.[90]

However, it can be argued,[91] when a defendant waives his right to a full trial and suffices with conviction in a plea-bargain, he is also waiving the requirement to prove guilt beyond reasonable doubt,[92] which is one of the principal mechanisms for preventing false convictions. This relates to the risk that the wide gap between the defendant's anticipated punishment if convicted at trial and the relatively lighter punishment if he confesses in the plea-bargain will lead not only the guilty but also the innocent to confessing, who are unwilling to take the risk of conviction at trial.[93]

Thomas described this problematic situation as ultimately deriving from the "failure to screen weak cases, many of which will involve innocent defendants, out of the system" and allowing prosecutors "free rein to offer very favorable plea bargains to get convictions when the case is weak. ... American plea bargaining thus creates huge incentives for the innocent people to plead guilty."[94] Thomas noted that society's "acceptance of this risk" leads to a prioritization of case-resolution over

---

[90] Stephanos Bibas, *Plea Bargaining Outside the Shadow of Trial*, 117 HARV. L. REV. (2004).

[91] Scott & Stuntz, *supra* note 88, at 1909, note: "Most legal scholars oppose plea bargaining, finding it both inefficient and unjust. Nevertheless, most participants in the plea bargaining process, including (perhaps especially) the courts, seem remarkably untroubled by it."

[92] *See, e.g.*, Kenneth Kipnis, *Criminal Justice and Negotiated Plea*, 86 ETHICS 93, 106 (1976).

[93] A well-known example of precisely this dilemma was raised by Albert Alschuler in his seminal article *The Prosecutor's Role in Plea Bargaining*, U. CHI. L. REV. 36, 61 (1968): a defendant accused of rape who was likely innocent told his lawyer that he will accept the prosecution's offer to reduce the charges to assault, which was made because they had no significant evidence against him, because he couldn't risk being convicted of rape. *See also* Stephen J. Schulhofer, *Plea Bargaining as Disaster*, 101 YALE L.J. 1979 (1992). Similarly, Lucian Dervan describes the outrageous case of Lea Fastow, who was forced to choose between short imprisonment before the long imprisonment of her husband and the risk of their both being sentenced to long, parallel imprisonments, which would have left their two young children without either of their parents, Lucian E. Dervan, *The Symbiotic Relationship between Plea Bargaining and Overcriminalization*, 7 J.L. ECON. & POL'Y 645, 653–55 (2011).

[94] THOMAS, *supra* note 2, at 12.

truth-finding.[95] Plea-bargains, he stated, remain "a troubling phenomenon" because they are "covert and informal"; thus there is no way of knowing "how many innocent defendants are 'sweet talked' into pleading guilty."[96] In a similar vein, the English Royal Commission on Criminal Justice ("Runciman Commission") Report stated, "it would be naive to suppose that innocent persons never plead guilty because of the prospect of the sentence discount."[97]

In the past, plea-bargaining was officially prohibited as a practice.[98] This prohibition was the legal expression of the morally questionable light in which many view plea-bargains, seen as distancing the law from justice.[99] On this background, Rule 11 of the Federal Rules of Criminal Procedure requires that judges ensure the voluntariness of a plea of guilty in the framework of a plea-bargain, by "addressing the defendant personally in open court, determining that the plea is voluntary and not the result of force or promises apart from a plea agreement." In its seminal 1970 *Brady* decision,[100] the Supreme Court ruled that even consent due to fear of the death penalty is to be considered voluntary, but at the same time, set certain limitations on plea-bargains: a plea-bargain can be made only when the evidence is overwhelming and the defendant unlikely to succeed at trial and can benefit from the opportunity to negotiate for a reduced sentence. Plea-bargaining, the Court further ruled, cannot be used to overwhelm defendants and force them to plead guilty when their guilt is uncertain. Finally, the Court stressed that if these constitutional limitations are not abided by, it would reconsider its approval of the plea-bargaining system.[101]

---

[95] *Id.* at 12 (quoting on this point Darryl K. Brown, *The Decline of Defense Counsel and the Rise of Accuracy in Criminal Adjudication*, 95 CALIF. L. REV. 1585, 1613 (2005)).

[96] *Id.* at 204.

[97] ROYAL COMM'N ON CRIMINAL JUSTICE REPORT: PRESENTED TO PARLIAMENT BY COMMAND OF HER MAJESTY 10 (July 1993) [hereinafter RUNCIMAN COMMISSION REPORT].

[98] Kipnis, *supra* note 92, at 101. See also Kipnis's interesting comparison of the plea-bargain to a situation in which an instructor suggests to a student that instead of bothering to mark the student's paper (which, from glancing at the first page, the instructor estimates would get a D-grade), the student can waive his right to having his paper checked and receive a B. The student agrees to this. *Id.* at 104–05.

[99] The waiving of the truth-finding process and the experience of doing justice is most prominent in the "Alford" and "nolo contendere" pleas: in the former, the defendant admits to the existence of sufficient evidence to convict him but asserts his innocence; in the latter, the defendant does not admit guilt but is willing to bear the punishment. *See* Stephanos Bibas, *Harmonizing Substantive-Criminal-Law Values and Criminal Procedure: The Case of Alford and Nolo Contendere Pleas*, 88 CORNELL L. REV. 1361 (2003); Albert W. Alschuler, *Straining at Gnats and Swallowing Camels: The Selective Morality of Professor Bibas*, 88 CORNELL L. REV. 1412 (2003); Stephanos Bibas, *Bringing Moral Values into a Flawed Plea-Bargaining System*, 88 CORNELL L. REV. 1425 (2003).

[100] Brady v. United States, 397 U.S. 742 (1970). *See also* North Carolina v. Alford, 400 U.S. 25 (1970).

[101] *Id. See also* Dervan, *supra* note 93, at 651–53.

The *Brady* rule ultimately failed, however. Today, it is generally acknowledged that innocent defendants are offered great enticements to falsely confess. Sometimes, everyone puts pressure on the defendant to confess: the prosecutor, the judge, and even the defense counsel.[102] This problem is further exacerbated by a potential conflict of interest and agency problem with the defense attorney (it is usually in the latter's best interest to convince her client to agree to a plea-bargain given the extensive work required by going to trial) and with the prosecuting attorney (prosecutors have personal considerations, such as career-advancement,[103] that could divert them from the public interest). As Stephen J. Schulhofer has shown, the agency costs of plea-bargains are significant.[104] Judicial discretion to reject a plea-bargain is too narrow; prosecutorial discretion to make a plea-bargain is too broad and powerful,[105] and is used to pressure defendants into pleading guilty or face severe sentences.[106] Moreover, the existing mechanisms for preventing unfounded prosecutions—namely, grand juries and preliminary hearings—are ineffective.[107] Grand jury proceedings are not presided over by a judge, and the defendant and counsel are not even present during the proceedings. All the prosecutor has to do is to persuade the grand jury of probable cause, bringing to mind the famous quip (attributed to a judge) that any prosecutor can get a grand jury to "indict a ham sandwich."[108] Prosecutors also suffer from "self-serving bias." The nature of their job leads them to conclude that defendants are guilty and to offer plea-bargains that reflect that assessment.[109] This can account for the practice of overcharging as a means of pressuring defendants to agree to a plea-bargain,[110] which is, in essence, blackmail.

In a plea-bargain system, it is sufficient for the case to be closed with a conviction that the defendant confessed. It is quite ironic that a common justification for

---

[102] *See* John H. Langbein, *Torture and Plea Bargaining*, 46 U. CHI. L. REV. 3 (1978) (claiming that torture and plea-bargaining are the criminal system's response to the failure of criminal procedure to address the needs of law enforcement). *But see* Wertheimer, *supra* note 88. In defense of plea-bargains, see Scott & Stuntz, *supra* note 88; *but see* Schulhofer, *supra* note 93.

[103] *See* Bandes, *supra* note 6; THOMAS, *supra* note 2.

[104] Schulhofer, *supra* note 93, at 1987–91.

[105] *See, e.g.*, Donald G. Gifford, *Meaningful Reform of Plea Bargaining: The Control of Prosecutorial Discretion*, 1983 U. ILL. L. REV. 37. *See also* THOMAS, *supra* note 2, at 204–05.

[106] Kate Stith, *The Arc of the Pendulum: Judges, Prosecutors, and the Exercise of Discretion*, 117 YALE L.J. 1420, 1422–25 (2008).

[107] Oren Gazal-Ayal, *Partial Ban on Plea Bargains*, 27 CARDOZO L. REV. 2295, 2349 (2006); Craig M. Bradley, *United States, in* CRIMINAL PROCEDURE—A WORLDWIDE STUDY 540–41 (Craig M. Bradley ed., 2007).

[108] THOMAS, *supra* note 2, at 30, 172, 202–04.

[109] Linda Babcock & George Loewenstein, *Explaining Bargaining Impasse: The Role of Self-Serving Biases*, 11 J. ECON. PERSP. 109 (1997).

[110] Gifford, *supra* note 105, at 47–49.

offering a plea-bargain is that the prosecution lacks strong enough evidence to convict at trial. The reality, however, is that false convictions occur also when defendants confess in the framework of a plea-bargain.[111] Indeed, plea-bargains are one of the central mechanisms facilitating false convictions. This system is a veritable convictions industry, of both the innocent and guilty. There is, of course, a close correlation between the high rate of convictions[112] and the rate of plea-bargains, which operates in both directions: On the one hand, as with plea bargains, the outcome is, by definition, conviction and not acquittal, they obviously contribute to the high conviction rate. On the other hand, as the rate of convictions is high, it is not surprising that almost all defendants prefer to confess in a plea-bargain, regardless of actual guilt or innocence, having lost hope of acquittal at trial.

To illustrate, in cases of widespread police corruption, such as the LAPD Rampart scandal[113] and Tulia scandal,[114] in which scores of innocent defendants were charged and brought to trial, the majority of the defendants pleaded guilty. In the Rampart scandal, for example, a corrupt police detective revealed how he and his colleagues had incriminated defendants by fabricating evidence and giving false testimony, among other things. Over a hundred defendants were convicted this way, with most pleading guilty to the charges. In the Tulia scandal, thirty-nine defendants were tried for drug offenses based on a single false testimony given by an undercover police detective. Most of these defendants pleaded guilty and were convicted.[115]

The Rampart and Tulia corruption cases prove that a very troublesome situation arises with plea bargains. Eighty-one percent of those convicted confessed in a plea-bargain, despite their actual innocence. Should they have done otherwise? Not necessarily. In the Tulia case, for example, a defendant who falsely confessed in a plea-bargain received, on average, a four-year prison sentence, as opposed to fifty-one years for a defendant who pleaded innocent.[116] The system thus imposes a heavy quasi-fine on those who insist on going to trial: a defendant who maintains his innocence is harshly punished, which impels the majority of defendants

---

[111] Brandon L. Garrett, *Judging Innocence*, 108 COLUM. L. REV. 55, 74 (2008). In a study conducted in Virginia, all cases in which DNA samples had been preserved in the laboratory were examined, without distinguishing between cases in which a plea bargain had been reached and those that went to trial. An examination of the DNA samples revealed that of those defendants who had agreed to a plea-bargain, some were also wrongly convicted. JOHN ROMAN, KELLY WALSH, PAMELA LACHMAN & JENNIFER YAHNER, POST-CONVICTION DNA TESTING AND WRONGFUL CONVICTION 4 n.6 (2012) (research report submitted to the U.S. Department of Justice).

[112] Thus, for example, the acquittal rate in 2002 stood at 1 percent. THOMAS, *supra* note 2, at 204.

[113] Gross et al., *supra* note 15, at 534–36.

[114] *Id.*

[115] *Id.*

[116] RUSSELL D. COVEY, MASS EXONERATION DATA AND THE CAUSES OF WRONGFUL CONVICTIONS (2011), *available at* http://ssrn.com/abstract=1881767 or http://dx.doi.org/10.2139/ssrn.1881767.

to confess regardless of actual guilt or innocence. In its recent *Frye* decision, the Supreme Court noted this phenomenon, citing Barkow: "[Defendants] who do take their case to trial and lose receive longer sentences than even Congress or the prosecutor might think appropriate, because the longer sentences exist on the books largely for bargaining purposes."[117] Yet for some inexplicable reason, the Court did not express any outrage over this reality of heavy "trial penalties."

In the exceptional cases that were exposed, such as Tulia and Rampart, the plea-bargains served the Hidden Accidents Principle in criminal law, according to which false convictions are usually never detected. Oren Gazal-Ayal and Avishalom Tor[118] recently conducted an interesting empirical study of the rate of innocent defendants who confess in the framework of a plea-bargain. Using data from the Innocence Project gathered by Gross et al.,[119] they compiled and examined a dataset of 466 exonerations based on new information pointing to the defendants' factual innocence. In 284 of the cases, the conviction was vacated based on DNA evidence, with the actual offender identified in 96 of the cases.[120] The authors arrived at two noteworthy findings. The one was that although the rate of plea bargains during the relevant period for similar crimes was approximately 90 percent, in only 7.9 percent of the exoneration cases examined in the study had the defendants originally confessed in a plea bargain.[121] The authors inferred from this (as well as from two earlier experimental studies[122]) what they term the "innocence effect," where in contrast to what is commonly presumed under the "looming shadow of the trial theory," here innocent defendants emerged as tending not to confess in a plea-bargain and preferring to go to trial.[123] The authors' second intriguing finding, which derived from the first, is that as the innocent do not tend to agree to a plea bargain, those who are convicted at trial receive particularly harsh sentences. Thus, according to this study's findings, although the rate of false convictions caused by plea-bargains is lower than what is generally thought, the plea-bargaining system nonetheless works to the detriment of innocent defendants in that it results in harsh sentences if they are convicted at trial—far harsher than those received by guilty defendants who agree to a plea bargain.[124]

---

[117] *See* Missouri v. Frye, USSC No. 10-444 (Mar. 21, 2012) (2012 U.S. LEXIS 2321, at 18) (quoting Rachel E. Barkow, *Separation of Powers and the Criminal Law*, 58 STAN. L. REV. 989, 1034 (2006)).

[118] Oren Gazal-Ayal & Avishalom Tor, *The Innocence Effect*, 62 DUKE L.J. 339 (2012).

[119] Gross et al., *supra* note 15.

[120] Gazal-Ayal & Tor, *supra* note 118, at 351–52.

[121] *Id.* at 352.

[122] *Id.* at 359–62.

[123] *Id.* at 345.

[124] *Id.* at 347–48.

There is, however, a methodological flaw to this interesting study. It is generally extremely difficult for someone who has been falsely convicted to obtain an exoneration, and even more so if he confessed, regardless of whether in a plea-bargain or not. Given a confession, exoneration will likely require scientific findings supporting the defendant's innocence,[125] and at times, even DNA findings will not suffice.[126] Accordingly, it is reasonable to assume that the rate of exoneration of defendants wrongly convicted in the framework of a plea-bargain is significantly lower than the rate of exoneration for defendants wrongly convicted after a full trial. Therefore, the fact that the exonerations studied by the authors included only a few cases involving a plea-bargain is not an indication that innocent defendants do not tend to agree to plea bargains, nor does it imply that the plea-bargaining system does not lead to many false convictions.[127] However, what this study does reveal is a compelling need for additional empirical research of plea- bargains in the criminal justice system, as one of the first steps toward making the system safer.

Last, as Oren Bar-Gill and Omri Ben-Shahar have shown, the assumption that without a plea-deal, defendants will be forced to go to trial is completely erroneous, for the prosecution does not have sufficient resources to conduct a trial for every indictment it files, but rather only for a small minority of cases. In practice, only 3 percent of all federal cases go to trial, and only 6 percent of state cases.[128] In the remainder, conviction is obtained through plea-bargaining. Without this system, and given the level of resources currently available to the prosecution, prosecutors would not be able to indict the majority of suspects and would have to instead do significant prescreening before charging suspects.[129] The screening process would likely take into account the severity of the offense in question (applying a standard resembling the de minimis doctrine, for example) and the strength of the evidence in each case. It can be assumed that in many cases, the evidence against an innocent defendant will be weaker than the evidence against another defendant; without the

---

[125] Garrett, *supra* note 111, at 91.

[126] Thus, for example, George Allen was imprisoned for a number of years even after DNA evidence supporting his innocence had been found. See Chapter 5 (section IV) on this.

[127] Another argument was raised by Gross: Samuel R. Gross, *Pretrial Incentives, Post-conviction Review, and Sorting Criminal Prosecutions by Guilt or Innocence*, 56 N.Y.L. SCH. L. REV. 1009, 1019 (2011–2012): "[T]he individual exonerations we know about consist almost entirely of a subset of the most serious false convictions for rape and murder. Inevitably, they underrepresent guilty pleas because most available resources (of courts as well as innocence projects and other defense attorneys) are devoted to potentially innocent defendants who have been sentenced to death or very long prison terms, and such sentences are much less likely after a plea bargain than after a trial."

[128] *See* Missouri v. Frye, USSC No. 10-444 (Mar. 21, 2012) (2012 U.S. LEXIS 2321); Lafler v. Cooper, USSC No. 10-209 (Mar. 21, 2012) (2012 U.S. LEXIS 2322).

[129] Oren Bar-Gill & Omri Ben-Shahar, *The Prisoners' (Plea Bargain) Dilemma*, 1 J. LEGAL ANALYSIS 737 (2009).

option of plea-bargaining, then, many cases against innocent defendants will not go to trial and will be closed. Hence, we can see how the plea-bargaining system is what facilitates the indictment of many defendants, and without this system, it is reasonable to assume that the majority would never be charged. Under this analysis, it seems patently wrong to presume that the plea-bargain system works to the benefit of defendants as a group—although it is possible that it works in favor of specific defendants in specific cases.

B. POSSIBLE SAFETY MEASURES

It is important to distinguish between a comprehensive transformation that does away with plea-bargaining altogether and proposals for specific changes and improvements to the existing plea-bargain system. I will first review some of the proposals made for improving the present situation, and will then consider the possibility of completely abolishing the plea-bargain system. I will stress that so long as there is no reporting duty, database, or empirical studies examining the effectiveness of the proposed changes in improving the system, we can only surmise as to whether they attain their goals. Accordingly, even if a particular proposal is adopted, modern safety theory requires that its impact on the system be assessed in order to decide whether to continue in its implementation.

(1) Possible Improvements to the Plea-Bargain System

To begin with, there is an urgent need to strengthen the current prescreening procedures for indictments,[130] with regard to all offenses and not only serious crimes.[131] Certainly, proof beyond a reasonable doubt cannot be expected in the framework of a plea bargain. However, it is, nonetheless, possible to require, in a law, that the police and prosecution investigation files be submitted to the court for review of whether the evidence of the defendant's guilt meets at least the preponderance of evidence (51 percent) standard.[132]

So long as the system revolves around plea bargains—97 percent of convictions in federal criminal proceedings and 94 percent of the convictions in state proceedings

---

[130] Gifford, *supra* note 99, at 48. *See also* THOMAS, *supra* note 2, at 184, 198–202.

[131] Joan Barkai, *Accuracy Inquiries for All Felony and Misdemeanor Pleas: Voluntary Pleas but Innocent Defendants?*, 126 U. PA. L. REV. 88 (1977).

[132] THOMAS, *supra* note 2, at 199. In German law, "judges receive, even before trial, the investigative file containing all the evidence gathered by the police and the prosecution .... Even a full confession made by the defendant in open court does not necessarily relieve the court of the duty to 'discover the truth.'" Weigend & Turner, *supra* note 2, at 84–85.

are obtained through plea-bargaining—[133] I propose recognizing *defendants' right to a fair plea-bargain offer.*[134] Plea bargains need not be dependent on the goodwill of a particular prosecutor toward a particular defendant or her defense counsel.[135] In the absence of such a right, the majority of defendants' rights are stripped of content, for the majority of criminal proceedings culminate in a plea-bargain rather than after a full trial, where presumably, certain defendants' rights are upheld. If a right to a fair plea-bargain offer is not recognized as part of due process, then the right to a fair trial recedes ex ante to apply in only 3 percent of criminal proceedings in the federal system and 6 percent in the state system, and the U.S. Constitution becomes virtually irrelevant in all the other criminal proceedings.[136]

Also necessary, I contend, is supervision of the prosecution's policy for determining the divergence between the punishment offered in a plea-deal and that expected if convicted at trial, so as to prevent the enticement of the innocent to confess. In practice, when the prosecution offers a defendant a much lighter punishment relative to the punishment expected if convicted after a full trial, this is strong indication that it lacks significant evidence against the defendant (although there are, of course, other possible reasons for a lenient offer), which points to a high likelihood of the defendant's innocence. In such circumstances, optimally the prosecution should not indict the defendant and try to get a conviction by offering a lenient plea-deal. Given this, Gazal-Ayal suggests a "partial ban on plea bargains," so that courts will reject overly lenient ones. In his estimation, this would influence

---

[133] *See* Missouri v. Frye, USSC No. 10-444 (Mar. 21, 2012) (2012 U.S. LEXIS 2321); Lafler v. Cooper, USSC No. 10-209 (Mar. 21, 2012) (2012 U.S. LEXIS 2322) (noting "the reality that criminal justice today is for the most part a system of pleas, not a system of trials").

[134] In the Supreme Court case law, the premise is that the accused is not entitled to such a right and that the prosecution has very broad discretion in this context. *Missouri*, USSC No. 10-444; *Lafler*, USSC No. 10-209.

[135] Under current law, the prosecution is not "under any obligation" to engage in any type of bargaining. Bradley, *supra* note 107, at 543.

[136] It appears that adopting this proposal would also solve the problem of the anomaly created by the majority opinion, which Justice Scalia pointed out in *Lafler v. Cooper*, USSC No. 10-209, and *Missouri v. Frye*, USSC No. 10-444. On the one hand, the majority justices assumed that the defendant does not have a right to receive any sort of plea-bargain offer from the prosecution, but on the other hand, they held that the Sixth Amendment right to counsel extends also to the negotiations leading up to the plea-deal. Thus, if this right was violated due to ineffective counsel (as in *Lafler*), and as a result, the case went to full trial, it is possible that in appeal, the verdict will be vacated and the court will order the prosecution to remake its plea-offer. If the right to counsel was violated due to ineffective counsel (as in *Frye*), and as a result the defendant was never informed of the prosecution's lenient plea-offer and later agreed to a harsher deal, it is possible that on appeal the court will vacate the verdict that gave force to the harsher plea-bargain. In *Frye*, the defense counsel failed to inform the defendant of the plea-offer. After the offer lapsed, the defendant still pleaded guilty, but on more severe terms. In *Lafler*, the client was informed of the favorable plea-offer but, on bad advice from counsel, rejected the offer, and in a full trial before a jury, he received a much harsher sentence than had been offered in the plea-bargain.

prosecutorial screening decisions and lead to a substantial decrease in the number of weak cases that prosecutors pursue.[137]

In German law, it is accepted that courts supervise the gap between the punishment offered to defendants in a plea-bargain and the punishment he can expect to receive if convicted at trial, and they do not accept overly lenient plea-deals that could serve to entice the innocent to confess.[138] Another practical way of achieving such result is to establish an external body to supervise prosecutors, given their tremendous power and the prevalence of false convictions. There should also be adoption of a policy not to make plea-bargains when there is no significant evidence of the defendant's guilt. In addition, Gazal-Ayal and Tor also propose restricting trial penalties,[139] that is to say, constraining judges in giving harsher sentences to defendants who chose not to waive their right to a trial. Diminishing this practice will also ex ante reduce the temptation for the innocent to confess in a plea-bargain due to the wide disparity between the plea-bargain punishment and expected punishment if convicted at trial. It will also, moreover, alleviate the injustice caused to innocent defendants who choose to go to trial and are convicted.

Schulhofer has suggested two important proposals for specific improvements to the current situation. The first is to expand pretrial discovery to approximate the civil model, "so that negotiating parties could more accurately estimate ex ante the likelihood of conviction at trial."[140] The second proposal—the more critical one in his opinion—is that the economic relationship between the defense attorney and his or her client be restructured.[141] For example, when defense attorneys receive the same fee for a case that ends quickly in a plea-bargain and a case that ends only after trial and requires considerably more work, they have a stronger incentive to reach a plea-bargain and convince the client not to go to trial. This asymmetry in representation in criminal proceedings has been depicted in the literature as "a contest between underfunded (and, too often, ineffective) defense attorneys and prosecutors who tend to believe that their duty to win supersedes their duty to do justice";[142] moreover, "the imbalance is so pervasive in the United States that it might be treated as a structural error."[143] Yet Schulhofer's most important recommendation does not

---

[137] Gazal-Ayal, *supra* note 107, at 2300.

[138] *See* Weigend & Turner, *supra* note 2, at 84–85.

[139] Gazal-Ayal & Tor, *supra* note 118, at 395.

[140] Schulhofer, *supra* note 93, at 1998. *See also* Andrew D. Leipold, *How Pretrial Process Contributes to Wrongful Convictions*, 42 AM. CRIM. L. REV. 1123, 1151–52 (2005); *but see* Easterbrook, *supra* note 88, at 1972.

[141] Schulhofer, *supra* note 93, at 1998–99. For additional support of this proposal, see Easterbrook, *supra* note 88, at 1973–74.

[142] THOMAS, *supra* note 2, at 170–71.

[143] Zalman, *supra* note 2, at 80.

relate to specific improvements of the system but, rather, the abolition of the system in its entirety.

(2) Abolition

Four well-known but very different descriptions of the plea-bargain system have been suggested in the literature. Robert E. Scott and William J. Stuntz have described it as a contract,[144] while Frank H. Easterbrook described it as a compromise.[145] John H. Langbein, in turn, compared it to (modern) torture: just as in medieval Europe, the accused had to choose between confessing and torture, today, defendants have to choose between pleading guilty and receiving a lenient penalty and going to trial and risking a long jail-term or even life imprisonment.[146] Finally, Schulhofer calls the plea-bargain system a disaster.[147] I contend that all four of these descriptions are thought-provoking. The first two, however, are applicable only with regard to a guilty defendant, for when an innocent person has been wrongly accused, the plea-bargain is a very unfair contract, and in no way a compromise but rather a terrible submission. When a defendant is innocent (and, probably, also in the case of a guilty defendant), plea-bargaining can be a terrible infliction of psychological torture. The law-enforcement system is unable to distinguish in advance between the guilty and the innocent and, in fact, does not even make a serious attempt at doing so; it therefore, offers plea-bargains to both the guilty and innocent. I thus hold that the plea-bargain system in its entirety is truly a disaster, particularly from the perspective of the need for safety from false convictions.

Unquestionably, the plea-bargain system is a poor one, and I, like Schulhofer and other scholars, view it as a disaster.[148] This is a system that should be abolished because, among other reasons, it leads to false convictions and fosters over-criminalization. Schulhofer has distinguished between two possible levels of abolition.[149] The first level is the abolition of concessions, which would eliminate all incentives for defendants to waive their right to trial; the second level is the abolition only of bargaining, so that concessions for pleas could still be offered, but they would be nonnegotiable incentives set in a statute or court rules.[150] Schulhofer compellingly demonstrated

---

[144] Scott & Stuntz, *supra* note 88.
[145] Easterbrook, *supra* note 88.
[146] Langbein, *supra* note 102.
[147] Schulhofer, *supra* note 93.
[148] *See id. See also* Stephen J. Schulhofer, *Is Plea Bargaining Inevitable?*, 97 HARV. L. REV. 1037 (1984); Albert W. Alschuler, *The Changing Plea Bargaining Debate*, 69 CALIF. L. REV. 652 (1981).
[149] Schulhofer, *supra* note 93.
[150] Suggesting similarly that a magistrate judge be in control of the process leading to a guilty plea and thereby "the coercion and unequal bargaining power that infects the American plea-bargaining system" will be avoided; see THOMAS, *supra* note 2, at 207.

that although abolition of bargaining is certainly an attractive, low-cost solution, abolishing concessions altogether is a no less viable, albeit more costly, strategy.[151]

How is it possible to abolish—either partially or fully—the plea-bargain system? Two possible ways that immediately come to mind are through legislation and through judicial rulings. Internalizing the need for safety in the criminal justice system in order to reduce the extent of false convictions requires that Congress, state legislatures, and judges act to eliminate the plea-bargain system or, at the very least, significantly restrict its scope. But there is also a third possible way of bringing about the abolition of the system: through an alliance of attorneys and defendants. As explained by Bar-Gill and Ben-Shahar, there is a certain paradox in the fact that despite common knowledge of the limited resources available to the prosecution, which means it cannot actually carry out its threat against all defendants and bring them all to trial, this threat nonetheless succeeds in the overwhelming majority of cases: defendants almost always agree to a plea-bargain.[152] The authors explain this with the prisoner's dilemma model: even though the plea-bargain system worsens the situation of defendants as a population (for without the ability to plea-bargain, the prosecution would be forced due to a lack of necessary resources to forgo the majority of indictments), every individual defendant is still likely to think that in his specific case, a plea bargain is to his advantage.[153] Bar-Gill and Ben-Shahar address the possibility of defendants and attorneys—particular public defenders—organizing to take a stand against the system in its entirety, or at least against harsh plea- bargains. In their opinion, however, such an endeavor would likely fail, primarily due to what Bar-Gill and Ben-Shahar describe as a collective action problem.[154] While I agree with the majority of Bar-Gill and Shahar's analysis, I contest their premise that the public defender's fiduciary duty toward a certain client may preclude such an organized effort. In my view, the public defender owes a fiduciary duty not only to each individual client but also to the entire population of defendants; it is possible, therefore, based on this latter duty, to break the vicious cycle of plea-bargains. The avenues explored by the authors, such as having willing defendants sign a letter of agreement not to accept a plea-deal, are, in my estimation, likely to succeed.[155] At the very least, they should be attempted. If the current reality in which millions of defendants, in the face of prosecutors' threats, are compelled to confess to the crimes they are accused of and waive a full trial is seen as an injustice to defendants (at least the innocent ones) by the law-enforcement system,

---

[151] Schulhofer, *supra* note 93, at 2003–09.
[152] Bar-Gill & Ben-Shahar, *supra* note 129, at 739, 744–46.
[153] *Id.* at 746–65.
[154] *Id.* at 758–65.
[155] *Id.* at 760–65.

then defense attorneys should not counsel defendants to accept plea- bargains and thereby assist prosecutors.

Finally, it is important to respond to the counterargument that the criminal law-enforcement system would collapse without plea bargains. The relationship between plea-bargains and over-criminalization is a reciprocal one.[156] On the one hand, plea bargains have allowed for a multiplicity of proceedings; on the other hand, as the system currently conducts too many proceedings, it is now incapable of doing so by determining guilt at trial and without plea-bargains. The criminal law has grown to monstrous proportions: it has taken over our lives. There is an erroneous presumption that every realm of life can be arranged by the criminal law, which was originally intended, of course, to address only the most dangerous antisocial phenomena. When anything can be considered criminal (the Talmudic phrase "*tafasta merube lo tafasta*" comes to mind—if you have seized too much, you have not seized anything at all), the stigma and shame of a criminal conviction fades: too many people are being deemed criminals.[157]

With the realization that the plea-bargains enabling millions of easy convictions annually have generated a process of over-criminalization, the threat of the collapse of the system becomes less alarming. Nothing, in my opinion, will collapse if the plea-bargain system is abolished or at least significantly constricted. Prosecutors will be forced to set priorities and focus on enforcing offenses that are genuinely criminal in nature,[158] and they will cease to use the criminal law to hound citizens over trivial matters. At the same time, constraining the plea-bargain industry will mean a return to a proper attempt at conducting full trials of justice. The phenomenon of wholesale convictions without any attempt at verifying defendants' guilt will come to an end.[159] And last, significant progress will be made toward a safer law-enforcement system.

---

[156] Dervan, *supra* note 101.

[157] *See* Sanford H. Kadish, *The Crisis of Overcriminalization, in* BLAME AND PUNISHMENT: ESSAYS IN THE CRIMINAL LAW 21 (1987); Jonathan Simon, GOVERNING THROUGH CRIME: HOW THE WAR ON CRIME TRANSFORMED AMERICAN DEMOCRACY AND CREATED A CULTURE OF FEAR (2007); DOUGLAS HUSAK, OVERCRIMINALIZATION: THE LIMITS OF THE CRIMINAL LAW (2008); GO DIRECTLY TO JAIL: THE CRIMINALIZATION OF ALMOST EVERYTHING (Gene Healy ed., 2004).

[158] *See also* Kipnis, *supra* note 92, at 106.

[159] An additional possible counterargument is that in the reality of full trials, defendants—including innocent falsely convicted defendants—will receive more severe sentences, for the courts currently give harsher punishments than those attained in plea- bargains. However, as Schulhofer rightly shows, as correction facility resources are limited, the level of the court-decreed punishments can be expected to drop to the current level of punishments offered in plea-deals. Schulhofer, *supra* note 93, at 2007–08. Moreover, those who refuse to waive their right to a full trial will no longer be punished for this choice.

C. APPLYING THE STAMP MODEL TO PLEA BARGAINS

If my central recommendation is adopted—namely, the abolition of the plea-bargain system—there will presumably be no need for a safety model for this system. However, the criminal justice system is currently still based on plea-bargains, and moreover, even if at some point, abolition is implemented, it is reasonable to assume that although the rate of plea-bargains will drop, they will not disappear altogether. And regardless, this will certainly be a long process. Thus, in the coming years and perhaps even decades, I estimate that the system will continue to be based on plea-bargains to some extent.

As more than 90 percent of criminal proceedings end in plea-bargains today, I will demonstrate how the System-Theoretic Accident Model and Processes (STAMP) safety model can be applied in criminal procedure specifically with regard to the plea-bargain mechanism, which is perhaps the central area of prevailing U.S. criminal law. Under Leveson's advanced STAMP model, which I elaborated on in Chapter 2,[160] for each of the hazards existing in the plea-bargain system, the safety constraints necessary in the criminal justice system for preventing these hazards must be defined; for each of these constraints, controls (and barriers) must also be defined, whose purpose is to enforce the safety constraints. This is analyzed in the following table.

TABLE 6.1

ANALYZING PLEA BARGAINS ACCORDING TO THE STAMP MODEL

Hazards	Safety Constraints & Controls
1. A plea-bargain leads to a false confession.	**Safety Constraints:** (a) A confession in the framework of a plea-bargain must be voluntary. (b) A confession in the framework of a plea-bargain must be credible. (c) A temptation to confess must not be created by offering a considerably lighter sentence to a defendant if he confesses in the framework of a plea-bargain than the expected sentence if convicted at trial. (d) The defendant must not be pressured to confess in the framework of a plea-bargain.
	Controls (and Barriers): (e) A plea-bargain must not be made with a defendant if there is no significant evidence against him. (f) A plea-bargain must not be made with someone prior to deciding to indict him. (g) A charge must not be included in the indictment as solely a negotiations tool. (h) A plea-bargain must not be made with a defendant who has no legal representation. (i) All of the evidence gathered by the prosecution must be disclosed to the de-fendant and his attorney, so that they can arrive at an informed decision.

(continued)

---

160 See Section XI of Chapter 2.

TABLE 6.1 (CONTINUED)

Hazards	Safety Constraints & Controls
	(j) The various stages of the plea-bargain negotiations and agreement must be documented.
	(k) Prosecutors must be taught about the hazards of violating Guidelines (a)–(j).
	(l) A supervisory mechanism must be instituted to ensure that prosecutors act in accordance with Guidelines (a)–(j).
2. A defendant is convicted based on a false confession attained through a plea-bargain.	**Safety Constraints:** (a) Judges must determine whether a confession was made voluntarily. They must hear a detailed explanation from defendants as to why they confessed. (b) Judges must not accept a confession if there are significant indications that it is false. Judges must instruct defendants to describe in detail the reasons for committing the crime they have confessed to. (c) A conviction must not be based on a confession if it is the sole piece of evidence (because the confession could be false). (d) A conviction based on a confession must have strong corroboration (not only with respect to corpus delicti but also with regard to the identification of the defendant as the perpetrator of the crime).
	Controls (and Barriers): (e) Judges must not accept a confession obtained through a significant violation by the prosecution of any of the above guidelines directed at the prosecution (1(a)–(j)). (f) Judges must receive from the prosecution a detailed description in writing of the negotiations process preceding the plea-bargain. (g) Judges must receive for review all of the prosecution's evidence materials so as to ensure that the additional pieces of evidence—aside from the confession—significantly implicate the defendant as the perpetrator of the crime. (h) Judges must be instructed in training workshops on the hazards of violating Guidelines (a)–(g). (i) In an appeal of a conviction, there must be close scrutiny of whether all the guidelines relating to the above two hazards were followed. (j) Following conviction, a plea-bargain must not be seen as a barrier to filing an appeal or moving for a retrial, and any new piece of evidence that is likely to indicate that the conviction was false must be examined.

It is important to clarify that this table is not intended as an exhaustive list of all the safety constraints necessary to make the plea-bargain system safe from the risk of false convictions. Moreover, it most certainly does not present all the controls (and barriers) that must be instituted to enforce these safety constraints. All of this must be determined through comprehensive groundwork by the SCJSI (Safety in the Criminal Justice System Institute). I have simply sought here to point to the general direction that systematic safety thinking should take in order to cultivate safety in the criminal justice system and reduce the risk of wrongful convictions.

IV. Post-Conviction Proceedings

A. CURRENT UNSAFETY

(1) General

It is extremely difficult to correct an error after conviction. First of all, given the Hidden Accidents Principle in criminal law, it is very hard to uncover mistakes and even harder to prove them. At times, the very cause of the miscarriage of justice is what perpetuates the injustice and prevents its rectification. Thus, in a case in which the police or prosecution concealed possibly exculpatory evidence, it can be very reasonably assumed that they will continue to withhold that evidence and obstruct its discovery, if only to prevent their own incrimination.

An additional, albeit innocent contributing factor is that once the indictment has been made, the police usually close their investigation. No additional investigation angles are explored, and they do not pursue any alternative suspects. The police assume that the defendant who has been charged with the crime is the actual perpetrator. Added to this is the natural reluctance of any person or institution to admit to a mistake. Hence, innocent suspects generally cannot expect the police to come to their rescue. This is even more so for innocent convicted inmates, for their conviction is accompanied by a presumption of their guilt, and conducting an investigation into their matter is therefore regarded as undermining the judicial system.

But if not the police, then who will find the true perpetrator of the crime and prove the innocence of the wrongly convicted defendant? The answer is: usually no one. The falsely convicted are usually completely powerless. They are sometimes financially destitute, particularly due to the huge amounts of money they have spent on the trial and appeal, with no source of livelihood while imprisoned.

A study conducted by Hugo A. Bedau and Michael L. Radelet found that in cases in which a miscarriage of justice was revealed, it was often by a conscience-driven attorney who had continued to work on the case free of charge for all the long years.[161] But although this was indeed the reality in the past, today the Innocence Project plays a central role in exposing false convictions in the United States, based on DNA comparisons.[162]

In the United Kingdom, the traditional conventional wisdom that false convictions do not occur was shaken to the core with the exposure of the wrongful convictions of Irish individuals due to the "predatory" investigations of the British police,

---

[161] Hugo A. Bedau & Michael L. Radelet, *Miscarriages of Justice in Potentially Capital Cases*, 40 STAN. L. REV. 21, 64 (1987).

[162] See the Innocence Project website at www.innocenceproject.org.

in the notorious "Birmingham Six"[163] and "Guildford Four"[164] cases. Following these revelations, the Runciman Royal Commission on Criminal Justice was appointed to investigate the English criminal justice system and to recommend improvements. Its final report in 1993[165] led to a drastic change in the English approach to the phenomenon of false convictions. The Criminal Cases Review Commission (CCRC) was also established pursuant to this report to review claims of false conviction.[166] An independent public body that serves as a mechanism of last resort, after the judicial process has been exhausted, the CCRC conducts its own inquiry into the cases and convictions and refers suitable cases to the court of appeal.[167] In a considerable number of these cases (twenty one a year on average), the courts have found a miscarriage of justice and have exonerated and released the wrongfully convicted inmates.[168]

The passage of time also works to the detriment of someone who has been the victim of a miscarriage of justice. The more time that passes, the harder it is to uncover the truth. Time is one of the greatest enemies of reconstructing the truth. Evidence gets lost; potential witnesses forget, move away, or die. The legal rules, including, first and foremost, the finality of proceedings rule, on which I elaborate below, hinder the rectification of miscarriages of justice. From the moment that a person is wrongfully convicted, it is very difficult to reverse the outcome. As I will show in what follows, the appeals procedure is very limited, tending to focus primarily on questions of law and constitutional issues and not on questions of fact, even though the majority of false convictions apparently stem from fact-finding errors. As I show below, even when the appellate court finds a defect in the original trial proceedings, it will most likely be deemed "harmless error." Thus, the finality of proceedings rule in fact already applies with the handing down of the verdict at trial, even before appeal. The main procedural mechanism intended for correcting miscarriages of justice is a motion for a new trial. But is this mechanism effective? This will also be considered below.[169]

---

[163] R. v. McIlkenny, (1991) 93 Cr. App. R. 287.

[164] R. v. Richardson, Oct. 20, 1989, 1989 WL 651412 (C.A. Crim. Div. 1989).

[165] RUNCIMAN COMMISSION REPORT, *supra* note 97.

[166] See the CCRC website at http://www.ccrc.gov.uk (last visited April 23, 2015).

[167] *Id.*

[168] From its establishment in April 1997 and up until March 31, 2015, the CCRC had transferred 586 files it deemed suitable to the court of appeals for reconsideration. Of those 550 have been heard by the appeal courts. 380 appeals were won (21 a year) and 154 lost. 874 cases are currently under review and 593 are awaiting review – *Id.* See also Lissa Griffin, *The Correction of Wrongful Convictions: A Comparative Perspective*, 16 AM. U. INT'L L. REV. 1241, 1275–78 (2001).

[169] There is a pessimistic estimation that the adjudicatory process has only limited capability to distinguish between accurate and inaccurate evidence and that "criminal verdicts are determined in the investigative phase, with the trial serving primarily as a ritual that delivers more symbolic than diagnostic value." DAN SIMON, IN DOUBT—THE PSYCHOLOGY OF THE CRIMINAL JUSTICE PROCESS 203 (2012).

(2) Finality of Proceedings Rule

Finality of legal proceedings is not a value in and of itself, but rather a means of attaining other goals. These goals must be closely examined so as to, on the one hand, justify the finality rule while, on the other hand, set its boundaries and exceptions. A central goal of the finality of proceedings rule is to preserve the *deterrence* generated by the verdict, by preventing additional appeal. Once a judgment has been rendered and the right to appeal exhausted, the tendency is to leave no hope of continuing the legal proceedings. The aspiration is to accord the judgment maximum stability, so as to sustain its deterrent effect. In addition, the knowledge that the legal determination is only temporary detracts from its value. It might also inhibit the healing of victims.

Efficiency considerations support the finality of proceedings rule. If a convicted defendant were allowed to appeal interminably, as long as he wishes, there would be no end to the process, the verdict judgment would have little value, and the overloaded courts would be incapable of fulfilling their role. There is both a general and administrative interest in legal proceedings coming to an end.

Nevertheless one may wonder whether the pursuit of the truth and doing justice can be abandoned only due to the costs of further investigation. The hazard that must be weighed against the justifications for the finality of proceedings rule is the horrific prospect of wrongful conviction and its possible outcomes: that the lives of the falsely convicted defendant and his or her family members will be destroyed; that the true criminal will roam free, and might even commit more crimes; and that public confidence in the justice system will be undermined. In my estimation, in the current legal situation, too much weight is accorded to the finality of proceedings rule.[170] As will be shown in what follows, in the context of motions for a new trial on a claim of actual innocence, upholding the rule comes at the expense of the inherent value of uncovering the truth.

(3) Appeal

In the American system, all convicted defendants have a right of first appeal.[171] However, the appeal cannot contest the evidence submitted at trial,[172] for it is aimed at correcting legal or judicial error and not errors of fact. Thus, appeals deal almost exclusively with procedural errors,[173] and the appellate courts usually lack the

---

[170] Even in capital cases, the courts emphasize the need for finality. *See id.* at 213.

[171] Bradley, *supra* note 107, at 546–47.

[172] Lissa Griffin, *Correcting Injustice: Studying How the United Kingdom and the United States Review Claims of Innocence*, 41 U. TOL. L. REV. 107, 109 (2009).

[173] THOMAS, *supra* note 2, at 214–19; Gross, *supra* note 127, at 1021.

authority to deliberate regarding new evidence or reverse a conviction due to jury error.[174] Despite a defendant's due process right not to be convicted on insufficient evidence, the Supreme Court ruled in *Jackson* that it is sufficient that "after viewing the evidence in the light most favorable to the prosecution, any rational trier of fact could have found the essential elements of the crime beyond a reasonable doubt."[175] Consequently, the appeal process does not efficiently ensure the exoneration of defendants who were wrongly convicted. As Thomas has asserted, "The notion of 'elusive truth' helps explain why American criminal appeals are almost exclusively about procedural errors rather than whether the convicted defendant was guilty of the crime. If truth is elusive, who can say that the jury was wrong?" He compares the American system to continental systems, where "getting the facts right is normally one of the preconditions to realizing the goal of the legal process."[176] In contrast, American appellate courts are strongly averse to intervening in the factual determinations made at trial.[177]

One explanation for the current ineffectivity of appeals in correcting wrongful convictions is the nature of the jury system. As the jury determines questions of fact and gives only a verdict of guilty or not-guilty, without any details or reasoning, it is indeed difficult for the appellate court to review and find error in the factual determinations that led to the conviction of an innocent defendant. Therefore, recommendations for improving the appeal process can be implemented primarily with regard to bench trials, where the fact-finder is a professional judge. But either way, the appeal procedure in its current form is not an effective mechanism for correcting factual errors that led to a false conviction.

(4) New Trial: Reality (DNA) or Dream ("Harmless Error")?

"Exoneration" is defined as "An official act declaring a defendant not guilty of a crime for which he or she had previously been convicted."[178] There are different sources of exonerations: acquittal in retrial, dismissal of conviction by the court based on new evidence, pardon based on innocence, and posthumous acknowledgment by the state that a prisoner who died in prison was factually innocent.[179]

---

[174] Griffin, *supra* note 168, at 1271; Gross, *supra* note 127, at 1021.

[175] Jackson v. Virginia, 443 U.S. 307, 318–19 (1979).

[176] THOMAS, *supra* note 2, at 1–2. *See also id.* at 172, 214–19.

[177] SIMON, *supra* note 169, at 212.

[178] Gross et al., *supra* note 9, at 524. .

[179] *Id.*

The harmless error doctrine is likely the biggest obstacle to obtaining a new trial. Even when faced with a constitutional violation,[180] appellate courts must deny relief if the prosecution can show, beyond a reasonable doubt, that the error was harmless (or, in habeas corpus procedure, did not substantially contribute to the conviction).[181] The rationale offered for this rule is that because convicted defendants are allegedly almost always actually guilty, there should be finality to a conviction. Thus, appellate courts can hold a constitutional error to be "harmless" if they find that other evidence presented to the jury could support the conviction.[182] In the legal literature, the doctrine of harmless error has been described as "basically a judicial assurance that nearly anything will be tolerated in regard to an obviously guilty defendant"[183] and as "create[ing] a firewall between constitutional rights and remedies" as an empirical matter.[184]

Strict retroactivity rules, moreover, preclude the application of changes in law to preexisting convictions.[185] Thus, the emergence of a "successful corrective system" is hindered by "the demanding standard of review used by U.S. courts, combined with strict retroactivity rules, a refusal to discover newly discovered impeachments evidence, and a reluctance to test convictions against developments in modern science."[186] Although a convicted defendant who has new evidence of his innocence has the right to apply for a new trial, the motion must be made before the same judge who convicted him, which inevitably leads to institutional bias.[187] Compounding all this are short statutes of limitations,[188] the high standard of proof the defendant must meet (namely, showing that the new evidence probably would have produced a different result at trial),[189] and the disallowance of impeachment evidence as a basis for relief in most state jurisdictions.[190]

If relief is unavailable in the state court, a wrongly convicted defendant can resort to a federal writ of habeas corpus. But federal courts award relief in only 0.4 percent

---

[180] Unless resulting from a structural defect; *see* Arizona v. Fulminante, 499 U.S. 279, 309–10 (1991). The Supreme Court has excluded structural defects in the trial mechanisms (such as the absolute denial of the right to counsel, judicial neutrality, unjustified dismissal of a jury member belonging to the same racial group as the defendant, denial of the right to self-representation, etc.) from the "harmless error" test.

[181] Brandon L. Garrett, *Claiming Innocence*, 92 MINN. L. REV. 1629, 1698 (2008).

[182] Garrett, *supra* note 8, at 36.

[183] *Id.* at 36 (quoting JOSEPH F. LAWLESS, PROSECUTORIAL MISCONDUCT: LAW, PROCEDURE, FORMS, at xii–xiii (2d ed. 1999)).

[184] *Id.* at 36 (quoting Sam Kamin, *Harmless Error and the Rights/Remedies Split*, 88 VA. L. REV. 1, 7 (2002)).

[185] Griffin, *supra* note 168, at 141. Compare: Dov Fox and Alex Stein, *Watersheds* (forthcoming, available at http://ssrn.com/abstract=2597301 (April, 2015)).

[186] Griffin, *supra* note 168, at 107–08.

[187] *Id.* at 134.

[188] *Id.* at 141–42.

[189] *Id.* at 137–40.

[190] *Id.* at 144–47.

of the noncapital habeas corpus cases.[191] Moreover, since *Herrera v. Collins*,[192] the Supreme Court has rejected factual innocence as a basis for relief, except in capital cases,[193] and holding that federal habeas review is intended only "to ensure that individuals are not imprisoned in violation of the Constitution—not to correct errors of fact."[194] Accordingly, the Court has never released a person on federal habeas grounds because he was actually innocent,[195] with considerations of finality and reliability suggested as underlying the Court's approach:[196] in the Court's words, "the passage of time only diminishes the reliability of criminal adjudications" due to the "erosion of memory and desperation of witnesses."[197] But *Herrera* preceded the DNA revolution, and reliable DNA evidence can be generated even decades after the crime was committed. Therefore, even though the *Herrera* rule itself has not been overturned, the federal legislature and most state legislatures have amended the procedural rules to allow convicts to get a new trial based on DNA evidence.

(5) New Post-conviction Proceedings Legislation

The Innocence Protection Act, 2004, led to three positive developments. First, it allows a convicted defendant in federal cases who is "under a sentence of imprisonment or sentence of death" to apply for post-conviction DNA testing, subject to certain limitations.[198] The Act requires that biological evidence in federal cases be preserved while an individual is imprisoned, and allocates federal funds to states to assist with the costs of post-conviction DNA testing.[199] The second improvement is that the Act allows for grants to states to "establish, implement, and improve an effective system for providing competent legal representation" to indigent capital defendants.[200] Third, the Act increased the amount of compensation that can be awarded to exonerated prisoners in federal criminal cases.[201]

Certainly, this legislation is a step in the right direction. Yet it amounts to only a partial solution. To begin with, only state defendants who have been charged

---

[191] SIMON, *supra* note 169, at 212.

[192] Herrera v. Collins, 506 U.S. 390, 416 (1993).

[193] House v. Bell, 126 S. Ct. 2064, 2087 (2006). *See also* Griffin, *supra* note 168, at 136; Thomas, *supra* note 2, at 166–67.

[194] *Herrera*, 506 U.S. at 400.

[195] Michael E. Kleinert, Note: *Improving the Quality of Justice: The Innocence Protection Act of 2004 Ensures Post-conviction DNA Testing, Better Legal Representation, and Increased Compensation for the Wrongfully Imprisoned*, 44 BRANDEIS L.J. 491, 500 (2006).

[196] Garrett, *supra* note 181, at 1699–704.

[197] *Herrera*, 506 U.S. at 403–04.

[198] Kleinert, *supra* note 195, at 501 (section 411 of the Act).

[199] *Id*. at 503 (sections 411–13 of the Act).

[200] *Id*. at 504 (section 421 of the Act).

[201] *Id*. at 505 (section 431 of the Act).

with a capital offense or sentenced to death benefit from the improvement in law-yering quality.[202] Moreover, all three new arrangements under the Act (ensuring post-conviction DNA testing, legal representation, and increased compensation for the wrongfully imprisoned) should not be limited to federal cases, but extended also to state convicts, all offenses, and all types of punishments. Most important, how-ever, as DNA testing is viable only in rare instances, the Innocence Act should apply to any type of new evidence with the potential of proving innocence.

Almost all states have enacted statutes allowing relief based on new evidence of innocence, usually DNA evidence.[203] But these statutes set arbitrary restrictions that deny DNA testing for some and preclude relief in many cases even where inno-cence has been shown.[204] Most of the state statutes allow only post-conviction DNA testing, for example, and not other kinds of evidence as the basis for relief. The most prevalent restrictions in these statutes are guilty-plea exclusions (which, in prac-tice, means the majority of criminal cases are excluded), custody requirements, due diligence requirements, and a requirement that the technology has advanced since the trial. Many states limit DNA testing to specified serious crimes or require that the petitioner be incarcerated or in custody in order to obtain testing. Some states, moreover, require that identity was an issue at trial, thereby precluding relief in cases where a guilty plea was made.[205]

As the empirical aspect of the exonerations was described by Gross:

> These are the exonerations we hear about in the news. But they are very uncom-mon—perhaps fifty a year, at present, in a country with over a million felony convictions annually, overwhelmingly in murder and rape cases, on average about ten years after conviction.[206]

B. POSSIBLE SAFETY MEASURES

There can be no doubt that significant changes are vital to change the legal real-ity of post-conviction proceedings, in line with the safety principles proposed in this book. First and foremost, safety must be implemented not only during the investigation and trial proceedings, but also after conviction. As conviction does not require certainty of guilt, the terms for allowing convicted defendants access to DNA testing should be lenient, for example, without setting any time limit on

---

[202] *Id.* at 508.

[203] Garrett, *supra* note 181, at 1716.

[204] *Id.* at 1717.

[205] *Id.* at 1679–80.

[206] Gross, *supra* note 127, at 1022.

this access.[207] Ensuring the preservation of DNA samples after conviction is also, therefore, vital. Second, given the proposed principle of an ongoing endeavor to exhaust all potential evidence so as to uncover the truth and in light of the overwhelming asymmetry between the state's power and defendants' power, I contend that defense attorneys (and defendants) should be allowed to submit potentially exculpatory evidence at all stages of the process: at trial, on appeal, and in motions for a new trial. This, of course, should not be limited only to DNA evidence but should rather extend to any evidence that can shed light on the truth. If the system truly seeks to uncover the truth, ensure that justice is done, and prevent further false convictions, it is duty-bound to implement the proposed safety rule.

Third, it is vital that claims of actual innocence be investigated at any stage that they are raised, without any time limit or procedural obstacles. The finality of proceedings rule has been given an inflated status in criminal law, and must be relaxed to facilitate comprehensive evaluation of actual innocence claims and the exoneration of falsely convicted defendants. Post-conviction proceedings must not be restricted to examining flaws of only a certain type, such as violations of constitutional rights. With all due respect to the Constitution, protecting the innocent from false conviction is no less of an important goal than protecting constitutional rights. Moreover, defendants' constitutional rights—such as the right to counsel, right to silence, and right to confront the prosecution's witnesses against her—are, it could be argued, intended primarily to protect the innocent. Regardless, however, these two important objectives should not compete against one another but rather complement each other.

A number of different recommendations have been made in the legal literature for reforming the system that, in my opinion, have great potential for improving the situation, although each one, of course, would have to be assessed for effectivity following implementation. To begin with, some scholars have proposed adopting the "unsafe verdict" standard in post-conviction proceedings in which a claim of actual innocence has been made. Under this standard, which is currently applied in English law, if the prosecution is unable to show that the conviction is "safe," the defendant is granted a new trial or immediate exoneration. As D. Michael Risinger has explained,

In virtually every American jurisdiction, when the sufficiency of evidence to support a verdict is attacked, the rubric is the same whether the case is civil or criminal. The party prevailing below is entitled to every inference that a

[207] INNOCENCE PROJECT, ACCESS TO POST-CONVICTION DNA TESTING, www.innocenceproject.org/Content/Access_To_PostConviction_DNA_Testing.php (last visited Oct. 7, 2014).

reasonable jury might have made given the evidence on the record considered in its most favorable light. This essentially means accepting at face value all testimonial evidence in favor of the verdict and assuming all testimonial evidence to the contrary to have been rejected on credibility grounds.[208]

Moreover, he notes that for "literally centuries," American courts have "insulated themselves from responsibility for protecting the factually innocent, hiding behind an artificial concept of evidentiary sufficiency, a misplaced apotheosis of direct witness testimony, and deference to juries. It is time they realized that, in regard to claims of factual innocence, justice demands more."[209] Lissa Griffin has similarly suggested broadening the U.S. standard for evaluating claims of innocence based on new evidence to resemble the standard currently applied in England. Under the expanded standard, a court would be able to vacate a conviction where the prosecution cannot show that conviction would have resulted even given the new evidence.[210]

Second, other scholars[211] have suggested establishing in the United States a publicly accountable body similar to the English Criminal Cases Review Commission, which was created following the recommendations of the Runciman Commission Report and has operated with considerable success over the years. The CCRC's mandate is to review claims of wrongful conviction and refer those cases it deems suitable to the court of appeal. The CCRC is authorized to conduct extensive independent inquiries into wrongful-conviction claims.[212] This includes the authority to subpoena public documents and seek disclosure of information that is not available to the defense, as well as to request independent reports from forensic and psychiatric experts. In practice, it does as much fieldwork as practical on its own.[213] I believe that establishing an autonomous body along the lines of the CCRC is likely to assist in contending with a number of the problems discussed here in this book, including the phenomenon of tunnel vision with regard to suspects' and defendants' guilt and police and prosecutorial misconduct.

A third suggestion made by scholars is to look to continental systems, such as the German legal system, where the appellate court "starts over from scratch": it hears

---

[208] Risinger, *supra* note 2, at 1313–14.
[209] *Id.* at 1335.
[210] Griffin, *supra* note 168, at 1308.
[211] The first one was probably Griffin, in 2001, at Griffin, *supra* note 168, and in 2009, at Griffin, *supra* note 172. *See also* Keith A. Findley, *Learning from Our Mistakes: A Criminal Justice Commission to Study Wrongful Convictions*, 38 CALIF. W. L. REV. 332, 344–48 (2002).
[212] Griffin, *supra* note 168, at 1275–78; Griffin, *supra* note 172, at 111–13. And see the CCRC website at http://www.ccrc.gov.uk (last visited April 23, 2015).
[213] Griffin, *supra* note 172, at 112–13.

witness testimony, it re-examines the evidence and relevant law, and it reaches its own independent determinations.[214] Such an appeal procedure is far more thorough than what is accepted in the American system, and the chances of correcting a wrongful conviction through such a procedure significantly greater. Inspired by the continental appeal procedure but presuming such a change to be too drastic for the American system, Thomas has proposed the following compromise: requiring appellate courts to determine from the trial transcripts whether the prosecution provided sufficient evidence of the defendant's guilt,[215] but leaving appeals of procedural errors to continue as present. Under Thomas's proposed solution, defendants would have the right to request that the court review the record and independently decide "if it has confidence in the conviction"; to this end, the court could even direct the trial judge to take new evidence if it finds it necessary. If the appellate court finds that guilt was not proven beyond a reasonable doubt, it will acquit the defendant.[216]

Fourth, some authors have suggested strengthening the clemency procedure, so that it will become an effective avenue for gaining the release of innocent-convicted inmates.[217] Echoing this aspiration is the *Herrera* Court's assertion that executive clemency is a meaningful safeguard against wrongful convictions.[218] The Court insisted, furthermore, that one of the roles of clemency is to prevent a miscarriage of justice when the legal process has been exhausted.[219]

Executive clemency is entirely discretionary, however, and generally not open to public scrutiny.[220] State governors often even fear that granting clemency will harm their chances of re-election. It is therefore hardly surprising that the empirical data show that clemency fails to serve as a safety net due, among other things, to political circumstances and forces.[221] On this background, it has been suggested that Congress and state legislatures establish review bodies resembling the CCRC to investigate, assess, and advise on clemency and pardon applications.[222]

On the one hand, I believe that the wrongly convicted deserve not only physical release from imprisonment, but also a full clearing of their name in the framework of legal proceedings, such as a new trial. On the other hand, so long as the present system is failing (and, at times, not even trying) to live up to this ideal, clemency should not be rejected as an alternative means of ending the injustice. However,

---

[214] THOMAS, *supra* note 2, at 216–17.

[215] *Id.* at 217. For a similar suggestion see Risinger, *supra* note 2, at 1313–14.

[216] *Id.* at 223–24.

[217] *See, e.g.*, Griffin, *supra* note 168, at 1299–300; Griffin, *supra* note 172, at 152.

[218] Herrera v. Collins, 506 U.S. 390 (1993).

[219] *Id.* at 411–12.

[220] Griffin, *supra* note 168, at 1299.

[221] *Id.* at 1306.

[222] *Id.*

after release from prison through clemency, the former inmate should be allowed, if he so desires, to pursue legal proceedings to reveal the truth and fully clear his name.

I will close this chapter with two final thoughts on the role of new trials. The one idea is that the weaker the guarantees of a fair trial, the greater the need to broaden the grounds for granting a new trial. As we saw in the discussion of procedural causes of false convictions, the existing guarantees of a fair trial are not strong enough. Given that the overwhelming majority of convictions are attained not through trial proceedings but through plea bargains, and that the appeals process is futile, principally because there is no scrutiny of the factual determinations made at trial, there is an urgent need for an effective new trial procedure.

The second point is that as we saw in the discussion of evidentiary causes of false convictions (in Chapter 5), there seems to be a historical pattern whereby with every new generation, there is an understanding that certain types of evidence considered in the past to be strong proof of a person's guilt are in fact not particularly reliable but erroneous, and that they mislead judges and juries. Thus, they should be given less weight than accorded in the past. The new trial mechanism can and should be used, then, to correct miscarriages of justice by reviewing past convictions and the evidence on which they were based from the current, up-to-date perspective.

Conclusion

THERE HAVE ALWAYS been, and always will be, accidents. In some aspects
of our life, this appears to be an inevitable reality. However, a high rate of accidents is not an unavoidable fact of life, but rather the product of human negligence and—when we are aware of the danger but do not act purposefully to reduce
it—even indifference.

In certain fields, the meaning of a "safety-critical system" is well understood,
and resources are, therefore, invested in modern safety methods, which reduce significantly the rate of accidents. This is the case, for example, in the field of pharmaceuticals and drugs, where in the first half of the twentieth-century, the need
for safety was already acknowledged and internalized, and the necessary powers
and authorities were granted to the FDA to ensure this. This was also the case in
the aviation field, which abandoned the obsolete "Fly-Fix-Fly" approach in the
mid-twentieth century and developed more advanced safety methods that generally
follow an "Identify-Analyze-Control" model and are aimed at "First-Time-Safe."
Modern safety approaches such as these were implemented in other fields as well,
such as transportation and engineering, and later on, in labor and medicine.
These safety systems are constructed on, among other things: safety education and
training, a culture of safety, a duty to report not only accidents but also incidents
(near-accidents), professional risk assessment, a process of perpetual improvement,

and the understanding that safety in each component of a system alone in detachment from the entire system is not sufficient for achieving system safety.

In the criminal justice system, too, accidents happen, of course: false convictions. For this reason, this system must also be classified as a safety-critical system. Yet in criminal law, a Hidden Accidents Principle governs. Thus, the overwhelming majority of false convictions are never detected, which led to the erroneous traditional and conservative assumption that they occur at an almost negligible rate and that the criminal justice system is "almost" perfect. Consequently, no thought has ever been given to safety in the system, and the criminal justice system, from a safety perspective, lags far behind other areas of life.

The patently flawed assumption of a low false-conviction rate has been challenged in recent decades. This has been primarily a result of the work of the Innocence Project, in which hundreds of cases of false convictions have been exposed through genetic testing, and empiric studies based on the Project's findings, which point to a very high false-conviction rate: at least 5 percent for the most serious crimes and an apparently even higher rate for less serious crimes.

On this background, this book has proposed a preliminary theory and some initial tools for incorporating modern safety into the criminal justice system. Alongside general principles, specific recommendations were made in the context of evidence, with particular attention to the central types of criminal evidence—confessions, eyewitness identification, DNA comparisons, and fingerprint comparisons—and the need to contend with "junk science"; and in the context of criminal procedure, with detailed focus on police and prosecutorial negligence and misconduct, plea bargains, and post-conviction proceedings. Among other things, I demonstrated how the innovative "System-Theoretic Accident Model and Processes" (STAMP) safety model can be applied in the criminal justice system, by developing constraints, controls, and barriers against the existing hazards in the contexts of plea bargains and of convictions grounded on the defendant's confession during police interrogation.

The criminal justice system produces countless convictions of the guilty but, unfortunately, also many convictions of the innocent. Creating safety from false convictions entails the investment of considerable resources, which can be coordinated in the framework of the Safety in the Criminal Justice System Institute I have proposed establishing. This institute will promote research on the criminal justice system, including the various types of evidence and procedures, with the goal of developing best practice protocols and modern safety techniques and methods. In the present situation, there is a systematic infliction and perpetuation of the greatest injustice that a state can cause to its citizens: the criminal conviction of the innocent. Fundamental reforms and changes are vital. Hopefully this book has contributed to taking some steps on that path to safety and inspired others to take up the challenge to further develop safety in the criminal justice system.